MODERN MUSIC AND AFTER

MODERN MUSIC AND AFTER

PAUL GRIFFITHS

OXFORD UNIVERSITY PRESS
1995

for Edmund

Oxford University Press, Walton Street, Oxford OX2 6DP
Oxford New York
Athens Auckland Bangkok Bombay
Calcutta Cape Town Dar es Salaam Delhi
Florence Hong Kong Istanbul Karachi
Kuala Lumpur Madras Madrid Melbourne
Mexico City Nairobi Paris Singapore
Taipei Tokyo Toronto
and associated companies in
Berlin Ibadan

Oxford is a trade mark of Oxford University Press

Published in the United States
by Oxford University Press Inc., New York

First published by J.M. Dent & Sons Ltd as
Modern Music; The avant garde since 1945 1981
First published by Oxford University Press 1995

British Library Cataloguing in Publication Data
Data available

Library of Congress Cataloging in Publication Data
Griffiths, Paul, 1947 Nov. 24–
Modern music and after / Paul Griffiths.
p. cm.
Rev. ed. of: Modern Music : the avant garde since 1945. 1981.
Includes bibliographical references and index.
1. Music—20th century—History and criticism. 1. Griffiths,
Paul, 1947 Nov. 24– Modern music. II. Title.
ML197.G76 1995 780'.9'04—dc20 95–13369
ISBN 0–19–816578–1 (cloth)
ISBN 0–19–816511–0 (pbk.).

1 3 5 7 9 10 8 6 4 2

Typeset by Hope Services (Abingdon)
Printed in Great Britain
at The Bath Press Ltd.
Bath, Somerset

MUSIC ACKNOWLEDGEMENTS

I am most grateful for the friendly help I have had over the years from numerous representatives of music publishing houses, including David Allenby, Susan Bamert and Janis Susskind of Boosey & Hawkes, Rosemary Johnson and Jane Wilson of Chester Music, Bálint András Varga of Editio Musica Budapest and later Universal Edition, Sally Cavender of Faber Music, Graham Hayter of Peters Edition, Avril James of Ricordi, Sally Groves and Ulrike Müller of Schott, Suzanne Stephens of Stockhausen Verlag, Christopher Saward of United Music Publishers, and Eric Forder of Universal Edition.

I am also indebted to the companies who have generously allowed me to quote from published scores as follows.

Ex. 1   **Boulez: Sonatina**
Reproduced by kind permission of Editions Amphion (Paris)/United Music Publishers Ltd.

Ex. 2   **Boulez: Piano Sonata No. 2**
Reproduced by kind permission of Editions Heugel et Cie. (Paris)/United Music Publishers Ltd.

Ex. 3   **Nono: *Variazioni canoniche***
© by G. Ricordi & Co. (London) Ltd., reproduced by permission

Ex. 4   **Cage: *Sonatas and Interludes***
Reproduced by kind permission of C. F. Peters Corporation (New York)

Ex. 5   **Cage: *Music of Changes***
Reproduced by kind permission of C. F. Peters Corporation (New York)

Ex. 6   **Messiaen: *Mode de valeurs et d'intensités***
Reproduced by kind permission of Editions Durand (Paris)/United Music Publishers Ltd.

Ex. 7   **Stockhausen: *Kreuzspiel***
Reproduced by kind permission of Universal Edition (London) Ltd.

Ex. 8   **Boulez: *Structures Ib***
Reproduced by kind permission of Universal Edition (London) Ltd.

Ex. 9   **Nono: *Y su sangre ya viene cantando***
Reproduced by kind permission of Schott & Co. Ltd.

Ex. 10   **Stockhausen: *Studie II***
Reproduced by kind permission of Stockhausen Verlag

Ex. 11   **Barraqué: Piano Sonata**
Reproduced by kind permission of Editore Bruzzichelli

Ex. 12   **Carter: String Quartet No. 1**
Reproduced by kind permission of Associated Music Publishers/G. Schirmer

Ex. 13   **Babbitt:** *Three Compositions for Piano*
Reproduced by kind permission of Boelke-Bomart/Alfred A. Kalmus

Ex. 14   **Babbitt:** *Post-Partitions*
Reproduced by kind permission of C. F. Peters Corporation (New York)

Ex. 15   **Stockhausen:** *Kontra-Punkte*
Reproduced by kind permission of Universal Edition (London) Ltd.

Ex. 16   **Stockhausen: Piano Piece III**
Reproduced by kind permission of Universal Edition (London) Ltd.

Ex. 17*a*   **Boulez:** *Le marteau sans maître*
Reproduced by kind permission of Universal Edition (London) Ltd.

Ex. 18   **Nono:** *Il canto sospeso*
Reproduced by kind permission of Schott & Co. Ltd.

Ex. 19   **Stockhausen:** *Zeitmasze*
Reproduced by kind permission of Universal Edition (London) Ltd.

Ex. 20   **Feldman:** *Projection II*
Reproduced by kind permission of C. F. Peters Corporation (New York)

Ex. 21   **Brown:** *December 1952*
Reproduced by kind permission of Associated Music Publishers/G. Schirmer

Ex. 22   **Cage:** *Concert for Piano and Orchestra*
Reproduced by kind permission of C. F. Peters Corporation (New York)

Ex. 23   **Nancarrow: Study No. 5**
Reproduced by kind permission of Schott & Co. Ltd.

Ex. 24*b*   **Boulez: Piano Sonata No. 3**
Reproduced by kind permission of Universal Edition (London) Ltd.

Ex. 25   **Berio:** *Circles*
Reproduced by kind permission of Universal Edition (London) Ltd.

Ex. 26   **Stravinsky:** *Movements*
Reproduced by kind permission of Boosey & Hawkes Music Publishers Ltd.

Ex. 27   **Messiaen:** *Réveil des oiseaux*
Reproduced by kind permission of Editions Durand (Paris)/United Music Publishers Ltd.

Ex. 28   **Messiaen:** *Sept haïkaï*
Reproduced by kind permission of Editions A. Leduc (Paris)/United Music Publishers Ltd.

Ex. 29   **Wolpe: Oboe Quartet**
© 1976 by Josef Marx Music Company, reproduced by kind permission of the publishers

Ex. 30   **Bussotti:** *Per tre sul piano*
Reproduced by kind permission of Universal Edition (London) Ltd.

Ex. 31   **Stockhausen:** *Kontakte*
Reproduced by kind permission of Stockhausen Verlag

Ex. 32*b*   Davies: *Taverner*
Reproduced by kind permission of Boosey & Hawkes Music Publishers Ltd.

Ex. 33   Berio: *Sinfonia*
Reproduced by kind permission of Universal Edition (London) Ltd.

Ex. 34   Stockhausen: *Hymnen*
Reproduced by kind permission of Stockhausen Verlag

Ex. 35   Birtwistle: *Verses for Ensembles*
Reproduced by kind permission of Universal Edition (London) Ltd.

Ex. 36   Kagel: *Match*
Reproduced by kind permission of Universal Edition (London) Ltd.

Ex. 37   Stockhausen: *Inori*
Reproduced by kind permission of Stockhausen Verlag

Ex. 38   Cardew: *Treatise*
Reproduced by kind permission of Peters Edition Ltd. (London)

Ex. 39   Cardew: 'Soon'
Reproduced by kind permission of the composer

Ex. 40   Berio: *Sequenza III*
Reproduced by kind permission of Universal Edition (London) Ltd.

Ex. 41   Boulez: *Domaines*
Reproduced by kind permission of Universal Edition (London) Ltd.

Ex. 42   Holliger: *Siebengesang*
Reproduced by kind permission of Schott & Co. Ltd.

Ex. 43   Lachenmann: *Pression*
Reproduced by kind permission of Breitkopf & Härtel

Ex. 44   Xenakis: *Evryali*
Reproduced by kind permission of Editions Salabert (Paris)/United Music Publishers Ltd.

Ex. 45   Stockhausen: *Prozession*
Reproduced by kind permission of Stockhausen Verlag

Ex. 46   Young: *The Well-Tuned Piano*
Reproduced from an article by Kyle Gann in *Perspectives of New Music*, by kind permission of author and editor

Ex. 47   Glass: *Music in Similar Motion*
Reproduced by kind permission of Dunvagen Music

Ex. 48   Reich: *Violin Phase*
Reproduced by kind permission of Universal Edition (London) Ltd.

Ex. 49   Boulez: *Eclat*
Reproduced by kind permission of Universal Edition (London) Ltd.

Ex. 50   Boulez: *Rituel*
Reproduced by kind permission of Universal Edition (London) Ltd.

Ex. 51   Ligeti: *Bewegung*
Reproduced by kind permission of Schott & Co. Ltd.

Ex. 52   Birtwistle: *Melencolia I*
Reproduced by kind permission of Universal Edition (London) Ltd.

Ex. 53   Stockhausen: *Mantra*
Reproduced by kind permission of Stockhausen Verlag

Ex. 54   Stravinsky: *Introitus*
Reproduced by kind permission of Boosey & Hawkes Music Publishers Ltd.

Ex. 55   Barraqué: *. . . au delà du hasard*
Reproduced by kind permission of Editore Bruzzichelli

Ex. 56   Hopkins: *Pendant*
Reproduced by kind permission of Clare Hopkins

Ex. 57   Xenakis: *Tetora*
Reproduced by kind permission of Editions Salabert (Paris)/United Music Publishers Ltd.

Ex. 58   Weir: *A Night at the Chinese Opera*
Reproduced by kind permission of Novello & Co. Ltd.

Ex. 59   Tan: *On Taoism*
Reproduced by kind permission of G. Schirmer

Ex. 60*a*   Stockhausen: nuclear formula for Eva
Reproduced by kind permission of Stockhausen Verlag

Ex. 60*b*   Stockhausen: *Pietà* from *Dienstag*
Reproduced by kind permission of Stockhausen Verlag

Ex. 61   Schnittke: String Quartet No. 3
Reproduced by kind permission of Boosey & Hawkes Music Publishers Ltd.

Ex. 62   Scelsi: String Quartet No. 4
Reproduced by kind permission of Editions Salabert (Paris)/United Music Publishers Ltd.

Ex. 63   Rihm: *Kein Firmament*
Reproduced by kind permission of Universal Edition (London) Ltd.

Ex. 64   Reich: *Different Trains*
Reproduced by kind permission of Boosey & Hawkes Music Publishers Ltd.

Ex. 65   Pärt: *Passio Domini Nostri Jesu Christi secundum Joannem*
Reproduced by kind permission of Universal Edition (London) Ltd.

Ex. 66   Adams: *Nixon in China*
Reproduced by kind permission of Boosey & Hawkes Music Publishers Ltd.

Ex. 67   Nono: *La lontananza nostalgica utopica futura*
© by G. Ricordi & Co. (London) Ltd., reproduced by permission

Ex. 68   Ligeti: Etude No. 1 'Désordre'
Reproduced by kind permission of Schott & Co. Ltd.

Ex. 69   Kurtág: *The Sayings of Péter Bornemisza*
Reproduced by kind permission of Universal Edition (London) Ltd.

Ex. 70*a*   Kurtág: *Twelve Microludes*
© 1979 by Editio Musica Budapest, reproduced by kind permission

Ex. 70*b* **Kurtág:** ... *quasi una fantasia* ...
© 1989 by Editio Musica Budapest, reproduced by kind permission

Ex. 71 **Holliger: 'Der Sommer (III)'**
Reproduced by kind permission of Schott & Co. Ltd.

Ex. 72 **Ferneyhough:** *Unity Capsule*
Reproduced by kind permission of Peters Edition Ltd. (London)

Ex. 73 **Ferneyhough:** *Etudes transcendentales*
Reproduced by kind permission of Peters Edition Ltd. (London)

Ex. 74 **Feldman:** *Three Voices*
Reproduced by kind permission of Universal Edition (London) Ltd.

Ex. 75 **Donatoni:** *Still*
© by G. Ricordi & Co. (London) Ltd., reproduced by permission

Ex. 76 **Benjamin:** *Antara*
Reproduced by kind permission of Faber Music

Ex. 77 **Cage:** *Two*
Reproduced by kind permission of C. F. Peters Corporation (New York)

Ex. 78 **Birtwistle:** *Ritual Fragment*
Reproduced by kind permission of Universal Edition (London) Ltd.

Ex. 79 **Berio:** *Formazioni*
Reproduced by kind permission of Universal Edition (London) Ltd.

CONTENTS

II. SIX WAVES AND FIVE MASTERS: THE 1960s AND 1970s

III. MANY RIVERS: THE 1980s AND 1990s

PRELUDE

I began this book—before arriving at the beginning now beginning—as a simple updating of my *Modern Music*, which I had finished in 1979. But the infant with whom that earlier survey had, to quote from its dedication, 'a race to delivery', is now nearing manhood, and a comparable change seemed to be demanded of the book—demanded by the last fifteen years of composition, by the progress of scholarship, and by the altered view of distance.

The original *Modern Music*, with a title that seemed either quaint or defensive in a world waking to postmodernism, viewed the period since 1945 as divided into two phases. One, lasting until around 1960, was governed by hopes for a constant progressive change in the nature of music, in the routines of composing, and in music's place within society. Because those hopes were widely shared, they encouraged an uncommon profusion of alliances—an urge that may have been intensified by the fact that so many of the leading composers of these years were men (rarely women) who were in their twenties, and therefore susceptible to fantasies of group identity. And because the hopes sometimes seemed more important than the music—as if what was written could only be a sketch towards some grand future project—they also generated a quite unusual quantity of verbal justification, in the form of analytical articles, treatises of composition, declarations of aesthetic intent, and polemical counterblasts. It was a time of vigorous bonding, fierce denunciation and conspicuous theorizing (there are close parallels with what was going on within the left-wing politics of the time). Only the energy of reconstruction—the drive to build a better musical future, to reach new promised lands—was beyond dispute. That energy, that drive, made the passage of time feel urgent and forward-moving, and something of the same dynamic was maintained when, as inevitably happened, the differences among composers began to overwhelm the mutualities, and the single history of the late 1940s and 1950s was succeeded in the next two decades by a knotted web of arrows—a web which the second part of *Modern Music* tried to expose in a sequence of traverses rather than a solitary narrative line.

This new version of the book maintains the earlier two-part structure, and adds to it a third part concerning music since the late 1970s. The three parts cover roughly equal periods of time, but not at equal length, for various reasons. With the passage of time, music grows, enriched by performance, by interpretation, by the effect it has on subsequent music: the music of the late 1940s and 1950s thereby commands more attention here than the spring grass of the 1990s. Also, that immediate postwar music is unusually big in its achievements, deep in its questions, and long in its implications. Just as a book on the music of the first half of the nineteenth century would have to give disproportionate weight to the period up to 1828, so this one is bottom-heavy. Reasons of convenience, too, have sometimes pulled later music into the first part—though they have also sometimes pulled earlier music into later parts. We live among many simultaneous histories: there is the chronology of when things get composed, when they get performed, when they get to seem important, when they get to seem important specifically to each of us. The book does not—could not—iron out these tangles.

The entire text has been radically overhauled, in order to take some account both of new research and of a broader view that now seems appropriate, even if the book's heart remains in much the same place. That broader view is necessary because not only has musical confusion—which one may at different times consider a cause for wonder, bewilderment or alarm—gone on increasing during the last decade and a half, but its effect has been to call into question the 1950s belief in musical progress. There has been time for alternative traditions to grow up and separate themselves, so that by now the pathways have forked so far that they have lost the memory of any common origin. Looking back from the present situation of, say, Arvo Pärt or Ellen Taaffe Zwilich, *Le marteau sans maître* might seem an alien curiosity: Vivaldi and Pérotin are nearer precursors for the one, Mahler and Shostakovich for the other. Where, in the 1950s, composers as diverse as Boulez, Cage, and Babbitt all recognized Schoenberg, Webern, and Varèse as among their godfathers, the only common view now is that there is no common view. Out of the muddled present we see a muddled past.

An observer may still believe that the challenges of the 1950s—the challenges of self-awareness, of commitment to change and discovery, of exacting precision—remain, and that 'modernism' is not just a style among others but an imperative that goes on being answered, however variously, in the music, say, of Babbitt, Birtwistle, Ferneyhough, Kurtág, and Ligeti. A historian, though, must record other possibilities, even if no history can hope to be other than partisan—as this history is for several reasons.

One of these must be, banally, the sheer quantity of serious music now being written. In the 1950s and 1960s the principal media of musical dissemination—records, radio concerts, festivals—were dominated by two dozen or so international figures. Most of those composers remain at the forefront: the big names of the 1950s are still the big names of the 1990s. But they have been joined by many thousands of composers whose works have at least intermittent exposure, with the result that nobody can claim familiarity with more than a small part of what is a constantly growing musical universe. Nor can we have too much confidence in time's winnowing. The experience of the last fifteen years has been rather that the repertory constantly increases, as a result both of living composers' activities, and of perpetual revivals from the immediate past. What anyone knows will be governed partly by nationality, partly by opportunity, and partly by taste.

The role of taste is something else that must render any history of modern music illusory. The great hope of the immediate postwar years was to eliminate the functioning of taste, either by establishing axioms whose historical necessity and rational fitness would be bound to command general agreement (as Boulez and Babbitt hoped) or by accepting any material as musical (which was Cage's only rule). But when music is so diverse, taste gains a worrying force over composers and listeners, and indeed over critics and historians. Admiration for—to return to an earlier example—*Le marteau sans maître*, can be justified on the grounds of the work's supremacy in answering what were current questions of compositional technique and aesthetics. But today, when it is hard enough to find the questions, subjective criteria of appreciation become overwhelming. The problem then—and it is a problem each one of us must address—is that of how to be more than a consumer at the great feast of contemporary music, how to create, almost as a composition itself, a listening life that is integrated and yet also responsive to the age's diversity and abundance.

PART I. BEGINNING AGAIN: FROM 1945 TO THE EARLY 1960s

Europe 1: Commencement, 1945–1951

Paris, 1945–1948

It was in Paris, during these immediate postwar years, that the last phase of modern music began—that the last effort to alter music radically, and even to set the art on a new course, had its most conspicuous and decisive origin. Though musical life had continued during the German occupation, the ending of the war was an incentive to breathe again, and then to change the world. In Paris, too, as throughout the previous Nazi empire, liberation made it possible to perform, discuss, and hear music that had been banned for being adventurous or Jewish or, to take the prominent case of Schoenberg, both. The moment, then, was right. And there were the right people to take possession of the moment. Olivier Messiaen (1908–92) during these years was composing his largest and most elaborate work so far, the *Turangalîla* symphony, a composition to crown his earlier achievements and at the same time display new concerns he shared with the young pupils who had gathered around him at the Paris Conservatoire. Pierre Boulez (b. 1925), the most gifted of those pupils, was meanwhile producing the first pieces by which he would wish to be known, graduating from the miniature *Notations* for piano (1945) to the four-movement Second Piano Sonata (1946–8), which brought his early style to a climax of formal sophistication and expressive vehemence. Finally, the year of the sonata's completion also saw the creation by Pierre Schaeffer (b. 1910), working in the studios of Radiodiffusion-Télévision Française, of the first essays in *musique concrète*, music made by transforming recorded sounds and composed not on to paper but on to the heavy black discs of the contemporary gramophone.

Boulez's Early Works

Boulez, who studied with Messiaen during the academic year 1944–5, later wrote an appreciation of his teacher which eloquently conveys the atmosphere in which musical revolution was being prepared: 'Names that were all but forbidden, and works of which we knew nothing, were held up for our admiration and were to arouse our intellectual curiosity . . . Africa and Asia showed us that the prerogatives of "tradition" were not confined to any one part of the world, and in our enthusiasm we came to regard music as a way of life rather than an art: we were marked for life.'[1]

[1] 'A Class and Its Fantasies', *Orientations* (London, 1986), 404; the piece was originally published as a tribute to Messiaen on his fiftieth birthday. See also 'In Retrospect', ibid. 405–6.

In the case of Boulez himself, at least, the admiration and the curiosity did not wash away—rather they intensified—a need to challenge, even to reject. It was through admiration and curiosity that Boulez was led to recognize his musical fore-fathers, but it was through challenge and rejection that he was led to recognize him-self. In his later career as a conductor, he has performed neither the *Trois petites liturgies* (1943–4) nor the complete *Turangalîla* (1946–8), preferring the scores Messiaen wrote in the 1950s and 1960s—scores arguably influenced by his own music. At the time, the echo of Messiaen's modes remained detectable in his com-positions only because those modes were being so punishingly negated, and for several years the pupil was expressly hostile to his erstwhile master. In a critical paragraph from one of his earliest essays, published in 1948, he concluded that Messiaen 'does not compose—he juxtaposes'.[2]

To some extent, the hostility was the display of a delayed adolescence; it was also a necessary fuel for the young composer's creative zeal. Boulez formed himself in explosive reaction against what he found around him—not just the dusty Conservatoire but Messiaen, Schoenberg, Berg, Bartók, Stravinsky, all of whom were furiously taken to task in the polemical articles he wrote during his twenties, just as they were being implicitly taken to task in his compositions of those years. His most typical way of arguing on behalf of his music was to show how it realized potentialities that had been glimpsed by his predecessors but fudged by them for want of perspicacity or intellectual bravery. For example, the same essay that criti-cizes Messiaen the 'juxtaposer'—an essay devoted to finding a way forward for rhythm—admonishes Bartók for having a rhythmic style 'much simpler and more traditional' than that of *The Rite of Spring*, Jolivet because 'his empirical technique has prevented him from going very far', Messiaen for failing to integrate rhythm and harmony, Schoenberg and Berg because they 'remain attached to the classical bar and the old idea of rhythm', and Varèse 'for spiriting away the whole problem of technique . . . [:] a facile solution which solves nothing'. Even Webern—whom the young Boulez took as a touchstone of unflinching modernism, and whom he was at pains to isolate from other members of that crucial grandfatherly generation as the only exemplar[3]—even Webern is glancingly, parenthetically chided for 'his attach-ment to rhythmic tradition'.

Messiaen recalled that during this period Boulez 'was in revolt against every-thing';[4] Boulez himself remembers that 'it was our privilege to make the discover-ies and also to find ourselves faced with nothing'.[5] The artist who is 'against everything' can, by virtue of that, look around him and find 'nothing'. Boulez's iconoclasm was perhaps extreme, but not exceptional for a self-confident young man in his late teens and early twenties. What was exceptional was the fact that

---

[2] 'Proposals', *Stocktakings from an Apprenticeship* (Oxford, 1991).

[3] See e.g. his 1952 essay 'Possibly . . .' (ibid. 114), and the conclusion of his 1961 encyclopaedia entry on Webern (ibid. 303).

[4] Claude Samuel, *Olivier Messiaen: Music and Color* (Portland, Oreg., 1994), 182.

[5] *Orientations*, 445.

musical history yielded itself to iconoclasm—that a composer in these years could set himself against not only the Milhauds and Poulencs but the Messiaens and Schoenbergs, and could find, in his contrariety, the spur to achievement.

There were perhaps several reasons, quite beyond anything in Boulez's psychology, why that could happen. One was the need, after the war, to build afresh, and the feeling that the future lay with a new generation—a generation unsullied by the compromises that had been forced on people during the 1930s and then during the war. Another, more particularly concerned with music, was the evident fact that a period of artistic upheaval—the few years before the First World War, the years of the first atonal compositions, of *Pierrot lunaire*, of *The Rite of Spring*—had been followed by thirty years during which the clock of progress had slowed, or even reversed. Yet another factor would have been the philosophical movement, centred in Paris, which viewed the individual as the creator of himself. References to Jean-Paul Sartre in Boulez's writings and lectures are rare, but many of his statements ring out with a cold, clear bravery as those of a Sartrian hero: 'There is no such thing as historical inevitability. History is what one makes it. I hold very firmly to this principle.'[6]

Of course there is a paradox here. On the one hand, composers of the two previous generations are criticized for not answering the call of history implicit in their own works; on the other, there is this claim that 'history is what one makes it'. Boulez could hardly have avoided the view—voiced by a century of avant gardes, and dignified by Schoenberg and Adorno—that history compels artists to move in a certain direction at a certain time: the whole modernist aesthetic, which he was insistently promoting, demanded that conclusion. However, it seems that he was also able to see his participation in history as a willed act. The need was there: a vacant hole of musical possibility, the 'nothing' with which he was faced. But the challenge required an active, determined champion to accept it.

Before that could happen, though, he needed to acquaint himself completely with the 'everything' that he was against, and here he was lucky. René Leibowitz (1913–72), a Polish-born musician who had studied with Webern in the early 1930s, came to Paris in 1945 and in February of that year conducted (presumably this was then necessary) a recording of Schoenberg's Wind Quintet that was broadcast immediately after the liberation of France. It is not clear whether what Boulez heard was the original performance or the broadcast, but in either event the piece seemed to answer all his dissatisfactions. 'It was a revelation to me. It obeyed no tonal laws, and I found in it a harmonic and contrapuntal richness, and a consequent ability to develop, extend and vary ideas, that I had not found anywhere else. I wanted, above all, to know how it was written, so I went to Leibowitz and took with me other students from Messiaen's harmony class.'[7]

In retrospect it is ironic that Schoenberg's Op. 26 should have been the work to provide this determining experience, for while Schoenberg's atonal works (Opp.

[6] *Conversations with Célestin Deliège* (London, 1977), 33.

[7] Quoted in Joan Peyser, *Boulez: Composer, Conductor, Enigma* (London, 1977), 32–3.

11–22) were to remain part of that select repertory Boulez deemed beyond reproach, he was soon to criticize the adherence to classical models of form in the serial pieces that followed, just as, with even more inevitability, he was to turn his pen against Leibowitz in 'Proposals', one of his earliest essays.[8] The bombshell might be more easily understood if this had been Boulez's first encounter with anything by Schoenberg, as it just about could have been. One might have supposed he would have met Schoenberg already in Messiaen's classes, but then one might have supposed he would have met serialism there too; the documentation of this whole period is weak. Perhaps the crucial point was that he was being introduced to Schoenberg and to serialism as sound. It had been the sound of Stravinsky's *Chant du rossignol*, heard over the radio, that had first opened his ears to 'modern music';[9] it was now the sound of the Schoenberg Wind Quintet that pointed him in a new direction. Perhaps in both cases the unexpectedness was decisive. Boulez's language in speaking of his formative experiences is almost that of religious conversion: the being 'marked for life', the 'revelation'. Nor need it have been irrelevant, even to an obstinately atheist pupil, that Messiaen understood music as a spiritual art, an art of large stakes. The shock of Schoenberg's Op. 26 was the shock of an unknown in which the young man, only nineteen or twenty at the time, suddenly discovered both an ancestor and himself.

A few published excerpts from Boulez's early compositions[10] hint at what happened. A Toccata—one of five piano pieces written in December 1944 and January 1945, and therefore before the confrontation with serialism—seems to be attempting to create a totally chromatic world by rapidly piling up motifs characteristic of Messiaen's modes. Particularly prominent are motifs including a tritone and a perfect fifth, whose diminishing echoes go on at least as far as the cantata *Le soleil des eaux* (1948). Also striking is the adumbration of two kinds of music on which Boulez was to base his First Piano Sonata, a long seventeen months later: relatively slow music that includes rapid gruppetti, and so displays a simultaneity of tempos more characteristic of extra-European traditions (as for instance in the nimble ornaments an Indian musician might introduce into preludial material, or in the overtone-related speeds of Indonesian percussion orchestras); and extremely fast music in which all qualities of harmony and contrapuntal relation are hammered towards uniform pulsation (here again the goal seems to be non-western, though this time Boulez had clear pointers available, especially in the toccata-style piano music of Messiaen—such as the 'chord theme' in the *Vingt regards sur l'Enfant-Jésus*, which Messiaen was completing when Boulez joined his class—and Bartók).

After the experience of Schoenberg's Op. 26, in the Theme and Variations for piano left hand (June 1945) and the first two movements of a Quartet for ondes

---

[8] For a study of the conflict, written from a viewpoint sympathetic to Leibowitz, see Reinhard Kapp, 'Shades of the Double's Original: René Leibowitz's Dispute with Boulez', *Tempo*, 165 (1988), 2–16.

[9] *New Yorker* profile of Boulez by Peter Heyworth, reprinted in William Glock (ed.), *Pierre Boulez: a Symposium* (London, 1986), 5.

[10] Accompanying Gerald Bennett's article, ibid. 44–52.

martenot (August–September 1945), we find a Boulez who has mastered Schoenbergian serialism, and added to it a quite non-Schoenbergian and already non-Leibowitzian rhythmic irregularity based on cells rather than metres, thereby attempting some union of Schoenberg and Messiaen (the flavour of Messiaen's harmony is perhaps more a residue than an attempt). The next step, which could have followed the discovery of Webern, was a sudden reduction of scale, in the *Notations* of December 1945, to flash views of musical worlds—worlds which include again interminglings of speed and slowness (No. 1) and a hectic toccata (No. 6), besides varieties of trapped ostinato.

Boulez dedicated *Notations* to Serge Nigg (b. 1924), who it seems was the liveliest of the bunch of contemporaries to have come with him through Messiaen to Leibowitz, and whose career arrestingly points up something that Boulez was not: political. Boulez's political indifference—perhaps his political atheism—is all the more remarkable given how the vocabulary of his reminiscences suggests not only Pauline conversion but revolutionary activism. To many of his contemporaries the connections were inescapable: the connections between rethinking music and rethinking society, both activities to be done on the basis of rational, egalitarian principles in determined opposition to the philosophical floundering that had gone before. In these few years before the full freeze of the Cold War, it was not disingenuous or merely idealistic to see the possibility of revolution spreading across Europe, and thereby providing the home for a new musical order. Soon, though, the happy alliance of socialism and serialism was to wither as a dream, and Nigg's political commitment—fully formed by the time of his four Eluard songs (1948) and cantata *Le fusillé inconnu* (1949)—led him along a familiar path towards musical conservatism in the interests of mass appeal. Nor was he by any means alone among western Europeans in reliving what had been the tensions of Soviet cultural policy in the first two decades after 1917: his exact contemporary Luigi Nono (1924–90) fought that fight.

To Boulez it might have appeared that abstention from politics was necessary in order for him to focus on the task of bringing about the musical revolution. (It could also be that the refusal of political engagement was allied with the rejection of Leibowitz.) Quite what he hoped for after the revolution is unclear, and perhaps was so then. The effort to generalize serialism—to apply twelve-note principles to domains other than pitch, such as duration, instrumentation, dynamic or, for the piano, mode of attack—was not explicitly voiced in his compositions or writings until 1951, by which time Messiaen had pointed the way in his 'Mode de valeurs et d'intensités'. Before then Boulez's expressed theoretical endeavour was rather more limited, to ensure—quoting again from the 1948 essay in which he had briskly surveyed his precedessors' contributions to rhythm—'that techniques as varied as those of dodecaphony can be balanced by a rhythmic element itself perfectly "atonal" '.[11]

---

[11] 'Proposals', 54.

The fact that Babbitt had devised a kind of rhythmic serialism—just the year before and quite independently—might seem to justify Boulez's Schoenbergian and Adornoesque belief in a historical imperative within music. It is not so relevant to this, but only characteristic of a period of forking paths, that the two composers had little to say to one another when opportunity arose: Babbitt was to express his disappointment with European serialism,[12] and Boulez's only evidence of reciprocal interest was a single performance (of Babbitt's *Correspondences* for string orchestra and tape in 1973) when he was at the head of the New York Philharmonic. Besides, there is the testimony of the pieces they were writing during this period, for though Boulez's longing for 'atonal' rhythm might seem a rather abstract desire, there was nothing cool or studious or even rational about his music. The works he produced between 1946 and 1948—the Sonatina for flute and piano (January–February 1946), the First Piano Sonata (May–June 1946) and the Second Piano Sonata (1946–8)[13]—show rather how his rebuilding was taking place through and within what Messiaen remembered as the dominant feature of his personality: revolt.

Creative violence in these works is associated, on one level, with the presence in all of them of the piano, since to the examples he had drawn from Messiaen's and Bartók's intemperate toccatas, Boulez could now add those of Schoenberg's Op. 11 pieces and *Pierrot lunaire*, in which he admired 'a kind of piano writing . . . with considerable density of texture and a violence of expression because the piano is treated . . . as a percussive piano which is at the same time remarkably prone to frenzy'.[14] He also accepted Schoenberg as an ideal of form in the Sonatina, jamming four movement-types—the specific model was Schoenberg's Chamber Symphony, Op. 9—into a continuous structure. One can understand why he might have been attracted by this idea. It offered a double-layered form to equal in complexity his treatment of pitch and rhythm as separate but joinable parameters. It enabled him to return, after the unusual brevity of *Notations*, to the expansiveness and dynamism of his earlier music. And it set him, at a time when he was still a member of Leibowitz's group, in the line of Schoenberg. For among its other revolts, the Sonatina is ruthlessly contra-French in showing how a quintessentially Gallic medium could give rise to music as opposed as possible to the elegant bittersweet neoclassicism of so many other flute sonatinas coming out of Paris in the 1940s.

But the piece is contra-Schoenberg too, inevitably. Example 1, from the opening of the 'first movement', shows a rare complete linear statement of the series, in the flute part. The series in this form contains a restricted variety of intervals: major sevenths, major thirds (plus one major tenth), tritones and fifths, including two

---

[12] See below, p. 00.

[13] Other works of this period have been long withdrawn (the Sonata for two pianos of 1948, incorporating two movements from the Ondes Martenot Quartet of 1945–6), revised (two cantatas to words by René Char: *Le visage nuptial*, originally from Sept.–Nov. 1946, and *Le soleil des eaux*, emanating from a radio score written early in 1948), or lost (the 1947 Symphony).

[14] *Conversations with Célestin Deliège*, 30.

expressions of the tritone-fifth motif, as B♭–E–A and D–A♭–E♭. These limitations, and the explicit division of the series into groups of five, five, and two notes, may indicate a wish to profit from Webern's example of using serialism as a control on interval content, but while loosening the reins a little. However, the piano does not provide a strict counterpoint to the flute, as it might have done in Webern, nor is it a complementary support, as it might have been in Schoenberg. There are places where the piano offers a close approximation to the pitch succession of the series, as, for example, in the sequence E–F . . . B–B♭ in bars 35–7, which is almost a statement of the series transposed down a semitone, or the immediately preceding sequence, which is almost equivalent to the inverted form between the same poles of F and B. But the opening gesture collapses the series into an ornament (the first hexachord of a serial form is read forwards, the second simultaneously backwards), and other features of the piano part—notably including the flagrant minor third in bar 33—are quite alien to the series. The passage is full of allusions, both rhythmic and intervallic, but the derivations are mostly hazy, remote, and momentary.

Ex. 1. Boulez, Sonatina (1946)

One important effect is to disrupt the flow of time. Not only is there no consistent pulse, but the two instruments pull and tug against each other in their spasmodic cross-referring. When it doubles the flute's note, the piano may coincide, echo or pre-empt. Motivic details, such as the frequent major sevenths, are allied with others which seem arbitrary. Webern's geometries are shattered and distorted over curves. The whole western ideal of music to be apprehended moment by moment, as purposeful growth, is countered, and the writing for both instruments—the suggestions of drums, xylophones and vibraphones in the piano, the use of the flute's extreme high register, with its inevitable breakdown of tone—points as much to traditions from beyond Europe. In that is perhaps the Sonatina's most radical departure: to be open to non-European music without recourse to any kind of exoticism.

What also contributes to the Asian or African quality of the piece is Boulez's understanding of theme as ostinato. Where the Sonatina is most thematic, in the quite unusually symmetrical and playful 'scherzo', it sounds drilled to be so, and the initial five-note idea in the flute part of Example 1, though a recurrent gesture, functions less as a theme than as a periodic signal. And while the whole series does appear again in the 'slow movement', it is buried as a trilling cantus firmus, overlaid by elements which seem unrelated to it and purely decorative: the texture is astonishingly predictive of Boulez's later music. At other points, as in the section beginning at bar 296, Boulez destroys the series wilfully and utterly, splitting it into dyads which he engages in a purely rhythmic development without reference to the pitch orderings in the series. This is typical of a work whose intensiveness comes partly from the antagonism between serial repetition and the perpetual quest for ways of transforming and disintegrating the series beyond recognition, and partly from those harsh metrical dislocations that derive from the kind of cellular rhythm inherited from Messiaen and from *The Rite of Spring*. Boulez's achievement here, in combining the lessons of his predecessors, in looking out from Europe, in expanding serial technique, and in conveying an unmistakable determination all his own, is extraordinary for a composer of twenty-one.

Second Piano Sonata

Boulez's position as the leader of the young Parisian serialists appears in retrospect to have been definitively established by 1948, the year in which he not only completed his Second Piano Sonata but also had a score performed on French radio (his music for René Char's *Le soleil des eaux*) and published two articles in the new journal *Polyphonie*. This was to be the pattern of his activity for the next several years— producing music, and arguments in support of that music—and it testifies to his self-chosen role as the head of a revolutionary phalanx. In 'The Current Impact of Berg',[15] prompted by a series of performances in Paris, he attacked the

---

[15] *Stocktakings*, 183–7.

'Romanticism' and 'attachment to tradition' he found in various works by the composer, his attack being stimulated particularly by a contemporary (and not only contemporary) tendency to praise Berg at the expense of Schoenberg and Webern as the master of atonality with a human face. The other essay was the already invoked 'Proposals', in which he not only called his predecessors to task but offered indications of the path forward with reference to his own recent works: the Sonatina, the Char cantata *Le visage nuptial*, the lost Symphony and the Second Piano Sonata.

The Second Sonata, a much weightier work than the Sonatina or the slim, two-movement First Sonata, is a half-hour piece in four movements, and shows, besides an extension of Boulez's divergent serial technique, a deeper involvement of rhythm as a functional participant in the musical fabric. The growth in scale is significant in its direction. Comparison of the sonata with Beethoven's 'Hammer-klavier' has long been a commonplace of Boulez criticism, and seems to have been invited by the composer in creating music of Beethovenian weight, density, and texture (this is a far more continuous, propelled piece than the Sonatina, as well as a heavier one), and in providing strong intimations of sonata form in the first movement and of fugue in the finale. Given that Boulez, when he wrote the work, was still in his early twenties and unknown outside a small Paris circle, his appeal to Beethoven bespeaks a certainty in his historical position that would have to seem absurdly presumptuous had it not been vindicated by his subsequent career, and in particular by the subsequent career of this piece. Its acceptance into the repertory of so discriminating a musician as Maurizio Pollini was one mark of its status. The work is also, with the Sonatina and the First Sonata, one of the few that Boulez has not suppressed or revised. Where the chronological places of, for example, *Le soleil des eaux* and *Le visage nuptial* have been confused by repeated recastings, the Second Sonata persists as a channel of direct access to the young Boulez in the heat of self-discovery.

Why he should have been attracted to the 'Hammerklavier' model—other than as a defiant challenge to himself and to others—is not hard to guess: the spirit of contrariety would have drawn him to a work which strains at the edges of its own form, and which does so to the extent of appearing to contradict what it executes. As he himself has recalled: 'I tried to destroy the first-movement sonata form, to disintegrate slow movement form by the use of the trope, and repetitive scherzo form by the use of variation form, and finally, in the fourth movement, to demolish fugal and canonic form. Perhaps I am using too many negative terms, but the Second Sonata does have this explosive, disintegrating and dispersive character, and in spite of its own very restricting form the destruction of all these classical moulds was quite deliberate.'[16]

Since Boulez was here speaking a quarter of a century after the event, he could have been influenced by how his work had come to be regarded in the interim.

[16] *Conversations with Célestin Deliège*, 41–2.

However, creative violence is strikingly expressed in the music's markings, especially in the last movement. Having asked, in his opening remarks, that the player should 'avoid absolutely, above all in slow tempos, what are customarily called "expressive nuances" ', he repeatedly requires in the finale that the sound be 'percussive', 'strident', 'exasperated', arriving near the end at the instruction to 'pulverize the sound'. Destructiveness is at least implicit, too, in what he wrote at the time in 'Proposals': the destructiveness of one whose only response to his musical forefathers was antagonistic, and the destructiveness of one whose ideal was ceaseless change. If there was to be a coherent relationship between pitch and rhythm, then, as he saw it, rhythm had to obey similar laws of instability and non-repetition to those which obtained in his serial universe: as he wrote in 'Proposals', 'the principle of variation and constant renewal will guide us remorselessly'.[17]

Ex. 2. Boulez, Piano Sonata No. 2 (1947–8): I

[17] *Stocktakings*, 57.

The most usual result of this principle in the Second Sonata is a tangled counter-point of cells, frequently in three or four parts, perpetually reinterpreting the pro-portions of a few basic motifs. Example 2*a* shows the initial two bars of the sonata and Example 2*b* a passage from later in the first movement, the latter redrawn in order to show the polyphony more clearly (the division into parts here is arbitrary). Among other correspondences, the semiquaver repeated-note element of Example 2*a* appears in Example 2*b* in units of semiquavers, triplet quavers, quavers, and triplet crotchets, each time to a different transformation of the same interval motif. In this last respect, the compositional technique is more logical than in the Sonatina, though of course that tendency is countered by the density and speed, speed being an especially important component of the passion and drive in early Boulez—the alarming sense of music going too fast, hurtling out of control.

Cellular counterpoint of this kind is alternated in the first movement with vigor-ous chordal charges (Tempo II) which serve to reinject the music with energy when-ever it shows signs of flagging or of coming to a dead end, and which themselves strive towards an even quaver motion that, once achieved, is suddenly galloped into triplets before the counterpoint returns 'rapide et violent'. A second opposition is created between passages in which the twelve notes are fixed in register, creating a feeling of obsessiveness or frustration, and others in which they are free; in Example 2*b* the C♯/D and G♯/A♭ are so fixed. Out of these two kinds of dialectic Boulez gen-erates the impression of a classical sonata allegro, but since the movement is at the same time constantly redrawing its basic thematic material, it manifests too a head-long rush away from any kind of formal definition.

The other movements are as described in the above quotation from the com-poser (only the third uses the same series as the first, the second and fourth having one of their own). The second movement, like the slow section of the Sonatina, looks towards the later Boulez, but now more in terms of form than of texture. A rel-atively simple first part is, though with considerable variation, repeated in retro-grade and interrupted by musical parentheses in faster or slower tempos: this is what Boulez meant by referring to the medieval practice of troping. Contrasting with this elaborate structure, the third movement is straightforwardly a scherzo with three trios,[18] though passed through the filter of variation form (the four scherzo sections are related as original, retrograde inversion, inversion, and retro-grade): the relatively simple style of this movement perhaps reflects its early date, for it was finished in May 1946, which might suggest that it was originally planned not for the Second Sonata but for the First. The finale is again a highly ramified con-struction. Starting with three and a half pages of desperate suggestion around the basic ideas, it plunges into the extreme bass for an ominous serial statement which gives rise to a quasi-fugal development in two phases, the themes being defined more by rhythm than by pitch.

[18] See *Conversations with Célestin Deliège*, 41. However, the original title was 'Variations-Rondeau' (see *The Boulez–Cage Correspondence*, ed. Jean-Jacques Nattiez (Cambridge, 1993), 77).

In most of this movement, as throughout those before, Boulez works with con-catenations of cells, but in one section (defined by the tempo of quaver = 126 and beginning at the bottom of p. 34 in the Heugel edition) he seems to be trying out a new arithmetical approach to rhythm—one that Messiaen had introduced in the movements 'Turangalîla II' and 'Turangalîla III' of his *Turangalîla* symphony.[19] Both composers used rhythmic values which are all multiples of a semiquaver; the Boulez passage has values between two and nine semiquavers, with some relation-ships between successions of values in different polyphonic lines. At one point, for example, the sequence 2–7–3–7–4–9–2 coincides with its retrograde, and though the moment is too brief for any firm conclusions to be drawn, the way is opened here towards the serial durations of the musical manifesto of total serialism (i.e. ser-ial organization of all parameters) that Boulez would provide four years later in the first book of his *Structures* for two pianos. It is noteworthy, and similarly significant in the light of Boulez's future development, that the pitch lines here do not show the same retrograde relationship. Following Messiaen's example, Boulez treats rhythm and pitch as separately composable elements, and as elements whose structures may even be placed in open conflict, provided there is the notional coherence of both having the same abundant freedom.

Example 2*b* has already suggested both the separateness and the intensiveness of Boulez's rhythmic development, but there are other places in the work, especially in the finale, where the rhythmic counterpoint is more orderly, at least in how it is notated. (In much of the music Boulez wrote in his twenties the notation serves to reveal aspects of compositional technique that a more practical orthography might obliterate, as if the music were intended not only to be played and heard but to give lessons to junior composers, and perhaps even to be discussed in histories of music.) At one point, for instance, a rhythmic canon is projected by lines made up of variants of two cells: one is distinguished by having two equal values plus a third which is dissimilar (e.g. dotted semiquaver – dotted semiquaver – semiquaver), the other by symmetry (e.g. semiquaver – semiquaver triplets – semiquaver: in Messiaen's terms such rhythms are 'non-retrogradable'). The modifications of these motifs are easy to follow, but the ties—not to mention the low dynamic level of this section, the speed, the density, and the absence of any parallel cross-refer-ences on the pitch level—thoroughly obscure what is going on. The highly evolved construction is obliterated as it is established.

Such negativity, as has already been indicated, is characteristic of Boulez's early music, and in particular of this sonata. The violence of the work is not just superfi-cial rhetoric but symptomatic of a whole aesthetic of annihilation, and especially of a need to demolish what had gone before. To quote Boulez again on this: 'History as it is made by great composers is not a history of conservation but of destruc-tion—even while cherishing what has been destroyed.'[20] The massively powered developments of the sonata's outer movements bring an autodestructive impetus

---

[19] See Robert Sherlaw Johnson: *Messiaen* (London, 1977), 92–3.
[20] *Conversations with Célestin Deliège*, 21.

to the classical moulds of sonata allegro and fugue in what is at the same time a determined refutation of Schoenberg's conservative practice with regard to form. Simultaneously Boulez effaces his own constructive means (while leaving traces for readers of the printed music), not only by piling up rhythmic cells so that they obliterate one another, as in Example 2, but also by pressing his proliferating serial method so hard that any unifying power in the basic interval shapes is threatened.

Char Cantatas and the *Livre pour quatuor*

Nothing could better illustrate the gap—but also the underlying alliance—between master and pupil than to place Boulez's Second Piano Sonata alongside Messiaen's precisely contemporary *Turangalîla* symphony. Where Boulez's work appears to have been consciously created as a contribution to musical history, within a context of Beethoven, Schoenberg, and Messiaen, Messiaen's symphony stands apart from the western tradition: it seems to need no background other than is supplied by the common human heritage, and one can imagine it being understood by people who had never heard any western music before. Where Boulez detonates traditional forms, Messiaen, the 'juxtaposer', assembles his materials in simple schemes of repetition and alternation. Where Boulez negates, Messiaen affirms and accepts. The symphony is a ten-movement cycle of celebration: a celebration of exhilarating pulsation, of radiant harmony, of the rich colours to be found in a large orchestra augmented by ondes martenot and by a solo piano at the head of a tuned percussion group also including glockenspiel, celesta, and vibraphone.

The similarities between the sonata and the symphony would have to include intermittent high speed, cellular rhythm (though of course regular pulse is the exception in Boulez), and perhaps also erotic impulse. In almost everything Boulez has said and written about his own music, the interlacing of creation and destruction is seen in quite abstract terms. However, of the two vocal works he produced during this period, the larger, *Le visage nuptial*, sets poems of intense sexual imagery, while the other, *Le soleil des eaux*, begins, in its definitive form, with a song of sensual longing. According to his own account, he was drawn to the poetry of René Char because of 'the clipped violence of his style, the unequalled paroxysm, the purity'.[21] But though this is borne out by the fact that similar phrases could be used to describe his music from the late 1940s, there is no explanation here for his particular choice of *Le visage nuptial*, nor for his response to those poems, which he set for two rapturously intertwined women soloists (soprano and contralto), with female chorus and orchestra in the final version. All the signs of explosion in the Second Sonata—the speed, the colliding detail, the rejection—have other referents in the poetry of *Le visage nuptial*, though of course it may be that Boulez selected those poems because they provided a metaphor for the musical project on which he

[21] Antoine Goléa, *Rencontres avec Pierre Boulez* (Paris, 1958), 99.

was engaged. Cleansing the house of music may always have been his first and only purpose.

It may nevertheless have suited him that the only unchanged records of that purpose should be abstract pieces: the Sonatina and the two sonatas. *Le visage nuptial*, originally set out in 1946–7 for soloists with two ondes martenot, piano, and percussion, was subsequently orchestrated and then substantially revised in the late 1980s. *Le soleil des eaux* was reinterpreted in three successive cantata versions in 1950, 1958, and 1965. With the historical place of these Char settings effectively neutralized, the remaining instrumental works could testify to an impatience that was prompted solely and vigorously by musical conditions, and the success of that image demonstrates how plausible it seemed that a young man in the late 1940s should have been totally engaged in advancing compositional thought.

It is in keeping with the persona of the single-minded musical revolutionary that he should have said so little of his expressive intentions: the remark about 'expressive nuances' at the head of the Second Sonata is indicative of his distaste. Only rarely has the austere silence been broken, as when he recalled how he had been 'struck in a very violent way' by the beauty of African and Far Eastern music (the music that Messiaen had taught him to admire), 'a beauty so far removed from our own culture and so close to my own temperament',[22] or when, at the end of 'Proposals', he acknowledged another French artist who had been 'struck in a very violent way' by extra-European cultures. 'I think', he wrote, 'that music should be collective hysteria and magic, violently modern—along the lines of Antonin Artaud.' But then immediately comes the recoil: 'I have a horror of discussing verbally what is so smugly called the problem of aesthetics . . . I prefer to return to my lined paper.'[23]

The work he returned to his lined paper to write was the *Livre pour quatuor* (1948–9), his first instrumental work without piano. The medium of the string quartet inevitably imposed, as he has said, 'a certain reticence',[24] but it also made available a wide variety of tone colour, for he took up effects to be found in the quartets of Debussy, Bartók, Berg, and Webern. Of the six projected movements, the even-numbered ones (except perhaps for IV, which has been neither published nor performed) are those in which attention is fixed most firmly on the development of rhythmic cells in an intensive manner proceeding from the Second Sonata. The odd-numbered movements are freer in feeling and motion, and often touch an abstracted sensuousness that also marks the opening song of *Le soleil des eaux*. But rhythmic complexity is a feature throughout, and no doubt accounted for the delayed and piecemeal première of the work: movements I and II were not heard until 1955, and III, V and VI followed only in the early 1960s. Partial performances are not, however, in contradiction with the nature of the *Livre*, for the players are invited to choose and order movements as they will—though there is some doubt as to whether this mobile conception was part of the original plan. In any event, by

[22] ' "Sonate, que me veux-tu?" ', *Perspectives of New Music*, 1/2 (1963), 34.

[23] *Stocktakings*, 54.   [24] *Conversations with Célestin Deliège*, 53.

the late 1960s Boulez had decided that the work could not be performed adequately without a conductor, and so he withdrew it (except for performances by quartets who had already learned it) and set about a version for large string orchestra, *Livre pour cordes*. However, the arrival in the 1970s and 1980s of new ensembles committed to modern works—notably the Arditti and Alban Berg quartets—prompted him to re-release the score, though during this period he also made a new version of the single movement (I) he had composed of the *Livre pour cordes*.

Here again, then, one finds circumstances—and the composer's own actions—altering history. Boulez's statements about history, such as have been quoted here, suggest a single, stable march of events, into which he strode, and whose tempo he made his own. The effect of his explanations, emphasizing the Sonatina and the sonatas as way stations towards the first book of *Structures*, has been to affirm that view, which became part of the ideology of new music in the 1950s and 1960s. This meant that other works of Boulez's passionately creative early twenties—*Le visage nuptial, Le soleil des eaux*, the *Livre pour cordes* and the long withdrawn Sonata for two pianos—were relegated to the margins. What thereby emerged as a zealous pursuit of historical necessity is therefore only a part of the truth of Boulez's artistic behaviour in the late 1940s. It is no less remarkable for that.

Musique concrète

The presence of the ondes martenot in the music that Boulez and Messiaen were writing at this time—Boulez's Quartet and *Le visage nuptial*, Messiaen's *Turangalîla*—can be understood in various ways: Boulez was a performer on the instrument, and Messiaen used its capacity to suggest a voice unearthly in its range, power, and wordlessness. Whether at the time they were concerned too with electronic music as a goal is unclear: Boulez's early writings suggest that the problems consuming him were those of *écriture*. However, there were others who were eager to explore new sound resources, and in May 1948 Pierre Schaeffer created the first example of what became known as 'musique concrète': *Etude aux chemins de fer*, a three-minute piece made by manipulating recordings of railway trains.[25]

Experiments with discs had been conducted before the war, notably (and independently) by Milhaud, Hindemith, and Varèse, but it remained to Schaeffer to discover and use the basic techniques of sound transformation: reversing a sound by playing its recording backwards, altering it in pitch, speed, and timbre by changing the velocity of playback, isolating elements from it, and superimposing one sound on another. Just as important as these possibilities was the change to the art of composition. Every example of *musique concrète* was an improvisation which the composer created by working directly with the sounds at his disposal: notation and performance were bypassed, and many of the traditional skills of composers—

[25] See Carlos Palombini, 'Machine Songs V: Pierre Schaeffer—from Research into Noises to Experimental Music', *Computer Music Journal*, 17/3 (1993), 14–19.

abstract imagination, acuteness of internal hearing, precision of notation—were irrelevant. Perhaps for those very reasons, electronic music was soon set on a path apart from other music, to become a sphere (too often regarded as a secondary sphere) with its own institutions and proponents.

At the time, though, Schaeffer's hopes, like Boulez's, would seem to have been more utopian. Both men were convinced that their innovations—techniques of sound transformation for the one, principles of rhythm and form adequate to serialism for the other—were historically inevitable and would provide a way towards the musical future. Schaeffer's aim was to use his techniques in order to free his material from its native associations, so that an event could become not just an evocative symbol but a pure 'sound object' amenable to compositional treatment: to have depended on the original associations would have been, in his terms, to create not music but literature, to make a drama of sound effects rather than a musical composition of rhythms and timbres. An important discovery was made when he remarked that the removal of the opening instants of a sound, the 'starting transient', could transform its character, so that a bell stroke, for instance, would be changed into something more like an organ tone. Armed with techniques of this kind, he hoped to employ an array of gramophone turntables as 'the most general musical instrument possible', providing facilities for altering any sound derived from the real world (hence the term 'musique concrète' to denote this music created from 'concrete' sound sources, though behind the choice of word there may also have been the hope that new materials would revolutionize the art in the way that reinforced concrete had revolutionized architecture—an optimistic analogy cherished by many composers in the decade or so after the war).

Schaeffer's early studies, which include not only the railway piece but also others created from piano chords (played by Boulez) and saucepans, were broadcast by French radio on 5 October 1948 in what was billed as a 'concert of noises'. The result was immediate interest from the public and from fellow composers. Several young musicians visited Schaeffer's studio, and one of them, the Messiaen pupil Pierre Henry, remained to collaborate with him on what was the first extended electronic composition, the *Symphonie pour un homme seul* (1949–50), which uses a wide variety of sounds—vocal, instrumental, and orchestral, as well as many from everyday objects—in eleven short movements of diverse character, by turns erotic, whimsical, and menacing. The work received its première at the first public concert of electronic music, given at the Ecole Normale de Musique in Paris on 18 March 1950. With the arrival of the tape recorder later that year to ease production, and with the formal establishment by French radio of a Groupe de Musique Concrète in 1951, the way was open for a wider dissemination of the means of electronic music. For Boulez and Messiaen, the possibility of a precise control over sound and duration came at the opportune moment when music itself seemed to be demanding pristine process.

Variations: Nono

1948 begins to appear a key year: the year of the first *musique concrète*, the year when Messiaen completed *Turangalîla* and Boulez his Second Sonata, and the year when another avenue of modernism opened with the arrival of Hermann Scherchen (1891–1966) to teach a course at the conservatory in Venice, where his class included Bruno Maderna (1920–73) and Nono, both Venetians and both ex-pupils of Gian Francesco Malipiero.[26] Scherchen was a great instigator. He had conducted *Pierrot lunaire* on its 1912 tour, and given the first performance of Berg's *Wozzeck* fragments, among many premières; since 1933 he had been living in Switzerland. He was active in the International Society for Contemporary Music, which during the decade or so after the war was still an important forum. And he had founded, in 1919, the most influential new-music review: *Melos*. Rather unusually for someone who had emerged from Schoenberg's circle, he had catholic tastes, and seems to have encouraged young composers—first Nono and Maderna, later Iannis Xenakis (b. 1920)—to stay independent of all orthodoxies. On Nono his influence was decisive, though also important at that 1948 course was the presence of Eunice Catunda, a Brazilian composer and communist, who introduced both Nono and Maderna to Spanish and Brazilian dance rhythms, and to the poetry of Lorca. The Latin rhythms and the Lorca were to have a driving importance in Nono's music of the early 1950s; the communist allegiance he already shared, for though it was not until 1952 that he joined the party, his first public work was a homage to one of Schoenberg's anti-fascist pieces, *Variazioni canoniche sulla serie dell'op.41 di Arnold Schoenberg* (i.e. the *Ode to Napoleon*).

The title could be misleading. Nono's interpretation of both variation and canon is unconventional, and the work is not serial: rather the series is the music's gradual discovery, taking control of harmony in the third variation and of melodic counterpoint in the fourth, at the end of which—in the closing bars of the piece—the harp at last presents the twelve-note succession complete. (There is a parallel here, though the musical circumstances are very different, with the Piano Sonata of Jean Barraqué.) Like Boulez at a similar point of close approach to Schoenberg (in the Sonatina), Nono immediately proves his separation and his individuality; but he does this not so much by contradicting Schoenberg as by hailing him from a distance, a distance expressed in features which were to remain characteristic. Among these are the treatment of the orchestra in choirs of like instruments (an old Venetian habit), the elemental simplicity, the Varèsian favouring of unpitched percussion for rhythmic messages, and the powerful drive. Hopkins mentions also 'that sense of mystery whereby Nono seems to be a conjuror drawing sounds from the air as from a hat'. Example 3, from the lead-up to the second variation, may indi-

---

[26] I am grateful to Nicolas Hodges for giving me the benefit of his unpublished essay 'Luigi Nono: Compositional Development from *Variazioni canoniche* (1950) to *Composizione n.2 per orchestra—Diario polacco* (1958–9)'. The best published introduction to Nono in English remains, G. W. Hopkins: 'Luigi Nono', *Music and Musicians*, 14/8 (1965–6), 32 ff.

cate many of these aspects. The drive and the elementalness are there in the way a short–long–short rhythmic figure is stamped by the timpani in the fifth bar from out of the whispering percussion, and then becomes, in a second wave, the subject of a timbral crescendo from timpani to brass to strings, harp and piano in octaves. The magic unpredictability is present in the repeated surprise of a sudden boldness.

Ex. 3. Nono, *Variazioni canoniche* (1950)

The work was composed in 1950, and Nono took it with him that summer when he went, as did Scherchen and Maderna, to the summer course that would provide the gathering European avant garde with an annual meeting-place: Darmstadt.

America 1: Silencing Music, 1946–1952

Rhythmic Structuring

The principal work of his own that Cage took with him to Paris in 1949 was his book of *Sonatas and Interludes* for prepared piano (1946–8), one of the largest of several compositions from that decade in which he adjusted the timbres of the piano by inserting foreign objects between the strings: the printed music includes a 'table of preparations' which gives instructions for the placing of screws, nuts, bolts, and pieces of plastic and rubber to alter the sounds of forty-five notes, so that the piano comes to make largely unpitched noises like those of drums, gongs, and rattles. Preparation of the piano offered the composer the opportunity to explore and transform his sound material in a very direct manner, by inviting an empirical mode of working similar to that being made possible by the electronic medium. Indeed, the prepared piano was perhaps consciously developed as a home-made substitute for the synthesizer of the future. In 1937 Cage had expressed his optimistic view of the potential electronic evolution of music,[1] and in 1942—after he had made his first electronic experiments, beginning with the 1939 *Imaginary Landscape No. 1*, for instruments including two variable-speed turntables with frequency recordings—he had been more specific: 'Many musicians,' he had written, 'the writer included, have dreamed of compact technological boxes, inside which all audible sounds, including noise, would be ready to come forth at the command of the composer.'[2] In this article he had gone on to describe the work he had recently done at a Chicago radio station, using electrical gadgets (buzzers, amplified coils of wire, a radio, and a gramophone) in various pieces made on to disc for broadcast.

If in their experimental approach to sound the *Sonatas and Interludes* relate to Cage's electronic essays, they also connect with his earlier works for his own percussion orchestra, such as the *First Construction (in Metal)* for six players (1939), since the prepared piano is effectively a one-man percussion group. This concentration on percussive sonorities was a central item of musical principle, for it dramatized the need, as Cage saw it, for music to be structured on the basis of duration (possessed by all kinds of sound, and by silence) rather than harmony (possessed only by pitched tones in combination). His 'Defense of Satie',[3] a lecture delivered soon after the completion of the *Sonatas and Interludes*, charges Beethoven with

[1] 'The Future of Music: Credo', in *Silence, Lectures and Writings* (London, 1968), 3–7.
[2] 'For More New Sounds', in Richard Kostelanetz (ed.), *John Cage* (London, 1971), 65.
[3] Ibid. 77–84.

the 'error' of defining structure by means of harmony, and applauds Satie and Webern for correctly using duration as the measure: 'There can be no right making of music that does not structure itself from the very roots of sound and silence—lengths of time'. Later in the same essay he insists that the purpose of a musical composition is 'to bring into co-being elements paradoxical by nature, to bring into one situation elements that can be and ought to be agreed upon—that is, Law elements—together with elements that cannot and ought not to be agreed upon—that is, Freedom elements—these two ornamented by other elements, which may lend support to one or the other of the two fundamental and opposed elements, the whole forming thereby an organic entity.'

In the *Sonatas and Interludes* he provided the most comprehensive demonstration of this combining of 'Law' and 'Freedom' in rhythmic structure. Each of the sixteen sonatas and four interludes is based on a number sequence which defines the durational proportions of the subsections and often appears also in smaller rhythmic units. In the case of Sonata I, for instance, the sequence is 4-1-3-4-1-3-4-2-4-2, and the movement, like all the sonatas, falls into two repeated sections which correspond in their lengths to this sequence, the first being of four, one and three double-dotted semibreves, the second of four and two double-dotted semibreves. Nor is this choice of the double-dotted semibreve as unit an arbitrary one, for the number sequence sums to twenty-eight, and the double-dotted semibreve is made up of twenty-eight semiquavers (sixteen plus eight plus four). So the entire sequence can be represented within any subsection. For example, the first subsection, with a length of four double-dotted semibreves, can equally be considered as containing twenty-eight crotchets, and so can express the sequence in terms of crotchets, as indicated in Example 4, which shows only the rhythm of this subsection. Here, it is clear, the proportions are to some degree masked by what one must take to be 'Freedom elements', though these often state fragments of the 'Law' in miniature: the ratio 1 : 3, for instance, features in bars 1, 3, 5, and 6, as well as in its rightful places at bars 2 and 4. The sonata therefore displays the same proportioning on three levels: in the subsectioning of the whole, in the rhythmic divisions of subsections, and in the fine detail of the rhythmic divisions.

Ex. 4. Cage, *Sonatas and Interludes* (1946–8): I

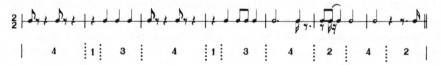

Cage had introduced this kind of self-repeating form in the *First Construction*, and continued with it in the works that came immediately after the *Sonatas and Interludes*, including the composition he began in Paris—the String Quartet in Four Parts (1949–50)—and the ensuing Concerto for prepared piano and orchestra

(1950–1). In the former, the guiding number sequence governs the relative lengths of the four movements, which form a seasonal cycle from summer to spring. It is to these movements that the title alludes and not to the medium's polyphonic nature, for the quartet is not really polyphonic at all but essentially in one part: Cage described it as 'a melodic line without accompaniment, which employs single tones, intervals, triads and aggregates requiring one or more of the instruments for their production'[4] (by 'aggregates' he meant chords more complex than simple intervals and triads). The harmonies, reintroduced after a spate of works for largely percussive resources, are not to be interpreted as functional—indeed,the slow progress of unrelated chords defies an understanding in terms of harmonic conse- quence—but are rather single and independent events, each chosen for its colour and caused to occupy the space allotted to it by the numerical pattern. The string quartet thus becomes a kind of enlarged prepared piano, able to offer a very differ- ent range of sonorities, but similarly to be used as a reservoir of unconnected sounds. Cage pursued this mode of composition in writing for an orchestra of twenty-two soloists in the Concerto, the players again contributing to a monorhythmic line of detached sound events.

As Cage recognized, his use of fixed-proportion rhythmic structures allowed him to place not only sound, noise, and silence on an equal footing but also east and west. Rhythm, not harmony, was what was fundamental to all musical cultures. And his own rhythmic practice related to the Indian concept of tala, or to the tiered speeds of Balinese gamelan music, which the work of Colin McPhee would have drawn to his attention in the 1930s. The sounds of his works for percussion ensem- ble and for prepared piano also suggested those of Balinese music, and the *Sonatas and Interludes* had deeper links with the orient, coming from the time when Cage said he 'first became seriously aware of Oriental philosophy'.[5] It was after reading the works of Ananda K. Coomaraswamy that he determined in the *Sonatas and Interludes* 'to attempt the expression in music of the 'permanent emotions' of Indian tradition: the heroic, the erotic, the wondrous, the mirthful, sorrow, fear, anger, the odious, and their common tendency toward tranquility'.[6] Then in the String Quartet he was stimulated by eastern associations of summer with preserva- tion, autumn with destruction, winter with peace, and spring with creation.

Given Cage's interests in rhythm and in eastern music, his relationship with Boulez in 1949 begins to make sense. For Boulez, here was a man whose use of rhythmic cells—albeit in strictly monophonic music—showed similar techniques of variation to his own, a man who was similarly iconoclastic (though, as it turned out, in his calm way far more ruthlessly so than the intemperate Boulez), and a man whose understanding of music was similarly global. Cage was, too, an American in Paris, the representative of a nation which had been partly responsible for liberat- ing France from its political and intellectual bondage, and the representative of a culture which might have appeared—to a young man seemingly immune to the

---

[4] Preface to the score.   [5] Kostelanetz (ed.), *John Cage*, 129.   [6] Ibid.

siren call of the Soviet Union—to hold the key to the future. Falling between Boulez and Messiaen in age, Cage could have impressed Boulez as an older brother, and a proof that he was on the right path. Boulez was particularly struck by Cage's use of square charts setting out the durational relationships to be employed in a work, by his escape from temperament in writing for noise instruments, and by his handling of complex sounds not as agents of harmonic meaning but as events in themselves, and as events that suggested a pitch analogue for the rhythmic cell. 'The tendency of these experiments by John Cage', he was to write in 1952, 'is too close to my own for me to fail to mention them.'[7] But by that time, when Boulez had made the break-through into total serialism, Cage's retreat from western rhetoric—to be observed progressively in the *Sonatas and Interludes*, the String Quartet, and the Concerto for prepared piano—had set him on a very different course.

Towards Silence

The deceptive—perhaps even self-deceptive—nature of the link between Cage and Boulez is manifest from a comparison of the former's Concerto for prepared piano (summer 1950–February 1951) with the latter's first book of *Structures* (1951–2). Both composers made extensive use of number charts, but where Boulez saw them as an aid in total serial organization, Cage found in them a way to attain non-intention. For Boulez, objective rule was a guardian against traditional values, a guarantor of independence: he as composer was master of the rule. For Cage, always more radical, mastery of the rule was an idle conceit: he was delighted by the possibility of removing his own creative wishes. 'I let the pianist express the opinion that music should be improvised or felt,' he said of the Concerto's first movement, 'while the orchestra expressed only the chart, with no personal taste involved. In the second movement I made large concentric moves on the chart for both pianist and orchestra, with the idea of the pianist beginning to give up personal taste. The third movement had only one set of moves [dictated by coin tossing[8]] on the chart for both, and a lot of silences . . . Until that time, my music had been based on the traditional idea that you had to say something. The charts gave me my first indication of the possibility of saying nothing.'[9]

The virtue of saying nothing was being borne in upon him by his studies of zen under Daisetz T. Suzuki at Columbia University in 1951. Opening his work to chance decisions gave him some inkling of how to reach the goal. Through a mechanical procedure—at first coin tosses to pick places on number charts—sounds would arrive in a composition without the composer's will or decision, and so without any deliberate connection to other sounds. Nobody would be intending them; no musical language would be giving them a meaning. One could 'make a composition the continuity of which is free of individual taste and memory

[7] 'Possibly . . .', *Stocktakings*, 135.   [8] See *The Boulez–Cage Correspondence*, 94.
[9] Note with Nonesuch H 71202.

(psychology) and also of the literature and "traditions" of the art. The sounds enter the time-space centered within themselves, unimpeded by service to any abstraction, their 360 degrees of circumference free for an infinite play of interpenetration. Value judgments are not in the nature of this work as regards either composition, performance, or listening. The idea of relation (the idea: 2) being absent, anything (the idea: 1) may happen. A "mistake" is beside the point, for once anything happens it authentically is.'[10]

For the rest of his life—a period of forty years after this statement was published in 1952—Cage never wavered from the view he had here expressed. In a sense, therefore, the Concerto for prepared piano is his last composition, the last composition in which he exerted his will, though dyingly. Yet there is a paradox here. Nonintention was itself an intention, and what allows us to go on speaking of Cage as a composer after the Concerto is the unparalleled determination with which he pursued that intention through an extraordinary variety of ways and means. This is where 'individual taste and memory (psychology)' make their remarkable return, for a determined absence of determination had already been the central characteristic of his music, an absence revealed in his treatment of time as unmotivated extension, his choice of simplicity and repetition (found at an early extreme in the 1947 prepared-piano piece *Music for Marcel Duchamp*), his avoidance of rhetoric. And the future was to prove, despite his immense and worldwide influence in the 1950s and 1960s, that nobody could make unmeant music as he could.

One of his earliest and boldest ventures in that direction was his *Imaginary Landscape No. 4* for twelve radio receivers, first performed in New York on 10 May 1951. In order to remove his own preferences from the composition he entrusted it to 'chance operations', using, as in the last movement of the Concerto, coin tosses to derive positions on his charts: the particular stimulus was the *I Ching*, of which the Wilhelm version had been published in New York the previous year. Where the *I Ching* invites the user to cast lots and so be directed to one of sixty-four oracular pronouncements, Cage substituted for the latter his charts, of eight-by-eight arrays of numbers which he could use to dictate musical parameters—in this case, the wavelengths, durations, and dynamic levels to be achieved with the twelve radios. All these parameters are notated, but of course there is no way of knowing what will be broadcast on any given wavelength at the time of performance. It might therefore seem that the scrupulousness is ironic, even comic; but to see Cage as clown or satirist misses the point of his work, and mistakes too the calm cheerfulness with which he went through life. His folly was a kind of devotion. To accept the data of chance was to welcome anything. And to present those data in the form of a score was to demand a similar selflessness, trust, and tenacity from performers, which may explain why his chance-composed works—so far from licensing irresponsibility—require and favour a rare degree of artistry.

[10] 'To Describe the Process of Composition used in *Music of Changes* and *Imaginary Landscape No. 4*', *Silence*, 59.

He was lucky in some of his colleagues. Alongside *Imaginary Landscape No. 4* he was at work on a big solo piano work for David Tudor (b. 1926), whom he had persuaded to give the first New York performance of Boulez's Second Sonata on 17 December 1950. Tudor was to remain one of his regular collaborators and friends; both men were associated with Merce Cunningham's dance company, and Tudor was the destined performer or co-performer of much of Cage's music for piano or electronics (towards which he moved in 1960). The work that started this musical alliance was the *Music of Changes* (the Wilhelm *I Ching* had been published as *The Book of Changes*), which maintains the fixed-proportion rhythmic structure of the earlier works, though time is here measured principally by lengths of stave. Such notation, often called 'space-time notation', was widely adopted during the 1950s, 1960s, and 1970s; for Cage it provided a way to symbolize time as a smooth extent, into which conventionally notated durations fall. The proportional rhythmic structure is now unregarded by the music: it simply provides passages of time to be filled, and the filling is dictated again by coin tosses that determine tempos, the number of simultaneous layers, dynamic levels, pitches, and sound categories (whether single notes, groups, aggregates, other complex events such as clusters, silently depressed keys, trills and glissandos on the strings, noises such as lid slams, or rests); durations were derived from the Tarot pack. Often the unwilled result is irrational: for instance, in Example 5, which shows the opening of the first of the four books into which the work is divided, the left-hand cluster gets in the way of other incidents. In such cases 'the performer is to apply his own discretion'.

Perhaps the only thing that was intended of the *Music of Changes* was that it should be a response to the Boulez sonata, with which it was paired at its first complete performance, in New York on 1 January 1952. Everything else was ruthlessly

Ex. 5. Cage, *Music of Changes* (1951): I

non-intentional—except, crucially, the ruthlessness. For one thing, few other musicians would have carried through the project of chance-composing every detail in a packed three-quarter-hour work, and of then going on in that direction: apologizing to Boulez in the summer of 1952 for the sketchiness of a letter, Cage remarked that 'I spend a great deal of time tossing coins and the emptiness of head that that induces begins to penetrate the rest of my time as well'.[11] The laborious mechanism of chance composition was not only a bulwark against creative intention: it withered creative intention. And yet by denying himself choice, Cage paradoxically intensified those features that had been most characteristic of his deliberate music: its openness to new and various sounds, and its cool unfolding, not troubled by passages of extreme activity or complexity, 'throwing sound into silence'.[12] Slowed beat in the String Quartet and the Concerto for prepared piano had already reduced the sense of music driving the machine of time. In the *Music of Changes*, by definition, there can be no moment-to-moment purpose. Time is a neutral expanse into which sounds come, and by offering it as such, Cage completed the revolution that Debussy had begun against musical progression.

He went on to apply coin-tossing methods to the electronic medium in *Imaginary Landscape No. 5* (1951–2) and *Williams Mix* (1952). Tape music was then in its infancy. The Russian-born Vladimir Ussachevsky (b. 1911), who taught at Columbia University, gave a demonstration of the new medium's potential in 1952, and he was soon joined in his endeavours by Otto Luening (b. 1900), who had studied with Busoni. They presented the first concert of electronic music in America, at the Museum of Modern Art in New York on 28 October 1952: representative of the pieces then heard are Ussachevsky's *Sonic Contours* and Luening's *Fantasy in Space*, based on the sounds of piano and flute respectively. Out of their efforts grew the Columbia–Princeton Electronic Music Center, which was formally founded in 1960.

Cage's interest in electronic music went back long before the Ussachevsky–Luening initiative to his 1937 essay and the works that had followed it; he had also had his enthusiasm reawakened by Boulez's news of working with Schaeffer.[13] But by now he was concerned not so much with new sounds as with tape as a holding medium. The notation of the *Music of Changes* already suggests a stretch of magnetic tape bearing sound imprints; *Imaginary Landscape No. 5*, devised for a dance, was to actualize that image, with the imprints taken from any forty-two source recordings. To make his own version he went to the studio of Louis and Bebe Barron (who in 1956 were to be responsible for the first electronic music for a commercial film, *Forbidden Planet*), and stayed on to create the vastly more complex *Williams Mix*, named in honour of the patron, Paul Williams, who had funded the work. *Williams Mix*, of which only a four-minute fragment was ever completed, required a host of coin tosses to determine the kinds and lengths of sounds to be spliced together onto eight simultaneous tracks, each sound belonging to one of six

---

[11] *The Boulez–Cage Correspondence*, 133.   [12] Ibid. 78.   [13] See ibid. 119 ff.

categories—'city sounds', 'country sounds', 'electronic sounds', 'manually produced sounds, including the literature of music', 'wind-produced sounds, including songs' and 'small sounds requiring amplification to be heard with the
others'[14]—and subjected or not to control of frequency, overtone structure, and
amplitude. For Cage, the work took him still closer to non-intentionality, since the
choices of sounds and controls could be made by other people, following the
chance-ordered plan. 'So that it is not "my" work.'[15]

But in another sense it is, for the usual reasons of discipline and openness, and
also for the characteristic generosity to the small. Other works from the remarkable
year of 1952 included *Water Music* (for a pianist also using a radio and other sound
sources), the first of the *Music for Piano* series (in which Cage discovered a quicker
way of creating chance music, by marking imperfections on a sheet of paper and
placing notes there) and the opening piece in another series, of time-title works:
4' 33". But the celebrated silence of this last also stands at the end of a road, as one
logical conclusion to Cage's quest for self-withdrawal from his work, and as a natural development from the yawning gulfs of the Concerto for prepared piano and
the *Music of Changes*. It also presents the paradox of non-intentionality with peculiar intensity. Stray intentions persist. Cage sometimes seemed to accept the view
that the piece is not silent at all, but rather a revelation of the sounds an audience
would normally disregard or treat as disturbance. It is also mute theatre, in that the
performer or performers (the première, at Woodstock, New York, on 29 August
1952, was given by Tudor, but the work was later made available to any forces) must
make it clear that a musical performance is taking place. But these things are by the
way. *4' 33"* is music reduced to nothing, and nothing raised to music. It cannot be
heard, and is heard anywhere by anyone at any time. It is the extinction of thought,
and has provoked more thought than any other music of the second half of the
twentieth century.

[14] From Cage's note on the work in Kostelanetz (ed.), *John Cage*, 109.
[15] *The Boulez–Cage Correspondence*, 132.

Europe 2: Total Organization, 1949–1954

The Moment of Total Serialism 1: Darmstadt 1949 and Darmstadt 1951

It was at this point that Messiaen, through becoming a pupil of his pupils, became again their teacher. Speaking generally of his students, he once observed that 'their questions compelled me to undertake studies I might not have dreamed of, had it not been for them':[1] uppermost in his mind, surely, must have been his relationship with Boulez in the late 1940s and early 1950s. However, his leap from the *Cinq rechants* (1949) to the *Mode de valeurs et d'intensités* for piano (1949–50) might indicate some other catalyst, given that Boulez's most recent work at the time was the *Livre pour quatuor*. Then again, the dateline of the *Mode de valeurs*, 'Darmstadt 1949', is momentous only in the light of Darmstadt's later history: that year, when Messiaen was teaching there, the courses were still dominated by Leibowitz, who had brought some of his pupils—though not Boulez, who was already opposing himself to what he considered 'academic' in Leibowitz's brand of serialism. Perhaps the *Mode de valeurs* was a Boulezian historical necessity. Or perhaps it was tripped by a new card dealt into the pack of French music in the spring of 1949: Cage.

Cage spent several months in Paris before returning to New York, and played his *Sonatas and Interludes* for prepared piano (1946–8) both for Messiaen's class on 7 June[2] and at a soirée when Boulez delivered a slightly circumspect introduction.[3] Boulez's reference here to 'duration, amplitude, frequency, and timbre—in other words, the four characteristics of a sound' echoes a statement of sound's quaternary nature in Cage's recent essay 'Forerunners of Modern Music',[4] and suggests that the definition of those four parameters, which provided the organizational basis for total serialism, came from Cage. The setting-up of compositional algorithms, another essential feature of total serialism, also has clearer origins in Cage's principle of rhythmic proportioning than in Boulez's turmoil of motivic extrapolations. All that was needed was to add the twelve-note principle to these Cageian elements—the four parameters, automatic operation—and the *Mode de valeurs* would be the almost inevitable result.

Messiaen's preface to the *Mode de valeurs* describes how the piece is composed as a three-part counterpoint, each part using a different set of twelve chromatic pitches and twelve 'chromatic durations'. These, following the principle of rhythmic arithmetic in the *Turangalîla* symphony, are on scales from a demisemiquaver

---

[1] *Music and Color*, 176.
[2] See *The Boulez–Cage Correspondence*, 5.
[3] Reproduced ibid. 27–32.
[4] *Silence*, 62–6; also republished ibid. 38–42.

to a dotted crotchet in the top part, from a semiquaver to a dotted minim in the middle part, and from a quaver to a dotted semibreve in the bottom part. Each of the thirty-six pitches is permanently associated with one of the thirty-six durations, and each also keeps the same values in the other two parameters, of which 'amplitude' is represented by seven dynamic levels and 'timbre' by seven different attack markings. Example 6 shows the opening of the piece, which continues in the same manner throughout its duration of three and a half minutes. As Richard Toop has demonstrated in an important article on the origins of total serialism, there is a tendency to maintain contiguous fragments of the duration scales (the two upper lines in the example, for instance, both begin one–two–three–four, and the one–two–three pattern is soon repeated in the middle part), but in no sense is the construction serial: decisions about the ordering of fragments appear to be based on the wish to avoid octaves and other overt suggestions of tonality.[5]

For Messiaen, the *Mode de valeurs* was at an extreme point of pre-compositional systematization. In the larger piano piece *Cantéyodjayâ* (1949) he had placed a fraction of similar music along with other elements in a dance of the possibilities open

Ex. 6. Messiaen, *Mode de valeurs et d'intensités* (1949–50)

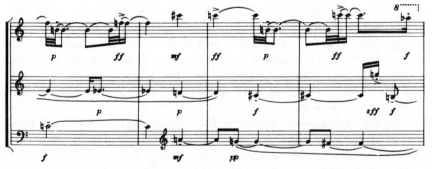

---

[5] 'Messiaen/Goeyvaerts, Fano/Stockhausen, Boulez', *Perspectives of New Music*, 13/1 (1974), 141–69.

to him after the *Turangalîla* symphony; in later works he used sets of chromatic durations again—notably in the piano piece *Île de feu II* (1950), the *Livre d'orgue* (1951), *La chouette hulotte* and *Le merle de roche* from the piano cycle *Catalogue d'oiseaux* (1956–8), the orchestral *Chronochromie* (1960) and the stigmata scene from *Saint François d'Assise* (1975–83)—but always with 'interversion' to make the haphazardness of the *Mode de valeurs* into decisive process. This technique he introduced in *Île de feu II*, where a sequence of twelve chromatic durations is permuted by taking values successively from the centre; that generates the first 'interversion', from which the second can be obtained by repeating the process:

Original	12	11	10	9	8	7	6	5	4	3	2	1
Interversion 1	6	7	5	8	4	9	3	10	2	11	1	12
Interversion 2	3	9	10	4	2	8	11	5	1	7	12	6

The operation can be repeated further until the original sequence is reproduced—in this case as the tenth interversion. *Île de feu II* unfolds the entire cycle, with less strictly organized episodes, but Messiaen later preferred sequences of thirty-two or sixty-four chromatic durations (the last piece in the *Livre d'orgue* has the title 'Soixante-quatre durées'), sequences whose interversions could intimate immense stretches of time.

Île de feu II and the *Mode de valeurs* were published with two other pieces as *Quatre études de rythme*, of which Messiaen made a commercial recording, and it was in this audible form that the *Mode de valeurs* returned to Darmstadt in 1951. Among the students there was Karlheinz Stockhausen (b. 1928), who was immediately attracted by what he called a 'fantastic music of the stars':[6] what excited him, as this image suggests, was the music's presentation of itself as constituted of single notes, 'existing for themselves in complete freedom,' as he went on to put it, 'and formulated individually in considerable isolation from each other'. Hitherto he had written twelve-note pieces in traditional thematic style, pursuing a Schoenberg–Hindemith synthesis that had rapidly become the common language of postwar Germany. Now the experience of the *Mode de valeurs*—and of discussions with two other young men at Darmstadt, Karel Goeyvaerts (1923–93), and Nono—set him in a new direction.

It is worth noting that Stockhausen was awestruck first by the sound of Messiaen's piece, not by its mechanism, for the physical substance and the sensuous impact of sound were to remain essential to his work. But he has consistently needed system too, and here Goeyvaerts could offer help. Goeyvaerts, after studies in his native Antwerp, had gone to the Paris Conservatoire and been a member of Messiaen's class in 1947–8, though apparently he had no knowledge of the *Mode de valeurs* before arriving in Darmstadt, bringing with him his Opus 1, a Sonata for two pianos (1950–1).[7] The detached notes ('points' in Stockhausen's terminology) of this piece must therefore be an independent evolution from earlier Messiaen

---

[6] K. H. Wörner: *Stockhausen: Life and Work* (London, 1973), 61.
[7] See Toop, 'Messiaen/Goeyvaerts', 162.

works, and surely even more so from the study of Webern's Piano Variations that Goeyvaerts had made in 1949–50, when he was still in Paris. (The possibility therefore arises that Goeyvaerts—as much as Boulez and Cage, and maybe more than either—was responsible for jolting Messiaen towards the *Mode de valeurs*.)

The Webern piece, though not itself definable as an example of total serialism,[8] proved to contain valuable pointers. Its second movement, for example, uses only three dynamic markings and five varieties of rhythmic cell; from this it was not too large a step to Goeyvaerts's use in the middle two movements of his sonata of seven duration values, seven modes of attack (as in the *Mode de valeurs*), and four dynamic levels. (The outer two movements, planned to contrast with the rationality within, are counterpoints of irrational cells derived more directly from Messiaen.) But the striking innovation of the sonata—certainly as far as Stockhausen was concerned—was its structural use of register, and this too had its roots in the Webern Variations, where pitch palindromes may be slightly upset by registral displacements of motifs, and in Messiaen ('Regard de l'onction terrible' from the *Vingt regards sur l'Enfant-Jésus*).

In the central movements of Goeyvaerts's sonata, cues from Webern and Messiaen are considerably developed. Initially a range of nearly five and a half octaves is available, gradually reducing to two and a half at the end of the second movement, and then widening again in the third. Two notes, A and D♯, remain fixed in register, but each time any other note recurs, it is transposed up an octave, or if that would take it over the registral ceiling of the moment, it is reintroduced in the bass. Thus where Boulez had used fixity and mobility of register as an alternative to harmonic dialectic in his Second Sonata (no doubt also under the influences of Webern—perhaps specifically of the first movement of the Symphony, Op. 21), Goeyvaerts's registral process created a form that depended neither on conventional models nor, as in the *Mode de valeurs*, on the composer's taste and judgment. Given a few simple rules, the music did not need to be 'composed' at all: the notes would be at play of themselves. Goeyvaerts had gone a step further even than Cage at this point towards music by algorithm, towards automatic composition.

Stockhausen's susceptibility to this could not have been predicted from the pieces he had written before going to Darmstadt in the summer of 1951: the shock of the encounter with Messiaen and Goeyvaerts is all there in the leap from the Sonatina for violin and piano, completed soon before, to *Kreuzspiel* for piano with percussion trio and two woodwind instruments, written in the immediate aftermath. One might even speak of a conversion, specially when what exhilarated both Stockhausen and Goeyvaerts was the spiritual dimension of their work: the possibility of liberating, more than creating, sound structures which would have nothing human in their composition, which would be images of divine unity.[9] Since at this point Stockhausen was a devout Catholic, the form and title of his first piece after

---

[8] See Peter Westergaard, 'Webern and "Total Organization": an Analysis of the Second Movement of the Piano Variations, Op. 27', *Perspectives of New Music*, 1/2 (1963), 107–20.

[9] See Richard Toop's review in *Contact*, 12 (1975), 45–6.

the Darmstadt experience cannot have been accidental, though the 'crossplay' is also a direct extension from Goeyvaerts's method of shunting single notes, an extension complicated and enlivened by parallel processes applied to Messiaen-style chromatic durations (hence the percussion), to dynamic levels, and to instrumental colours (hence the woodwind). The necessary link between formal process and instrumentation may well have been, for Stockhausen, a further sign of deep wholeness.

Example 7 shows the opening of the first of the three main sections, up to the end of the opening statements of the pitch series and two different duration series in triplet semiquavers: one pattered out by the tumbas in even values, the other presented by the piano (11–5–6 . . .) and by the tom-toms in 'transposed inversion' (2–8–7 . . .). Each of these serial forms, whether of pitches or of durations, goes through a cross-over process which completes the section. In succeeding twelve-note sequences, notes progressively move towards the edges of the row, and then reappear at the middle. At the same time, they move in register. To begin with, as shown in the example, they are evenly divided between the lowest possible placement and the highest; then, starting at different times, they move, according to the pattern 0–1–5–2–3–4–1–6 or its retrograde. As they reach the middle register, they are taken over by one of the two woodwind instruments, oboe and bass clarinet. So around the centre of the section most notes are played by the woodwind, while at each end the piano predominates.

In the second section the processes of registral and instrumental transfer are turned inside-out, so that the music starts at the woodwind centre, moves out to the extremes of the keyboard, and then returns, though there is the complication of an additional process playing itself out in trichords on the piano. The third section then combines the other two: piano and woodwind project a retrograde of the convergent–divergent crossplay of the first section, while the piano also retrogrades the divergent–convergent mechanics of the second. In the pure symmetry of this scheme, as well as in its development of the cross-over idea, the piece reveals its debt to the Goeyvaerts exemplar, while the influence of the 'star music' of the *Mode de valeurs* is there in the piano points (the very first pitch might be construed as a homage to Messiaen) and in the attachment, within any section, of each note to a particular duration (though there are structural exceptions to this rule, such as the progressively increasing duration of C in the second section).

However, this is, already, a characteristic Stockhausen piece, not only in its perfect digestion of its models but also in its intriguing introduction of discrepancies, its delighted newness, and its brio. Apart from the durational changes just mentioned, the discrepancies include disturbances to the pitch pattern when a pitched attack coincides with one in the percussion: Stockhausen may have been concerned to make some connection between the two streams; certainly the melding of pitched and unpitched sound was to become a priority in many subsequent works, notably *Kontakte*. As for the newness, out of the new system comes a new way of listening, though perhaps not directly. It cannot be contemplated that the

Ex. 7. Stockhausen, *Kreuzspiel* (1951)

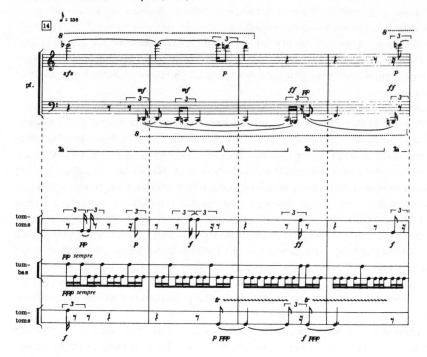

crossplays described are to be followed by the listener: their effect, rather, is of a ruthlessly channelled disorder, of unseen hands moving notes according to unknown rules, as if one were observing a complex game with no prior knowledge of its etiquette. Where order is glimpsed—for instance in repetitions of intervallic motif—it will likely be adventitious. *Kreuzspiel* flies free from the thematic–harmonic continuity that Schoenberg had wanted to preserve, and does so not by punishing that continuity, as Boulez had done, but by ignoring it.

In this lies one of the work's connections with non-European musical traditions: another would be its instrumentation, suggestive more of African or Asian ensembles than of German chamber music. Where such connections were deliberate in Boulez, in Stockhausen at this point they may still have been accidental; if the instrumentation, for instance, was not wholly a concomitant of the musical processes, its feel could have come from the modern jazz of the time. Jazz, too, is evoked—again, perhaps inadvertently—by the rhythm, the irregular accents within uniform pulsation (though the boogie-woogie slow movement of the Violin Sonatina is a long, long few months in the past). This uniform pulsation, which arises inevitably from the superimposing of lines in chromatic durations (and is, of course, emphasized by the tumbas of the first section), was something that Stockhausen soon became anxious to avoid, but in *Kreuzspiel* it makes a decisive contribution to the streamlined glide of process, and gives the game a tension of direction.

During the last two months of 1951, immediately after the composition of *Kreuzspiel*, Stockhausen went on to apply similar structural principles not to isolated points but to whole melodic and harmonic units, resulting in the movement later published as *Formel*, for twelve each of wind and strings with pitched percussion. This brought him a commission to complete an orchestral piece for the 1952 Donaueschingen Festival, and with the promise of a fee he set off for Paris in January 1952, there to study with Messiaen.

Interlude: The Patrons of Modernism

The names of Darmstadt and Donaueschingen have already suggested the importance those places had in propagating new music between the late 1940s and the early 1960s, and to a lesser extent thereafter. Each owed that importance to the determination of a music critic, to the fresh-start mood in the western sectors of Germany immediately after the war, and to the willingness of public authorities (local government agencies and radio stations) to sponsor new music—a willingness that some competitiveness among localities might have helped foster. Wolfgang Steinecke (1910–61) started the Darmstadt summer courses in 1946, and vigorously supported the turn of events that took them, from the mid-1950s onwards, out of the hands of men of his own generation (Hindemith, Leibowitz, Messiaen) into those of Boulez, Maderna, and Stockhausen. Heinrich Strobel

(1898–1970), who had spent the war years in France, returned to his post in 1946 as editor of *Melos*, and the same year became head of music for the Südwestfunk (SWF), stationed in Baden-Baden.

In 1950 the Donaueschingen Festival became part of his responsibilities, and he soon made its annual October weekend of concerts the most important public event in the new-music calendar: works first performed there under his jurisdiction included not only Boulez's *Polyphonie X* in 1951 and Stockhausen's *Spiel* in 1952 but also the former's *Livre pour quatuor* in 1955 (first two movements), *Poésie pour pouvoir* in 1958, *Tombeau* in 1959, second book of *Structures* in 1961, and *Pli selon pli* in 1962, and the latter's *Punkte* in 1963, as well as Messiaen's *Réveil des oiseaux* in 1953, Xenakis's first acknowledged work, *Metastaseis*, in 1955, and Ligeti's *Atmosphères* in 1960.[10] It was through his influence that Boulez was encouraged to conduct the SWF orchestra regularly from 1958 onwards, and to make his home in Baden-Baden from the beginning of 1959. (Previously, between 1946 and 1955, Boulez had earned his living principally as music director for the theatre company run by Jean-Louis Barrault and Madeleine Renaud.) Meanwhile Stockhausen found his principal benefactor in the Westdeutscher Rundfunk (WDR) of Cologne, the city near which he was born, and in whose vicinity he has stayed: not only was he engaged at the electronic music studio from 1953 onwards, but the WDR presented the premières of his *Kontra-Punkte* in 1953, *Gruppen* in 1958, and *Momente* in 1962.

The munificence of the SWF and the WDR provided an example to other radio stations, in Germany and elsewhere, to the extent that the leading composers of the Boulez–Stockhausen generation in western Europe were all supported by broadcasting organizations—either directly as employees (usually in electronic music studios) or indirectly through the provision of the means for performance and recording. Their sole responsibility, therefore, was to create. (Only in the 1970s did Europe begin to bend towards the American pattern of maintaining composers as university teachers.) Had that not been the case, it is hard to imagine that Stockhausen, in particular, could have achieved such a volume and intensity of compositional work, or could have felt free to pursue his instincts through the remarkable transformations his music was to undergo during the next two decades.

The Moment of Total Serialism 2: Paris 1952

In Paris, Stockhausen decided that *Formel* was too thematic, a cul-de-sac; it became relevant again only when he returned to thematic composition in the 1970s. (If this was indeed his process of thought, it indicates how his strategy was to draw up a scheme, follow it through, and then look at the results. Such an approach to composition would justify the use of such terms—much vaunted at the time—as 'experiment' and 'research', and would partly explain the pattern of Stockhausen's

[10] Recordings of many of these performances are presented on Col Legno AU 031 800, together with premières from the 1970s and 1980s of works by Holliger, Lachenmann, Rihm, and others.

output, which to some extent has continued: a pattern of one-offs.) So to Donaueschingen he sent only the two subsequent movements as *Spiel*. Here he returned to points, and added to the *Formel* orchestra a large array of unpitched percussion instruments, used in the first movement to provide a vast repertory of attacks to coincide with the notes, which gradually come together in melodies (in this process, as in *Formel*, the vibraphone has a guiding role), and in the second to generate clouds of resonance out of which sustained points arrive as droplets of pitch condensation. This second movement, consistently slow, relates to his contemporary statement that the new 'through-organized' music demanded a kind of 'meditative' listening: 'One stays in the music . . . one needs nothing before or after in order to perceive the individual now (the individual sound).'[11] Here is confirmation of what was said above about *Kreuzspiel*, that the process enacted in the music is a way of making it, not a way of hearing it. For the listener, the process lies hidden, and what is heard is a succession of heterogeneous instants, just as, for the observer of the world, elementary laws of physics and genetics—laws which Stockhausen might have preferred to interpret as the purposes of God—are concealed behind and within a seeming chaos of phenomena.

The same paradox of rational, purposeful process and irrational, haphazard effect remains throughout the large body of work Stockhausen achieved during his year in Paris: *Spiel*, a quartet for pianist and timpanists (later revised as a trio), *Punkte* for orchestra (also later revised, and re-revised), the first four of a continuing sequence of piano pieces, a study in *musique concrète*, and the beginnings of *Kontra-Punkte* for ten players. Paris provided him with new opportunities, and new encounters—not only with Messiaen, but also with Boulez, who by this time was at work on total-serial projects of his own: two *musique concrète* studies and the first book of *Structures* for two pianos.

Like Stockhausen, Boulez was struck by Messiaen's *Mode de valeurs*, but perhaps more as a display of discipline than as a sound ideal. In the summer of 1951 he had quickly written the first chapter of *Structures*, using the 'first division' of Messiaen's three-part mode as a twelve-note series (E♭–D–A–A♭–G–F♯–E–C♯–C–B♭–F–B), combined with a twelve-duration series in demisemiquavers, again as in the Messiaen model. By its nature, the piece lies completely open to analysis—or at least to the analysis of how it was put together; the untangling that György Ligeti (b. 1923) published,[12] shortly after leaving Hungary and before he was well known as a composer in the west, is as much a classic document as the piece itself, and an almost inevitable companion to it. As Ligeti demonstrates, Boulez obtained his duration series by applying numbers to the pitch series, and then translating all the other serial forms into number sequences by using the same pitch-number equivalences: thus the retrograde inversion B–F–C–B♭–A– . . . translates as 12–11–9–10–3– . . . Boulez also arranged the number sequences—twelve for the prime forms, twelve

[11] *Texte*, i (Cologne, 1963), 21.
[12] 'Pierre Boulez', *Die Reihe*, 4 (1958, English edn. 1960), 36–62.

for the inverted forms (retrogrades can be simply read off backwards)—in two twelve-by-twelve squares, and obtained series of dynamic markings by reading the squares diagonally and interpreting the numbers on a scale from 1 = *pppp* to 12 = *ffff*.

Structures Ia is quite simply a presentation of the forty-eight forms of the pitch series, each with a different form of the duration series (so that pitches do not always have the same durations, as happens in the *Mode de valeurs* and generally within each major section of *Kreuzspiel*), and each with a particular dynamic level and attack marking. The serial forms are laid out in fourteen sections, these defined by the number of simultaneous forms (from one to six), the registral space, and the tempo. The sectional form owes something to the exposition from the Sonata for two pianos (1951) by Michel Fano (b. 1929), who had become a pupil of Messiaen the previous year, and whose piece is in some measure the missing link between the *Mode de valeurs* and *Structures Ia*[13] (though Fano was soon to turn from abstract composition to working in cinema as a musician and film-maker). The rest of the Fano Sonata, however, is a polyphony of rhythmic cells rather in the manner of Boulez's Second Sonata or *Livre pour quatuor*, if at a lower temperature of change. *Structures Ia*, on the other hand, retains its purity as a total serial construction, though one made not as an image of the pristine divine, it would seem, but rather as a way of approaching automatic composition. To quote Boulez himself on this: 'I wanted to give the first *Structure* . . . the title of a painting by Klee, "At the limit of fertile land". This painting is mainly constructed on horizontal lines with a few oblique ones, so that it is very restricted in its invention. The first *Structure* was quite consciously composed in an analogous way . . . I wanted to use the potential of a given material to find out how far automatism in musical relationships would go, with individual invention appearing only in some very simple forms of disposition—in the matter of densities, for example.'[14]

What Boulez here terms 'individual invention'—putting together a kit of serial forms that have almost invented themselves—is responsible for the shape of the piece, established by a palindromic arrangement of tempos, an increasing and increasingly stable density, and a variation in the fixing of notes within particular registers.[15] This last technique produces a markedly different effect here from the sense of desperate insistence or worrying it created in the Second Sonata: the impression is of something more abstract, of what Ligeti aptly calls 'knots' in the serial web. But what is most revealing in Boulez's statement is his dualism of the automatic (seen as generated by an impersonal process) and the individual (seen as resulting from the composer's free act of will). The virtue of automatism, for him, was that it provided an escape from tastes and learned techniques: there was no danger, for instance, of imitating past ways of shaping melodic ideas, because the shaping was done by the scheme. To that degree, it was an experiment that did not have to be repeated. Having been obliged to consider each note as an element in a

---

[13] See Toop, 'Messiaen/Goeyvaerts'.   [14] *Conversations with Célestin Deliège*, 55.
[15] See Ligeti's analysis; and Griffiths, *Boulez* (London, 1978), 22–3.

schematic design, the composer could now consider each note for his own purposes.

But for Stockhausen, and even more so for John Cage, objective process and automatic mechanism were by no means so momentary or so negative in their implications. For example, where Boulez in *Structures Ia* grasped at what liberties remained in order to create an arbitrary form, a defiant display of his own hand, Stockhausen in *Kreuzspiel* took pleasure in making forms that were themselves automatic, and that sprang from how the material was constituted and deployed. It is a difference that he neatly stated in a remark on his contemporary: 'His objective is the work, mine rather the working.'[16] Both composers saw a need to generalize the serial principle, but for Stockhausen this entailed deriving single, through-composed forms from the basic ideas (*Spiel* was to be his last work in distinct movements until the mid-1970s), whereas Boulez was concerned to establish the foundations of a musical language, rules of musical grammar and vocabulary which composers could use to write scripts that would be their own.

Boulez's anxieties about total serialism may be reflected not only in his suspicion of his own achievement in *Structures Ia* but also in his rapid withdrawal of his *Polyphonie X* for eighteen players (1950–1) after its performance at the 1951 Donaueschingen Festival. This piece was the only one he completed of a projected volume of instrumental polyphonies—a volume that would seem to be an early example of an open work, allowing a free choice of pieces to be conjoined in any performance.[17] Its particular title indicates that it was an essay in 'cross polyphony', in the 'diagonal' thinking that had captured Boulez's imagination from the first. As in Stockhausen's independently conceived works, the crossing involved exchanges of musical characteristics between two ideas from one point in time to another, as well as a reciprocity between melodic and harmonic composition, a kind of continuous arpeggiation on the grandest scale (this Boulez derived from Webern, and in particular from the Second Cantata). Beyond that, *Polyphonie X* was again an exercise in total serial control, though of a different kind from that shown in *Structures Ia*. The rhythmic organization, following the Second Sonata and the *Livre pour quatuor*, is based on quasi-serial transformations of cells rather than on chromatic durations: there are seven basic cells, and seven ways of altering them. Instrumentation, too, is numerically organized, there being, again, seven groups at any time.[18]

What Boulez later criticized in *Polyphonie X* was its 'theoretical exaggeration' and in particular its instrumentation by numbers,[19] but though it certainly contains moments of abrupt delivery, which caused some merriment at the first performance,[20] the composer may well have been just as unhappy at the time with the

---

[16] Wörner, *Stockhausen*, 229.   [17] See *The Boulez–Cage Correspondence*, 80.

[18] See Boulez's essay 'Possibly . . .', *Stocktakings*, 111–40. The work is also discussed, with brief examples, in Jean Barraqué, 'Rythme et développement', *Polyphonie*, 9–10 (1954), 47–74; and Goléa, *Rencontres avec Pierre Boulez*, 141 and 143.

[19] See *Conversations with Célestin Deliège*, 58–9.   [20] Recorded on Col Legno AU 031 800.

generally slow tempo of the piece and with its quantities of motivic imitation and recall—the same features that disappointed Stockhausen in *Formel*. Instead of advance there was regression, to patterns that seemed defunct (but that might subsequently become relevant again). So one moved on, as Boulez now moved on from *Polyphonie X* and from the endgame of *Structures Ia* to another piece for the latter book, *Ic*. *Ia* may have seemed a setback most of all for its mechanical rhythms, and especially for the tendency towards even pulsation that has been noted also in *Kreuzspiel* as a result of working with chromatic durations (and that Stockhausen typically turned into a plus), since *Ic* has a much livelier feel, even though it is still a bald presentation of serial forms.[21]

Structures Ib, the last piece of the set to be composed, is much the longest and most complex (becoming, in a little symptom of Boulez's concern for arranged form, the centrepiece of a symmetry rather than the finale of an explosion). It is also a piece of much greater weight, if not of greater historical moment, than the exceptional but crucial *Ia* (whose existence may have started Boulez wondering whether his purpose was to create paradigms or art). Boulez returns to his earlier breadth and secrecy of serial usage, not laying out twelve-note sequences but using the series to generate 'a certain texture of intervals', one in which the minor second and its octave transpositions inevitably have pride of place, since there are five such

Ex. 8. Boulez, *Structures Ib* (1951–2)

---

[21] See Philip Bracanin, 'The Abstract System as Compositional Matrix', *Studies in Music*, 5 (1971), 90–114.

intervals in the series. He returns also to the flexibility of motion he had reached in the late 1940s, reintroducing grace-notes, irrational values, and, as in the slow movement of the Second Sonata, pauses to isolate what may be regarded as interpolated commentaries. All these features are shown in Example 8, a not untypical passage which may suggest how much Boulez had honed his former self on the rigours of total serialism, which are still evident in the detailed markings and perhaps too in moments of idealism (such as the coincidence of *fff* and *pp*).

The example shows how the two-piano medium is now used for its antiphonal qualities, and not merely as a way of sounding six serial forms at the same time. Formally, too, the piece takes up what had earlier been a characteristic way of balancing different kinds of musical motion. Short sections of two-part counterpoint in a strict fast tempo are alternated with longer and more convoluted passages allowing mobility within a slow tempo range (Example 8 illustrates of course the latter type). The contrasts of tempo are extreme, but there is a disparity between written and experienced tempo because the predominant note values also change wildly. The opening 'Très rapide', for example, sounds slower than the 'Lent' which follows it. In this way Boulez brings about, as in later works, a double sensation of tempo: the possibility of very fast slow music or of slow fast music.

Those various ways of generalizing serialism that Boulez had discovered in *Structures*, in *Polyphonie X* and in his two studies in *musique concrète* were set out—though curiously without acknowledged reference to those works—in his article 'Possibly . . .',[22] first published in a special issue of the *Revue musicale* that marked a grand festival of contemporary art in Paris, 'L'Œuvre du XXe siècle'. (Messiaen and Boulez played *Structures Ia* at the festival, whose more prestigious events included an *Oedipus rex* conducted by Stravinsky and staged by Cocteau.) In this article Boulez insisted that 'any musician who has not experienced—I do not say understood, but truly experienced—the necessity of dodecaphonic language is USE-LESS'. One might pause over the parenthesis: Boulez was perhaps implying that commitment to serialism was a matter of intuition, even passion, not logic, and thereby siding with *Structures Ib* rather than with its predecessor. About the message, though, or about the path forward, there was no doubt.

The Human Voice 1: Nono

In the summer of 1952, when the Darmstadt summer courses reconvened, they were intellectually dominated not by Leibowitz and Messiaen but by Stockhausen, Nono, and Boulez, with the premières of *Kreuzspiel* and *España en el corazon* (the first part of Nono's triptych *Epitaffio per Federico García Lorca*), and with performances of Boulez's Second Sonata and tape *Etudes*. Among other works from the new generation were what seems to have been the first piece combining live and

---

[22] *Stocktakings*, 111–40.

electronic sounds, Maderna's *Musica su due dimensioni* for flute, cymbals, and tape. But while the young composers at Darmstadt were united in their zest for the new and their opposition to compromise—especially the compromise of neoclassicism—they were no monolithic group. Nono, in particular, could not go along with his fellows in their pursuit of total serialism and their resulting fragmentation of texture. 'Pointillism', as he later put it, 'is contrary to my technique of sound *relations*.'[23] His emphasis was accordingly not on separate organizations of the parameters but on new, vigorous connections among them, and his *Polifonica–monodia–ritmica* for five wind players, piano, and percussion (1951) partitions the components only in order to propound continuity. In the first section, polyphonic lines edge out from repeated notes and fragments of the chromatic scale; in the second, a long melody works towards a fierce climax; and in the third, with the wind instruments silent, xylophone, piano and percussion play against a persistent 3/4 metre.

It is not clear whether Nono's two works of 1951—this triptych and the orchestral *Composizione*—were written before or after his meeting with Stockhausen and Goeyvaerts at Darmstadt, but the evidence of his next pieces is that their ideas, projects, and achievements had remarkably little effect on him. In most elements of style and technique, his music of 1951–3 proceeds directly out of his *Variazioni canoniche*. There is the same handling of instruments in 'cori spezzati' (the *Composizione* introduces the orchestral groups one by one: tuned percussion, strings, noise percussion, wind), the same use of non-serial chromatic segments and big formal gestures (the *Composizione* is composed entirely of nine notes until the percussion finale, where the timpani revel in the three notes that remain), the same unabashed display of figures rather than points: motifs, reiterated notes, vivid chords, powerfully urged metres (the finale of the *Composizione* is again in 3/4).

Nono now applied these principles on a larger plan in his first two published vocal works: *Epitaffio* for soloists, chorus and orchestra (1952–3) and the ballet *Der rote Mantel* (1953), both fruits of his sense of a fraternal alliance with Lorca (the ballet is based on Lorca's play *Don Perlimplin*; *Epitaffio* sets his poetry along with a Neruda lyric that also treats of the Spanish Civil War). Just as Nono's orchestral writing had thrust unpitched percussion into prominence, so *Epitaffio* highlights speaking singers, using a simplified form of the *Sprechgesang* notation Schoenberg used in *A Survivor from Warsaw*, a work whose actuality and commitment may have provided him with a model. The epitaph—a memorial to Lorca and implicitly to all Republican victims of the war—is a set of three works, of which the first, *España en el corazon*, is itself a triptych. Its first section is a gentle piece for the soprano and baritone soloists entwining with clarinet over percussion; its third is similarly quiet and reflective, setting the soprano in *Sprechgesang* against a larger ensemble. But the centrepiece vocalizes the violent, protesting manner of the *Variazioni canoniche*, and looks forward to the intensive third part of *Epitaffio*,

---

[23] Quoted in Michael Gorodecki, 'Luigi Nono: a History of Belief', *Musical Times*, 133 (1992), 10–17.

Ex. 9. Nono, *Y su sangre ya viene cantando* (1952)

Memento. In between these vocal panels comes a chamber concerto for flute, a wordless setting of Lorca's lament *Y su sangre ya viene cantando*, in which the three stanzas of the poem are represented by three musical sections in a fast–slow–fast pattern. Example 9, from the middle section, may illustrate Nono's tense hold on melody at a time when his contemporaries were finding melody impossible, and also his adoption of Schoenbergian complementarity, the tuned percussion supporting the flute by playing the notes it omits. Also characteristic is the use of a defective chromatic mode (omitting B and C♯) in the flute part, and the high tremor of suspended cymbal tone, which continues with the held string harmonics almost throughout this section.

Nono's insistence on melodic line (*Y su sangre* was exactly contemporary with Stockhausen's *Kontra-Punkte*: see Example 15) is one measure of the primacy of expressive force in his thinking. For him, melody could survive the absence of tonality and the loss of its function as theme; it could even gain thereby, and become, though passionate, objective. Free and unrepeating, it could speak of a hope for freedom, in a personless voice. And Nono made his music speak for the generality, too, in his use of the chorus, not only in *Der rote Mantel* and the flanking parts of *Epitaffio* but also in *La victoire de Guernica* and—a rare removal from combat music—the *Liebeslied* he wrote for his wife. Just as he would use percussion instruments to give his orchestra power and actuality, so he would have his chorus (though not in the *Liebeslied*) speak. And when their music was less eruptive it would be—again as in the orchestral works—fundamentally melodic, not contrapuntal: a line in unison, or (so characteristic of Nono) a line threading itself from one vocal part into another. Atonality, being central to his anti-traditional, anti-bourgeois activism, required a vigilance in the handling of pitch—a vigilance neatly displayed in the *Liebeslied*, where each half of the piece uses just five notes until the arrival of another to complete the hexachord. But there was still, remarkably, no question of serialism.

Electronic Music

One major problem with applying serialism to all the parameters had been the lack in other domains of anything corresponding to the equal-tempered scale or to the principle of octave equivalence: Messiaen's system of chromatic durations was an obvious cobbling—though undeniably useful to the composers of the *Mode de valeurs*, *Kreuzspiel*, *Structures I*, and *Polifonica–monodia–ritmica*. Boulez in 'Possibly . . .' had suggested that tempo might help. One could define twelve durations which reproduced the frequency ratios of the chromatic scale (to a rough approximation the major triad would thereby have its durational equivalent in the threesome of, say, crotchet, crotchet plus quaver, and dotted crotchet), and then these basic durations could be 'transposed' by changing the tempo, a doubling of speed being equivalent to octave transposition.[24] But clearly this is still an arbitrary set-up, since there is no true equivalence, in either psychoacoustical or formal mathematical terms, between change of tempo and pitch transposition. Most importantly, there is no durational counterpart here to the interval: a major third is always a major third, but Boulez's duration intervals (if such things may be conceived) would vary from one 'transpositional level' to another. Babbitt at this point was working on more sophisticated approaches to serial rhythm, but as yet, in the early 1950s, his work was little known in Europe.

If rhythmic serialism was fraught with difficulties, then the serialization of timbre presented still more intractable problems. It was reasonable enough to establish a scale of attacks in piano music—from intense to gentle, as Boulez had done in the first book of his *Structures*—but there was no obvious way in which one might place in order, for example, the sound qualities of harp, cello, flute, and horn. Twelve-piece ensembles, such as Babbitt had used, could not provide anything more than artificial one-off solutions; nor was the basic problem of ordering addressed by the grouping schemes of Boulez's *Polyphonie X* and Stockhausen's *Formel*. One had to be able to 'tune' timbre, to control it. Stockhausen made an effort in that direction in *Spiel*, but seems to have realized that the solution would only come when composers could create timbres on tape. At the same time, the tape medium would make it considerably easier to realize durations with precision, and so to create a serial rhythm, whatever that might be, uncompromised by the needs, wishes and habits of performers. The same impetus that led to total serialism therefore rapidly took composers into electronic music.

Schaeffer's studio provided the first stop, since it was virtually the only place where tape music was being made professionally in Europe in the early 1950s. Messiaen, Boulez, Barraqué, and Stockhausen all composed tape pieces, though Messiaen's *Timbres-durées*—a title expressive of what concerned all these composers—was put together by Henry. Something of the excitement of the adventure springs from the pages of Schaeffer's essay 'L'objet musical', published in the same

---

[24] *Stocktakings*, 126–8.

special issue of the *Revue musicale*[25] that contained Boulez's 'Possibly . . .'. Following up earlier suggestions of his own, but almost certainly influenced also by the group of young collaborators he had acquired, Schaeffer proposes serial manipulations of sound objects, objects which could be transformed in precise ways; he even theorizes about procedures that were to engage Stockhausen's attention throughout the next decade, such as the conversion of a complex event into a single sound, or the treatment of duration as a variable with the same capacity for complex relationships as pitch.

For the moment, though, the overriding concern was serial organization in all the parameters. In his *Etude sur un son* (1951) Boulez drew scales of timbre out of a recording of a sansa stroke, and in the ensuing *Etude sur sept sons* went on in the same direction. However, the equipment was insufficient for Boulez's purposes, and both studies have an uncharacteristically inert sound. Boulez emerged from the studio totally disenchanted with its facilities and personnel,[26] and his continuing espousal of the need for electronic means seems to have been tempered—even during the decade and more when, much later, he was running his own studio—by misgivings.

Stockhausen, by contrast, learned from his experience with *musique concrète* that he would need other means: not transformation but electronic sound synthesis.[27] A new musical architecture demanded new material, not refashionings of the old. The work of Helmholtz and Fourier had suggested that any sound could be analysed as a collection of pure frequencies, of sine tones, and this was something that Stockhausen though the had confirmed, in analysing instrumental sounds in Paris. So it seemed reasonable to suppose that the process could be reversed, that timbres could be synthesized by playing together a chosen group of sine tones at chosen relative dynamic levels. One could thereby form a repertory of artificial timbres related in defined ways, and so suited to serial composition. This Stockhausen tried, working with a sine-wave generator at the postal headquarters in Paris, but the practical problems were insuperable. Instead, in December 1952, he turned to using initial moments from prepared piano sounds in his first electronic composition, the *Etüde*.[28]

The following spring he returned to Cologne. Herbert Eimert and Robert Beyer had begun experiments at the radio station, with which he had already had contacts before going to Paris (he had been a student in Cologne), and there he found the equipment that enabled him to make the first sine-tone composition, his *Studie I* (1953), in which each sound is constructed from up to six pure frequencies taken from a table based on the proportions 48 : 20 : 25 : 15⅝ : 37½ : 30, that sequence

[25] Issue 212 (1952).   [26] See his 'Concrète (Musique)', *Stocktakings*, 226–7.

[27] See his 'The Origins of Electronic Music', *Musical Times*, 112 (1971), 649–50—though this needs to be read as what it is: self-vindication rather than history.

[28] See Richard Toop, 'Stockhausen's *Konkrete Etüde*', *Music Review*, 38 (1976), 295–300; and 'Stockhausen and the Sine Wave: the Story of an Ambiguous Relationship', *Musical Quarterly*, 65 (1979), 379–91, of which the latter throws doubt on the above chronology, where Stockhausen's account has been followed.

being derived from the frequency ratios in the succession of falling minor tenth (12 : 5), rising major third (4 : 5), falling minor sixth (8 : 5), rising minor tenth (5 : 12), falling major third (5 : 4). The same sequence governs the rhythmic construction, and other six-unit series, made up of the first six whole numbers, determine other aspects: the number of sine tones packaged into each sound, their intensities, the dynamic curve applied, and the durations of pauses.[29] Nothing could better illustrate Stockhausen's will to achieve an image of perfect unity.

However, the sine tones obstinately failed to gel into the hoped-for new timbres, and so in his next electronic composition, *Studie II* (1954), he tried another tack.[30] Again there is an artificial frequency gamut, this time a simpler one of eighty-one frequencies each related to the next by the ratio $1 : \sqrt[25]{5}$ (approximately 1 : 1.07), chosen to produce an octave-less scale with uniform intervals of slightly more than a semitone. But now instead of simply superimposing the sine tones, as he had in *Studie I*, Stockhausen spliced them together, always in groups of five, played the spliced tape in a resonant space, and then re-recorded the reverberation of the mixture. This brought a greater degree of fusion, though still the work's success in synthesizing unified timbres is modest.

Failures of aim and technique, however, do not disqualify these pieces as objects of historical curiosity, and indeed of aesthetic contemplation. *Studie I* offers a surface of ringing chimes and deeper thuds: a slow percussion piece etherealized by the absence of sharp attacks. *Studie II*, by contrast, is brief and dynamic, its scintillating bundles of frequencies leaping about the novel pitch framework. Example 10, taken from the published score (this was the first electronic composition to appear in print), may give some impression of the piece at its most excited. The blocks in the upper part show the frequencies used in each note mixture; the numbers indicate durations in centimetres of tape (the speed being 76.2 centimetres per second); and the jagged lower part shows the dynamic envelopes imposed on the mixtures.

The Cologne studio's emphasis on synthesis from sine tones led to the coining of the term 'Elektronische Musik', partly to distinguish their work from the *musique concrète* of Paris, and for some years there was a mutual antipathy between the two institutions and their different ways of proceeding. There was no doubt, however, about which camp claimed the loyalty of the young composers who were starting to hear about the work of Stockhausen and Boulez, and to find something compelling in their vision of music reborn—composers like Henri Pousseur (b. 1929), who came to Cologne to work and learn. On 19 October 1954 the Cologne radio station broadcast a selection of compositions already produced in their studio, including pieces by Stockhausen, Eimert, Goeyvaerts, and Pousseur. Eimert's vision of a 'real musical control of Nature'[31] may have been unduly arrogant, as Stockhausen's experience had proved; and the early Cologne pieces may seem quaint in the light of the subsequent history of electronic music, which has been so much a history of performance rather than of music sealed for all time on tape. What was important,

[29] See *Texte*, ii (Cologne, 1964), 23–36.   [30] See preface to the score, repr. ibid. 37–42.
[31] 'What is Electronic Music?', *Die Reihe*, 1 (1955, English edn. 1958), 1–10.

Ex. 10. Stockhausen, *Studie II* (1954)

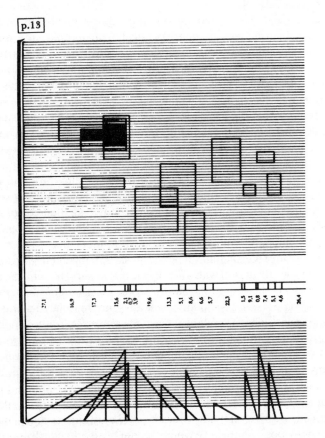

rather, was the commitment to building music from its most basic components, and that commitment had repercussions far beyond the half hour of the 1954 Cologne broadcast.

The Human Voice 2: Barraqué

But among the young European composers of the early 1950s there was one who viewed the current necessity of music as something other than the building of a bold new future—who may have shared some of Boulez's premises, but who worked with an unfashionable concern (even an imperative) to make musical statements in the grand manner, guaranteed not by total organization but by total purposefulness. (It followed that those statements would be few.) Jean Barraqué was also a pupil of Messiaen, and it was while under Messiaen's tutelage that he began his first acknowledged works, the Piano Sonata (1950–2) and *Séquence* for soprano and nine players (1950–4).

The latter, begun before the sonata but thoroughly revised afterwards, shows at once the scale of Barraqué's thinking. Not only is it an unbroken movement lasting for almost twenty minutes, but the writing for both voice and ensemble has an ampleness quite without parallel in the contemporary works of Boulez or Stockhausen. And it is entirely characteristic of Barraqué that this ampleness should be so often and so unpredictably cut off, as if the music were striving for a Romantic rhetoric that the composer knows to be at once essential and unattainable, or indefensible. The instrumental ensemble—a traditional grouping (piano trio) vastly expanded or exploded by the addition of pitched and unpitched percussion—both permits this vision and gives the work a distinctive sound world, while the choice of poetic texts from Nietzsche, arranged by the composer for his purpose, makes it clear that the work's extraordinary blend of magnificence and impotence, eloquence and muteness, comes from a conviction that creative effort is at once irresistible and vain. Barraqué's vocal writing is fiercely demanding, with its wide intervals, different kinds of articulation, and moments of violence, but lyricism persists. From a melancholic hyperaesthesia the singer moves in the latter half of the work to identify herself with a stock figure of musical history, the abandoned Ariadne, and the ending comes, somewhat as in *Erwartung*, with an evaporation. The music becomes bone dry; flooding melodies turn to isolated points.

The Piano Sonata takes a similar course, and carries itself with a similar continuity and desperation, though it is twice the length. It is clear that Barraqué was impressed by Boulez's Second Sonata, and by its cellular conception. But where Boulez's rhythmic style tends to either obscure cells in polyrhythm or throw them against a steady pulse, Barraqué maintains an irregular momentum through great lines of dissimilar cells, and thereby gains a compelling thrust. Tempo is not imposed on the music, as in Boulez, but executed by it, and the antagonism of powerfully urged tempos becomes the work's sonata-style dialectic. Example 11 shows a typical passage in which the cells do not deny but rather establish, however uncertainly, a feeling of progression, to which imitations of rhythmic or intervallic contour lend weight. Also noteworthy here is the registral locking of pitches, which is

Ex. 11. Barraqué, Piano Sonata (1950–2)

again a principle derived from the Boulez sonata, though here the fixing on a median range gives rise to a more intense, more vocal frustration.

The first part of the work is a quasi-sonata development of two kinds of music: a 'free' type, marked by a more virtuoso use of the keyboard, by the presence of quintuplet figures, and by the absence of registral locking; and a 'strict' type, in which register fixing goes along with a more sober musical growth (Example 11 comes, plainly, from music of this second sort). The separate development and the interpenetration of the two reaches a climax when the musical continuity is devastatingly interrupted by a sequence of progressively lengthening pauses. In the second part the role of silence becomes ever larger as sections from the first part are brought back, reversed and greatly decelerated (the slow movement of the Boulez sonata may have had an influence here, though the comparison shows how far Barraqué is from Boulez's poise). In the poetic but apt language of André Hodeir, whose book did much to communicate Barraqué's importance: 'Whole slabs of sound crumble and vanish in the silence which engulfs all. Only the twelve notes of the series remain, and these are plucked off, one by one.'[32] The sonata, while being a huge creative accomplishment, turns at the end into self-extinction, as if it had all been for nothing. But this was not what the young soldiers of total serialism wanted to hear.

[32] *La musique depuis Debussy* (Paris, 1961), 173.

America 2: Classic Modernism

The war had brought to the United States not only Schoenberg and Stravinsky but also Wolpe, Hindemith, Krenek, Martinů, and a host of other composers, leaving Europe comparatively bereft of senior figures. Another difference between the continents was that North America had not suffered enemy occupation or the bombing of cities. Perhaps both factors played a part in the alternative form that innovation took on the western side of the Atlantic, where there was more respect for the established masters, less feeling that music could or should be built anew. Schoenberg's own example, voiced in his words and in his music, was one of rooted growth. A late prose fragment, dating from 1950, begins by restating a thought constant in his writings: 'I am at least as conservative as Edison and Ford have been. But I am, unfortunately, not quite as progressive as they were in their own fields.'[1] His works of his last years, while retasting the freedom and edge of the *Erwartung* period, by no means betray his lifelong commitment to orderly development and integrity of voice.

The orderliness, at least, communicated itself to many of his American pupils and followers, among whom Milton Babbitt (b. 1916)—a follower, never a pupil—soon became one of the leading exponents of twelve-note music, both as a composer and as a professor at Princeton University, where his classes included James K. Randall (b. 1929), Donald Martino (b. 1931), Peter Westergaard (b. 1931), and Fred Lerdahl (b. 1943); Stephen Sondheim (b. 1930) was also a student. Babbitt's contemporary George Perle (b. 1915) promoted the same cause of rational twelve-note composition through his work as a teacher, theorist, and composer. His classic textbook *Serial Composition and Atonality* (1962) was followed fifteen years later by *Twelve-Tone Tonality*, an introduction to his own system, by which a twelve-note series structures relationships among notes, intervals and chords, allowing for the possibility of key feeling, and even diatonic triads, within totally chromatic music; his musical output, chiefly of instrumental works, includes sequences of wind quintets and of string quartets. From the same generation, Leon Kirchner (b. 1919), who studied with Schoenberg in Los Angeles, developed into a twelve-note composer able, like his teacher, to command the rhetoric of tonal symphonic music. His music, too, is mostly for orchestra (two piano concertos and a concerto for violin and cello with wind and percussion) or chamber ensemble (three quartets). One might also see the later music of Stravinsky, a US citizen since 1945, within the con-

---

[1] 'My Attitude towards Politics', in H. H. Stuckenschmidt, *Schoenberg: His Life, Work and World* (London, 1977), 551–2.

text of this American serial school, though in his case the impulses came more from Europe.

Against the picture of even progress from Schoenberg (or more particularly in Perle's case from Berg and Bartók) there might seem to stand the example of another Schoenberg pupil, Cage. Yet Cage's work is not so much an exception to this view as a challenge to it. The continuities from Schoenberg to Babbitt and beyond may have been overstated. Perhaps there was indeed a revolution, if one that took place against the drift of what Babbitt and some of his colleagues said they were doing. After all, Babbitt was defiantly un-Schoenbergian in his belief in the importance of method. (Something that Babbitt in his frequently expressed admiration of Schoenberg has left out of account is Schoenberg's repeatedly and joyfully indulged wish to compose again in the 'old' diatonic style.) And it is in this commitment to method that all those who came to the fore after 1945, both Americans and Europeans, seem most at one.

Indeed, there is no period in musical history when, so much as between 1945 and 1960, the attention of so many composers was focused so vigorously on basic matters of compositional technique. It is as if the Second World War had brought about a large-scale failure of musical nerve. Composers could no longer rely on their own sensibilities and a given language (tonal, serial, neoclassical or whatever) to guide them: music had to be rethought from fundamental principles, and every creative decision justified on the basis of that rethinking. Theoretical writings—the essays of Boulez, Cage, and Babbitt, and Messiaen's *Technique de mon langage musical* (1944)—became not only common but even central, as if the compositions were incomplete without some justification of their system. The half-decade after the war was a great age of pure music: Boulez's sonatas, Cage's *Sonatas and Interludes*, Babbitt's *Compositions*. But in another sense no music was pure; it was all technical demonstration, and incomplete without its manifesto or analysis.

What is also remarkable is how much the new generation—that of Babbitt, Boulez, and Cage—affected composers who had already established their own voices. Among European composers, the phenomenon can be seen clearly in Messiaen. Among Americans it influenced, for example, two of his outstanding contemporaries, Elliott Carter (b. 1908) and Stefan Wolpe (1902–72), the one a New Yorker, the other from among the immigrants of the 1930s. And for men of their age and experience, the new lessons were more likely to be intertwined with the old, to provide images of modernism relating less equivocally to what was past.

Schoenberg

As the Second World War came to an end Schoenberg was seventy. He had not left Los Angeles since arriving there in 1933, nor was he to travel during the remaining six years of his life. But friends, pupils, and colleagues made sure he was informed of his music's revival in Europe, where ideology or apathy had kept it from being

heard since his emigration. Correspondents told him, for example, about performances of the Six Little Piano Pieces for Salzburg radio in September 1945, of the
Second Quartet for Berlin radio in 1946, and of the First Chamber Symphony in
Munich in 1947.[2] There were other marks of esteem. In 1946 he was named hon-
orary president of the International Society for Contemporary Music and invited by
the Bürgermeister to return to Vienna.[3] He also had news of the Darmstadt courses,
to which Leibowitz asked him in 1949. Whether he was aware, too, of how his ideas
were being adapted, extended, and rebutted by a new generation of composers is
unsure: had he gone to Darmstadt in 1949 he would have met Messiaen and some
of Leibowitz's young pupils (though not Boulez).

His music of these last years is sparse. In August–September 1946 he was seriously ill, and saved by injections into the heart: the illness, and the injections, were
reflected in the String Trio he wrote during these months. Thereafter he was effectively an invalid, and his last works, all quite short, were achieved in brief bursts: in
August 1947 came *A Survivor from Warsaw*, in June the next year a set of three folksong arrangements for unaccompanied chorus, in the spring of 1949 the Phantasy
for violin and piano, the choral piece *Dreimel tausend Jahre*, sketches for another
choral work (*Israel Exists Again*), and the beginnings of a string quartet, and in
June–July 1950 a settling of Psalm 130 in Hebrew. His final year was devoted to the
words and music of a set of 'modern psalms', of which only one was partly composed.

For whatever reason—illness, age, recollection, the resuscitation of his music in
Europe—he recaptured in these concluding works something of the brevity and
fierceness of his first atonal pieces, though still with the insistent motivic echoing
that the twelve-note method had encouraged. The shadows of returning tonality in
the *Ode to Napoleon* and the Piano Concerto (both 1942) fall away, and there are no
more large-scale tonal compositions, such as had played a large part in his output
during the previous dozen years (the last tonal relics are just the folksong triptych
and a final canon). At the same time the links with standard forms and genres atten-
uate. The final chamber work is not a quartet but a trio, belonging to a much rarer
repertory, and though the music is often patently developmental, parts of it are dislocated and the whole adheres to no traditional scheme: the single movement
returns finally to its point of origin, having been interrupted by two self-contained
episodes and several shorter divagations. A similar wheeling course, but over a
reduced and smoother circuit, is taken by the only other instrumental work of this
period, the Phantasy for violin and piano.

In terms of rawness, though, the String Trio's only companion is its more immediate successor, *A Survivor from Warsaw*. A narrator, delivering Schoenberg's own
English text in *Sprechgesang*, recalls a brutal experience from the Warsaw ghetto:
semiconscious, in darkness, he hears trumpets, and a German officer demanding

---

[2] For these and other details see ibid. 474 ff.
[3] See Erwin Stein (ed.), *Arnold Schoenberg Letters* (London, 1964), 239.

the inmates come out and number off. The orchestral accompaniment is a patch-work of ostinatos and sudden gestures, closely keyed into the text in the way of *Erwartung*, until the final surge that brings the men's chorus on to carry the work home. The narrator refers near the start to 'the grandiose moment when they all started to sing': it is to this that the work looks forward and builds. The message, unequivocally, is one of triumphant defiance; it is also, for the music, one of pur-poseful achievement, with the majestic Hebrew hymn rising up as a twelve-note chant from the earlier disintegration.

Schoenberg's next choral works were all concerned with another new creation, that of the state of Israel, to which he dedicated his setting of Psalm 130 for six-part speaking and singing chorus. The unfinished 'modern psalm' that followed was, characteristically, a prayer about the possibility of prayer—a prayer that could have been voiced by the Moses of the opera, and is similarly projected by a man through *Sprechgesang*, the words being taken up and illuminated by a choir with orchestra. Schoenberg kept hoping he would be able to complete both *Moses und Aron* and *Die Jakobsleiter*, but nothing was added to those scores, and the *Modern Psalm* lapses at a corresponding point, where the words ask for the music of union with God.

Carter

The postwar tide of change hit—or was expressed in—no music more forcefully than Elliott Carter's. His self-reinvention came before Stravinsky's: his First Quartet, the signal of arrival in new terrain, was completed in September 1951, the month when Stravinsky's still resolutely neoclassical opera *The Rake's Progress* was being performed for the first time. And in his music change was not only a symptom but the prime subject. From the First Quartet onwards he was to work with materi-als in constant evolution: materials in which stability in one or more domains is necessary only to support and show the urgent movement in others. What the First Quartet also introduced was a polyphony of such dynamic streams, and in particu-lar a polyphony of tempos, so that the music moves at several different rates simul-taneously. Change does not happen simply because time is moving on; change is deliberately engineered and motivated.

There is a connection here—a connection of objectivity and rationalism—with the nevertheless very different music Carter had written before the late 1940s. Like other Americans of his generation, born in the first decade of the century, he had studied in France with Nadia Boulanger, and learned from her a reverence for the neoclassical Stravinsky. But what was ironic and suppositional in Stravinsky became candid in the music of Boulanger's pupils, who seemed confident of a restabilization, and a renewal of contact with an audience predisposed by taste and education to music of the eighteenth and nineteenth centuries (American neoclas-sicism often carried this subtext of democratic utopianism). Carter swam with that stream as far as his ballet *The Minotaur* (1947), where the allegiance is to Stravinsky's then recent Symphony in Three Movements, but his chamber pieces of 1948–9 began to introduce the new polyphony in characteristic terms of a polyphony of musical personality: the Cello Sonata, in particular, has this dialogue nature. Then he left New York to spend a year on a Guggenheim fellowship in the Arizona desert. 'I decided for once to write a work very interesting to myself, and so say to hell with the public and with the performers too.'[4] That work was his First Quartet.

Thus where his almost exact contemporary Messiaen (just a day older, born on 10 December 1908) would seem to have gained encouragement from the young pupils who surrounded him in the late 1940s and 1950s, Carter moved forward most rapidly when he was artistically alone. American popularism gave way to American independence, and did so in the music too, where a sense of self-propelled movement asserted itself—a sense in this quartet of up to four separate lines of activity. Ives may have provided a spur here. Carter, born into a wealthy New York family, had been introduced to Ives by his school music teacher, and would surely have been familiar with Ives's Second Quartet, a work 'for 4 men—who converse, discuss, argue (in re "politick"), fight, shake hands, shut up—then walk up the mountain-side to view the firmament.'[5] The essential difference in his own First Quartet is that the characters are not psychological, and certainly not identifiable consistently with the players, in the way that Ives's second violin enacts the role of his despised Rollo, the imaginary guardian of musical propriety. Instead the flows at play in Carter's First Quartet are characters existing only in and as music—characters which may be introduced by particular instruments, but which can carry uninterruptedly from one voice into another. They are abstract characters, defined by their musical constituents—intervals, tempo, pulse unit—rather than by anything describable as mood. This may be another inheritance from neoclassicism; it is certainly a primary marker of Carter's music. He is a dramatist of energies, not of human figures. Since 1945 he has written very little vocal music, preferring to work with the currents of musical movement that can be steered through instruments in small groupings (especially the string quartet) or through combinations of soloists and ensembles in works for orchestra (where Ives may again have provided an example: Carter's orchestral style is an abstraction of Ives's, with all the quotations and the local references taken out, to leave only the colliding textures and motions).

Almost any dozen bars from his First Quartet would show its coursing, ranging polyphony; Example 12 comes from near the midpoint of the work, and suggests how different kinds of musical motion can be cross-related both vertically and horizontally. At the beginning of the example, cascading 9/16 semiquavers pass from the first violin into the cello, where they come to a halt on the one note, C♯, untouched during the four-bar, five-octave descent in major and minor seconds.

---

[4] Allen Edwards, *Flawed Words and Stubborn Sounds: a Conversation with Elliott Carter* (New York, 1971), 35.

[5] Note on the manuscript.

Ex. 12. Carter, String Quartet No. 1 (1950–1): II

Simultaneously another train of thought, in pizzicato 3/8 quavers, transfers in the opposite direction, while the pulse units in the viola are drawn out, under the influence of the syncopated second violin, from three semiquavers to five, which the change of metre to 2/4 then reinterprets as four. This change of metre is an example of Carter's 'metric modulation', whereby a new metre is introduced as a translation of an old one, opening up the possibilities of pulses which would not have been easily available before, just as harmonic modulation changes the temporary tonic and thereby the pitch repertory. In this particular case, pulse ratios at the start of 2 : 3 : 9 per dotted crotchet in 3/8 (viola : cello : violin I) give way in the final momentary stalling to ratios of 8 : 15 : 20 per five semibreves in 2/4 (violin I : violin II : viola), where the 8 under the new dispensation is equivalent to 1.2 under the old. The music is performable because of regularities that bridge across: the quaver pulse that carries over from 3/8 to 5/8 in the first violin, or the pulse that stays the same across the change of tempo and metre at the double barline. These are classic means, extended from the two-against-three cross-rhythms of music from Brahms onwards. To that extent—as in the measure of his harmony, and his attachment to standard genres and weights of work—Carter is still a neoclassicist. But the jostling rushes of the First Quartet are new and distinctive, and were to be exuberantly taken further in the music of the next forty years and more.

Revolutions usually require some kind of radical simplification, and so it is here, in that Carter found it necessary to identify each of his pulse layers by keeping it regular: always quavers in the first violin in the six bars before the double barline, always triplet minims in the second violin from that point onwards. In later works he would be able to make the movement inside each layer more flexible, without losing the identity of the layer, and also without damaging the sense that each layer is itself concerned with change, with executing a process. The vestiges of theme that remain in the First Quartet and the Variations for orchestra (1953–5) would then dissolve away, to leave pure mobility and development within musical layers identified by speed, instrumentation, and interval content. And the relatively simple processes of the First Quartet—represented by the elements of ostinato and scalewise movement in Example 12—would give place to more complex sways and surges.

Carter's polyphony, in the First Quartet as in his later music, is one proof against subjectivity: because the music is happening in several speeds simultaneously, it has no speed of its own, and therefore allows no presumption that it speaks or sings (or, given the abundant pulsed rhythms, dances) the thinking of one person at one time. In form, the First Quartet celebrates this liberation from psychological time. It begins with several bars for the cello alone, and ends as a balancing, answering solo for the leader. At these points it has indeed a single voice—though the status of that voice is less certain at the conclusion, after so much polyphony of contradicting voices. Nobody is thinking this music. It is thinking itself.

The work's polyphony of tempos also has an effect on the notion of what constitutes a musical movement. Tempo in Carter is not something applied to music;

tempo is enacted by the music as it becomes sound. A slow movement or a scherzo is a mode of behaviour, and can only take hold by means of a clearing away or suppression of other modes of behaviour. So it is here. There are four movements—a fantasia, a scherzo, an adagio, and a set of variations—but the music flows from one into the next, and the two interruptions dramatize the fact by cutting almost arbitrarily into the scherzo and into the variations (Example 12 comes from the portion of the variations before this second break). Within the movements, too, the continuity of change removes the music from any normal pattern of recurrence: the themes of the variations, for instance, are not only several but tumbled into a process of swirling acceleration.

In its objectivity, and in its dancing rhythms, the First Quartet may still be Stravinskian, but it was also the first work in which Carter placed himself within the context of a wider divergence of modern masters: Ives, Debussy (whose *Jeux* and orchestral *Images* provided nearer examples of multiple tempos under supreme control), Schoenberg (for formal continuity and a disciplined atonality, though Carter had no use for the stabilization of motif implicit in classical serialism). Unlike Boulez, however, Carter never associated his music with a programme of modernist advance, and unlike Babbitt he has done little teaching. In an age of polemic and controversy, there was no suggestion from him that his works instanced preferred aesthetic or theoretical criteria. Instead, for the two decades or so after the First Quartet he just went on producing a new big instrumental piece every few years: the Variations in 1955, the Second Quartet in 1959, the Double Concerto for harpsichord and piano, each with its own chamber orchestra, in 1961, the Piano Concerto in 1965, the Concerto for Orchestra in 1969, the Third Quartet in 1971, the Duo for violin and piano and the Brass Quintet both in 1974.

These works can be seen to develop from the First Quartet in various ways. All of them are hectic musical conversations. The idea of the string quartet as composed of four differently minded individuals was taken further, and closer to the Ives model, in the Second Quartet, and then the Third deployed the ensemble as a double duo—a strategy instituted in the Adagio of the First Quartet, where the viola and cello are played off against the two violins. The orchestral works, meanwhile, increasingly project a conception of different temporal drifts—different kinds, speeds, and directions of movement—occurring in different departments. And the emphasis on movement, on change, brings a diminishment of theme, an abstraction in the direction of music defined by harmonic and rhythmic character.

The Concerto for Orchestra is the most complex piece of this period, and the most joyous: with Carter, complexity is a kind and a source of joy. The orchestra is reconceived—and repositioned on the platform—as a collection of four ensembles, each focused on a different register, and each in turn taking the lead in one of the four joined and intercalated movements: the tenor group (cellos, bassoons, piano, harp, marimba, percussion) in the opening of grand but failing gestures; the treble group (violins, flutes, clarinets, metal percussion) in quick, flowing music; the bass group (double basses, trombones, tuba, timpani) in solemn, rousing phrases; the alto group (violas, oboes, trumpets, horns, drums) in fast, affirmative pulsation. These four groupings, and four different sorts of music, are rival winds that blow through the music they bring into being. The metaphor comes from the composer, who related the work to St John Perse's poem *Vents*, a vision of winds gusting across the United States, and who declared his wish for 'the wind to blow through the music' when speaking of the variations of his First Quartet.[6] Wind—energy without visible substance, movement of great variety in speed, force, and direction, power with no purposes or destinations—provides the nearest natural image for the ways and forms in which Carter's music has travelled.

And has gone on travelling. Since the mid-1970s he has maintained the flow of big instrumental compositions, and the interpenetration of musical winds. In *A Symphony of Three Orchestras* (1976) each of the groups now has four different types of music, the twelve being braided together. Other works explored diverse alliances on a smaller scale: the Triple Duo (1982) is a comedy of partnerships for flute and clarinet, violin and cello, and piano and percussion, *Penthode* (1984–5) a drama for five mixed and dissimilar quartets. And there were more contributions to the two classical genres predisposed to Carter's kind of musical discourse: a Fourth Quartet (1986) and chamber concertos for oboe (1986–7) and violin (1990). Since the mid-1980s, too, Carter has produced a number of miniatures—usually for soloists or small combinations, but including also the *Three Occasions* for large orchestra (1986–9).

The more surprising innovation was the introduction of the solo singing voice in a triptych of chamber cantatas, collaborations with American poets close to Carter in terms both of time and of mentality: Elizabeth Bishop in *A Mirror on Which to Dwell* for soprano (1975), John Ashbery in *Syringa* for mezzo (1978), where a bass-baritone adds an audible substratum of ancient Greek verse in the original, and Robert Lowell in *In Sleep, in Thunder* for tenor (1981). What was surprising here was not only the return to vocal composition, after a lapse of more than thirty years, but also the interposing of a lyric voice in the work of a composer whose voices, as exemplified in the First Quartet, had been manifold and mutable. The polyphony, however, remains. Carter's choice was of poets whose works are themselves poly-phonic: self-questioning, spinning with references, sliding among different sorts of rhetoric. What he creates in his sung lines is, too, a constructed sort of lyricism, not unlike Stravinsky's in the Shakespeare settings and later songs—a sort of lyricism in which one hears both the voice and the assembly of the voice. There is also the sense of the singers as slightly apart from the musical action, which they hear a moment before the audience, and comment upon. Then in *Syringa* there is the real polyphony of two singers who not only come from two different times but spear-head—like the soloists of the Double Concerto—two different understandings of musical time: incantatory in the case of the bass-baritone, whose line often oscil-lates across wide intervals, and conversational in the case of the mezzo. The osten-

---

[6] See David Schiff, *The Music of Elliott Carter* (London, 1983), 161.

sible subject of *Syringa* is the story of Orpheus, which is patched together in the bass-baritone's anthology and mused on by the mezzo. But the story of Orpheus is also the story of time: the striking nearness of the past and yet the impossibility of return, the constant onrush of moments and yet the eternal present of love, the vanishing of music which can yet always be performed again. The two voices, those of oracle and dinner-party guest, sing mostly about the busy world in which they both astonishingly exist.

Carter's fecundity in his seventies and eighties is a measure of his mental alertness and gaiety (he is often present at performances of his music on both sides of the Atlantic, always a concerned and delighted observer). It may also reflect how the works of his forties, fifties, and early sixties—works that each required a hefty stretch of time in the composing—were needed to launch him into a more rapid creativity. Alternatively (or additionally), the condition of music since the early 1970s, with the decline of modernism as a progressive force, may perversely have stimulated a composer for whom the modernist achievement was something to be celebrated rather than joined. There was always this posteriority. For Carter, coming of age at a time when the great modernist advances of Stravinsky, Schoenberg, and Ives were recent history, the great need seems to have been one of clarification and triumphal commemoration: one could compare his historical position with Bach's, as a master of order (despite the fact that what he was ordering was dynamic movement) after a period of wholesale musical revolution. Change may be his principal subject, but the elation in his music is the elation of arrival.

Babbitt

Babbitt was a Schoenbergian from an early age. According to his own account,[7] it was for the sake of Schoenberg that he went to New York to study with Marion Bauer in the early 1930s; that gave him the opportunity to meet Schoenberg when the latter was staying in New York, in 1933–4. But during the next dozen years he composed rather little and published nothing: the release came only after the Second World War, when he began a regular pattern of composing and teaching (chiefly at Princeton University). His first published works were, he has remarked, 'concerned with embodying the extensions, generalizations, and fusions of certain techniques contained in the music of Schoenberg, Webern and Berg, and above all with applying the pitch operations of the twelve-tone system to non-pitch elements: durational rhythm, dynamics, phrase rhythm, timbre, and register, in such a manner as to preserve the most significant properties associated with these operations in the pitch domain when they are applied in these other domains'.[8] That final clause, implying a search for congruence among the organizational means used for the different parameters rather than for separation and conflict, draws attention to the fundamental division between Babbitt and Boulez.

---

[7] See his *Words about Music* (Madison, 1987), 5 ff.   [8] Note with CRI 138.

Something of how Babbitt went about fulfilling his self-imposed programme may be illustrated with reference to the *Three Compositions for Piano* (1947), his earliest acknowledged work, and one in which the principles of rhythmic serialism differ essentially from Boulez's techniques of unrestrained cellular variation and manipulating chromatic durations. Example 13 shows the start of the first *Composition*, which has been analysed by George Perle.[9] The serial forms have been marked here in accordance with the convention that 'P' represents a prime form, 'R' a retrograde, 'I' an inversion and 'RI' a retrograde inversion, the superscript numbers showing how many steps above C are needed to reach the first note.

Ex. 13. Babbitt, *Three Compositions for Piano* (1947): I

No analysis is needed to notice how the music, in its even progress and its wit, is totally at odds with Boulez's contemporary Second Piano Sonata: despite the debt to Schoenberg, there is more connection with the oriental serenity of Cage's *Sonatas and Interludes* or his String Quartet. Babbitt and Cage were alike, too, in needing a precise reason for every creative decision. Cage found reason in his use

---

[9] See his *Serial Composition and Atonality* (1978), 99–101, 135–6, 139–41.

of number sequences and charts, then later—the reason of no reason—in making choices according to dice-throws or other chance procedures. Babbitt has found reason, throughout a creative career of half a century, in the techniques of twelve-note composition. And those do need some analysis to untangle.

Babbitt characteristically bases his pitch organization on bringing together fractions of serial forms to produce 'aggregates', a term he uses to mean collections which contain all twelve pitch classes, but which are not instances of a work's series. (A pitch class—the term is again Babbitt's—is a virtual pitch, not yet ascribed to any register. A twelve-note series is a series of pitch classes, because a C in a series can be any C. Babbitt's nomenclature, more systematic than that of earlier serial composers, is required by music which is similarly more systematic.) In this case the fractions are simply hexachords, and it is easy to see how in each bar a pair of hexachords from different serial forms is combined to create an aggregate. The principle in operation here, developed from Schoenberg's use of hexachords in complementary relationships, is that of 'combinatoriality' (another key term in Babbitt's theory), specifically that of hexachordal combinatoriality. A twelve-note series exhibits this property if one of its hexachords can be combined with a hexachord from another form of the same series to produce an aggregate. Clearly, any prime form of any series will be combinatorial with the retrograde form that comes back to the same pitch class, and similarly any inversion with the retrograde inversion that takes the same path backwards. The possibilities are extended when a prime form is combinatorial with an inversion, a retrograde inversion or a transposition, as will happen when there is some symmetry between the hexachords.

In the case of the *Three Compositions*, each of the two hexachords consists of a chromatic group of four notes together with a note at each end a tone away (E, F♯, G, A♭, A, B and B♭, C, D♭, D, E♭, F, as they are in P_4). This series is particularly rich in combinatorial relationships, since a given serial form is hexachordally combinatorial with a transposition (the association of bars 1–2), an inversion (bars 3–4), a retrograde (bars 5–6) and a retrograde inversion (bars 7–8). A set of this kind is said to be 'all-combinatorial', and it provides a whole network of connections which the composer can use in ordering serial forms so as to ensure a perpetual circulation of the chromatic total and to achieve, as here, a density of correspondence that does not depend on thematic allusions.

Not only does the combinatorial property suggest which serial forms are to be superimposed, it also provides a clue for linear thinking. In Example 13, for instance, each hand proceeds from one serial form to another in accordance with a combinatorial relationship: the second hexachord of P_4 forms an aggregate with the first of R_{10} (right hand, bars 2–3) and so on. There thus emerge what Babbitt refers to as 'secondary sets',[10] formed when one hexachord from a particular serial form is joined to a complementary hexachord from another. In this case the secondary sets are not emphasized, but in many later works they take on more importance.

---

[10] 'Some Aspects of Twelve-Tone Composition', *The Score*, 12 (1955), 53 ff.

The combinatorial counterpoint and the secondary-set liaisons exemplify how Babbitt's world is a world of musical punning, in which particular elements (hexachords in this case) can be interpreted in more than one way. This may be one source—together with the rhythmic nimbleness—of his music's most characteristic feature: its humour.

Example 13 also displays the use of non-pitch parameters to elucidate and mesh with the pitch organization according to Babbitt's stated principles. Four dynamic levels are associated with the four varieties of serial form—*mp* with the prime, *mf* with the retrograde, *f* with the inversion, and *p* with the retrograde inversion—and these associations are retained throughout the development that follows (they are 'transposed down' by two degrees, to *pp*, *p*, *mp*, and *ppp* respectively, in the eight bars that symmetrically close the piece). The organization of rhythm also proceeds in step with that of pitch. Babbitt chooses a basic set of 5–1–4–2, which may be interpreted in terms of duration (crotchet tied to semiquaver, semiquaver, crotchet, quaver) or may alternatively, since it sums to twelve, be projected in the number of serial notes gathered together in bundles: 'durational rhythm' and 'phrase rhythm', to repeat Babbitt's terms, can both be organized serially, with reference to the same set.

It is phrase rhythm that is so organized in Example 13, where the prime form of the rhythmic set occurs with the prime form of the pitch set (bars 1–2) and the rhythmic retrograde (2–4–1–5) with the pitch retrograde (right hand, bars 3–4, and left hand, bars 7–8). Rhythmic inversion may be more difficult to imagine, but the process of intervallic inversion does provide a model for a rhythmic counterpart. If the notes of a series are numbered according to their distance above C in semitones (e.g. C–D–A♭ . . . becomes 0–2–8 . . .) then the inversion can be derived by complementing these numbers to twelve (12 [i.e. 0]–10–4 . . . being C–B♭–E . . .). Thus, by a similar process of complementation to six, the set 5–1–4–2 can be inverted to yield 1–5–2–4, with a corresponding retrograde inversion of 4–2–5–1. As may be seen in Example 13, these are indeed the rhythmic sets given to the inversion and retrograde inversion forms of the pitch set.

That eight bars of music may demonstrate so much evidence of control is some measure of Babbitt's ability to make everything in his compositions serve a constructive function, and to have a reason for everything. However, a persistent criticism of his music has been that the functions and the reasons cannot be discriminated by ear, except after considerable training: the same criticism was often made of Boulez and other European serialists, and has only diminished with the ebbing of serialism as a consideration in composers' self-pronouncements. In Europe, such doubts about the audibility of serial operations—doubts often voiced by composers themselves—contributed to the disintegration of what had been a concerted thrust to regenerate music in the 1950s, but in the United States the case was less contentious.

One factor may have been the success of Schenkerian analysis in the United States, for if tonal masterpieces—symphonies and sonatas by Beethoven and

Brahms—could be shown to be full of structure unsuspected by the naive listener, it might well be possible that consciously evolved serial structure, though not identifiable by the unaided ear, nevertheless would contribute to perception of the music as homogenous and purposeful. This seems clearly to be so in the relatively simple case of Example 13. The combinatorial relationships and the rhythmic serialism may not be noticed as such when the music is played and heard, but they surely contribute to the impression of lucidity, elegance, and pleasure the piece conveys. There is something watertight about the music: every detail has an immediate answer, suggesting that every eventuality has been prepared by the composer. What must also have contributed to the way in which Babbitt's music has been received is the fact that his arguments on behalf of his music and methods have the same complete intellectual integrity: his writings compel trust.

Those same writings, however, appear to assume that the comprehension of his music depends neither on some passive recognition of order nor on faith but rather on an active, conscious awareness of the rules of the game. That might explain why he took so long to establish the rules before he started to play, why he has been so concerned to keep to the same basic rules, and why he has felt able to apply the rules in gradually more complex and covert ways. Moreover, his demands for rigorous composition and rigorous listening need not be construed as idealist: they may rather be a composer's perfectly rational response to finding himself in a musical world where the general concert public has little use for Schoenberg or Schoenbergians, and where the audience for advanced serial music is most likely to consist of fellow composers, musicologists, and committed lay adherents. That audience may be presumed to admire, and to wish for, complexity. The complexity of Babbitt's music is, therefore, not a display of intellectual expertise and disdain, but rather a reaction of classical obedience to the wishes of what is the real audience.[11]

The second of the *Three Compositions for Piano* shows a further central element in Babbitt's technical repertory: the use of 'derived sets'. Following the example of such works of Webern as the Concerto, Op. 24, he makes use of sets which contain internal symmetries, these sets being derived from a parent by proliferation from a single fragment of two, three or four notes. For instance, the first three notes of the form RI_{11} from Example 13 (F–D♭–C) can be used to generate a derived set if they are combined with their own inversion (B♭–D–E♭), retrograde inversion (A–G♯–E) and retrograde (F♯–G–B). This is the set presented in the right hand at the opening of *Composition II*, a set full of identities: by definition, each of its four trichords contains only one each of two different intervals. With derived sets the composer is thus able to explore, systematically, different harmonic areas contained within the original set: as *Composition II* proceeds, it unfolds and develops derived sets obtained from each trichord of the parent series in turn.

---

[11] For a fascinating analysis of Babbitt's logic as a response to left-wing intellectual life in 1930s New York, see Martin Brody, ' "Music for the Masses": Milton Babbitt's Cold War Music Theory', *Musical Quarterly*, 77 (1993), 161–92.

The techniques of the *Three Compositions for Piano*—those of rhythmic serial-ism, combinatoriality, secondary sets, derived sets, and so on—were pursued in the *Composition for Four Instruments* (1948), the *Composition for Twelve Instruments* (1948), and the *Composition for Viola and Piano* (1950), each again with a title whose implications of 'abstractness and "formalism"' Babbitt declared himself happy to accept.[12] Where Boulez and Messiaen, in such works as the former's Second Piano Sonata and the latter's *Turangalîla* symphony, were producing music of great expressive force and dynamism, Babbitt and Cage were making their music as objective as possible. This difference at least balances the similarity between Boulez and Babbitt as serial composers, or that between Cage and Messiaen as anti-polyphonic musicians.

Babbitt's divergence from Boulez and Messiaen is further suggested by his abandonment of scales of twelve chromatic durations (which he had introduced, independently of the two French composers, in the *Composition for Twelve Instruments*) in favour of a rhythmic practice which would correspond more closely with pitch-class serialism—a practice which would, in particular, provide rhythmic counterparts to interval and to octave equivalence. Hence his notion of 'time points', introduced in two works of 1957: *Partitions* for piano and *All Set* (a typical title in showing how Babbitt's puns can be verbal as well as musical) for jazz ensem-ble.

The time point of a musical event is a measure of its position within the bar. Thus if the time signature is 3/4 and the unit of measurement is the semiquaver, a note attacked on the first beat is said to occur at time point zero, a note attacked a semi-quaver later is at time point one, and so on. Where the 'interval between two dura-tions' is a concept of obscure meaning, the interval between two time points is quite simply a duration. And where there is no justification for regarding twelve durations as completing a durational octave, the time-point equivalent to the octave is very present in the bar. For example, the interval between time points zero and six, in the case just outlined, is six semiquavers; if the second time point is delayed until the next bar, then this interval becomes a bar plus six semiquavers.

However, it needs an obvious effort from both composer and performer to make the time-point system explicit, and something of their responsibilities may be illus-trated with reference to the opening bar of *Post-Partitions* for piano (1966), repro-duced in Example 14. The twelve-note aggregate here is partitioned into dyads, each struck twice, so that there are twelve attacks. These attacks occur at twelve dif-ferent time points in six simultaneous metres, a feature that the dynamic levels are designed to clarify. Throughout the piece a direct relationship is maintained between dynamic level and time point on the scale $pppp = 1$, $pppp = 2$, ... $fffff = 12$ (i.e. 0): this is necessary when the conflux of metres cannot be rendered by rhyth-mic means alone, either notationally or in performance. The 4/4 barring in the example applied only to the triplet quaver units: on the triplet-semiquaver level,

[12] Note with CRI 138.

Ex. 14. Babbitt, *Post-Partitions* for piano (1966)

there are two notational bars in the example, and on the quintuplet-semiquaver level there are one and two-thirds.

The dynamic levels make it clear that, for instance, the first C in Example 14 is at time point one (metre counted in units of a triplet quaver) while the A♭ occurring with it is at time point two (metre counted in triplet semiquavers), and the second occurrence of the same dyad is at time point four (metre counted in quintuplet semiquavers). In this bar, two time points are struck in each of the six metrical streams: eight and zero in the semiquaver stream (each a low bass C), for example, or three and seven in that of septuplet semiquavers. These 'time-point dyads' are the rhythmic equivalents of the pitch-class dyads introduced, if the latter are numbered according to the usual convention that C is zero, C♯ one, and so on; hence, for example, A♭–C has the numbering eight–zero, and E♭–G is three–seven. There is thus a cohesiveness between the dispositions of pitch classes and of time points in the example, with the dynamics following the latter. Since there is significance, too, in the registral placings and in the durations, Babbitt has an array of ways to increase the density of meaning in his music.

But development has gone so far in the two decades between these two illustrations, from the *Three Compositions* and from *Post-Partitions*, that we seem to be in quite new territory. Recognition of the difference between, say, *fffff* and *ffff* is obviously hazardous, and yet it is on such fine discriminations that Babbitt depends for his time points to be communicated. Moreover, the ostensible time-point structure cuts against a much more obvious way of understanding the passage, as an overlapped sequence of two-note repetitions, the staggerings and the repetitions being at subtly different time intervals. Babbitt's earlier works, such as the *Three*

Compositions or the streamlined Second Quartet (1954), had suggested a smooth complicity between the composer and his audience—a relationship in which the music enacts and displays the processes by which it was composed, so that the composer manifests his thinking. But the structural puns at the start of *Post-Partitions*—the repetitions that, in time-point terms, are not repetitions—speak from a world of deliberate frustration that can appear teasing or, viewed more negatively, obfuscatory: writing about his Third Quartet (1969–70), for instance, the composer almost congratulates himself that the music 'does not instance any cherished surface "formal" pattern'.[13] Where the works of Babbitt's first two composing decades open themselves of themselves, welcoming an understanding that will span from small-scale connections of interval and motif to larger continuities, those from around 1965 onwards generally avoid explicit correspondences, except, as in *Post-Partitions*, to lay false trails for the unwary. The earlier music stands disclosed. But perhaps Babbitt then reacted to uninterest and misunderstanding by making sure that his works would be approached only by performers and listeners with the necessary qualifications.

Alternatively, and perhaps more optimistically, one can accept *Post-Partitions* as an exemplary instance of music which listeners have to grasp in ways quite different from the composer's. Just as one need not be aware of ionic forces and molecular geometries when admiring a crystal, so the thinking necessary to create such a work as *Post-Partitions* may not have to be in the listener's mind. One may be impressed more by the pianistic virtuosity and alacrity so vividly placed in evidence, or by the jittery rhythms of slightly uneven repetitions (a Babbitt characteristic), or by the use of extreme registers—the sense that all of the piano's notes remain constantly available (again typical of Babbitt's later music). This perpetual implicitness of the whole pitch repertory—coupled with an unvarying tempo of unfolding, however irregular the rhythmic detail—gives to Babbitt's later music a distinctive quality at once febrile and mechanical. Control is felt, but so is unpredictability. All this is to assume, though, that the music will indeed have listeners who are not composers, analysts or students. Babbitt's own ways of talking and writing about his work may be, as already suggested, more realistic.

An example would be his article[14]—one of rather few he has devoted to individual works—on an orchestral piece from the same period as *Post-Partitions*: *Relata I* (1965). In this essay he explains how the work, like *Post-Partitions*, has a time-point structure based on divisions of the crotchet into units of a third, a quarter, a fifth, a sixth, a seventh, and an eighth, all of which process within an unchanging tempo, the perceived speed being altered by shifts in the number of simultaneous streams and hence in the density of events. But the availability of a large ensemble makes possible an organization, unlike that of the piano work, in which timbre can play a rich part. Babbitt's orchestration—if one can generalize from a repertory that includes only two other works for large forces, *Relata II* (1969) and the Piano

---

[13] Note with Turnabout TV 34515.   [14] 'On *Relata I*', *Perspectives of New Music*, 9/1 (1970), 1–22.

Concerto (1985)—proceeds in majestic homogeneous blocks: again there is the awesome simultaneity of system and unpredictability. In the case of *Relata I*, there is a different instrument or like group for each of the forty-eight serial forms. Yet though Babbitt in his introduction emphasizes such ' "atomic" musical features', he also hints at how large sections of the work are connected together in ways that parallel the smaller relationships of the music, right down to those of its pre-compositional data.

In this respect *Relata I* may be regarded as leading towards what John M. Peel[15] has distinguished as Babbitt's 'third period', following on from the lucidity of his first composing decade and the abruptness of his second. According to Peel, the music of this period is preoccupied 'with polyphony, that is, fundamental "lines" or "voices" (in whatever musical dimensions these be interpreted) contributing ordered subsets or segments to form a larger, more complex, ordered set which itself may then be regarded as a new or derived line subject to the same transformations and the same interpretation in a musical dimension as a fundamental line'. This sort of writing, maintaining accuracy at the risk of appearing defensive, has taken command of most discussions of Babbitt's music, but it fails to reflect the clarity and humour of his own prose (in the same way that many of his composing imitators have missed those same qualities in his music). Peel's point, though, is reinforced by the hope the composer has expressed of his Third Quartet that 'further recalling should lead the listener from those local coherences and immediate modes of progression and association which are instantly apparent through those analogously constructed and related larger units which subsume them, on to the total foreground as a totality'.[16]

A ramified construction of this kind inevitably imposes severe burdens on the performers: the example from *Post-Partitions* has already intimated how much precision in the playing of rhythms and dynamics is expected. For a soloist or a small ensemble the demands are perhaps still within the bounds of the practical, and more often than not Babbitt has composed for dedicated instrumentalists (especially the pianists Robert Taub and Alan Feinberg) or chamber groups. However, an orchestra, under present conditions of work, is most unlikely to be able to give a fair account of a score as detailed as *Relata I*, and Babbitt drew a bitter lesson from the first performances, noting that 'only about 80 per cent of the notes were played at all, and only about 60 per cent of these were played accurately rhythmically, and only about 40 per cent of these were played with any regard for dynamic values'. Until things can be improved, he concludes, 'composers of such works who have access to electronic media will, with fewer and fainter pangs of renunciation, enter their electronic studios with their compositions in their heads, and leave those studios with their performances on the tapes in their hands'.[17]

This was another manifestation of Babbitt's realism: if complex polyphony could not be prepared by orchestras, a solution was at hand, and there need be no regrets

---

[15] In 'Milton Babbitt: String Quartet No. 3', *Contemporary Music Newsletter*, 8/1 (1974), 1–2.
[16] Note with Turnabout TV 34515.   [17] 'On *Relata I*', 21–2.

about the loss of live performance. Something quite general about Babbitt's music is implicated here. The performance of his compositions is the realization of what is notated, the transference of printed marks into sounds; the opportunity for performers to mould the music with their own sways and gestures is minimized— partly by rapidity of change, partly by the fact that, as in the opening of *Post-Partitions*, the composed structure goes against what a performer would probably take as the natural way to play a passage (in this case as six repetitions). This is not to say that Babbitt is unresponsive to the sounds of instruments and combinations: on the contrary. But one can understand how a composer who values accuracy might prefer to make his own electronic realization rather than submit his intentions to the hazards of orchestral performance.

All Babbitt's electronic pieces have been created with the aid of the RCA Synthesizer at the Columbia–Princeton Electronic Music Center in New York.[18] This machine, which has little in common with the voltage-controlled synthesizers developed later in the 1960s, can generate a wide variety of sounds or else alter sounds in quite precise ways. Oscillators and noise generators provide the raw materials which the composer, giving the synthesizer its instructions on a punched paper roll, can obtain at will with a high degree of control over pitch, timbre, and volume. The apparatus is a kind of super-organ, with an enormous range of stops, and it appears most happily employed when used to form, as in Babbitt's compositions, quasi-orchestral polyphonies within the equal-tempered twelve-note scale: his first two works wholly on tape were the *Composition for Synthesizer* (1960–1) and *Ensembles for Synthesizer* (1962–4), of which the former moves to a climax that shakes at a single chord, while the latter, in keeping with the development in his music at the time, is a composite of many tiny and ingeniously worked fragments, one that begins as an alternation between short counterpoints and chords from which notes are successively removed, then continues as a closely integrated mosaic of more diverse 'ensembles'. Babbitt has acknowledged the instrumental character of his electronic music, and voiced reservations about works which, like Stockhausen's *Gesang der Jünglinge* or *Kontakte*, are based on postulates particular to electronic means. 'Perhaps', he has written, 'a system founded on the unique resources of the electronic medium, and on premises hitherto unknown and not as yet even foreseeable, will be discovered and vindicated. Meanwhile, if it is only meanwhile, there is still an unforeseeably extensive domain in which the electronic medium uniquely can enrich and extend the musical systems whose premises have been tested, and whose resources barely have been tapped.'[19] What speaks here is his wariness not only of Stockhausen but of that whole generation of European composers, whose serial extrapolations he could not but find unsystematic and therefore, in his terms, illegitimate.

---

[18] See his 'An Introduction to the R.C.A. Synthesizer', *Journal of Music Theory*, 8 (1964), 251–65.

[19] 'Twelve-Tone Rhythmic Structure and the Electronic Medium', *Perspectives of New Music*, 1/1 (1962), 49–79: 79.

Yet his caution did not keep him from taking advantage of the dramatic possibilities of electronic music in his *Philomel* for soprano and tape (1963). This work—a scene for the soloist to an invisible accompaniment of recorded soprano and synthesized sounds—is set at the instant when the tongueless Philomel of the Ovid story undergoes metamorphosis into a nightingale. That transformation can be accomplished in the mirror of the loudspeakers, the voice coming now from the human soloist, present in the flesh, now from a disembodied entity cousin to her; there is an echo song for the two. At the same time the dense interweaving of electronically synthesized polyphony gives the work an imposing musical continuity while also making a poetic contribution in evoking the night forest through which Philomel flees and flies. There is, also, a sympathy between the intensive punning of John Hollander's text—'Feel a million filaments; fear the tearing, the feeling trees, that are full of felony'—and the perpetual reinterpretation of basic elements that is central to Babbitt's music.

His other vocal works show the same taste for texts packed with patent phonetic and metrical structure: poems by Gerard Manley Hopkins in *Two Sonnets* for baritone and trio (1955), by Elizabeth I and her court poets in *An Elizabethan Sextette* for a female madrigalian consort (1979), and by Hollander again in *The Head of the Bed* for soprano and quartet (1982). In *Vision and Prayer* for soprano and tape (1961), the direct but different predecessor of *Philomel*, and also in the *Composition for Tenor and Six Instruments* (1960), each vowel is associated with an accompanimental timbre. *Vision and Prayer* also shows various kinds of musical correspondence with the forms of Dylan Thomas's stanzas, patterned on the page in diamond and hourglass shapes. In *Sounds and Words* for soprano and piano (1960) and *Phonemena* for soprano and piano (1969–70) or tape (1975) the approach is different: both these works set nonsense phonemes associated with pitches according to rules of twelve-note organization, so that here music gives rise to a 'text' instead of conforming to one already existent.

Europe 3: Achievement, 1953–1957

From Points to Groups

Punke (1952), unperformed in its original version,[1] had apparently convinced Stockhausen that composing with points had its limitations: technical limitations, in that there was no way to order timbre when working with standard instruments, and aesthetic limitations, in that an orchestra of points became an undifferentiated mass, in the same way that, as both he and Boulez had found, layers of chromatic durations combined into regular pulsing. In the 1960s, in a sequence of revisions, he redrew the score for a larger orchestra, though one confined still to pitched instruments, and converted most of the original points into melodic lines, chords, and swarms of sound, so that the title became the relic of a history the piece had outgrown. More immediately he presented a creative criticism of the earlier score in *Kontra-Punkte* (1952–3), scored for an ensemble of ten players rather like that of Webern's Concerto, and carrying a title that may be understood as signifying 'Against Points', and even 'Against *Punkte*', as well as 'Counterpoints'. It was the first composition since *Kreuzspiel* in which Stockhausen found the musical means to keep pace with his intellectual élan, and he gave it the distinction 'Nr. 1' in his catalogue of works. It was also one of the first pieces to become widely disseminated. The Viennese firm Universal Edition, the publishers of most of Schoenberg, Berg, and Webern, printed the score in 1953 as part of a policy of promoting what their director, Alfred Kalmus, might well have seen as the twentieth century's second musical avant garde (they also became the publishers of Boulez, and later Pousseur, Berio, Birtwistle, and others), and a recording was issued in 1956.

Kontra-Punkte—one of the few Stockhausen pieces for which Boulez was to profess unguarded admiration—expanded the range of thinking at this fiercely analytical time, and did so with a proud dramatic sweep that has remained characteristic of the composer, and that was surely relevant to his commanding position among his colleagues from the mid-1950s to the late 1960s. In this case the drama comes about partly because the music's process is, at least in some measure, laid out to view. As it proceeds, so the instruments fall silent one by one, the six 'families' of the opening—flute plus bassoon, clarinet plus bass clarinet, trumpet plus trombone, piano, harp, and violin plus cello—giving place to the single timbre of the piano. At the same time, the ranges of dynamic level and rhythmic value are gradually

---

[1] For a note on this version, and a page from the score, see Robin Maconie, *The Works of Karlheinz Stockhausen* (Oxford, 1990), 38–40.

curtailed, and a texture that begins with isolated points ends with two-part counterpoint.

What chiefly distinguishes the piece, though, is the move from points to 'groups'. (It was a feature of the time that changes in technique had to be manifested as changes in terminology.) A group, for Stockhausen, was a collection of notes considered as an identity: if spread out through time, it was to be felt as an extended instant, and in order for that to happen, the texture of *Kontra-Punkte* consists largely of rapid arpeggiations, which give the piece an electric dynamism, realizing what Boulez had perhaps hoped to achieve in *Polyphonie X*. Example 15 shows a representative passage of counterpointed groups, and suggests how Stockhausen acquires the compelling small-scale continuity of the piece. The groups here set out more or less distinct harmonic fields, whose antagonisms are resolved in the large piano group at the end of the example—a group referring in bar 345 to the preceding harp group, in bar 346 to the clarinet group, and in bar 347 to the piano's own *sforzato* chord and group, while in the extreme bass there is a varied transposition of the flute group. Four 'families' are thus conjoined, in a miniature image of what happens in the entire piece; the cello is perhaps to be considered as going its own way; the sixth 'family', the brass duo, has by this stage dropped out. The working with allusive harmonic connections relates to Boulez, who had of course been doing this at least from the Sonatina onwards, but *Kontra-Punkte*, in a manner typical of Stockhausen, sets out as if from nothing but its own material, presenting a new world with joy and confidence.

As in *Kreuzspiel*, Stockhausen creates systems which result in vivacity. For example, the usual chromatic durations are combined with a division of the unchanging bar into up to twelve equal parts: hence the abundant demisemiquavers of Example 15—unless of course this effect preceded its supposed cause, and the system was chosen in order to justify a glittering rapidity. Another echo of total serialism lies in the zig-zags of dynamic markings, which again may act to enliven performance. Less obvious in a brief example is the way in which a fixed system of proportions—of the sort described in the case of *Studie I* and present in all Stockhausen's works of this period as a guarantor of unity—governs the profusion of ideas. What we have, in the composer's words, is 'not the same shapes in a changing light [a description perhaps of his distant model, the Webern Concerto]. Rather this: different shapes in the same, all-pervading light.'[2]

Contemporary with *Kontra-Punkte* and *Studie I* are the first four of Stockhausen's Piano Pieces, opening a projected cycle of twenty-one. The scope of the cycle was presumably determined by some ordering of the first six whole numbers—an obsession in Stockhausen's early music (see the above discussion of *Studie I*)—but after sets of four, six, and one, all produced in the 1950s, any such system broke down, and the subsequent piano pieces arrived much later as scenes in *Licht*, the operatic heptalogy he began in 1977. The first piece to be written, in Paris in 1952,

[2] *Texte*, i. 37.

Ex. 15. Stockhausen, *Kontra-Punkte* (1952–3)

was the one published as III, which is so brief that it can be quoted complete (Example 16) and serve as a small model for exploring Stockhausen's formal procedures.

The organization of pitch here is not easy to determine: Robin Maconie[3] proposes a hearing in terms of three overlapping chromatic segments (D–F, F–G#,

---

[3] *The Works of Karlheinz Stockhausen*, 63–4.

G#–B), whereas Dieter Schnebel,[4] Jonathan Harvey,[5] and David Lewin[6] would all see the five-note set of the first bar as the structural determinant, but neither approach is entirely satisfactory. There is also the common phenomenon of the difference between composing and hearing, between intention and result—a

4 'Karlheinz Stockhausen', *Die Reihe*, 4 (1958, English edn. 1960), 121–35.
5 *The Music of Stockhausen* (London, 1974), 24–6.
6 *Musical Form and Transformation* (New Haven, 1993), 16–67.

Ex. 16. Stockhausen, Piano Piece III (1952)

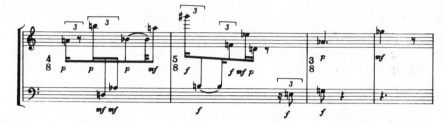

phenomenon that appears quite as acutely in the serial music of Boulez and Stockhausen as in the precisely contemporary chance music of Cage. Hence the possibility that both kinds of composing may produce aurally similar results: an order that goes unheard may, in certain cases, be heard as disorder (as in Stockhausen's hearing of the *Mode de valeurs*), just as order may be found—perhaps always will be found—in what has been composed by chance operations. If one were to approach the music expecting a congruence of means and effects—a congruence such as seems to have characterized diatonic music—then this divergence might be a problem. However, the obscuring of means and the qualification of intention were essential to postwar modernism: this was when it was discovered that the emancipation of dissonance had permitted discord not only in what music is but in how it is understood.

The sophistication of Lewin's analysis lies partly in its awareness of the uncertainty and partiality that must attend any analytical effort, and its clarity is partly that of an approach which, fixed on comprehending the result, leaves matters of intention in abeyance, almost as if the piece were a natural phenomenon (in which regard the analysis is indeed attuned to the objective intentions of many composers at this period)—though, to be sure, the sophistication and the clarity are there too in the findings. Lewin asks us to hear the piece as a sequence of four passes through an elegant network of transformations of its five-note set—or rather through a network of networks. The smaller networks consist of sets related by inversion preserving the chromatic tetrachord (e.g. the opening A–B–D–Ab–Bb and the partly overlapping Bb–A–G#–B–F) and of those related to these by transposition through a tritone (e.g. F–Eb–D–E–Ab in bars 2–3 and the largely simultaneous B–F–Eb–D–E); the larger network is a grouping of four of such foursomes. Lewin provides a pitch-set abstract of the piece, a kind of chorale, as an exercise in teaching the ear to hear what he hears. By training ourselves in this way, we might think, we are being led to hear Lewin rather than Stockhausen: a particular photograph of a landscape that remains mute. So it may be, but the objection is invalid if it suggests we can ever come directly to the landscape itself, to the piece unfiltered by the commentaries and interpretations of others, and by the prejudices we bring ourselves. (This, too, this dissolution of the musical work, has been a key theme of the period.) As Lewin notes at the end of his analysis, after remarking—not without some dismay—divergences between his version and the more eclectic treatment of the piece by Nicholas Cook:[7] 'The differences in segmentation between Cook's analysis and mine should not be problematic, I think, except for those who believe that form is "a Form", something a piece has one and only one of in all of its aspects.'

If we are intent, still, on discovering Stockhausen's intentions, they may sound more loudly in the projection of the piece into existence than in how that piece progresses—in the joy of discovery more than in the nature of what is discovered. Perhaps one should understand the precise definition of pitch here as an illusion—a necessary illusion, since the pianist must be given something to play (improvisation at this point in Stockhausen's career would have been ideologically unthinkable, and could not in any case be expected to produce such a curt and eruptive result)—for what any analysis in terms of pitch-class sets must leave out of account is the twinkling of ambiguities between clear intervals (especially thirds and sixths, sevenths and ninths) and uncertain leaps, where the sensation of pitch is attenuated by isolation or extreme register. It may also be that the notes are sometimes to be understood more as programmes for action than as pitches, their placing on the keyboard in relation to one another being important for its effect on timing and attack. As Stockhausen has said, his concern in all four of these first piano pieces was with 'imparting a new way of feeling time in music, in which the infinitely subtle "irrational" shadings and impulses and fluctuations of a good performer often produce what one wants better than any centimetre gauge'[8]—though this may have been more a response to how his music worked than a reason for its creation. In experimental art, the fortuitous need not be discounted, but rather welcomed and celebrated.

If Stockhausen was indeed coming to recognize a fundamental difference

---

[7] *A Guide to Musical Analysis* (New York, Braziller, 1987), 354–62.   [8] Wörner, *Stockhausen*, 32.

between synthesized and performed music—a distinction that was to be transcended in his next electronic works, *Gesang der Jünglinge* and *Kontakte*—he was still, at least in the composing of Piece III, able to transfer into the instrumental world an electronic phenomenon, that of time reversal. In the fifth bar he progressively builds up a three-note chord, as is common; in the seventh bar he progressively relinquishes notes, which is less usual. There are numerous more complex instances of this effect in Piece II, suggesting he might have been trying out something discovered in Schaeffer's studio, rather as Piece IV, in Maconie's plausible view,[9] finds him leaning over Boulez's shoulder at the worktable of *Structures* (though at this moment the two composers were so close that priorities are as hard to establish as they are irrelevant).

'We are all', Stockhausen wrote, 'more or less treading on ice, and as long as this is the case, the organizational systems being put forward represent guidelines to prevent the composer from faltering. And one has to face the fact that there are as many systems as there are grains of sand, systems that can be dreamed up and set in motion as easily as clockwork. Their number is probably infinite, but certainly only a very few of them are acceptable systems, compatible with their means of expression, and applicable without self-contradiction to all the dimensions of music. Of these, still fewer are so perfectly prefigured that they yield beautiful and interesting music.'[10] This was the big difference from Boulez. Where Boulez wanted one grammar to support a variety of idiolects, Stockhausen went in search of a new system in each piece, each time setting new conditions out of which a new musical universe could evolve. Music's ability to elaborate itself of itself, which Boulez wanted to control, Stockhausen was content to enable.

Systems of Organization

The mid-1950s confirmed Stockhausen and Boulez as the leaders of a movement whose influence was almost inescapable, touching not only many thousands of younger musicians but also the man who was almost universally regarded as the greatest living composer: Stravinsky, whose *Movements* for piano and orchestra (1958–9) reflects his admiration for *Kontra-Punkte*. The workshop period was over; it was a time for music of great ambition and public intent, music such as Boulez's *Le marteau sans maître* or Stockhausen's *Gesang der Jünglinge* and *Gruppen*. From 1956 both Boulez and Stockhausen taught regularly at Darmstadt, where student composers could also learn from Berio, Pousseur, Kagel, and Maderna. Boulez and Maderna, out of their performing work at Darmstadt, emerged as conductors, and

---

[9] *The Works of Karlheinz Stockhausen* (1st edn.), 67. In the 2nd edn. this view is tacitly withdrawn.

[10] *Texte*, i. 47. An unusually complete elucidation of a Stockhausen system is provided by Richard Toop in his analysis 'Stockhausen's "Klavierstück VIII" ', *Contact*, 28 (1984), 4–19.

began to gain a place for new music in the repertories of leading orchestras.[11] New journals—notably *Die Reihe*, whose first issue appeared in 1955—were founded to publish articles by and about composers of this group, and festivals and radio stations continued to provide them with a forum. Their music appeared in print, very often from Universal Edition, and increasingly on record. The Véga company, for example, issued recordings of many of the new works introduced at the Domaine Musical, the concert series which Boulez founded with Barrault's backing in Paris in 1954: Stockhausen's *Zeitmasze*, Nono's *Incontri*, Berio's *Serenata I*, and Boulez's own *Marteau* were all presented under his direction and recorded during the first three Domaine seasons.[12] (The Domaine was soon imitated in Milan with the founding of the Incontri Musicali by Berio and Maderna in 1956, in Vienna with the formation of the Die Reihe ensemble by Friedrich Cerha and Kurt Schwertsik in 1958, and elsewhere, in company with a compositional progression from such singular devisings as the septet of *Le marteau* to what became in the 1970s a standard line-up of wind and string soloists with piano and percussion.) Rarely can composers who were still in their twenties or very early thirties have exerted themselves so prominently in musical life.

All this has helped to generate an impression in retrospect of something monolithic, even totalitarian, though that may not have been how it appeared at the time. The experience of total serialism—a brief experience, confined to a few pieces written by Boulez and Stockhausen in 1951–2—had left composers with a determination to take nothing on trust; the intellectual excitement of the Darmstadt summers had a full measure of doubt and dispute. Boulez, in a 1954 essay,[13] chided his colleagues, and indeed his former self, for galloping too readily, too thoughtlessly, towards what he could only see as an illusory goal of total organization: 'One soon realizes', he wrote, perhaps with his own *Structures Ia* in mind, 'that composition and organization cannot be confused without falling into a maniacal inanity.' He went on to state his present wish for 'a dialectic operating at each moment of the composition between a strict global organization and a temporary structure controlled by free will' (which would explain the appeal to him of Stockhausen's *Kontra-Punkte*). Of course, it went without saying that the 'strict

[11] Boulez gave his first orchestral concert with the Venezuelan Symphony Orchestra in Caracas on 16 June 1956 (far from European view, he was on tour during his last year with the Renaud–Barrault company), in a programme of Debussy (*Jeux* and *Ibéria*) framing Prokofiev's 'Classical' Symphony and Stravinsky's Symphonies of Wind Instruments. He next faced a large orchestra in Cologne on 4 December 1957, when he took over the first performance of the expanded *Le visage nuptial* from Hermann Scherchen. In 1958 and 1959 he worked with several German radio orchestras, principally that of the SWF, in twentieth-century programmes; his career as a general conductor began in 1960 with the Concertgebouw.

[12] Boulez first conducted the Domaine during the 1955–6 season; the initial 'Concert du Petit Marigny' (named after the theatre where these events took place, before the introduction of the familiar name), on 13 January 1954, was conducted by Scherchen, with a programme of the *Musical Offering*, Nono's *Polifonica–monodia–ritmica*, Stockhausen's *Kontra-Punkte*, Webern's Concerto, and Stravinsky's *Renard*: that mixture of early music, new music, and modern classics was to be characteristic of Boulez's programming, not only with the Domaine. For a full history of the institution see Jésus Aguila: *Le Domaine Musical: Pierre Boulez et vingt ans de création contemporaine* (Paris, 1992).

[13] 'Current Investigations', *Stocktakings*, 15–19.

global organization' would in some way come out of total serialism. Organization would provide possibilities, among which the composer could direct himself by an alert marriage of intellect and instinct, with the late works of Debussy now admitted as potentially more useful models than Webern. Boulez's preference had always been for complexity and multiplicity—for Klee rather than Mondrian, as he had put it in a 1951 letter to Cage[14]—and it was to Debussian allusiveness rather than to Webernian strictness and symmetry that he appealed in *Le marteau sans maître*.

In the same essay Boulez also points the way towards the aleatory principles that were to occupy him later in the decade. He speculates about the possibility of a composition existing as a set of 'formants', each linked to the organizational bases of the work as the formants of a timbre are linked to the fundamental, and yet each independent: the *Polyphonie* idea is reasserting itself, behind the guise of terms borrowed from acoustical analysis, and was to be partially realized in the Third Piano Sonata, a work predicted in the following passage, highly characteristic of Boulez's wish for fluidity, ambiguity and freedom: 'Let us claim for music the right to parentheses and italics . . . a concept of discontinuous time made up of structures which interlock instead of remaining in airtight compartments; and finally a sort of development where the closed circuit is not the only possible answer.'

Such a labyrinthine conception, though manifested more obviously in the Third Piano Sonata, is already present in *Le marteau sans maître*, as indeed it had been in the Second Piano Sonata or the Sonatina. After *Structures Ia*, Boulez had immediately returned to what had been his earlier practice: that of using principles borrowed and extended from Schoenberg and Webern in order to proliferate intervallic motifs and rhythmic cells in a whole variety of ways. The apparatus of total serialism remains in *Le marteau*—the dynamic levels which change almost from note to note, the chromatic durations—but more than two decades passed before Lev Koblyakov uncovered the serial construction of the work.[15] Boulez's serial techniques, as described in what has been published of his Darmstadt lectures,[16] are so multifarious that almost anything could be derived from anything else, and his horror of the obvious makes a secure understanding of his compositional processes irretrievable.

Ligeti, who had abandoned the idea of analysing *Le marteau* before tackling the transparent *Structures Ia*, pointed out in a later article for *Die Reihe*[17] that the original conventions of serialism—and even those of total serialism—had been so far adapted in the immediately subsequent works of Pousseur, Stockhausen, Boulez, and others, that to describe those works as 'serial' would be almost meaningless. At best, only the essential principles—those of ordering a set of elements, and transforming that ordered set according to rules—remain. Babbitt felt this too, and

---

[14] *The Boulez–Cage Correspondence*, 116–17.
[15] His doctoral thesis (1975–7) is published as *Pierre Boulez: A World of Harmony* (Chur, 1990).
[16] *Boulez on Music Today* (London, 1971).
[17] 'Metamorphoses of Musical Form', *Die Reihe*, 7 (1960, English edn. 1965), 5–19.

recalled how, after his hopes had been aroused by news of endeavours seemingly similar to his own being carried out in Europe, his presumed comrades' 'music and technical writings eventually revealed so very different an attitude towards the means, and even so very different means, that the apparent agreement with regard to end lost its entire significance . . . Mathematics—or, more correctly, arithmetic—is used, not as a means of characterizing or discovering general systematic, pre-compositional relationships, but as a compositional device . . . The alleged "total organization" is achieved by applying dissimilar, essentially unrelated criteria of organization to each of the components, criteria often derived from outside the system, so that—for example—rhythm is independent of and thus separable from the pitch structure; this is described and justified as a "polyphony" of components, though polyphony is customarily understood to involve, among other things, a principle of organized simultaneity.'[18]

Babbitt's distress, not unmixed with self-congratulation, is occasioned by little more than the fact that his European colleagues did not share his view of what constituted 'general systematic, pre-compositional relationships': one could as well criticize Berlioz for not being Bach. But at least his diatribe points up the great gulf at the time between composers in America and those in Europe with regard to the serial heritage. That gulf might be illustrated by comparing *Kontra-Punkte* or *Le marteau sans maître* with his Second Quartet—a work of the same period, written soon before the essay just quoted. The Babbitt piece is lucid about itself: it is a demonstration of how it was composed. Its all-interval series is introduced interval by interval, as it were, with each new arrival initiating a development of the interval repertory thus far acquired, each development being argued in terms of derived sets. Important landmarks in the continuous progress are firmly underlined: Babbitt calls upon harmonic octaves at the points where new intervals are brought into play, brings in a rare solo line when the first hexachord has been completed (bar 114), and has the first complete serial statement begun by all four instruments in unison (bars 266–8). It is all far away from Stockhausen's new systems as grains of sand—each, one must guess, unlike any other, and certainly unlike any systems familiar from the past. It is equally far away from Boulez's 'notion of a discontinuous time achieved thanks to structures which will become entangled'.

Le marteau sans maître

Just as Boulez returned after *Structures Ia* to earlier musical ideals, so he returned to earlier poetic metaphors, but in both cases within a colder climate. In 1953, beginning his first new work after the book for two pianos, he went back again to René Char, but this time to an earlier collection, *Le marteau sans maître*, where the verse is very much more concise, more abruptly obscure, more objective. In all

---

[18] 'Some Aspects of Twelve-Tone Composition', *The Score*, 12 (1955), 53–61.

these respects the poems suited Boulez's purpose, which was not so much to set them to music, in the way that he had set the very much longer texts of *Le visage nuptial*, but rather to make them the seed of an elaborate musical form—a form in which purely instrumental movements would be necessary, and not merely as interludes.

As he had before, Boulez wrote an essay about his new work without naming it.[19] What mattered in music's contact with poetry, he declared, was structure: 'Structure: one of the key words of our time.' (This sentence alone conveys a thought, more poetic than analytical, to which every one of Boulez's compositions adds its commentary.) The poem must be more than 'a frame for the weaving of ornamental arabesques'; it must become ' "centre and absence" of the whole body of sound': 'centre' because everything in the music is derived from the words, and 'absence' because the process of musical composition has completely consumed them. By applying himself thoroughly to the text, the composer would uncover 'a whole web of relationships . . . , including, among others, the affective relationships, but also the entire mechanism of the poem, from its pure sound to its intelligible organization.'

It was perhaps disingenuous of Boulez to assume that earlier composers of vocal music had not been excited by matters of 'pure sound' or 'intelligible organization' in the texts they chose to set: as so often, he conjures up a caricature of the Romantic artist in order to affirm his otherness. It was also disingenuous of him to imply that the 'expressive' qualities of the Char poems were somehow secondary, for the odd combination of violence and vagueness was essential to him—perhaps especially the vagueness, since *Le marteau* as a setting of transparent, explicit texts is unthinkable. However, his emphasis on sound and structure was true to his practice, and true to the conscious concerns of many of his contemporaries. For example, Berio's responsiveness to verbal sound is evident right from his setting of three poems from Joyce's *Chamber Music* for female voice and trio, a work which dates from 1953 (the year before he was drawn into the Darmstadt circle through meeting Maderna, Pousseur, and Stockhausen), and which shows in its monotone second song a great number of patterns of timbre and rhythm suggested by patterns in the words. And as far as 'intelligible organization' is concerned, Babbitt's 'Spelt from Sybil's Leaves', one of the pair of settings of Hopkins sonnets for baritone and trio (1955), exhibits a neat parallel between the rhyme scheme and the serial forms used. Boulez himself was to derive musical reflections of sonnet form in later works based on Mallarmé, but the Char texts of *Le marteau* are brusquely irregular, and the music seems not so much to echo them as to channel them into its own structural processes.

Partly that must be because of how the work cuts down the importance of its ostensible soloist, in contrast with what happens in such widely differing examples of vocal chamber music as *Pierrot lunaire* and Ravel's Mallarmé poems: this is just

---

[19] 'Sound and Word', *Stocktakings*, 39–43.

one of its revolutionary features. Only four of the work's nine movements are vocal; two purely instrumental movements arrive before the singer enters; and the drama of the finale is the drama of the voice's being extinguished: first made wordless and a regular member of the ensemble, then replaced as principal part by the alto flute. There are no songs here, for the vocal movements are often dominated by instrumental qualities of rhythm, texture, and phrasing, and even the most song-like of them, 'L'artisanat furieux', is a duet in which the alto flute has a comprimary role. The voice is a potential danger, which the music has to limit. Or, to put it another way, vocal expression has to force itself through a mill of musical purpose. It is not that the instrumental movements extend and elaborate the vocal settings, but rather that the voice and the Char texts offer commentary on what seems most essentially an instrumental action.

Boulez's wariness of the voice—at least in the period between the seductive 'Complainte du lézard amoureux' in *Le soleil des eaux* and the fluid ornamented melismata of the *Improvisations sur Mallarmé*—was possibly a sign of a deeper wariness of music's ability to comport itself as if with a voice. His disdain of 'accompanied melody' in Messiaen,[20] his shattering of legato line in the Sonatina, and his insistence on polyphony—preferably on a polyphony of polyphonies, in which musical parameters are differently adjudicated—all point to this. In *Le marteau* music tumbles forth, but from no source that we can project: it is too fast, too flickering in colour, too jagged in outline, too prone to sudden stops and changes of course. One virtue of these Char poems, besides their brevity, was that the voice they intimate (two of them include the first person singular pronoun) speaks intensely of things disconnected, and of things disconnected from itself.

There are three poems, each contributing, or contributed to, a cycle of movements. 'L'artisanat furieux', sung in movement III, has a prelude (I) and a postlude (VII); 'Bourreaux de solitude' (VI) comes amid a chain of 'commentaries' that occupy the other even-numbered places; and 'Bel édifice et les pressentiments' (V) has a 'double', or variation, at the end of the work. The interweaving of three separate cycles recalls Messiaen's practice in the *Turangalîla* symphony, except that in Boulez's case the interweaving goes further. Not only does the last movement explicitly recall moments from all three cycles, but the characteristics unique to each cycle—such as the pulsed rhythms and the suspended continuities of the 'Bourreaux de solitude' group—are compromised by distinctions that cut across the cycles (notably the distinction between vocal and purely instrumental movements) and by general features of the work.

Among these, most important is the instrumentation, which opened new possibilities for western chamber music without there being subsequently any diminishment to the work's clang of novelty. The scoring is for contralto voice with alto flute, viola, guitar, vibraphone, xylorimba (a xylophone with an extended lower range), and unpitched percussion (one player), a grouping of diversities into a new

[20] See 'Proposals', ibid. 47–54.

unity, enabled partly by a common middle–high register, partly by bonds of sound, and partly by an abrupt removal of the instruments into a special world of speed, dash and harmonic restlessness. Also, heterogeneity is itself a unifying factor. Since none of the instruments is supported by any other, their gathered separations become a specific of the piece: this is music that is defined, and perhaps even made possible, by hazardous tanglings.

Its ancestries are also numerous. Derivation from *Pierrot lunaire* is acknowledged in the presence of a voice–flute duet (the setting of 'L'artisanat furieux'), and Boulez has also suggested that the vibraphone relates to the Balinese gamelan, the xylorimba to the music of black Africa, and the guitar to the Japanese koto,[21] to which one might add that the ensemble, like that of *Kreuzspiel*, is flavoured with the modern jazz of the period. *Le marteau* is thus a pioneering essay in the 'music of the whole world' that Stockhausen was to take as an ideal[22]—though it draws away from embracing exotic qualities of modality, rhythm, or ritual presentation: refusal is still what partly gives Boulez's music its energy, and this particular piece its quick temper.

As for the liaisons between instruments, those too have been described by the composer, in noting that the voice connects with the flute as an instrument of breath (so that the flute can seamlessly but also awesomely assume the vocal role at the end), the flute with the viola as an instrument able to sustain sounds, the viola (pizzicato) with the guitar for its plucked strings, the guitar with the vibraphone as a resonator, and the vibraphone with the xylorimba as an instrument to be struck.[23] The unpitched percussion (used only in the 'Bourreaux de solitude' cycle and the omnium-gatherum finale) he leaves out of account as 'marginal', though the xylorimba's high noise-content establishes some rapport.

Boulez's commentaries on *Le marteau* have concerned themselves only with these matters of apparatus and descent, and the very elusiveness of his published Darmstadt lectures is enough to suggest a view of detailed compositional technique as something to be withheld. The cause for this need not be interpreted as artistic pudeur, still less as a wish to protect trade secrets. Boulez's privacy is, rather, a silent statement of principle—of the principle that the creative means are, and should be, engulfed in the final work, so that to retrieve the compositional process would be impossible or, if it could be done, futile. Koblyakov's painstaking retrieval is, correspondingly, an astonishing detective achievement, and a resounding disproof of the impossibility, if not the futility, since the question remains as to how the process confers or determines the work's meaning and value. After all, *Le marteau sans maître* had been installed as a modern masterpiece—and hailed by Stravinsky, who attended a performance Boulez conducted in Los Angeles in 1957[24]—long before anyone but its composer had any knowledge of its compositional plan.

Example 17*a* shows the opening of the work, and Example 17*b* an indication,

[21] 'Speaking, Playing, Singing', *Orientations*, 330–43.

[22] See, for example, his note on *Telemusik* in Wörner, *Stockhausen*, 57–8.

[23] See 'Speaking, Playing, Singing', *Orientations*, 330–43.

[24] See Igor Stravinsky and Robert Craft, *Memories and Commentaries* (London, 1960), 123; and Craft (ed.) *Stravinsky: Selected Correspondence*, ii (London, 1984), 350.

based on Koblyakov, of how the basic series can be 'multiplied' by any one of its five constituent groups to yield a new series in which every original note is replaced by a transposition of the multiplying group onto that note. (It is unclear whether this was Boulez's independent extension from Webernian serialism or his formalization of Stockhausen's group technique.) In this case the 'factor' is group *c*, the minor third, and the new series is transposed as a whole up a semitone so that the new *dc* is equivalent to the old *c*. The music is in two parts, one shared between the alto flute and the vibraphone, the other between the guitar and the viola, and this latter part begins with groups *a*, *b* (the D has to be borrowed from the vibraphone), *ac* (the C has to be borrowed, again from the vibraphone), *dc* (the same C must do duty here too) and *bc* (with the A and the E♭ borrowed from the flute), while the flute–vibraphone line also moves through *bc* (beginning of the second bar) and *e* (beginning of the third bar), among other groups.

Koblyakov's analysis, carrying across the entire length of the work, is far more convincing than may appear in reference to a short extract, and its formidable detail defies summary. However—and not only on the historical grounds of the work's prior valuation—one must doubt that the music is heard as a succession of multiplied serial units. Not only is the division into such units not always clear (the C–E♭, split between vibraphone and guitar, and involved in both parts, is a case in point), but even the nature of the music as two-part counterpoint is constantly being jeopardized by the crossings of parts and the splittings of lines between dissimilar instruments, especially when the speed is such that triplet quavers are gone in a tenth of a second (both the prelude and the postlude to 'L'artisanat furieux' race at double the speed of the setting, as if they were harmonics of the vocal movement). Pace and fracturing, one might conclude, are more at issue here than polyphony—though with the polyphony vital for the pace and fracturing to be felt. Also, polyphonic order is expressed in the music most directly not by chains of serial multiplication products but by correspondences of shaped motif.

In Example 17 one may note the prominence of rising thirds (usually minor), with or without falling ninths or sixteenths (usually major): it is almost as if the alto flute were announcing a three-note motif, one to be answered successively, in Webernian fashion, by the guitar (though with mild distortion) and the viola (in retrograde inversion) along a time line of consecutive quavers, a time line that then continues as far as the middle of the third bar. Regularities, of motif and of pulse, are played against irregularities, in ways that echo, though they do not precisely duplicate, the compositional process of taking units from a mechanical scheme (the successions of units in Koblyakov's analysis come from diagonal traverses of five-by-five squares of multiplied series) and then interpreting them with apparent freedom in matters of note order, registration, rhythm, and dynamics. In Boulez's terms, the basic elements were produced automatically; it was then necessary to author them by what musical means remained. There had to be this dialectic between process and freedom, between organization and composition, between the rational and the irrational.

Ex. 17a. Boulez, *Le marteau sans maître* (1953–5)

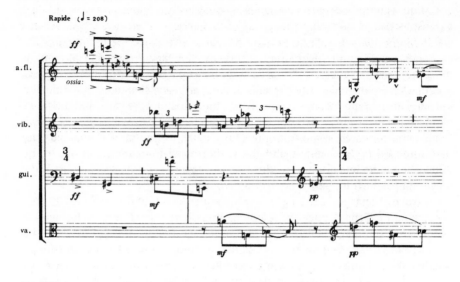

Ex. 17b.

Boulez has been consistent about such dichotomies, and about their irreplaceability. 'One used to find, especially in country towns, cafés where two walls with mirrors ran parallel. And when you entered these cafés you saw yourself into infinity; but if you took one mirror away, you saw only one reflection. I think that the imagination is situated between irrational and rational invention just as between two mirrors: if it deprives itself either of the irrational or the rational, then it can see itself only once.'[25] Even his unusually candid illustration of irrational invention, in this same article, finds excitement in an opposition: 'When you are out walking you can see the play of light on the leaves of the trees, and if you look at the leaves intensely enough you may suddenly be struck by the play of one structure in comparison with another. I have selected the example of leaves because I have seen for myself the relationship between one fixed arrangement of light and the flexible arrangement of leaves.' *Le marteau sans maître*, on many levels of pitch, rhythm, and instrumentation, is Boulez's most complex and endlessly fascinating, endlessly frustrating play of such relationships between the fixed and the flexible.

A more violent description of such an encounter comes at the end of his 'Sound and Word', where he invokes Artaud again—'hearing him read his own texts, accompanying them with shouts, noises, or rhythmic effects, has shown us how to

[25] 'Music and Invention', *Listener* (22 Jan. 1970), 101–2.

make the phoneme burst forth when the word can no longer do so' (a striking indication of what the effect of *Le marteau* should be, but has been less and less in Boulez's four successive recordings[26])—and concludes: 'I increasingly believe that to create effective art, we have to take delirium and, yes, organize it.' No doubt this is what he would have wished: to compose with the daemon upon him, and to wrest from the struggle a form. However, his procedure in *Le marteau sans maître* suggests much more someone taking organization and throwing it into delirium, and his awareness of this—his awareness that he belonged to a different class of artists, those needing a conscious structure to wield or fight against—may have been responsible for the decline in his output, and the virtual extinction of his ability to commit himself to a finished work, after the first performance, when he was thirty, of what was to remain his most signal achievement.[27]

Sound and Word

Le marteau sans maître was one of three closely contemporary works that Stockhausen discusses, along with Nono's *Il canto sospeso* (1956) and his own *Gesang der Jünglinge* (1955–6), in what is a rare document in showing a composer of this time (or indeed any time) observing his fellows.[28] As he intimates, his views of his colleagues are coloured by his own preoccupations: in particular his concern with treating the comprehensibility of words as a variable. It was characteristic of him that he could not be satisfied with Boulez's and Berio's derivation of music from verbal sound and structure: there must be some general principle, which a single work would be enough to demonstrate completely—some system which a work could bring into being. Such a system he found in the organization of degrees of comprehensibility, across a range from the plainness of speech to the total incomprehensibility of wordless music. This would require electronic means. He needed 'to arrange everything separate into as smooth a continuum as possible, and then to extricate the diversities from this continuum and compose with them',[29] and he found the way to do that through attending, between 1954 and 1956, classes in phonetics and information theory given at Bonn University by Werner Meyer-Eppler. Since, as he there discovered, vowel sounds are distinguished, whoever is speaking, by characteristic formants (emphasized bands of frequencies), it seemed it ought to be possible to create synthetic vowels out of

---

[26] See Paul Griffiths, 'Le marteau de son maître, or Boulez selon Boulez', in Josef Häusler (ed.), *Pierre Boulez: eine Festschrift zum 60. Geburtstag am 26. März 1985* (*Vienna, 1985*), 154–8.

[27] The work was scheduled for the 1954 Donaueschingen Festival but shelved, apparently because it stretched the guitarist. Boulez then revised it before the first performance several months later, on 18 June 1955 at the ISCM Festival in Baden-Baden, though the original version had already been published. For an anecdote from that première, see Elliott Carter, 'For Pierre on his Sixtieth', ibid. 12–13.

[28] 'Music and Speech', *Die Reihe*, 6 (1960, English edn. 1964), 40–64.

[29] Ibid.

electronic sounds, so that synthesized music could begin to function as language.[30] Working from the other end, the whole repertory of tape transformations was available to alter spoken or sung material and so move it towards pure, meaningless sound.

Thanks to these techniques Stockhausen was able to create in *Gesang der Jünglinge* a model union between music and language. The synthesized electronic sounds are composed according to principles analogous to those operating in vocal sounds, and the recorded voice, that of a boy treble, is carried into the electronic stream by studio alteration and editing: superimpositions creating virtual choruses, reverberations to suggest great distance, scramblings of words and parts of words, changes of speed and direction. Nothing on either side, therefore, is quite foreign to the other, and Stockhausen invites his audience to attend to degrees of comprehensibility by using a text with which he could expect them (the work was intended for projection in Cologne Cathedral) to be familiar: the German translation of the prayer sung in the Apocrypha by three young Jews in Nebuchadnezzar's furnace (hence the title, 'Song of the Youths'). Even so, the choice of this particular prayer—rather than, say, the 'Our Father', which would have been even more familiar—cannot have been uninfluenced by what Stockhausen could have envisioned would be the imagery of the piece, with the boy's singing surrounded by flames of electronic articulation.

In using natural alongside synthetic sound, Stockhausen mediated not only between speech and music but also between the *musique concrète* of Paris and the *Elektronische Musik* of Cologne, opening the middle ground for exploration. His example—in this as in so many other things—was widely followed. Berio, for instance, transformed a passage of recorded recitation from Joyce's *Ulysses* to produce a stream of comprehended and half-comprehended utterance in his tape piece *Thema–omaggio a Joyce* (1958), though with a physical, sensuous handling of the female voice that connects more with the vocal writing of his concert works, such as *Chamber Music*, than with the ecstatic purity of the treble in *Gesang der Jünglinge*. Ligeti, too, was impressed by Stockhausen's achievement, and in his *Artikulation* (1958) made a more ambivalent, half-comic essay in electronic sound mimicking language.

Equally influential was Stockhausen's introduction of a spatial dimension into electronic music. *Gesang der Jünglinge* was originally prepared for five tape channels, later reduced to four, and its ebullience is greatly enhanced by antiphonal effects. Stockhausen himself was to apply in many later works the discoveries he had made here in the treatment of language and of space, of which the latter was already claiming his attention in *Gruppen* for three orchestras. But perhaps the deepest lesson of *Gesang der Jünglinge* was that music of all kinds, whether naturally or electronically produced, is made of sounds rather than notes, and that the

---

[30] See Stockhausen's 'Actualia', *Die Reihe*, 1 (1955, English edn. 1958), 45–51, in which he adopts Boulez's way—perhaps designed to convey the authority of objectivity—of discussing a work without naming it; see also his 'Music and Speech'.

first task of the composer is to listen. 'More than ever before', Stockhausen wrote, 'we have to listen, every day of our lives. We draw conclusions by making tests on ourselves. Whether they are valid for others only our music can show.'[31]

Il canto sospeso, the third work Stockhausen considered in his essay on music and speech, is a setting of fragments from the farewell letters of condemned political prisoners—characteristically highly charged material, which Nono projects in characteristically highly charged music for soloists, chorus, and orchestra. There is certainly no Boulezian suspicion of 'expressive relationships' here, though at the same time Nono contrasts movements whose words can be understood (such as the fifth, for tenor and orchestra) with others in which the sense is almost wholly confounded by his serial mechanics. He adopts this latter course, Stockhausen interestingly suggests, when the words are such as would shame musical interpretation.

Example 18 shows the start of the second movement, which is the usual example, since in this piece for unaccompanied chorus the composer's procedures are transparent.[32] The movement is characteristic, however, in that the meaning of the text—'I die for a world which will shine with such a strong light and with such beauty that my sacrifice is nothing'—is obscured by having the four contrapuntal lines divided across the eight-part chorus. The contrapuntal lines move in units of quintuplet semiquavers, semiquavers, triplet quavers, and quavers, in each case in units from the Fibonacci series, 1–2–3–5–8–13, which in Stockhausen's music of this period, too, was often used to define proportions. All four lines are drawn into a single unfolding of pitches, simply repeating one of Nono's favoured all-interval series in which the intervals expand wedgewise: A–B♭–A♭–B–G–C–F♯–C♯–F–D–E–E♭. There is also a quite separate quasi-serial organization of dynamic levels. What Boulez saw as a problem—the struggle between organization and invention—becomes in Nono a dramatic emblem of his subject matter, as if we were hearing not so much prisoners as a prison itself singing.

A further, again different example of language becoming music was provided by Mauricio Kagel (b. 1931) in his *Anagrama* for four singers, speaking chorus, and eleven players (1955–8), which was one of the first works he completed after arriving in Cologne from his native Buenos Aires in 1957. Kagel's relationship with Stockhausen was evidently close at this time, and mutually beneficial: what Kagel took from *Gesang der Jünglinge* Stockhausen recovered with interest in *Momente*. His contribution was a fresh perspective—he seems to have developed avant-garde interests by himself in Argentina—and a satirical slant, so that working with degrees of comprehensibility creates absurd theatre. All the singers and speakers treat the text, in four languages, as phonetic more than meaningful material, and bring to it a wide variety of vocal techniques: whispering, shouting, and so on. This was new, as was the similar variety of effect in the instrumental parts, and the score

---

[31] 'Actualia'.

[32] For a very much more far-reaching analysis, see Kathryn Bailey, ' "Work in Progress": Analysing Nono's *Il canto sospeso*', *Music Analysis*, 11 (1992), 279–334.

Ex. 18. Nono, *Il canto sospeso* (1956): II

contributed decisively to the explosion of interest in the impurities and extremities of which both voices and instruments are capable.

. . . how time passes . . .

'Music consists of order-relationships in time.' So begins Stockhausen's essay '. . . how time passes . . .' (1957), whose title perhaps punningly speaks of bemusement at what had happened within the space of six years, as well as of his recent and present concerns with tempo (on the large scale), with the momentary fluctuations and vibrations of sound (on the small scale), and with relationships across the divide. These were the concerns of the fruitful phase that had followed *Kontra-Punkte*, the concerns of *Gesang der Jünglinge*, of the second set of Piano Pieces (V–X, though V was revised, VI and VII were replaced,[33] and IX and X were not finished until 1961), of *Zeitmasze* for five woodwind, and of *Gruppen*.

Work on his electronic *Studien* had given Stockhausen a practical demonstration of how pitch and duration—the two parameters whose parallel ordering had been such a problem to total serialism—are aspects of a single phenomenon, that of vibration. A vibration of, say, 32 Hz will be perceived as a pitched note, whereas one of 4 Hz will be heard as a regular rhythm, and somewhere in between the one will merge into another. So for different reasons—to do with acoustics rather than mathematics—Stockhausen came to the same conclusion that Babbitt had reached a little earlier, that some deep coherence had to be sought between the principles applied to pitch and to rhythm in forming a work. The scale of chromatic durations was inadequate, in Stockhausen's view, because it contradicted acoustical reality, being an additive series and not a logarithmic series such as lay behind the chromatic scale of pitches; moreover, it led to absurdities and inconsistencies, such as the tendency towards regular pulsation when many lines are superimposed, or the undue weight of long durations.

To be troubled by these things was not, of course, new. Boulez in *Le marteau sans maître* had developed his techniques of transformation to the point where he could range from strongly pulsed music to plastic counterpoint propelled by irregular beats or to completely ametrical movement: rhythmic variety, to which he had been led before by intuition and a sense of history, could now be justified within the system. Nono in *Il canto sospeso* had broken up regularity simply by overlaying streams in different units. Stockhausen himself, in *Kontra-Punkte* and Piano Pieces I–IV, had added equal divisions of the bar to chromatic durations. But now he wanted to base his organization on the nature of sound. To create a true confluence with the phenomenon of pitch, he introduced a logarithmic scale of twelve tempos—a scale which could be 'transposed' by altering the rhythmic unit: for example, a change from crotchets to semibreves, and therefore a deceleration by a factor of four, would be the equivalent of a downward shift of two octaves. Within this system, the obverse of the one proposed earlier by Boulez,[34] a rise of a perfect twelfth would have its analogue in a change of tempo in the ratio 3 : 2 (the frequency ratio of a perfect fifth, if one discounts the small discrepancies of temperament) coupled with a halving of the rhythmic unit. So any pitch line could be turned into a duration–tempo succession, a melody of rhythm, and one could also change the timbre of the rhythm, as it were, by adding 'partials' in the form of other duration–tempo successions going on at the same time, their number limited only by

---

[33] For remarks on the earlier versions of VI and VII see Richard Toop's articles 'On Writing about Stockhausen', *Contact*, 20 (1979), 25–7; and 'Stockhausen's Other Piano Pieces', *Musical Times*, 124 (1983), 348–52. For a presentation of V and VII see Karlheinz Stockhausen, 'Clavier Music 1992', *Perspectives of New Music*, 31/2 (1993), 136–49. This item is particularly valuable as a seemingly unedited transcript of the composer's speech.

[34] 'Possibly . . .', *Stocktakings*, 126–8.

the practicalities of performance. For instance, the first group of *Gruppen* has a 'fundamental' represented by minims in the violas, combined with 'overtones' of crotchets (cellos), triplet crotchets (harp), quavers (wood drums), and so on up to the 'tenth harmonic' (flutes). In this way each group in the work is composed as the image of a particular pitch in a particular octave with a particular timbre: as Jonathan Harvey has shown, the whole rhythmic structure is the vast amplification of a serial melodic thread.[35]

This equivalence leads naturally to the work's novel layout, for if different 'fundamentals' are to be heard at once—if the melody is to branch or be harmonized or counterpointed—there must be some way of maintaining different tempos simultaneously, and if each 'fundamental' is to have a rich spectrum of 'overtones', there must be a generous supply of instruments: hence *Gruppen* for three orchestras, each separated from the others and having its own conductor. But having derived the need for orchestral antiphony from his structural scheme, Stockhausen was characteristically drawn to take advantage of the opportunities for spectacle, notably in the sonorous climax where a brass chord is hurled from one orchestra to another across the auditorium. Or perhaps one should regard structure and spectacle as simultaneous imperatives: Stockhausen's artistic success, and his prowess among his peers, depended partly on this knack of discovering systems that would unfold into impressive and unprecedented results. *Gruppen* also belonged securely in his history as an exploration—despite its scale—of relatively small, highly variegated ensembles: this had been his preference in the *Drei Lieder* (at least to judge from the published revision), *Formel*, *Spiel*, and *Punkte*, and it seems to have been stimulated by a wish he shared with his colleagues, a wish to avoid the traditional string-based orchestra, to use different colours as freely as different notes, and to bring forward the percussion. Each orchestra of *Gruppen* is accordingly made up of three dozen players, about half of whom are strings, the rest being constituted equally of woodwind, brass, and percussion, both pitched and unpitched. The articulation of a new kind of rhythmic structure becomes—has to become, in obedience to that structure—a virtuoso exercise in orchestral sound.

As with *Kontra-Punkte*, the new work's innovatory exuberance powerfully impressed Stockhausen's contemporaries. Nono and Berio both wrote pieces for orchestras in groups: the former's *Composizione per orchestra No. 2: Diario polacco* of 1958 and the latter's *Allelujah II* of 1956–7. So, in his *Doubles* (1957–8), did Boulez, who was one of the conductors at the first performance of *Gruppen* (Cologne, 24 March 1958), when the piece brought together three leading composers of the new wave (Maderna was the third) in what could be seen as not only a new assault on space and time but also a symbol of fraternal co-operation.

[35] *The Music of Stockhausen*, 59–61; see also Gottfried Michael Koenig, 'Commentary', *Die Reihe*, 8 (1962, English edn. 1968), 80–98.

Statistics

Hardly less influential than *Gruppen* on the orchestral sound of the late 1950s was the music of Iannis Xenakis, whose promptings came not from acoustics but from architecture (of which he had practical experience at this time, working in Le Corbusier's studio) and mathematics. After arriving in Paris from Athens in 1947, he had some lessons in composition—in Messiaen's class, and as a protégé of Hermann Scherchen, who conducted several of his early performances—but he was always an independent, and not least in his rejection of his contemporaries' methods of working. His article 'La crise de la musique sérielle',[36] is a remarkable document for its time in denouncing directions that, at the moment of *Le marteau sans maître* and *Gruppen*, were commanding widespread enthusiasm. 'Linear polyphony', Xenakis wrote, with implicit reference to such works as Boulez's *Structures*, 'destroys itself by its very complexity; what one hears is in reality nothing but a mass of notes in various registers.'

Of course, this was precisely what had attracted Stockhausen to the 'star music' of the *Mode de valeurs*: Xenakis's criticism was only a statement of how the recent music of his contemporaries departed from traditional linear consequence, and its object was not so much the music itself as the justification of that music in terms of serial order and grammar. For him, though, the conclusion had to be that another theoretical base was needed. If the effect was to be 'nothing but a mass of notes', the means to produce that effect should be sought in the branch of mathematics that had been developed to deal with such statistical phenomena: in 'the notion of probability, which implies in this particular case, combinatory calculus'. He therefore turned to the laws of stochastics, which describe phenomena that can be defined only in the large (Xenakis gives as examples 'the collision of hail or rain on hard surfaces, or the song of cicadas in a summer field'[37]), and so derived 'stochastic music'. By interpreting curved planes—his architectural speciality—as massive overlays of glissandos, as if the strings of an orchestra were playing a blueprint, he had introduced a new and widely imitated texture in his first published piece, *Metastaseis* (1953–4). His second, *Pithoprakta* (1955–6), initiated stochastic music with highly differentiated textures calculated according to laws of probability.

Stockhausen was interested in those laws too, and again the starting point was his work with Meyer-Eppler on the nature of sound. One could, he had learned, define the formant spectrum of a complex sound—such as an unpitched percussion stroke, of the kind he had been using keenly since *Spiel*—without being able to know just which frequencies would be present at any particular instant. *Gruppen* suggests how he may have wanted to express this by having some frequencies (in their rhythmic embodiments) present throughout, while others make only a fleeting contribution. In the case of this work the image is fixed, as indeed it is in *Pithoprakta*, so that the score is in the nature of a photograph of something

---

[36] *Gravesaner Blätter*, 1 (1955), 2 ff.   [37] *Formalized Music* (Bloomington, 1971), 9.

potentially in motion: to realize the motion—to create a score open to macroscopic rhythmic uncertainty—would be hazardous in works for large forces. But it would be possible with soloists or small groupings, and it was this ideal of a constrained mobility that Stockhausen went after in his second set of piano pieces and in *Zeitmasze*.

Writing these compositions after a period of intensive work in the electronic studio on his *Studien*, he was determined also to take advantage of musical possibilities peculiar to live performance, among which rhythmic freedom coincided with the tendency in his theoretical thinking. It was perhaps only after the fact that he had been able, in the case of the first group of Piano Pieces, to delight in performers' rhythmic imprecision. In *Zeitmasze* and the new piano pieces such imprecision is made part of the structure, in that tempos (and in *Zeitmasze* the relative tempos of the five players) are here dependent less on notational prescription than on limitations of technique and feasibility. *Zeitmasze* becomes an elastic play of five time-strands, each of which mixes passages in strict tempo with others whose speeds are determined by, for example, the musicians' capacities to play as fast as possible, or as slowly as possible within one breath (hence the need for this to be a wind piece: aim and medium mesh in a manner characteristic of Stockhausen).

Each of the Piano Pieces in the V–X set similarly combines fixed rhythms with elements whose rhythmic characters will depend on the player's dexterity; each also brings together determined pitch structures with others which contradict these, or which contribute only a generalized effect: Stockhausen had been impressed by David Tudor's extension of piano technique in performing Cage, during the European tour the two American musicians made in 1954, and he dedicated the set to Tudor. The massive clusters and cluster-glissandos of Piece X are among the most striking of the statistical phenomena, or super-groups, where the character of the whole matters much more than the detailed contents. But this piece is unusual only in its flamboyance: its companions also uncover new techniques and sonorities, or formalize what had come out of Tudor's Cage. Piece VII, for instance, beautifully exploits the resonance effects obtained when strings are freed by silent depression of the keys.

Notwithstanding the Piano Pieces' qualities of sound and shapeliness, *Zeitmasze* is Stockhausen's most ambitious work in integrating metronomic definition with free tempo, and fixed metre with scatterings of notes. At the same time, like some of the piano pieces, it mixes points and groups in what the composer—again wanting to present musical decisions as instituting new modes of practice—called 'collective form'.[38] Example 19 gives some indication of this, and also of the work's counterpointing of time layers, as well as its profusion of cross-references in matters of interval and contour (compare, for example, the cor anglais and clarinet lines). Clearly such music poses great problems of coordination; at the same time it liberates the bounding energy of the ideas. No work better displays the self-confidence

---

[38] *Texte*, i. 235.

felt by Stockhausen and his colleagues at this point, nor the exhilaration they felt in pursuing and capturing new possibilities in sound.

Ex. 19. Stockhausen, *Zeitmasze* (1955–6)

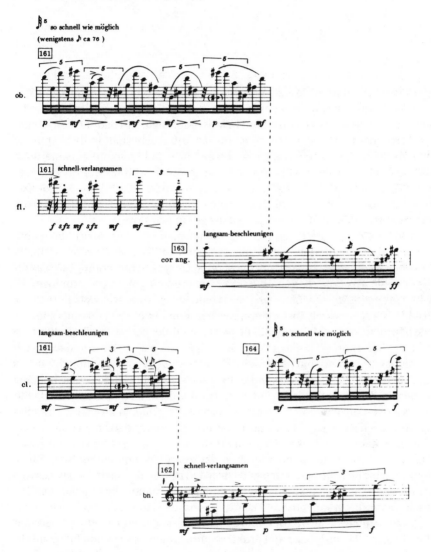

America 3: After Silence, 1952–1961

The Cage Circle

Cage's rapid evolution in 1951–2—from the Concerto for prepared piano to *4' 33"* in eighteen months—may have been encouraged not only by zen studies but also by support from fellow artists with whom he was associated. In Tudor he had a dedicated performer (hence so much piano music) and an assistant in the electronic studio. In Robert Rauschenberg, whom he met in 1948,[1] he found a painter with similar concerns for the small currency of experience. And in Morton Feldman (1926–87), Earle Brown (b. 1926), and Christian Wolff (b. 1934) he discovered younger composers willing to join his pursuit of non-intention: Feldman and Wolff came into his orbit in 1950; Brown joined the group two years later.

Some of Wolff's first pieces use radically limited materials: just three notes within the minimal chromatic range of a major second in his Duo for violins (1950). Meanwhile Feldman was taking an almost opposite tack in prescribing pitch as little as possible. His *Projections* and *Intersections* are series of 'graph' compositions in which, as in the *Music of Changes*, time is represented by space, and in which the spaced boxes specify only instrument, register, number of simultaneous sounds, mode of production, and duration. The two series differ in that the *Projections* are to be consistently quiet, while in the *Intersections* 'the player is free to choose any dynamic at any entrance but must maintain sameness of volume'—though 'what is desired in both . . . is a pure (non-vibrating) tone'.[2] Example 20 shows the opening of *Projection II*, where the dashed lines mark off units of a second; the first sound heard is a five-note chord in the extreme bass of the piano, followed by a middle-range trumpet note, a note in the mid-treble of the piano, and so on. In other works of the same period, such as the *Extensions* series or *Structures* for string quartet, Feldman used conventional notation in order to achieve non-compulsion differently, by having delicate figures repeated over and over again. But the ideal is essentially the same: as Cage pointed out, 'Feldman's conventionally notated music is himself playing his graph music'.[3] The exceptions to his world of low-density, low-speed, low-volume music were few and extreme: the hectically eventful *Intersection III* for piano, or the unrealized and probably unrealizable *Intersection* for tape.[4]

---

[1] See David Revill, *The Roaring Silence: John Cage: A Life* (London, 1992), 96.

[2] Statement by Feldman republished in *The Boulez–Cage Correspondence*, 104.

[3] Michael Nyman, *Experimental Music: Cage and Beyond* (London, 1974), 45.

[4] See n. 23 to Heinz-Klaus Metzger, 'Essay on Prerevolutionary Music', published with EMI C 165 28954-7.

Ex. 20. Feldman, *Projection II* (1951)

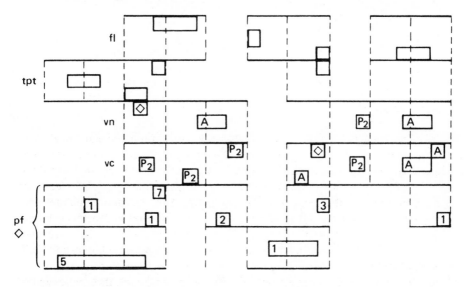

The fact that Feldman had such a thing as a personal sound-world is emblematic of his distance from Cage; Brown's objectives were different again, and perhaps formed most by what he learned from the visual arts. By his own account, he was stimulated by 'the integral but unpredictable "floating" variations of a Calder mobile and the contextual rightness of Pollock's spontaneity and directness in relation to the material and his particular image of his work'.[5] His aim was not the empty space of Cage, nor the quiet space of Feldman, but the decisive object—not the extinction of the composer, nor the liberation of the performer, but the creation of a well-made piece, one that would have a sure identity for all the variability of form and detail introduced by means of indeterminate notation. The more indeterminate the notation, the more the identity of the piece would have to be visual, until, very rapidly, he arrived at *December 1952* (Example 21), which is at once the earliest, the most enigmatic (there being no instructions about how these shapes are to be realized as sound) and the most elegant of graphic scores. *4′ 33″* had elided the gap between music and life; *December 1952*, less ambitiously, elided the gap between music and design.

After Silence

4′ 33″ appears to have been followed soon by a much longer silence in Cage's output, one of several months.[6] Perhaps it seemed that no more music was needed,

---

[5] Quoted in Nyman, *Experimental Music*, 48.   [6] See *The Boulez–Cage Correspondence*, 143.

Ex. 21. Brown, *December 1952*

that everything had been said in the saying of nothing. But there were endless ways of saying nothing, as Cage might have observed in the mute abundance of nature, from the mushrooms to the stars. There was, too, still a notional infinity of sounds waiting to 'become themselves', and it was perhaps on their behalf that he returned to composition—to the highly purposed business of creating music without purpose. He did so, between 1953 and 1956, exclusively on two fronts: in the *Music for Piano* series (still using the method of marking paper imperfections[7]) and in a collection of pieces measured to precise, chance-determined durations, a collection he referred to privately as 'The Ten Thousand Things'.[8]

The first of these were tiny, around a minute long, but those of 1954–6 became huge virtuoso exercises: *34' 46 776"* and *31' 57 9864"* for Tudor, *26' 1 1499"* for any four-stringed instrument, and *27' 10 554"* for percussionist. As in the *Music of Changes*, what is on display here is the complexity of chance phenomena: like the shapes of a broken glass, beyond what anyone could conceive, are the similarly wild and irregular occurrences that enter these compositions. It necessarily followed that, though Cage was utterly simple in his bearing and in his behaviour as an artist, the demands he placed on performers were stringent, in works from the *Music of*

---

[7] See 'To Describe the Process of Composition Used in *Music for Piano 21–52*', *Silence*, 60–1.
[8] See Revill, *The Roaring Silence*, 178.

Changes to such late pieces as the *Freeman Etudes*, and not least in 'The Ten Thousand Things', whose titles betoken a utopian accuracy of performance. The use of ancillary instruments, as in *Water Music*, adds further to the impression these pieces create of performance as action—of rhythm defined by rapidity of bodily movement, and of music becoming abstract theatre. Tudor gave the first performances of *34' 46 776"* and *31' 57 9864"* while on a European tour with Cage in October–November 1954: among the many European composers who were fascinated, Stockhausen dedicated his Piano Pieces V–VIII to Tudor (though V had already been performed).

This was another case, though, of Europeans mistaking the effect of Cage's music for its intention. If the exacting notation of 'The Ten Thousand Things' had any purpose, it was perhaps to screen off the habits and hopes of performers, just as chance operations screened off the habits and hopes of the composer. Having to offer so much attention to instructions, the players of these pieces could not at the same time offer any intention. Unaccustomed requirements—to play on the piano's strings or woodwork, use accessory instruments, deal with unusual notations—increased the defamiliarization, and Cage used all of these in his next major work, the *Concert for Piano and Orchestra* (1957–8).

He wrote in his programme note for the first performance—given as the climax of his silver jubilee concert at Town Hall, New York, on 15 May 1958—that his 'intention [*sic*] in this piece was to hold together extreme disparities, much as one finds them held together in the natural world, as, for instance, in a forest or on a city street.'[9] Accordingly the work is an encyclopaedia of notational possibilities, laid out in parts for piano and thirteen other instruments, any or all of which may be used in performance, together with other material (pieces from the *Music for Piano* series could also be overlapped at will). 'I regard this work', his note concludes, 'as one "in progress", which I intend [again] never to consider as in a final state, although I find each performance definitive.' This Joycean notion of the constantly continuing work had been part of 'The Ten Thousand Things',[10] and suggests that after *4' 33"* Cage had to consider his compositions as endlessly mutable, though it was only at this point in his career, after the *Concert*, that the emphasis in his music shifted from the solo piece to the unsynchronized ensemble.

At the same time there was a shift from relatively conventional notation to new forms requiring a contribution from the performer. Example 22, from the solo part of the *Concert*, provides an instance. The player has to draw perpendiculars from either the upper or the lower horizontal line to the slanting lines. Measurements from the base line to the points of intersection with the wavy lines are then used to determine values for the four musical parameters (pitch, duration, dynamic, attack) according to scales which the player also determines. The numbers show by their differences the time available for sounds derived from references to each of the slanting lines: 11.5 seconds in the case of the first, for example.

---

[9] Kostelanetz (ed.), *John Cage*, 130.   [10] See *The Boulez–Cage Correspondence*, 143.

Ex. 22. Cage, *Concert for Piano and Orchestra* (1958): solo

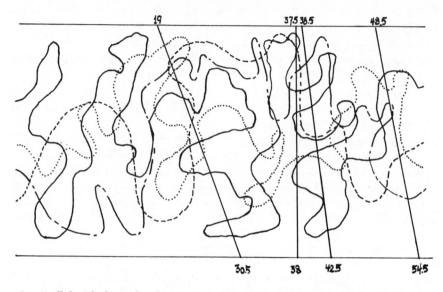

In parallel with these developments in his music—towards increasing multiplicity and new notations—Cage began in the late 1950s to concern himself again with electronic media, for which he found opportunities in Europe during a six-month tour in 1958–9. He produced a tape version of *Fontana Mix* (a kit composition rather in the manner of Example 22) at the RAI electronic music studio in Milan, and created two more realizations of *Fontana Mix* for himself to perform on Italian television: *Water Walk* and *Sounds of Venice*. By now, theatre was not just a by-product of his music but a prompting force: back in the United States he created *Theatre Piece* (1960), for eight performers in multifarious activities, as well as *Cartridge Music* (also 1960), in which he invented live electronic music.

Cartridge Music has several players generating sounds by inserting objects into gramophone cartridges or by acting on pieces of furniture to which contact microphones have been attached. The aim, so Cage said, was not only to create the possibility of electronic performance (indeed, one might add, of electronic theatre, since the sounds are out of proportion to the actions one sees), but also 'to bring about a situation in which any determination made by a performer would not necessarily be realizable. When, for instance, one of the performers changes a volume control, lowering it nearly to zero, the other performer's action, if it is affected by that particular amplification system, is inaudible. I had been concerned with composition which was indeterminate of its performance [because of the overlay possibilities of the *Music for Piano* series and the *Concert*, for instance]; but, in this instance, performance is made, so to say, indeterminate of itself.'[11]

The 1960s: Everywhere and Nowhere

Cage could now go no further—unless to allow the total indeterminacy of improvisation, which he had always resisted as an immediate return to personal taste. Here were more paradoxes. The publication of his first collection of lectures and essays, *Silence*, in 1961, installed him as the guru of a new libertarian avant garde, who heard his message that everything could be music but ignored the disciplines he had adopted to keep self at bay. In New York this avant garde was represented by the Fluxus group: La Monte Young (b. 1935), an early member of that group, had come into contact with Cage at Darmstadt in 1959, and went on the next year to produce a sequence of beguilingly simple pieces, opening out from the fascination with sounds of long duration that went back, so he has said, to listening to the wind from inside the loghouse in which he grew up. His first compositions had been fully notated, though with minimal materials. The new pieces of 1960 went quite beyond notation:

Turn a butterfly (or any number of butterflies) loose in the performance area.

When the composition is over, be sure to allow the butterfly to fly away outside.

The composition may be any length but if an unlimited amount of time is available, the doors and windows may be opened before the butterfly is turned loose and the composition may be considered finished when the butterfly flies away.[12]

Improvisation by butterflies perhaps would have met Cage's demands for music to be non-volitional; however, in his own pieces he had always required a rigorous control of action, the control being necessary not least to ensure that the action would be prevented from manifesting itself as meaning.

It was also in 1961, the year of *Silence*, that Cage's scores began to appear from the C. F. Peters Corporation in New York, greatly improving the dissemination of his music to cope with the increasing worldwide demand. And yet his production of new works slowed almost to silence.

Home-made Music: Partch and Nancarrow

Right from the start Cage had found and made his creative opportunities outside the norms of musical life, writing pieces for himself to perform, for close friends, for dancers: his 1949 String Quartet had been a rare venture into the traditional concert world. In the *annus mirabilis* of 1961 there was another, when the Montreal Festival Society commissioned an orchestral score and received *Atlas eclipticalis*, but it was not until the mid-1970s that he began to write regularly for conventional media. He was therefore able to avoid many of the most frequently discussed problems of contemporary music—concerning the morality and practicality of the composer's

[12] Composition 1960 No. 5.

participation in bourgeois musical life—until those problems had been talked into extinction.

In circumventing the usual routes and the usual public he was not alone, especially among American composers: Ives had done that, though differently, and the huge, multifarious output of Henry Cowell (an acquaintance of Ives and teacher of Cage) forestalls official culture's passions to delimit and define. Where western American composers closer to Cage in age are concerned, unorthodox musical behaviour becomes almost an orthodoxy. Harry Partch (1901–74), largely self-taught, devoted his life to designing, building, and writing for his own instruments made to a scale of forty-three justly tuned degrees per octave. Conlon Nancarrow (b. 1912) similarly concentrated, throughout a long period of his life, on an unconventional medium: the pianola, or, in American terminology, player piano. The music of Lou Harrison (b. 1917) suggests more a continuation from Cowell (who was his teacher too) in its abundance, its generous simplicity, and its complete lack of European hauteur with regard to the instruments, forms, and tunings of other cultures.

Partch had come upon the gate to his independent road in Hermann Helmholtz's book on acoustics, translated into English by A. J. Ellis as *On the Sensations of Tone*. In the early 1930s he had written a few pieces for voice with 'adapted viola' (an instrument with a lengthened neck, and with its fingerboard marked to facilitate performance in just intonation), but it was only during the late 1930s and 1940s that he began to assemble a collection of instruments, and most of his works date from the period between 1949 and 1966. They consist principally of musical dramas, since for him just intonation and instrument construction were imbricated in an aesthetic of 'corporeal' music—of music as founded in natural vibration, and of music as a narrative art, rooted in speech. The history of western music was, with rare exceptions (Musorgsky, for example), a contrary history of 'abstraction': closer to his ideals, he thought, were the musical cultures of ancient China and Greece, in which sound, display, word, and gesture were welded and magically potent. (There is a striking kinship here with Artaud's ideas, which appealed so much to Boulez at just the time Partch was beginning to realize his first major projects.)

The instruments which Partch made or adapted include reed organs, plucked strings (kitharas, zithers, koto), marimbas with wooden or bamboo keys, and other struck percussion instruments made with found objects of glass or metal. To these might be added regular instruments, but the sound-world would usually be dominated by the special percussion—as would the stage, for Partch clearly designed his instruments with an eye for spectacle.[13] He also gave them wonderful names: Mazda Marimba (made from light bulbs of different sizes), Spoils of War (including brass shell casings), Cloud-Chamber Bowls (of glass). In writing music for them, he tended to prefer simple textures, regular pulsation, and ostinato, for which his reasons might have included the need to work with student performers (his major performances were at universities in Chicago and Los Angeles), a wish to show off

---

[13] There are colour and monochrome photographs in his book *Genesis of a Music* (New York, 1974).

sonority, a way of working with stretches of music that—being equal in length and similar in rhythm—could be superposed, and a desire for elemental expression.

Two of his full-length dramas—all of which seem to call for dance and stylized action within the arena of the instrumentarium—are based on Greek plays: *Oedipus* and *The Bacchae* (transplanted into contemporary America in *Revelation in the Courthouse Park*). Of the others, *The Bewitched* is a sequence of scenes intended to reveal human conditioning ('We are all bewitched, and mostly by accident: the accident of form, color, and sex; of prejudices conditioned from the cradle up'[14]), and *Delusion of the Fury* is based on a Noh play in which vengeance gives way to enlightenment, with the appendage of a farce after an African tale.

Partch's combination of subtle intonation with primitive rhythm is neatly balanced by Nancarrow's pursuit of rhythmic intricacy using a medium which rules out any sophistication of tuning. But there are also parallels, and not only in the way both men existed outside musical convention—Partch scratching a hand-to-mouth existence in southern California for much of his life, Nancarrow living since 1940 in isolation in a suburb of Mexico City. Both started to make serious progress in the 1940; both began to achieve wider recognition late in life—Partch in the later 1960s, when his independent spirit and his magic dance dramas with resonant percussion instruments began to seem central and sympathetic, Nancarrow in the 1980s, when his patent complexity (as opposed to the concealed complexity of Boulezian serialism) could be recognized as in tune with a computer-orientated understanding of art and the mind.

Nancarrow began to compose for the player piano in order to realize tempo overlappings that proved beyond the performers he had to deal with at the time, and he returned to more normal media when his late-found fame brought him the virtuosos of a new age (his Third Quartet was written for the Arditti Quartet in 1987, and has the four instruments travelling at speeds related at 3 : 4 : 5 : 6). But the player piano was more than a functional interim. It allowed him to create rhythmic canons (and most of his player-piano studies are canonic) in which the voices move at far more complex relative speeds: in Study No. 37, to take an extreme case, there are twelve voices, at tempos in the ratios $1 : \frac{15}{14} : \frac{7}{8} : \frac{5}{6} : \frac{3}{4} : \frac{5}{8} : \frac{7}{8} : \frac{1}{2} : \frac{5}{8} : \frac{5}{6} : \frac{1}{4} : \frac{15}{16}$ (a rhythmic encoding of a twelve-note scale in just intonation). Also, the studies exult in possibilities of keyboard sound beyond any keyboard player or combination of keyboard players: not only twelve-part canons, but colossal, precisely simultaneous chords and immense glissandos, all moving at speed with perfect accuracy.

The prodigious rapidity and precisely executed extravagance of the music are among its joys and comedies: the joys and comedies of heavy loads lightly carried. For Nancarrow is one of the few great musical humorists. His techniques can be compared with those of animation, in that the preparation is an exercise of handicraft requiring concentration on items extracted from the continuity into which they will be absorbed (still pictures, single notes punched into the paper rolls that

---

[14] Ibid. 335.

are the player piano's software) and that the laboriousness of this procedure results in an inherent disproportion between cause and effect (more than a year may be taken up in creating a five-minute piece[15]). Such disproportion is itself comic: so is the existence of worlds in which anything can happen, but everything must be pre-ordained in detail. It may be for these reasons that animation lends itself most readily to comedy, and that Nancarrow's studies have the humour, as well as the dimensions, of the cartoon short (the longest of them play for around ten minutes; most last for between one minute and five).

They also resemble animated comedies in bringing brisk, simplified designs into movement, since Nancarrow's canons are not only abstract formal processes (often determinedly audible, at least up to the point—frequently reached and surpassed—at which the mind can no longer juggle with the number of lines in play) but also rules of behaviour for the small musical figures he commonly uses. To take a relatively straightforward example, Study No. 5[16] sets in play a variety of elements: an idle sort of vamp which lurches lopsidedly up to a cadence (it is characteristic of Nancarrow that humour should be present, as here, at the level of motif), twirls that are part way between scale and glissando, a fanfare of chords. Each of these ideas is on its own temporal plane: the vamp, for instance, repeats regularly throughout the piece, whereas other figures recur at increasingly shorter intervals. Example 23 shows a passage from about two-thirds of the way into the piece, and illustrates the polymetric density and the full keyboard texture Nancarrow can attain: at the beginning of the example, bars that have already begun have their time signatures placed in brackets; the repeating vamp is in 35/16, in the middle of the keyboard. The impression is of musical entities playing some game, dodging each other, while all the time more and more entities enter the game, to the point where, growing in frequency and in number, they meld: the whole process takes just over two and a half minutes. What also contributes to the comedy of the studies is the fact that an ignoble and outmoded machine is being used to create amazement.

Indeed, the studies are doubly mechanical: delivered by a mechanical instrument, and delivered too by machineries of rhythm in the form of mensuration canons. But, again like cartoon films, they thoroughly flout the notion that what is mechanical is *ipso facto* dead. Nancarrow's taste for complex cross-rhythms can be traced not only to his admiration for Stravinsky but also to his experience as a jazz trumpeter, and his ideas often have the syncopated spring of blues, ragtime or boogie woogie. Letters written in vernacular style are posted along elaborate and sophisticated networks; material which high culture would deem debased is fantastically rescued and celebrated. And this rescue effort is in itself humorous.

[15] See Charles Amirkhanian's note with Wergo 6168.

[16] The numbering of the studies is problematic and their dating uncertain: I am most grateful to Kyle Gann for helping me understand just how problematic and how uncertain. The earliest datable study, according to Gann, is No. 3, which was completed in 1948. The remaining studies up to No. 30 had all been made by 1960, which might suggest a date early in the 1950s for No. 5. Eighteen more studies, up to No. 50 (there being no Nos. 38–9), were composed between 1965 and 1988. Since 1992 have come further pieces for prepared piano: Study No. 3750, *For Yoko* and *Contraption No. 1*.

Ex. 23. Nancarrow, Study No. 5

Europe 4: Mobile Form, 1956–1962

Mobile Form 1: Stockhausen and Boulez

Hitherto Cage's impact on European music had come in short though perhaps decisive, shocks: in 1949, when he had made his music and his thinking known to Boulez and Messiaen in Paris, and in 1954, when he and Tudor had given performances in several European cities, and when Stockhausen had met them. But by the mid-1950s many of the most prospering musical developments in Europe—Stockhausen's concern with statistical events, Boulez's pursuit of open form, Kagel's and Berio's extensions of instrumental and vocal technique, almost everyone's effort at electronic music and so at ways of composing untempered sounds—were making Cage seem far more relevant than could have been the case earlier. In 1957 Maderna discussed Cage's work at Darmstadt, and an issue of *Die Reihe* included, between Stockhausen's '. . . how time passes . . .' and an elucidation by Pousseur of the current state of his technique, a short piece in which Cage described the compositional process required to create his *Music for Piano 21–52* (1955) by means of chance operations[1]—this in what had been the journal of total organization. Change was in the air, and the next year Cage and Tudor were themselves at Darmstadt.

By now it was clear that the interests of Stockhausen and Boulez were differently based, even though the Darmstadt comradeship continued until 1965,[2] the last year when Boulez was present. Stockhausen was driven on by what he could learn about the nature of sound, whereas Boulez's essays of the mid-1950s speak of aesthetic issues and models from literature. Both their closenesses and their differences are revealed in the extraordinary conjunction of Stockhausen's Piano Piece XI (1956) with Boulez's Third Piano Sonata (1955–7), the two first classics of open form in European music.

Stockhausen's piece presents the player with nineteen groups disposed on a single large sheet of paper. According to the instructions, the performer 'begins with whichever group he sees first', 'casts another random glance to find another of the groups', and continues in the same manner until a group has been reached for the third time. There is thus no guarantee that all the groups will be played, and similarly their order is entirely free, though Stockhausen makes some effort at linkage into what he may have seen as a Markov chain, 'a sequence of mutually dependent

---

[1] No. 3 (1957), 41–3.　　[2] See Dominique Jameux, *Pierre Boulez* (London, 1991), 117.

symbols',[3] since at the end of each group he gives a 'registration' of what tempo, dynamic level, and mode of touch must be used for the next, whichever that may be. Whether or not this is a borrowing from information theory, Stockhausen characteristically identifies his work as something new in musical history, having nothing to do with earlier examples of mobile form in the music, say, of Cage, Brown or Henry Cowell (whose 'Mosaic' Quartet dates from 1934), everything to do with research into sound. 'Piano Piece XI', he has said, 'is nothing but a sound in which certain partials, components, are behaving statistically . . . As soon as I compose a noise . . . then the wave structure of this sound is aleatoric. If I make a whole piece similar to the ways in which this sound is organized, then naturally the individual components of this piece could also be exchanged, permutated, without changing its basic quality.'[4]

Perhaps for the first time in their relationship, Boulez was mistrustful of one of Stockhausen's new departures, finding in it 'a new sort of automatism, one which, for all its apparent opening the gates to freedom, has only really let in an element of risk that seems to me absolutely inimical to the integrity of the work'.[5] That word 'automatism', conjuring up the stalemate of *Structures Ia* and the disappointments of Cage, suggests how deeply Boulez was worried. Leaving any aspect to chance produced exactly the same effect as being forced by some scheme: the composer's presumed liberty of action was compromised. This Boulez would not countenance, and yet there seemed no way to justify the composer's freedom other than by recourse to the mystique of the individual imagination, which again was not very satisfactory. Boulez's technique was presenting him with multiple possibilities, but no grounds for choice. However, by a far-reaching development of the open forms of Cage and Stockhausen, it might be possible to defer choice to the point of performance: to present the work with its alternatives intact, and to ask the performer or performers to choose from among them.

In a crucial article on aleatory composition,[6] Boulez proposes that chance can be 'absorbed' in musical structures dependent on a degree of flexibility, perhaps in tempo: there were already examples of such structures in his own music (*Structures Ib*, *Le marteau sans maître*) and in Stockhausen's (*Zeitmasze*, Piano Pieces V–X). Chance could also be accommodated, he ventures, in mobile forms, and that possibility he explored most deeply in his Third Piano Sonata, which could even have been intended as a creative criticism of Stockhausen's Piece XI. The performer is now asked not to give a 'random glance' but rather to prepare a way through the options provided, and the work is—or rather was planned to be, since only two of its five 'formants' have been published[7]—a compendium of opportunities for alternative route, *ossia* and *ad libitum*.

---

[3] For a different approach to Markovian music see Xenakis, *Formalized Music*, 43–109.

[4] Jonathan Cott, *Stockhausen* (London, 1974), 70.

[5] Goléa, *Rencontres avec Pierre Boulez*, 229.   [6] 'Alea', *Stocktakings*, 26–38.

[7] A fragment from another, *Antiphonie*, was published as *Sigle* in 1968 in a Universal Edition piano compendium.

Boulez's return to the term 'formant' is a reminder that his thoughts on open form go back to before Piano Piece XI—to his 1954 report 'Current Investigations',[8] and perhaps even to the *Polyphonie* enterprise—and that he too, in this respect at least, was open to ideas presenting themselves in the nature of sound. He has also suggested that there might be 'développants'—other movements 'complete in themselves but structurally connected with the original formants'.[9] However, the essentially literary nature of his approach is revealed by the layouts of the two printed formants, *Trope* and *Constellation–Miroir*. The former is a ring-bound sheaf of four items to be played in various possible orders—a 'Texte' which is the subject of a 'Parenthèse', 'Commentaire' and 'Glose', while *Constellation–Miroir* ('mirror' because what we have is, for reasons undisclosed, the retrograde of a notional *Constellation*) sprinkles fragments over several large pages, and so recalls the appearance of Mallarmé's *Un coup de dès*, which Boulez had planned to set in 1950.[10] At that time, instead of *Un coup de dès*, he had written *Structures Ia*: now *Constellation–Miroir* would take up Mallarmé's invitation towards a music of immanent variability in a different way, and find a route, in its teeming variety of routes, to defy compulsion.

The structural link between the formants is at the level of the basic series, which in *Trope* is considered as a succession of four units suggesting cyclical concatenations of serial forms (see Example 24a)[11] and also serving as the germ of the formant's circular mobility. Two of the serial units together, *b* and *d*, make up a transposition of *a* down a minor third; the foreign group *c*, a symmetrical pairing of minor thirds, is a 'trope' which both imitates and interrupts the larger symmetry. The formant is a vast magnification of this material, not only in its cyclical permutability but also in its inclusion of commentaries that are interpolated into the skeleton structure or else superimposed upon it. Not only are three of the large sections commentaries on the root 'Texte', but they contain within themselves parentheses and glosses that are sometimes obligatory, sometimes optional: Example 24b, from the opening of 'Parenthèse', shows one of the latter inserted into a straightforward serial chain, which is that of Example 24a.

The music's movement by allusion is a characteristic that goes back to the Sonatina of a decade before, and beyond that to the late Debussy that Boulez had invoked as a model in his 1954 essay '. . . Near and Far'.[12] For example, one may notice the accelerando run of *c* units within the brackets referring to the preceding *c* group marked 'un peu précipité', or the parenthetic *d* groups similarly relating to the corresponding group in the main text, or the registral fixing of the A–G minor seventh. What is unusual here—though repeated later in *Domaines* for clarinet and ensembles (1961–8)—is the clear demarcation between a strict framework of serial

---

[8] *Stocktakings*, 15–19; see above, p. 00.   [9] ' "Sonate, que me veux-tu?" ', *Orientations*, 143–54.

[10] *The Boulez–Cage Correspondence*, 80.

[11] See *Boulez on Music Today*, 73–4; and Iwanka Stoïanowa, 'La *Troisième sonate* de Boulez et le projet mallarméen du Livre', *Musique en jeu*, 16 (1974), 9–28.

[12] *Stocktakings*, 141–57.

Ex. 24*a*.

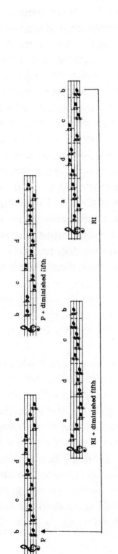

Ex. 24*b*. Boulez, Piano Sonata No. 3 (1956–7): *Trope*

unfolding and its vast possibilities of extension: that demarcation is even emphasized by the move out to another world of tempo, rhythmic variety, and density, and then by the return, through what may be sensed as a correction when the obligatory music repeats an E–F fall just heard in the free material. But if the formant is, in this regard, doctrinaire, that may have been in its purpose as a teaching instrument and example. It is the *Structures Ia* of aleatory form, and *Constellation–Miroir* the *Ib*.

This other piece, planned as the central sun around which the four smaller formants revolve (in that their placings were to have been variable), is considerably more ambiguous about the strategies by which simple material ('points': sequences made up essentially of single notes) is related to more complex ('blocs': massive chords and arpeggios). There is a brief mixture of the two types at the start, followed by three sections of 'points' alternated with two of 'blocs', and this large form is fixed. But within each section Boulez provides numerous possible ways of linking the fragments, so that the player 'must pick his way through a close network of paths' as he confronts what the composer has likened to a map of an unknown town.[13] More subtly and ambiguously than in *Trope*, unforeseen connections infiltrate the paths, and give any performance of the formant some sense that it is indeed the traverse of a maze, though hardly less important to the musical effect is the fluidity of movement (a controlled rubato is generally demanded) or the wide variety of sounds obtained by means of scrupulously marked pedallings and resonance effects. There were intimations of these in Example 24*b*, where, for example, the depression of the sustaining pedal near the start of the bracketed material, just after the fortissimo arpeggio has been played, captures the echo from the strings. But *Constellation–Miroir* has many more, so that the visual distinction of the printed music, which uses red ink for 'blocs' and green for 'points', is matched by its sonorous appeal.

Mobile form 2: Boulez and Berio

Apparently it was only after completing the first version of the Third Sonata that Boulez came to know of Mallarmé's dream of a Book that would be endlessly mutable, a Book whose segments could be chosen and ordered at will for public readings. Learning of this could only have intensified his feelings of proximity to a poet who had overturned existing grammar and trodden a similar path to his own between chance and necessity, and almost inevitably a large-scale Mallarmé setting was his next major project—not a return to *Un coup de dès* but an assembly of poems into a new book: *Pli selon pli* for soprano and orchestra (1957–62). The Third Sonata is related to this work rather as the first book of *Structures* is related to *Le marteau sans maître*, in that both later compositions give voice to poetic implications and discoveries that had already arrived in purely musical form. In principle, *Pli selon pli* is

---

[13] ' "Sonate, que me veux-tu?" ', *Orientations*, 151.

considerably less open in structure—partly for the practical reason that the sonata's multitude of options could not be imitated in a work for large forces without loss of the control Boulez was zealous to maintain. However, the work's revisions, continuing into the 1980s, kept it alive to change, even while gradually rescinding the original formal liberties.

The five moments, if all are to be played, must be given in a set, symmetrical order, beginning and ending with pieces for large ensemble in which the voice is present only momentarily (*Don* and *Tombeau*), and reaching inwards to a song for soprano and nine-piece percussion ensemble (*Improvisation sur Mallarmé II*). Revisions of the other two movements, the first and third *Improvisations*, increased their scale to enhance this palindrome, and at the same time deprived *Improvisation III* of its status as the work's one great area of unpredictability, withdrawing the performers' freedom to choose and order material. The work's elasticity thus became much more a matter of variable tempos, and of the superimposition of orchestral streams flowing at different rates, as in *Gruppen*, though requiring only one conductor. (And requiring, one might almost add, the composer himself to be that conductor, since most of his works since the late 1950s, when he began to give concerts regularly, have needed his own kinds of precisions and virtuosities: perfect ensemble playing, exact rhythm, and the ability to respond quickly to alternatives.)

For the outermost movements Boulez chose one of Mallarmé's earliest published poems ('Don du poème') and one of his last ('Tombeau', his homage to Verlaine). These movements therefore represent the birth and death of a poet, and stand too for the birth and death inherent in art: the birth of the creative impulse, and its death to the artist once it has been expressed. 'Don du poème' is further the celebration of a literary birth, in that it looks forward in metre and imagery to the poet's 'Hérodïade', and Boulez's *Don* similarly looks forward to the remainder of *Pli selon pli*. There is a dedicatory setting of the opening line of the poem, and then the text disappears (becomes 'central and absent', to recall Boulez's terminology); the music goes into the state of nascence that the silent words are at once describing and illustrating—a state, as musically interpreted, of suspended chords, through which prefigurings of the four movements to come are drawn forward in reverse order and lost. In *Tombeau*, completing the symmetry, the singer emerges at the end with the final line of the text, and the piece is extinguished by a *sforzato* chord which recalls the opening crack of *Don*. The end is as the beginning; a window is opened and shut.

The *Improvisations sur Mallarmé*—improvisations only for Boulez himself as composer and, in their fluidity of tempo, as conductor—allow the poem to be present as well as central (though this was not entirely the case in the early versions of the third), and so there can be a little less doubt about how the music relates to the words.[14] As in *Le marteau sans maître*, the relation takes place simultaneously in

[14] For Boulez's own explanations see his 'Constructing an Improvisation', *Orientations*, 155–73; and also *Conversations with Célestin Deliège*, 94–5.

different levels of imagery and structure, the former represented by, for example, the ornate vocal melisma for the undulating lace curtain of 'Une dentelle s'abolit' in *Improvisation II*, or the use of registral fixing now to give a stationary effect for reasons traceable to the text, or the choice of a scintillating, resonant instrumentation to correspond with metaphors of coldness, transparency, whiteness, and reflection. Meanwhile, perhaps a little naively, Boulez reacts to verbal structures with changes from melismatic to syllabic singing at formal junctures (all of the poems except 'Don du poème' are sonnets), or by deploying different compositional principles for masculine and feminine endings, or by musical eightnesses for the eight syllables of the lines.

Lessons from *Pli selon pli*—lessons concerned with the musical matching of verbal sound and sense, with the exploration of stationary harmonic fields, and with the notion of the work as a collection of fascicles—were absorbed and developed by Berio in an important group of pieces composed during the same period. Also crucial, to him and to others, was a lesson dramatized in *Le marteau sans maître*: the rediscovery, following the fragmentation of the heyday of total serialism, that an instrument (specifically the flute) could command the rhetoric of a voice. (Nono alone had no need to learn this lesson, since instrumental vocality and drama had been manifest in his music all through—not least in his flute concerto *Y su sangre*.) The flautist Severino Gazzelloni, a regular performer in *Le marteau*, was one of the first star soloists of the European new-music circuit, and responsible for the prominence of the flute in the music of that world; for him Berio wrote two chamber concertos, *Serenata I* (1957) and *Tempi concertati* (1958–9), as well as *Sequenza I* (1958), the first of a continuing series of virtuoso solos concerned with dramatizing performance.

Tempi concertati is a drama too. The 'concerted tempos', and the disposition of the orchestra into four groups, suggest another look at *Gruppen*, albeit on a smaller scale than in *Allelujah II* (where again the flute had a determining role), but *Tempi concertati* proceeds in quite a different fashion (and in quite a different fashion from *Serenata I*) as an interplay between solos and choruses, an interplay of declamation and revolt, suggestion and response, song and silence, in which the flute's primary place has to be held against solo activities from members of the groups, especially the violin and the two pianos. Together with the contemporary works of Kagel (different anyway in their concerns with debasement and criticism rather than brilliance and play), the piece stands at the head of a modern tradition of instrumental theatre.

After these three flute-centred works Berio returned to the voice of his wife Cathy Berberian (1925–83), who was another of the small group of performers devoted to new music in the 1950s (a short list would have to include also the names of David Tudor and Yvonne Loriod), and the singer on whose voice he had already created *Chamber Music* and *Thema*. In his next work for her, *Circles* with harpist and two percussionists (1960), he turned from Joyce to cummings, and set three poems, two of them twice, to make a palindrome $ABCB'A'$. Since the poems are, in the order

A–C, of increasingly dislocated syntax, one circle of the work is from words as information to words as sound and back again, and that circle is repeated in different aspects of the musical design. For example, both settings of the first two poems use conventional rhythmic notation, whereas *C* is in the proportional notation that Cage had introduced (Berio had already used this in *Sequenza I* and *Tempi concertati*), and *A* and *A'* feature the harp (in the latter case with mostly pitched percussion), whereas *C* is altogether noisier. Example 25, a passage from this central section, shows its typical qualities as well as the work's more general response, in instrumental as much as vocal writing, to the phonemes and meaning of the text: particular instances include the white noise of hi-hat and suspended cymbal connecting with the sibilants in the voice, or the drumrolls which unashamedly answer the text, or, still more obviously, the outburst at the word 'collide'.

The percussion notation in this passage, and elsewhere, owes something to Stockhausen's recent solo piece *Zyklus* (1959), with which the work also shares a combination of circular with directed form, though where Stockhausen had taken up Boulez's idea of ring-binding to create his cyclical composition, *Circles* has a fixed starting point: the circling is left implicit in the palindrome, a palindrome being a circle opened and stretched out. As for the directedness, that comes in the treatment of the voice. The ornamented lyricism of the first setting is progressively stripped away as the work proceeds towards its centre, with a change to syllabic singing in *B* and the introduction of speech and rounded Italian kinds of *Sprechgesang* in *C* (see Example 25, where the rectangular note heads indicate approximate pitch and the open ones speech). But then, instead of recovering its embellishments, the voice is drawn more and more into the musical ambits of the instruments in *B'* and *A'*, and this integration is demonstrated on the concert platform by having the soloist move to positions nearer the ensemble. (The mobile performer was as much a phenomenon of the period as instrumental theatre, and a phenomenon reaching its apogee in the actor–musicians on stage in Stockhausen's *Licht*.)

Berio's use of different vocal styles to articulate a form—a technique dependent on Berberian, whose mimic agility Cage had exploited in his *Aria* (1958)—is on show in three works completed soon after *Circles*: *Epifanie* for voice and orchestra (1959–61), the theatre piece *Passaggio* (1961–2), and *Folk Songs* for voice and septet (1964). These works also display Berio's range, from provocation to charm. *Folk Songs* is a garland of numbers from around the world, delightfully done (Berio's involvement with folk music was to go much deeper in such later works as *Coro* and *Voci*); *Passaggio* is ostensibly an attack on bourgeois society, an attack in the form of a mirror. The unnamed protagonist, She, moves among different stations, as in *Circles*, each station being associated with a different musical–dramatic aura: she is prisoner, prostitute, performer, and the audience discovers that their expectations of the theatre singer—expectations focused during this period on such women as Judy Garland, Edith Piaf, and Maria Callas—are what the piece is about. Choruses of singers and speakers, the latter placed among the audience, identify and exag-

Ex. 25. Berio, *Circles* (1960)

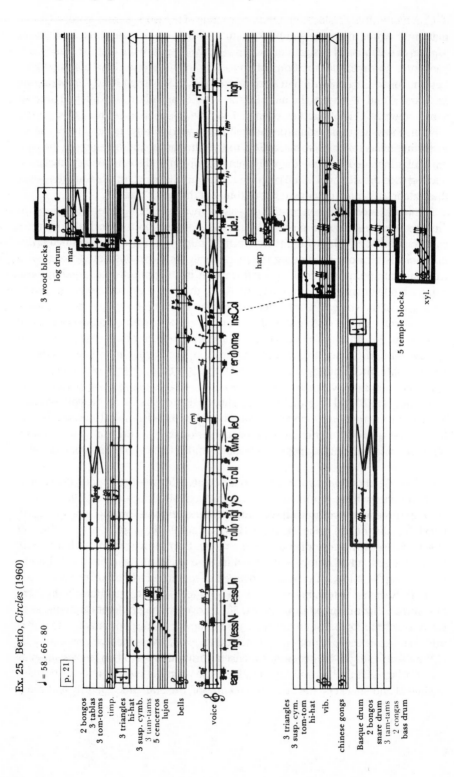

gerate modes of response (the work was evidently designed to instigate and to accommodate uproar), but though this might suggest an alignment with Nono's political art (recently brought to a larger public through the performance of his opera *Intolleranza 1960*), Berio, as always, is more concerned with means of communication than with messages. *Passaggio* is a play of different soprano-esque ideals (heroine, victim), of different relationships between words and music, of different avenues of response from the audience.

In that respect it is, as David Osmond-Smith has suggested, an 'open work' of the sort defined by the composer's longstanding friend and collaborator Umberto Eco, an example of works which 'although physically completed, are nevertheless "open" to a continuous germination of internal relations that the spectator must discover and select in the act of perceiving the totality of stimuli'.[15] This is the kind of indeterminacy—an indeterminacy of meaning, brought about by a use of languages (verbal and musical) of high ambiguity, by an avoidance of finality in any statement, and by rich networks of cross-reference operating both within the work and across to other works of the composer's own or by other composers (hence Berio's endless fascination with arrangement and recomposition)—that Berio preferred to a Cageian indeterminacy of sound or a Boulezian indeterminacy of form. His interest was not so much in a new language as in all languages, old and new, and he was therefore disinclined—disinclined too, perhaps, by temperament—to resist echoes of tonality. The thirteen-note series of his orchestral piece *Nones* (1954), for example, had emphasized major and minor thirds, through which he achieved a suaver harmonic texture than most of his colleagues would have countenanced, though he avoided Henze's path towards a restoration of tonal kinds of form and behaviour. This is a sophisticated world in which tonal harmonies can be found among many others, and favoured not so much out of nostalgia as for their ease and sensuousness of sound. There seems to be a similar amenability in the material when Berio works with electronic resources, as in *Perspectives* (1956) and *Momenti* (1957).

Another of his electronic pieces, *Visage* (1961), is again based on Berberian's voice. Following the example of *Gesang der Jünglinge* (but not of his own *Thema*, which had used only vocal sounds), Berio here presents a *mélange* of the vocal and the purely electronic, with the difference that the voice by no means resists interpretation as a character. She is heard in a natural recording almost throughout, but only at two points does she stumble towards verbal expression, towards verbal expression at an emblematically elementary level (of all words she retains only 'words' itself, in Italian 'parole'). For the rest she laughs, moans, sighs, cries, and gabbles in nonsense language, creating a fluid stream of musical–dramatic suggestions on a private and intimate level to contrast with the public agony of *Passaggio*. Both *Visage* and *Thema* were composed at the RAI electronic studio in Milan, where Berio and Maderna were directors, and where guest composers included Cage in the winter of 1958–9 and Nono in the 1960s. Another work Berio prepared there was

[15] Quoted in Osmond-Smith's notes in the programme book for the Berio festival held in London in January 1990.

Différences for quintet and tape (1959), concerned with borderlands not between vocal sense and senselessness but between live instrumental playing and the widened possibilities of the same ensemble subjected to electronic processing. Again the piece is an open work in Eco's sense, though Berio did also achieve one example of the Boulezian open form in *Epifanie*.

This was a collection of seven orchestral pieces, which could be played separately as *Quaderni* ('exercise books'), and five vocal items to texts by various European writers set in their original languages, all twelve sections to be performed in one of several possible sequences. But where for Boulez, in the Third Sonata, mobile form was an acceptance that order had ceased to matter, in *Epifanie* order mattered very much. 'The chosen order', Berio noted, 'will emphasize the apparent heterogeneity of the texts or their dialectical unity', and in his recording he preferred the latter, creating 'a gradual passage from a lyric transfiguration of reality (Proust, Machado, Joyce) to a disenchanted acknowledgement of things (Simon)'[16] and so to Brecht's warning that words should not be allowed to seduce us from deeds. However—and this is why the past tense has been necessary here—his definitive revision of the score, to create *Epiphanies* in 1991–2, set the music in a fixed succession. There is a striking parallel with Boulez's revision of *Improvisation sur Mallarmé III* to remove variability, and indeed with a general disenchantment with mobile form after the mid-1960s.

But in the late 1950s and early 1960s this was still a hot topic. Alongside the Third Sonata and *Pli selon pli*, two other works were occupying Boulez's attention then: the orchestral piece *Figures–Doubles–Prismes*, which was mobile only in the sense that most of its rare performances found it revised and extended, and the second book of *Structures* for two pianos, which is inherently an open form, begun in 1956, the year after the sonata. It may be that Boulez saw these two major keyboard projects, embarked upon as his period with Barrault's company was coming to an end, as material for recitals, and that their long (in the case of the sonata, indefinite) deferral came about because his performing medium changed during the late 1950s from the piano to the orchestra. He gave the first performance of the sonata at Darmstadt in 1957 (apparently all five formants were represented), and the same year played *Structures* (including some of the second book) with Yvonne Loriod in London and Germany. The new book of *Structures* was finished in 1961—or perhaps abandoned then, since several years passed before it was published, and its flexible plan could accommodate other 'chapters' besides the two provided. Since this book is based on the second division of Messiaen's pitch mode for the *Mode de valeurs*, there remains the possibility of a third book based on the last division.

Boulez's use of the term 'chapters' is another sign of the literary bent of his thinking in the later 1950s; he has also described the second book of *Structures* as 'a fantastic succession, in which the "stories" have no rigid relationship, no fixed order',[17]

---

[16] Note with RCA SB 6850.

[17] Programme note for the definitive first performance, again by Boulez and Loriod, at the 1962 Donaueschingen Festival.

and Robert Piencikowski has suggested the influence of the *nouveau roman*, especially of the work of Michel Butor, himself influenced by new music and especially by Boulez.[18] In the first chapter mobility remains implicit—implicit in the 'fantastic succession' of fragments, some of which are in strict time and require the exact co-ordination of the players, others being solo breaks loosened by the flurries of grace-notes that permanently entered Boulez's music in this work and the *Improvisations sur Mallarmé*. Usually these solo passages—ranging in length from a short bar to the substantial cadenzas that both pianists have soon after the middle of the chapter—are accompanied or supported by sustained resonance, and the two kinds of sound are linked by shared or overlapping harmonic fields, these fields being built up by the multiplication technique. So music which is newly played, present, and visible to the audience, subject to momentary whim or error, falls into line with music which is reverberating, past, and invisible, fixed. This is a source of great beauty, of flashing events reflected in still pools; but there is also a hopelessness in the music's inability to break free from the ice trap of what has been: the beauty and the hopelessness are those of the Mallarmé sonnet set in the first *Improvisation*, and they seem to combine in what is both an image and a demonstration of Boulez's predicament. The rushing evolution of the past decade had brought him the means for one masterpiece, *Le marteau sans maître*, but beyond that he had come again to 'the end of fertile land', where he was condemned to magnificent repetition.

The work's second chapter, fully mobile, has one notional stream of continuity that begins as a glacial succession of chords in both pianos (both with bass strings freed by the sostenuto pedal to reverberate) and opens into arpeggios in the second piano, among and over which the first piano introduces self-contained items, which can be played at different points in accordance with a system of musical cueing, or which may in some cases be omitted. These items, like the fragments of the first chapter, are distinguished by harmony, rhythmic character, and register: the two longest of them, both to be performed as fast as possible, are confined respectively to the extreme treble and the extreme bass, tightening Boulez's toccata manner to a point where energy is turned by the harmonic fixing into whirling rotation, where fury is all manner. For the splendour of its piano writing (vacant though that splendour is becoming), for the reflections it sets up between the pianos, for its stimulating and influential projection of performers as sportsmen and signallers, and for its loneliness as the single work from the two decades between *Le marteau* and *Rituel* that Boulez completed and left unaltered, the second book of *Structures* is a key work, and perhaps unsurpassed in all Boulez's career since 1955.

[18] See Piencikowski's note with Sony MK 42619; and Butor's essay 'Mallarmé selon Boulez', *Melos*, 28 (1961), 356 ff.

Elder Responses

The success of the avant garde—especially the European avant garde—in the 1950s and early 1960s can be measured not only by the festivals, courses, studios, journals, and record series that provided the new music with its matrix, but also by the impact the music had on composers who were already well established. There seems no parallel for this, that artists still in their twenties should have motivated masters of their parents' and grandparents' generations to change direction. Stravinsky, perhaps, was a special case: a composer with a constant inquisitiveness and intellectual rapacity. Messiaen, too, was maybe in an unusual position as the man who had had both Boulez and Stockhausen in his classroom, and whose prestige as a teacher brought him into daily contact with young composers. But there were so many others whose music grew leaner, less diatonic, more contrapuntal, and often more systematic: Carter, Wolpe, Britten, Tippett, Lutos awski, Dallapiccola, Scelsi, Dutilleux. In some cases—Carter's and Scelsi's, for example—the change would seem to have come about independently. Nevertheless, change there certainly was.

Stravinsky

The Stravinsky works that fall into the time frame of this book—works which include the Mass, *The Rake's Progress*, the Shakespeare songs, *Canticum sacrum*, *Agon*, *Threni*, *Movements*, *Abraham and Isaac* and the *Requiem Canticles*—would, if merit could be measured in pages (or, indeed, measured at all), occupy a large proportion of the volume. As time passes, the security of these achievements comes to seem one of the rare absolutes of music since 1945: in particular, Stravinsky's relationship with the new European avant garde begins to have a different sense. Where *Movements*, for example, was once viewed almost as an appendage of recent Stockhausen and Boulez—even as a regrettable display of old age in pursuit of fashion—now the arrow turns, and the piece starts to appear as a pristine realization of possibilities hazy and latent in the younger composers' works. However, and partly for these reasons of Stravinsky's primacy even in his seventies and eighties, there are numerous other sources of information, and this section will attempt no more than a sketch.

The pattern of Stravinsky's composing was not immediately changed by the ending of the war: he continued to write orchestral pieces of diverse kinds (the *Ebony Concerto* for jazz band, the Concerto in D for strings, the ballet *Orpheus*), and he completed the Mass for choir and wind he had started in 1944. But the Concerto in D and *Orpheus* begin to suggest a stylistic development towards more angular melody, tauter harmony, and sparser texture—a development partly derailed by the composer's decision to embark on a large-scale vocal piece (his first encounter with song, as distinct from chorus, since *Perséphone* in 1933–4), and to make that piece a parody of a Mozart opera: *The Rake's Progress* (1947–51).

This is in many respects an unsettling work. It is by some way Stravinsky's longest composition, and yet it lacks the definitiveness which that status would imply. It presents itself as a morality play, and yet offers no ground from which moral judgements might be made: the closing 'moral', delivered by the cast, is a surely deliberate sham, whose main function is to confirm a kinship with *Don Giovanni*— another amoral morality. And the relationship with Mozart is a further cause of worry for the audience. Stravinsky's 'neoclassicism' is typically promiscuous, and this work spreads its favours too: its allusions range over the operatic repertory from Monteverdi to Donizetti, and the libretto, by Auden and Kallman, encourages references to English styles of pastoral song, ballad, and elegy. But the presence of the Mozartian model, and particularly of *Don Giovanni*, is constant. This is the only piece in which Stravinsky imitated another composer's orchestration, simply adding piccolo and cor anglais as doublings. The piece also adheres to its model in alternating scored numbers with harpsichord-accompanied recitative (at least in the first act; this is one of the ideals that deliquesce). Moreover, it puts Mozartian, even *Giovanni*-esque, people on the stage: most noticeably, Nick Shadow, the devil of the plot, amalgamates Don Giovanni's pursuit of pleasure with Leporello's life of service. Previously Stravinsky's allusions had provided a frame; now it is the frame that sings. *The Rake's Progress* is accordingly unanchored in time: too much a work of the eighteenth century to be credible as a twentieth-century opera, too much a product of the mid-twentieth century to be accepted as a homage.

Stravinsky's progress at this moment was both forwards and backwards. Within the sphere of his own music, new compositions had to come about in company with revisions of earlier scores, and though many of the 'new versions' that followed his acquiring of American citizenship (in 1945) were made for copyright reasons, some were indeed new, like the rescoring of *Petrushka* in 1946, or the several arrangements made during the 1950s for Lawrence Morton's chamber concerts in Los Angeles. Within the world of music generally, his interests widened out to embrace the Renaissance and modernism, Gesualdo and Webern. His first work after *The Rake's Progress* was the Cantata on English poems of the fifteenth and six-teenth centuries (1951–2); his next was the Septet (1952–3) prompted partly by hearing Schoenberg's Suite for septet. In moving both ways he was helped by Robert Craft, who had joined his household in 1949, and who rapidly became his closest musical adviser. He was obviously intrigued, too, by the news from Europe.

During his first postwar European tour, in the summer and autumn of 1951, he was occupied with the first performance of *The Rake's Progress* (in Venice) and with concerts and recordings, but in May–June 1952 he was in Paris for the twentieth-century festival (at which he conducted *Oedipus rex*) and heard Boulez and Messiaen give the first public performance of *Structures Ia*.[1] But though the knowledge of movement in Paris may have provided the right kind of echo, the more important impulses to change must have come at this point from Craft, from Craft's performances of Schoenberg and Webern, and perhaps from Carter. His next composition after the Septet was his first with ordered sets, the springtime triptych of Shakespeare songs for female voice with a slightly Webernian trio of flute, clarinet and viola (1953), after which came his first to use the same set throughout: *In memoriam Dylan Thomas*, a song for tenor and string quartet between 'dirge-canons' for four trombones (1954).

The poet's death had come just as Stravinsky and he were about to embark on an opera, whose subject could not have been more suitable for Stravinsky's music at this point: the piece was to have been about the reinvention of language following a catastrophe, and these first serial songs are beautifully careful essays in the renaming of features that had long been characteristic of Stravinsky—features such as repeated notes (which alone place his serial music at a distance from Schoenberg and Webern, though not from Babbitt), verse–refrain forms, counterpoint in two or three parts, wide-gapped chords, and sprung rhythm. One talks of influences, but these songs—like the songs Stravinsky had written nearly four decades before, during the early years of his Swiss exile—are moving essays in self-education.

Another signal quality of *In memoriam Dylan Thomas* is quite straightforwardly that it is a memorial. Many of Stravinsky's ensuing serial compositions were also to be monuments (*Epitaphium*, *Introitus*, *Requiem Canticles*); others were to be sacred commemorations (*Canticum sacrum*, *Threni*). One of the values of serialism was that it suggested fixity, order and objectivity—that it offered exactly that canonical rule which 'neoclassicism' had been supposed to provide. So Stravinsky's evolution during the 1950s—though perceived as a defection by those for whom modern music was divided between Stravinsky as neoclassicist and Schoenberg as serialist—was more an arrival than a new departure. The fundamental Stravinsky–Schoenberg dichotomy was between block form and development, pulse and metre, objectivity and subjectivity, and here nobody can change sides.

But Stravinsky's serial constructions were not all funerary or religious: *Canticum sacrum* (1955), an exercise in twentieth-century Venetian music, was written during an interlude in the composition of the abstract ballet *Agon* (1954–7), whose long gestation helped make it a meeting ground of the explicitly tonal and the explicitly twelve-note, of the French Baroque and of the modern Viennese. And his next work, the solemn, ceremonial *Threni* (1957–8), was followed by a nervy piano concerto, *Movements* (1958–9). Whether by accident or intention, there were severe sacred pieces for Europe (*Threni* too was written for Venice, where Stravinsky spent the late summer each year from 1956 to 1960), and lively instrumental designs for the United States.

---

[1] See Robert Craft (ed.), *Stravinsky: Selected Correspondence*, ii (London, 1984), 349, from the section in which Stravinsky's letters and Craft's notes elucidate the composer's relationship with Boulez.

However, *Movements* is a European work in being the site of Stravinsky's closest contact with the Darmstadt-centred avant garde. In November 1956 Boulez, Stockhausen, and Nono had visited him in hospital in Munich, and for a few years thereafter he and Boulez were in regular communication. He was present when Boulez conducted *Le marteau sans maître* in Los Angeles in March 1957, and when Boulez, Stockhausen, and Rosbaud rehearsed *Gruppen* in Baden-Baden in October 1958; presumably he was also brought into contact with the music of these composers when Craft recorded *Le marteau* and *Zeitmasze* in the early months of 1958, in which case these encounters might have provided the trigger, since *Movements*, which begins as if with a triggered release, seems to have been begun soon afterwards.

Two strikingly new features of the piece are its polyrhythms and its flickering instrumentation, both illustrated in the closing bars, which are shown in Example 26, and both suggesting how Stravinsky's new-found admiration of Webern[2] was conditioned by his experience of Stockhausen and Boulez. The music ends, as it had begun, with a statement of the basic series, but much of the work is built up from elements derived by non-standard means: rotating notes within hexachords, overlaying four serial forms to obtain a sequence of four-note sets.[3] These are Stravinsky's own techniques, but the effect of them is like the effect of Boulez's techniques in *Le marteau* or Stockhausen's in *Kontra-Punkte*: to create a field of action so broad that almost any move (and *Movements* is a sequence of moves as in a game, as well as a chain of five miniature musical movements and a succession of different speeds, different ways of moving) can be justified in terms of the 'system'. What actually happens, then, is likely to be determined by the composer's aims and tastes—by those matters of intention and personality that Cage (and briefly Boulez) had wanted to eradicate. In the particular case of *Movements*, Stravinsky's authorship is evident in many features: the remaining weight of strong beats in barring that is much more than a notational convenience; in parallel with that, the remaining weight of intervals and chords from the vocabularies of his earlier works (the chord heavily affirmed in the 9/16 bar is surely not an arbitrary choice); the role of the piano as more obbligato than solo; the light counterpoint; the deployment of the orchestra as a nesting set of ensembles; the projection of music as abstract drama (a drama whose most spectacular event in Example 26 is how the piano disappears, only to reappear, like Petrushka, in ghost form, as the celesta, unheard since near the work's beginning). What is equally typical of Stravinsky is that new circumstances should have produced a new composer.

---

[2] See the interview with him printed as an introduction to Hans Moldenhauer and Demar Irvine (eds), *Anton von Webern: Perspectives* (Seattle, University of Washington Press, 1966).

[3] See Stephen Walsh, *The Music of Stravinsky* (London, 1988), 246–54; and Claudio Spies, 'Impressions after an Exhibition', *Tempo*, 102 (1972), 2–9.

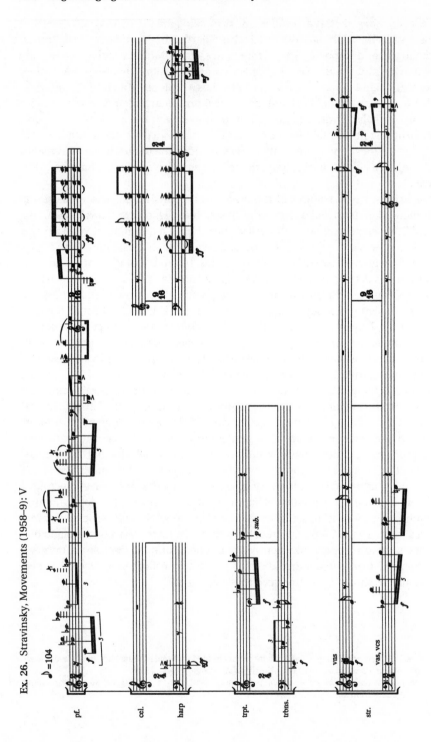

Ex. 26. Stravinsky, Movements (1958–9): V

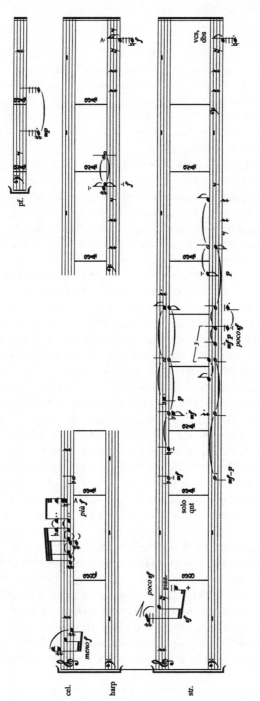

Messiaen

Messiaen's direct participation in his juniors' enterprises was brief—limited in the case of electronic music to *Timbres-durées* and in the case of total organization to the archetype, the *Mode de valeurs et d'intensités*, as well as to elements in some of the piano and organ pieces that immediately followed. By 1951 the phase was over, and in that year he made a first step into a new world, of music made from birdsong: this modest but crucial reinitiation was *Le merle noir* for flute and piano, which was followed by *Réveil des oiseaux* for piano and orchestra (1953), *Oiseaux exotiques* for piano, wind, and percussion (1955–6), and the *Catalogue d'oiseaux* (1956–8), consisting of thirteen piano pieces with a total duration of over two hours.

The departure was not entirely new: there are birdsong imitations in earlier works, including notably the *Quatuor pour la fin du temps* and *Turangalîla*. But making birdsong the sole substance of a work certainly was new. *Réveil* has no other material than that which Messiaen himself collected in the field, and though both *Oiseaux exotiques* and the *Catalogue* admit other kinds of music, birdsong is still the overwhelming source, and everything else has to be justified either as armature (the percussion engineering with Greek and Indian rhythmic patterns which underlies large sections of *Oiseaux exotiques*) or else as descriptive context (the occasional passages in the *Catalogue* where a sway of chords is introduced to convey, in Messiaen's usual synaesthetic manner, the colour of plumage or landscape). The reasons for this recourse to nature surely included those he gave himself: that he took great joy in the songs of birds, that he saw their music as a cornucopia of divine creation, that he understood them—being winged, aerial, and beautiful—as earthly harbingers of the angels. 'I do not believe one can find in any human music, however inspired, melodies and rhythms which have the sovereign liberty of birdsong.'[4] But none of this quite explains the sudden conversion of 1951, which may have been a reaction to the implication of the *Mode de valeurs*, the implication that composition required the separate ordaining of each note. Under such conditions, human melodists would have to fall mute, leaving only the birds singing.

In the case of *Réveil*, nature provides not only the material but also the form. According to the score's preface, the music replays birdsongs heard in springtime between midnight and noon, though it does so through time that is doubly bent: accelerated fortyfold in order to compress nature's half-day into twenty minutes in the concert hall, and simultaneously decelerated so that rapid songs can be brought down, in both tempo and tuning, to a human scale of hearing. Messiaen explained how his transcriptions of birdsongs—nearly always based on field observation—had to be slowed, reduced in pitch and expanded uniformly in interval size for the necessities of human performers and listeners, and he likened his procedures to those of composers of *musique concrète*.[5] Calls which seem by nature already adapted to human time he tended to avoid: the cuckoo and the turtle dove, for

---

[4] Antoine Goléa, *Rencontres avec Olivier Messiaen* (Paris, 1960), 234.   [5] See *Music and Color*, 95.

instance, never appeared again in his music after their débuts in *Réveil*. The songs he preferred were the florid roulades of warblers, thrushes, and larks, and the strident cries found more often among tropical than temperate species—preferences which may have been prompted by the greater challenge these songs presented to the composer as listener and reinterpreter, having to register long melodies in the one case and complex timbres in the other. After all, if he had wanted simply to make use of birdsongs as musical material, he could have done so in the *musique concrète* studio: the point was to exercise his own artistry, in company with the birds, to celebrate with them, and to do so, as they did, extra-personally, to achieve a creaturely innocence in the rendering of nature. The art of composition became the art of imitation, of copying nature not from a consistent viewpoint, in the manner of a landscape painter or the composer of a symphonic poem, but item by item, piece by piece: not a Sibelian scene with cranes but a *Catalogue d'oiseaux*.

Réveil des oiseaux, the first of Messiaen's major birdsong pieces, is an extinction of creative personality as complete as its great contemporary 4' 33", and as incomplete. In principle, material and form are given; however, fingerprints mark the choice of found material and its handling. Silence was already Cage's signature, and performed silence still more so. Messiaen, in choosing birdsongs from all the sounds of nature, chose in accordance with the history of his own music, which was in part a history of quasi-neumatic repetitions of rhythmic–melodic formulae in music of toccata-style speed and insistence; at the same time, he revealed his authorship in the way he treated birdsongs. Several songs in *Réveil*, shown in Example 27, conform to the same setting of one of his most characteristic modes, the 'second mode of limited transpositions': C–Db–Eb–E–Gb–G–A–Bb–C. And though in later works his birdsong transcriptions became modally more complex and often more fastidiously defined and decorated, links to his particular harmonic world would remain; besides which, by the end of the 1950s he had effectively defined instrumental birdsong imitation (just as Cage had defined silence) as his realm. But this was by inadvertence. The essential was the effort, which he shared with Cage and in some respects with Boulez, to make art objectively, even if it would be impossible to make art objective. By endeavouring to reflect back, perfectly, the perfection of creation, Messiaen's birdsong pieces of 1951–60 (including the orchestral *Chronochromie*) participate in his spiritual project, even though this period was unique in his output for its lack of explicitly religious subject matter.

The birdsong pieces also belong with the rest of Messiaen by virtue of their objectivity of pattern and form: their adherence not to the experiential time of smooth onward flow but to a non-human time of cyclic repetition, abrupt change, and potentially endless continuity—not one arrow but many arrows. If repetition and alternation (of pitch, of rhythmic value, of motif) are important in the birdsong detail of *Réveil des oiseaux*, its larger plan is also one of oscillation, since Messiaen interprets the midnight-to-midday span as a sequence of solos for the piano (nightingales at midnight, a blackcap after sunrise, later a blackbird, and a medley at midday) interspersed with choruses for piano and orchestra. After the work's first

Ex. 27. Messiaen, *Réveil des oiseaux* (1953)

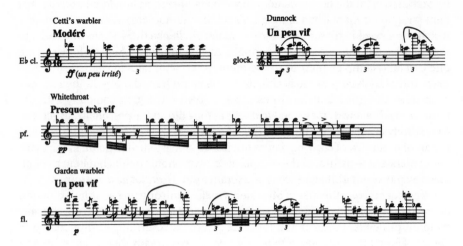

performance—at the 1953 Donaueschingen Festival, signifying Messiaen's abiding status as a senior member of the avant garde—there was a silence of very nearly two years before the beginning of *Oiseaux exotiques*, perhaps because *Réveil* appeared to its composer a solution that left no possibility of development. He found that possibility by releasing the solo–chorus antiphony from its descriptive intentions, providing it in part with underlays of rhythmic mosaic formed from the ancient Greek and Indian figures that had long featured in his music, removing the strings from his orchestra, and extending his ornithological frontiers to include, as the title intimates, birds from many different countries. *Réveil* had perhaps been too simple-minded an attempt to copy nature; *Oiseaux exotiques* exults in the possibility of attaining objective form by other means—by the reiteration and accumulation of musical objects—and of releasing the bounds of verisimilitude in the dynamic scale and the conjoining of species. Birds from India, the Far East, the Canaries and North America sing together, and sing loudly. The work also makes more assertive use of signal cries, especially the jubilant E majorish calls of the Indian shama which clamour for the music to close.

The *Catalogue d'oiseaux* ostensibly returns to the naturalist intentions of portraying birds—all French birds—in their habitats, but there are the same structures of alternation and palindrome, along with further infiltrations of non-birdsong material. Usually this material is justified as illustrative, but the mechanisms of illustration are codes peculiar to Messiaen, the most important being his equivalences of colour and harmony. For example, E major seems to represent the blazing gold of the oriole and of summer sunlight in 'Le loriot', just as it worked similarly in *Oiseaux exotiques*, and A major conveys the blue of the sea and of the bird's plumage in 'Le merle bleu'. Black, absence of light, has no chord to represent it, since chords in Messiaen's vocabulary are instances of resonance, and resonance is the sounding image of light. The dark of night in 'La chouette hulotte' ('The tawny owl') is introduced rather as a three-part counterpoint in a mode of pitches, durations, and intensities, so that what had been, just a few years earlier, the whole thrust of Messiaen's endeavour—towards a music of abstract speculation—is now the antithesis, the contrary to his music of reimagined nature and of colour.

Abstraction—especially the abstraction of musical arithmetic effected by rhythmic cells or chromatic durations—can alternatively be a frame for birdsongs, as it was in *Oiseaux exotiques* and 'Soixante-quatre durées' from the *Livre d'orgue*, and as it is in several of the *Catalogue d'oiseaux* pieces and in *Chronochromie* (1959–60)'. Though this last work is a final climax to the birdsong period, Messiaen's title, backed by his pronouncements,[6] insists on it as an exercise in colouring time, in marking out segments by percussion attacks and identifying them with the colours of string chords (the combination of resonance with continuous tone may reflect an awareness of Stockhausen's efforts at timbre synthesis). This is what happens in the two 'strophes' of the score, in each of which interversions of a sequence of thirty-two durations are laid out under birdsongs. More birdsongs—those of two Messiaen favourites, skylark and songthrush—alternate in the corresponding 'antistrophes', and the ensuing 'epode' is a tangle of eighteen birdsong lines for solo strings. The strophe–antistrophe–epode triad follows the form of Greek choral odes, a model Messiaen had previously used in 'Le chocard des alpes' from the bird catalogue; in *Chronochromie* not only are the strophe and antistrophe doubled (repeated with variation) but the whole assembly is placed between an introduction and a coda, which again are doubles of each other. And these outer sections add more, non-avian elements to the composer's imitation of nature: fortissimo chromatic chords hurled in rapid interchange from different orchestral sectors to represent rocks, and a 'torrent' passage in which, according to a note in the score, 'the tumbling sound of the water is rendered principally by the violas and cellos' and the trills of violins and basses are 'vapour and confusion'. Following one of Messiaen's preferences among the works of nature, *Chronochromie* is a mountain walk of music, where birds from Japan, Sweden, and France can all be heard, and time is parcelled out in moments of harmony. 'For me', Messiaen has said, 'the only real music has always existed in the sounds of nature . . . The harmony of wind in trees, the rhythm of waves on the sea, the timbre of raindrops, of breaking branches, of stones struck together, the different cries of animals are the true music as far as I am concerned.' Cage might have said the same, except that his interpretation of 'nature' would have included the human and the industrial, and that his aim was to imitate not nature's sounds but nature's selflessness. These are differences on which one might ponder in comparing another pair of near-coincident scores, *Chronochromie* and *Atlas eclipticalis*.

[6] See *Music and Color*, 135–6.

The first performance of *Chronochromie*—again at the Donaueschingen Festival, in 1960—was again succeeded by a hiatus in Messiaen's composing. Then came another septenary, the *Sept haïkaï* for piano and small orchestra (1962), stimulated by his first visit to Japan, and including, besides two birdsong movements in the alternating solo–chorus manner of *Oiseaux exotiques*, one of his rare attempts to make a similar sketch of human music: 'Gagaku', in which a piece from the repertory of the imperial court ensemble is transcribed as if it were a birdsong or the rush of a mountain stream—alien sound whose imitation would divert the composer's art along the objective pathways of record (the melody for the shawm-like hichiriki is taken by a trumpet with oboes and cor anglais in unison, while eight violins reproduce the accompanying chords of the sho, a mouth organ). Large parts of the *Sept haïkaï* are again hung on frames of rhythmic patterning measured out by percussion: an Indian scheme in the introduction and coda, interversions of thirty-two chromatic durations once more in 'Gagaku' and in 'The Park at Nara and the Stone Lanterns' (the first of two movements compacting elements from Japanese landscapes), Greek metres elsewhere. What is unusual for Messiaen in the arithmetic of this work is the presence of so much irregular rhythm, suggesting that, like Stravinsky, he was impressed by the recent work of Stockhausen. Example 28, from 'The Park at Nara', illustrates this, and illustrates too how the music is often composed of several independent temporal layers. Such compound textures recur in Messiaen's music from the 'Crystal Liturgy' of the *Quatuor pour la fin du temps* onwards, and they help, as in so much music of this period, to split the viewpoint— to provide, in this instance, an impression of things heard and seen (the piano and the prominent marimba, however much the latter recalls Messiaen's 'style oiseau', might suggest the stone lanterns, the chromatic clarinets the enveloping darkness) with no person in the picture hearing and seeing them.

Contact with Japan might have reinforced—if that had been possible— Messiaen's taste for simultaneous alterities, for the eternities of slow motion and repetition, for a long view of tradition. In his interviews with Claude Samuel, he speaks of Japan almost as if it were paradise: 'It's a country where everything is noble: in the streets in Japan, one sees no drunks, no beggars . . . [What struck me] was also the beauty of the men and women—their marvelous black hair, which remains black as ebony to the ends of their lives . . . Nara . . . has several temples and, in the parks surrounding them, immense thousand-year-old trees . . . In these parks, does, stags, and fawns roam freely and approach visitors with no apprehension.'[7] In Europe, in the resolutely positivist Europe of the 1950s, he might easily have felt himself out of place and out of time: that would have been another reason for his recourse to given musical material, and for the unusual gaps in his output. Japan showed him that he was not, after all, alone (though that lesson was now coming from Europe and North America, too, with the increasing appreciation of his music from the early 1960s onwards). Japan was a new home, and an old one: a

---

[7] See *Music and Color*, 99–100.

Ex. 28. Messiaen, *Sept haïkaï* (1953): II

place that had suffered no Renaissance to uproot its art from sacredness, and yet a place that was fully attuned to new ways of thinking and working. Japan—it would have the same effect for Stockhausen a little later—restored him.

His next work after the *Sept haïkaï* was based on a similar ensemble of piano, clarinets, and tuned percussion, but with orchestral brass instead of the eight violins: *Couleurs de la Cité Céleste* (1963). There are similarly constancies and changes in the musical material: still present are the birdsongs, the chords of colour, the chromatic durations, and the Indian and Greek rhythmic patterns; gone are the irregular rhythms; newly arrived (or restored) are the plainsong quotations and the breadth of form, the work playing continuously for over a quarter of an hour. Also new, or returning, is the exalted subject, which is the subject of several earlier and later works: the life of the resurrected, especially as revealed in the last book of the New Testament. The 'colours of the Heavenly City' are those of the precious stones which St John describes as forming the foundations of the New Jerusalem, and which Messiaen interprets as harmonies that similarly anchor his work, whether they are presented resplendent as chords or used to enhance the chants and birdsongs: sardonyx, chrysoprase, emerald, sapphire, amethyst, and the rest. At the same time, the colours of the work are its fragments, studded together like the pieces of coloured glass in the windows of Chartres or the Sainte Chapelle—to suggest an analogy which his own admiration for those windows makes inescapable. In that respect, the illustrations of the subject—the harmonic gemstones, the alleluias of the heavenly host, the 'star which holds the key to the abyss' (a musical pictogram of piano appeal, lightning stroke and fortissimo strokes of low gongs and tam-tams)—dissolve into the swirl of lit sound. Messiaen's participation in the avant garde, as teacher and taught, had vastly widened his scope during the fifteen years since the *Turangalîla* symphony, and made it possible for him to move from that work's powerful harmonic surges and rhythmic pulsations into the fractured time of *Couleurs de la Cité Céleste*—a structure appealing at once to the verse–refrain forms and antiphonies of the Middle Ages and to modern predilections for sudden shift and ceaseless change.

Varèse

In several ways Edgard Varèse (1883–1965) was Messiaen's dialectical opposite: American rather than European (though both were born in France), secular rather than sacred, urban rather than rural, spasmodic in creativity rather than continuous, solitary rather than being revered by hundreds of pupils and devoted performers. But the similarities outweigh. Both were impressed by ancient cultures. Both produced some of their best work for ensembles of wind and percussion. Both took from Stravinsky the principle of construction in disjunct blocks. Both were attracted by the ondes martenot, and both used ideas from electronic music (reversal through time, change of speed and register, sound synthesis) in works for instruments. Both—to pick up a tiny point of what seems to have been convergent evolution rather than borrowing—used an ensemble of violins to imitate the Japanese sho (the Varèse piece was his unfinished *Nocturnal*). Both, finally, enjoyed a creative renewal around 1950.

In Varèse's case it is hard to know how much this depended on the rising generation. As a member of the 1950 Darmstadt faculty he would have encountered Nono, but he seems to have had no meeting with Boulez until 1952, in New York,[8] or with Stockhausen until December 1954, in Paris, when *Déserts* was given its first performance with Boulez introducing the piece and Stockhausen controlling the tape relay[9]—a prime moment in the history of the avant garde. Besides, he had started *Déserts*—the key work in his regeneration: his first new achievement since 1936[10]—before the summer of 1950. Of course, he must have known of Cage's work

---

[8] See Fernaud Ouellette, *Edgard Varèse* (London, 1973), 177–8.

[9] See Michael Kurtz, *Stockhausen: a Biography* (London, 1992), 76.

[10] Discounting the unpublished *Etude pour 'Espace'*, which has had no performance since its 1947 première, and the tiny 1949 dance score for Burgess Meredith.

before this, but by far the overwhelming stimulus for *Déserts* surely came from *musique concrète* and from the access to a tape recorder he gained in 1952.

The plan of *Déserts*, unprecedented, was that electronic and orchestral music should be brought face to face: three sequences of 'organized sound' on tape are interpolated into a composition for an orchestra of wind, piano, and percussion. Babbitt has drawn attention to the subtlety with which Varèse assembles timbres from his ensemble,[11] and indeed much of the scoring suggests an almost Webernian care for timbre-melody—something quite new in Varèse's music, the instruments being used, for example, to vary the colours of the sustained pitches that are stations of polarity in the musical progress.[12] The correlative qualities of moderate speed and passivity provide a striking contrast with most of Varèse's earlier music, whose assertive gestures, repeated here, now fail to initiate movement. Their forcelessness may be understood in the light of his intention to refer to deserts of all kinds: 'All those that people traverse or may traverse: *physical* deserts, on the earth, in the sea, in the sky, of sand, of snow, of interstellar spaces or of great cities, but also those of the human *spirit*, of that distant *inner* space no telescope can reach, where one is alone.'[13] (And here is another contrast with Messiaen, the world of nature for Varèse being silent and alien, typified by the desert, whereas Messiaen at the same time was rehearsing the forests in *Réveil des oiseaux*.)

Varèse's further intention for *Déserts* was that it should be experienced in company with a film, one which would have to be 'in opposition with the score. Only through opposition can one avoid paraphrase . . . There will be no action. There will be no story. There will be images. Phenomena of light, purely . . . Successions, oppositions of visual planes, as there are successions and oppositions of sound planes.'[14] Varèse's horror of 'paraphrase' between sight and sound was typical of the time: it was shared by Cage and Cunningham in their collaborations, and reflected in the seeming desuetude of opera. Post-1945 modernism was distinguished by separation—the separation of notes, the separation of rhythm from pitch contour, the separation of vision from sound—since only through separation, so it was thought, could phenomena be defined and structured. But Varèse's dream of a grand simultaneity had its realization in the superior *son et lumière* show that took place at the 1958 Brussels Exposition, in a futuristic pavilion designed for the Philips company by Le Corbusier (with the help of his assistant Xenakis). Varèse's contribution to this was his *Poème électronique* (1956–7), which stands with *Gesang der Jünglinge* and *Kontakte* in the rather small repertory of electronic masterpieces. By contrast with the tape inserts for *Déserts*, the *Poème* is strongly defined, exuberant, and rich. It includes electronically generated melodies, wedges of distorted organ sound (a potent image that also occurs in the *Déserts* interpolations), industrial noises, and fragments from the recording of the *Etude pour 'Espace'*. The drive that presses through material so diverse and so expressively resonant is irresistible;

---

[11] See 'Edgard Varèse, a Few Observations of his Music', *Perspectives of New Music*, 5/1 (1966), 93–111.
[12] See Arnold Whittall, 'Varèse and Organic Athematicism', *Music Review*, 28 (1967), 311–15.
[13] Quoted in Georges Charbonnier, *Entretiens avec Edgard Varèse* (Paris, 1970), 156.   [14] Ibid. 66.

in its original location, relayed through numerous loudspeakers and experienced with projections, it must have been overwhelming.

For Varèse, who had been looking forward to electronic music since the First World War, it was the appropriate culmination. Between 1954 and 1958 he had spent a good deal of time in Europe, working on his two major electronic works in Paris and Bilthoven, and perhaps not resisting the role of adoptive grandfather thrust on him by Boulez and Stockhausen. He then returned to New York, put away his tape machine, and spent his last years on various projects connected with themes of night and death, of which *Nocturnal* was completed by his pupil Chou Wen-chung.

Wolpe

Like Stravinsky—but a year before, in 1938—Wolpe moved to the United States after previous travels, which in his case had taken him from his native Berlin to Palestine. Like Varèse, he settled in New York. Like Messiaen, he became an important teacher (of Feldman among others). And like all those colleagues, he changed his music, or found his music changing, during the immediate postwar years. From Berlin and Vienna (where he had studied with Webern) he brought with him a mind set on counterpoint and chromaticism, but he was determined too on constant freedom to give motifs the stamp of character and to let them develop with vigour but without force. These are aspects of his music that he best expressed himself, for, as so often with composers, his prose accords with his music not only in its content but in its manner: even his problems with the language become solutions to the greater problem of creating a personal voice, rather as eccentricities in his music become essential, even natural. 'I very much like', he wrote, 'to maintain the flexibility of sound structures (as one would try to draw on water). That leads me to the promotion of a very mobile polyphony in which the partials of the sound behave like river currents and a greater orbit spread-out is guaranteed to the sound, a greater circulatory agility (a greater momentum too). The sound gets the plasticity of figures of waves and the magneticism and the fluid elasticity of river currents, or the fire of gestures and the generative liveliness of all what is life (and Apollo and Dionysus, and the seasons of the heart, and the articulate fevers).'[15]

The onwardness and the energy of his music have something to do with his appreciation of jazz, which he had known since his Berlin days, but which came closer up behind the surface of his music in the United States, most explicitly in his Quartet for the modern-jazz ensemble of tenor saxophone, trumpet, percussion, and piano (1950). In other works of this period, such as the sonata-weight *Battle Piece* for solo piano (1947) and the Violin Sonata (1949), the resemblance is not so much to the colour of jazz as to the unpredictability within a strongly forward

---

[15] Note on the Violin Sonata, quoted in note with Koch 3 7112 2H1.

movement. Wolpe typically sets up a regular, physical pulse, often at a brisk walk-ing pace, even while lines of motivic development are going along in seeming inde-pendence of each other. As was soon to happen in Carter's music, a musical section (the Violin Sonata has four; *Battle Piece* is continuous) may not be identifiable as a 'movement': the music keeps the freedom to alter and contrast speed and charac-ter, almost from moment to moment. A collection of 'interval studies' (1944–9)—short contrapuntal essays 'for any instruments'—appears to have been the exercise book in which the composer devoted himself to the postwar demand for logical reconstruction.

But the moves in Wolpe's creative life were as bold (and as fully engaged, as whole-hearted) as those in his music. During the summers of 1952–6 he taught at Black Mountain College in North Carolina, where fellow members of the faculty in his first year included Cage, Cunningham, Tudor, and Harrison. The works he wrote there, including *Enactments* for three pianos (1953) and the Quartet for oboe, cello, percussion, and piano (1955), bring an intermingling of the experimental into his recently developed style, as may be glimpsed in Example 29, from near the end of the quartet. The pianist, in the last bar of this extract, is directed to get up from the

Ex. 29. Wolpe, Oboe Quartet (1955): IV

keyboard, turn to the audience, and stamp 'in a dance-like movement' with left foot, then right; the percussionist repeats the stamps. Yet the effect, like the elementary ostinatos and the singing, is welded into the music's rhythm: something is flowing through this extraordinary passage on into more usual sorts of instrumental interplay. At the same time, the oboe part (and the oboist is effectively the work's soloist) shows a characteristic achievement of individual rhetoric—summons, playfulness—from elements of pitch and rhythm shared with the group: in that respect, jazz is still the ideal.

In the late 1950s and early 1960s Wolpe went regularly to Darmstadt, to teach and to learn, and this again brought a change in his music: a greater abstraction (though he would accept, as he had in the Black Mountain works, his music's development towards the world of some other composer or style), sometimes a greater density, and an effort to organize aspects of tempo, rhythm, and instrumentation in parallel with his ways of using pitch cells. But what remained, as forcible as ever, was the push of musical implication in the motifs of which his music was made.

Shostakovich and Music in Eastern Europe

The situation of music in eastern Europe, especially during the period before Josef Stalin's death in 1953, cannot be considered without multiple kinds of unease, because Soviet cultural politics had instituted music as a discourse of state: ever since the attack on Shostakovich in 1936, prompted by his opera *The Lady Macbeth of the Mtsensk District*, Soviet composers had been enjoined to adhere to a programme of 'socialist realism', which in fact was about spreading wishful thinking and downright unreality. The model was provided by Nazi Germany, and the enemies were the same: any departure from a middlebrow reading of national tradition and tonal practice, and anything to do with expatriates (notably Stravinsky in the case of Russia). With the tightening of Russia's grip on her neighbours during the immediate postwar years, the same model was forced on the German Democratic Republic, Poland, Czechoslovakia, and Hungary, to name the four countries with the most active musical cultures. In Hungary, for example, most of Bartók's music vanished from performance or discussion, and a more naive handling of folk tunes became the required mode. There could be no question of participating in the musical adventure associated with Boulez, Nono, and Stockhausen: only by means of western radio broadcasts could their music—or most of Schoenberg, Berg, Webern, Varèse and Stravinsky—be heard.[16] In a grotesque distortion of promise, revolutionary music was barred in precisely those countries professing a commitment to revolution, and the achievements of October 1917 had to be hymned in music that would have seemed blithely polite to an audience of Tsarist officials and businessmen.

[16] For a firsthand account see Ligeti's reminiscences in Paul Griffiths, *György Ligeti* (London, 1983), 19–22.

The inevitable result was to make double-think a way of life for composers, as for other artists. Either you went forward on two fronts simultaneously, writing acceptable music for performance and unacceptable music for export, private dissemination or a bottom drawer, or else you contrived to realize both at once, making the acceptable surface a concealment for unacceptable protest. Music, lacking explicit subject matter, was particularly amenable to irony of this kind, and Shostakovich rapidly found, through Tchaikovsky, Mahler, Musorgsky, and Stravinsky, ways to create music that scoffed at its own pomposity, that undercut serenity with melancholy, and that could give voice at once to the rejoicing crowd and the alienated observer. The essence of irony, however, is that it is a secret weapon, and the larger irony was that Shostakovich's duplicity of tone was not generally remarked upon until after his death.[17] Not only did Soviet authorities, under Stalin, Krushchev, and Brezhnev, find no reason not to parade him as the outstanding exponent of 'socialist' art, but his music was widely accepted in the west as a viable continuation of the symphonic tradition, with nothing contrary to that tradition suspected. His satire was read as high spirits, his ostensible conformity as reassuring.

Such ways of responding to Shostakovich can be understood in terms of the positivism which, at the same time, underlay the otherwise so dissimilar work of the Darmstadt composers, and which was also revealed in the move towards basing performance in the text rather than in traditions of interpretation (the 'Urtext' movement was paving the way, during the 1950s, for the full-scale pursuit of 'authentic' practice). Music was to be found in the material, not in the thoughts that anyone—composer, performer or listener—might have about it. Boulez, in proclaiming 'structure' to be 'one of the words of our time' (1958),[18] was talking not only about *Le marteau sans maître* but about the reformation of Bach performance and the perception of Shostakovich.

After his Ninth Symphony (1945)—perhaps a deliberately insufficient, inconsequential expression of joy at the end of the war—and particularly after a severe official denunciation of him and other Soviet composers in 1948, Shostakovich concentrated for the present on public canvases (film scores, patriotic choral pieces) and private music (string quartets, a set of preludes and fugues in all the keys), while holding in reserve for more propitious times a single abstract orchestral composition, his First Violin Concerto. The gap of eight years to his next symphony was the longest in his career; that symphony was also one of his biggest—big enough to contain not so much the relief he might have felt at Stalin's death as the pain, discomfort, and self-contempt he had been storing up: there are quotations from several of his recent works along the way, and the personal voice is inscribed into the music in the form of a coded monogram (D–E♭–C–B: in German nomenclature D–Es–C–H, for D. Sch.).

In 1955 he released the violin concerto, and in 1956 he revised *The Lady Macbeth*,

[17] The change of view came after the publication of Solomon Volkov's *Testimony: the Memoirs of Dmitry Shostakovich* (London, 1979), whose reliability has since been questioned.

[18] 'Sound and Word', *Stocktakings*, 40.

but there was no sudden shift in Soviet cultural policy: the new version of the opera was not performed until 1963, and Shostakovich returned to quartets (including in 1960 his Eighth Quartet, which again asserts itself as autobiography by incorporating self-quotations and the monogram) and film scores. His two next symphonies, No. 11 (1957) and No. 12 (1961), are almost film scores without films, each of them following a programme drawn from the events of a year notable in the history of the Russian revolution (1905 and 1917 respectively).

Elsewhere in eastern Europe, though, there was a political and cultural thaw in the mid-1950s, a thaw that Russia might suppress, as in the case of Hungary's attempt at independence, but that might be permitted if it seemed only decorative: hence the remarkable arrival of a Polish avant-garde school (not a contradiction in terms, given the conditions of the time, for Darmstadt was providing the image of an avant-garde school). The Warsaw Autumn, founded in 1956, soon became one of the main staging posts on the circuit of modern-music festivals: Nono and Stockhausen were both there in 1958. With his ears opened, Witold Lutos awski (1913–94) moved away from mildly Bartókian neoclassicism to a more deliberate, quasi-serial assembly of materials in his *Funeral Music* for strings (1954–8) and then—following Cage, but discreetly—to unsynchronized orchestral textures in *Venetian Games* (1960–1) and many subsequent works. Meanwhile younger composers, including Henryk Górecki (b. 1933) and Krzysztof Penderecki (b. 1933), took on board the new sounds in Stockhausen, Ligeti and Xenakis, and drew from them a brute expressive force that had not been on the Darmstadt agenda. The legacy of totalitarianism, still for them as much as for Shostakovich, was that affect mattered—even that affect was all that mattered, as their later works might seem to want to suggest.

Europe 5: Disintegrations, 1959–1964

Reappraisal: Ligeti

There is something emblematic in Boulez's recourse to the personal in the works he began during the second half of the fifties: to the solo voice, even to song (the cantabile of the *Improvisations sur Mallarmé* has no precedent in *Le marteau sans maître*), to music for himself to perform (*Le marteau* dates from before the beginning of his concert-hall career; *Pli selon pli* and *Figures–Doubles–Prismes* developed in parallel with that career, and became repositories for practical discoveries in terms both of the orchestra and of his own performing skills as the pianist of the Third Sonata and *Structures* grew into the international conductor), to a personal world of brilliantly figured, static sound. The idea of the work as a model embodiment of new musical thinking—the idea behind the first book of *Structures*, *Le marteau*, and everything Stockhausen had written from *Kreuzspiel* onwards, an idea that belonged with the Darmstadt notion of the composer as his juniors' examplar—was perhaps harder for him to sustain as it became clear that there was no such thing as 'the avant garde', that the years of mutual interests were passing, and that composers were going their own ways.

Xenakis's earlier criticism had come from outside the central group, and so perhaps could be brushed off, but in 1960 Ligeti made some of the same points within the pages of *Die Reihe*,[1] citing examples from Boulez, Stockhausen and others to show how serial principles had either proved self-defeating or been replaced by 'higher order' principles, such as those governing the temporal structure of *Gruppen*. Out of this analysis he derived the notion of 'permeability' in music: a musical structure is said to be 'permeable' if it allows a free choice of intervals and 'impermeable' if not (he gives the example of Palestrina's music—a symptomatic choice for a contrapuntalist—as being strictly defined by harmonic rules and hence 'impermeable' to an unusual degree). But permeability and impermeability could also be features of texture, rather than harmony, as was the case in contemporary music. Using the example again of *Gruppen*, he noted how 'a dense, gelatinous, soft and sensitive material can be penetrated *ad libitum* by sharp, hacked splinters . . . "Soft" materials are less permeable when combined with each other, and there are places of an opaque complexity beyond compare'—beyond compare, that is, in late 1958, when Ligeti wrote the article. By the next year he had completed his orchestral piece *Apparitions*, whose first performance, at the 1960 festival of the

[1] 'Metamorphoses of Musical Form', *Die Reihe*, 7 (1960, English edn. 1965), 5–19.

International Society for Contemporary Music, caused so much stir among composers as to indicate that something significant was taking place: a challenge to the orthodoxy of complexity.

Until this point Ligeti had been known in the west as an associate of Stockhausen's at the Cologne electronic studio and as the painstaking analyst of *Structures Ia*: a composer, therefore, firmly at the centre of advanced music. Perhaps what bothered his colleagues about *Apparitions* was not so much the resort to orchestral clusters and the reduction of music to shifting or contrasted types of sound as the rationale provided by his essay: Stockhausen in *Carré* (1959–60) had arrived at a similar handling of the orchestra (if without the dramatized weirdness and comedy), and 'texture music' was in vogue—as witness the works that suddenly established Penderecki, such as his *Threnody—to the Victims of Hiroshima* for string orchestra (1960), in which Xenakisian cluster glissandos are given a searing affect. But for a composer of the Darmstadt–Cologne axis to wonder about the musical disciplines of the last several years was troubling.

Ligeti went on to develop his cluster technique more thoroughly and masterfully in his *Atmosphères* for orchestra (1961) and *Volumina* for organ (1961–2), in which there is no longer any attempt to deal with units of pitch, duration, loudness, and timbre in a serial manner, or indeed any other. Ligeti's conclusion was that musical atoms could not, or could not yet, be composed into meaningful structures, by which he presumably meant that the kind of compositional method he had revealed in *Structures Ia* was not intelligible in performance. What he left out of account was the possibility of meaning introduced subsidiarily, whether by the composer (as one would guess to be the case with the quasi-motifs at the start of *Le marteau*), by the performer (who might—perhaps must—present a particular view even of such recalcitrant material as that of *Structures Ia*) or by the listener (whose ways are the most difficult to determine). The sound of these massive exemptions is there in the music, in the suppression of differentiations that *Atmosphères* solemnly accomplishes. Rhythmic movement is eliminated by staggering instrumental entries (a technique for which Ligeti introduced the term 'micro-polyphony'), emphasizing sustained sounds (the work, unusually for this period, is for an orchestra without percussion), and avoiding all sense of pulse; harmony is held in suspension by the use of clusters. All these effects of continuity provoke an experience of sound as texture—the sort of experience that Ligeti had indicated in his 1960 essay (in the terms of that essay, the textures of *Atmosphères* are peculiarly permeable). Along a different route he had arrived at the position of Boulez in *Structures Ia* or Cage in the *Music of Changes*: he had reacted to the immediate past by effacing it, clearing the ground for his later works to make a progressive rediscovery of modes of particularization which might be, in his terms, comprehensible.

Music and Graphics and Theatre: Bussotti and Kagel

The beauty of *Atmosphères* must depend on the fastidiousness of its scoring, but when writing for a soloist, in *Volumina*, Ligeti could achieve similar effects by simply blocking in areas of the keyboard graphically. Here again he was marching with others. At Darmstadt in 1959, the year following Cage's visit, it had become clear that introducing chance into composition would have much more far-reaching consequences than those allowed in the mobile forms of Stockhausen and Boulez that had been heard for the first time there two years before. A course in 'music and graphics' included performances of Cage's *Concert*, and of European pieces that had been stimulated by Cage's innovations in notation and Tudor's style of playing, among them Kagel's *Transición II* for pianist, percussionist, and tapes (1958–9), *Five Piano Pieces for David Tudor* (1959) by Sylvano Bussotti (b. 1931), and Stockhausen's *Zyklus* for percussionist (1959). There was also a lecture by Stockhausen[2] in which he spoke of a 'music for reading' made conceivable by the 'emancipation of the graphic from the acoustic element', a feature he detected in the scores of Cage and Bussotti. As if to demonstrate that emancipation, Cage had already the previous year given an exhibition of his scores as pictures, when the art critic of the *New York Times* had found in them 'a delicate sense of design . . . that transcends the purely technical matter of setting down music'.[3]

But of course that was not Cage's intention. Nothing was Cage's intention. Whether the pages of his *Concert* look beautiful (as one may easily agree they do)— whether the work sounds beautiful—has to do with the observer: like a flower or a cloudscape, such a piece does not strive for beauty. And the new kinds of notation— far more various than one illustration (Example 22) can indicate—arose directly from new kinds of compositional method. It was different with Bussotti. Example 30, from his *Per tre sul piano* (one of his *Sette fogli* of 1959), may work as 'music for reading', but the aim is surely much more to excite the performers' imaginations. Cage was concerned with action, Bussotti with feeling. In this particular case the piano becomes, in Richard Toop's words, 'a prone body, alternately caressed, cajoled and assaulted by its suitors'.[4] (The eroticism was to remain characteristic of Bussotti's work, representing a self-consciously excessive satisfaction of what bourgeois culture desires of artists, so that decadence turns into social criticism.) In a prefatory note to the published edition of *Sette fogli*, the composer remarks that he had originally planned an explanatory apparatus (such as many scores carried during this period of rapid notational change), but that the works had established their own performing tradition during the decade which passed between composition and publication.

---

[2] 'Musik und Graphik', *Texte*, i. 176–88.
[3] Dore Ashton, 'Cage, Composer, Shows Calligraphy of Note' [the paper's headline style has not changed], *New York Times* (6 May 1958), reprinted in Kostelanetz (ed.), *John Cage*, 126.
[4] Note with EMI EMSP 551.

Ex. 30. Bussotti, *Per tre sul piano* (1959)

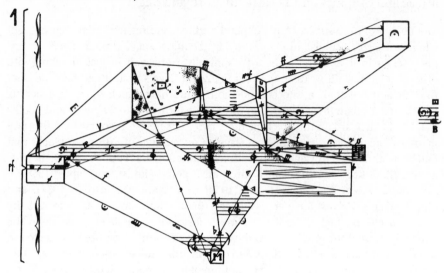

(To the extent that this performing tradition has been interrupted, Bussotti's music will go on surviving only in the form of recordings: it is, as much as Stockhausen's *Studien,* a set of fixed electronic objects. But it is not alone in this regard. Remarkably few works by young European composers of the 1950s and early 1960s continue in regular performance: outside the works of Boulez, Stockhausen, and Berio, almost none. One can regret this. One can regret especially the neglect of Barraqué and Nono. But there are obvious reasons, both in the difficulty posed to performers and in the expense of preparing pieces for non-standard formations; there may be a less obvious reason in the philosophy of composition at this time. Since the emphasis was on being at one with the historical moment, the resulting works were inevitably dated to that moment: to styles of performance and, perhaps most importantly, to conditions of friction with the musical establishment. Such pieces as *Kontra-Punkte* or *Le marteau sans maître* are fresh with the discovery that isolated events, speedy and precise, can outweigh the calls of continuity, and once their claims about music began to be generally accepted—as they certainly were by the 1970s, when it was possible for Boulez to be conducting Beethoven, and when the early-music movement was releasing Bach and Mozart from the continuity of traditional interpretation—their essential contrariness was compromised. So recordings of these works from close to their time may—perhaps must—be more faithful than subsequent performances, even if those subsequent performances are more literally accurate. The presentation of a modern classic cannot easily be also a gesture of revolt. Perhaps the whole history of music since the introduction of the LP record, around 1950, has been swayed by the existence of a means whereby not only could listeners repeatedly hear the same piece—which would be an encouragement towards subtlety and complexity—but also the performing criteria of the time would be permanently emplaced in the music.)

Bussotti's casting of the musician as seducer or rapist was a theatrical extension of what Tudor had shown possible in performing the most recent Cage: exploring the whole body of the piano for the sounds it can produce, and so extending earlier work by Cowell and Cage himself. Kagel was also stimulated by this, as well as by Cage's calligraphy, but instead of pressing player and instrument into a sensual encounter, he preferred to view the behaviour of the investigatory performer with a certain ironic detachment, and to enjoy the other irony of highly detailed notation giving rise to impure results. In its outlandish sophistication, with rotatable discs and moveable slides, the score of his *Transición II* proceeds from that of Boulez's Third Sonata, while its promised intention to fuse 'in one single declension' the musical present (heard in performance) with the past (returning on tape) and the future ('pre-experienced' in the form of previously prepared recordings of music to come) suggests a Stockhausen-like will to compose with time itself.[5] And yet in performance the work could hardly fail to seem an absurd spectacle in which two musicians, operating on a piano, undertake meticulous actions in the service of musical aims which remain obscure, and in that respect the piece—as much as *Anagrama*—presents itself as a caricature of contemporary avant-garde endeavour.

Kagel's exposure of musicians as actors continued to convey a more comic and critical attitude than could be found at the same time in the instrumental theatre of Bussotti or Berio. Often he showed too, as he had in *Anagrama* and *Transición II*, an interest in neglected possibilities of sound. *Sonant* (1960), scored for the unusual ensemble of guitar, harp, double bass and drums, comes near Feldman in its unsynchronized parts and its absorption with extremes of quiet, but the players' bashfulness also has a theatrical import quite alien to Feldman, and Kagel went still further in taking the then unusual step of requiring his musicians to speak. Also from this period is *Sur scène* for bass, mime, speaker, and three keyboard players (1958–60), whose fundamental idea was 'to create a spectacle out of elements borrowed from traditional musical life: instrumental playing, exercises which precede performance (scales, vocalises, etc), the commentaries of a musicologist . . . Music becomes a character on stage, which represents the reversal of the situation in opera.'[6] Almost from the first then, Kagel's satires and explorations were directed into the wider musical culture and not only into the areas of his colleagues' immediate concerns.

---

[5] See the composer's note with the recording on Mainstream 5003; and also his articles 'Tone, Clusters, Attacks, Transitions', *Die Reihe*, 5 (1959, English edn. 1961), 40–55; and 'Translation–Rotation', *Die Reihe*, 7 (1960, English edn. 1965), 32–60.

[6] Jean-Yves Bosseur, 'Dossier Kagel', *Musique en jeu*, 7 (1972), 88–126.

Exploiting the Moment: Stockhausen

Stockhausen's tendency to describe himself as an originator, influencing many but influenced by none, is understandable in view of the way his works from *Kreuzspiel* to *Gesang der Jünglinge* were received, by composers from the very youngest to the most distinguished of the time, Stravinsky. But it seems possible that the arrival of Kagel, Ligeti, and the young English composer Cornelius Cardew (1936–81), all of whom came to live in Cologne in 1957, had an effect on him: at least it extended his circle, which also included the critic Heinz-Klaus Metzger, the poet Hans G. Helms, various people in the art world, and colleagues from the early days of the WDR electronic music studio, notably the composer Gottfried Michael Koenig. In such an intellectual environment, questions of priority are undecidable: things that appear first in scores by Ligeti or Kagel might have been provoked by suggestions from Stockhausen, and vice versa. Indeed, Stockhausen's whole career, since *Kreuzspiel*, had shown how he could seize opportunities provided by encounters with others, and his success in the electronic studio (the high place of *Gesang* in the electronic repertory seems unassailable) was probably helped by his skill in teamwork. The important difference now was that Cologne, where Stockhausen was living until he moved out in 1964 to the house he had designed at Kürten, began to provide what Darmstadt had before: a forum of debate and artistic stimulation.

Inevitably there was a change in what he was producing. The completion of *Gruppen*, also in 1957, brought an end to a phase of highly detailed and rapidly changing music; the next group of works—*Zyklus* for percussionist (1959), *Refrain* for a chiming trio of piano, celesta, and vibraphone (1959), *Carré* for four choral–orchestral groups (1959–60), *Kontakte* (1958–60), an electronic piece to be played either alone or with pianist and percussionist, and Piano Pieces IX and X (1961)—shift the centre towards slowness, more complex sounds, and greater latitude in the execution of detail. Also noteworthy is the move from works which would have to be played on mixed programmes to works that chosen performers (Tudor and other pianists, especially Aloys Kontarsky and Frederic Rzewski, and the percussionist Christoph Caskel) could perform at all-Stockhausen concerts. There were the beginnings here of the ensemble which regularly presented his music between 1964 and the early 1970s, and for which most of his works from that period were written. For him, as for Boulez, contributing to a movement was becoming less important than pursuing individual explorations.

Zyklus was Stockhausen's masterpiece of graphic invention, using indeterminate signs for indeterminate sounds—sounds that cannot be completely defined by conventional notation (marimba and vibraphone, the two instruments of precise pitch, are used only in glissandos), and that may be prescribed merely as a scatter of attacks on a particular instrument within a given time. Characteristically, Stockhausen establishes a scale of nine degrees of uncertainty that may exist within an event, and uses that scale to mediate between what is prescribed and what is loose. Equally characteristically, he creates the piece as the image of a sound, a complex vibration in which nine constituents follow staggered cycles of growth and decay: in the musical metaphor there are nine chief instruments, and the player turns to them in turn as he moves through a circle inside his battery. Spiral binding, as in Boulez's *Trope*, makes it possible to start the circuit at any point. The need to complete the cycle gives *Zyklus* an onwardness that Stockhausen had wanted to avoid in Piano Piece XI, but at the same time the freedom in the notation, including a freedom to introduce optional elements, means that the implicit dynamism can be either endorsed or countered by the performer, whose wheeling, clock-like movement makes this Stockhausen's first contribution to manifest instrumental theatre. However, the greater visual achievement is the score's, and Stravinsky's reservation ('very attractive to look at, too—one almost wishes it didn't have to be *translated* into sound'[7]) was perhaps shared by Stockhausen himself, with his talk of music for reading.

Refrain is also an elegant package, but a simpler and sharper design in letting chance into a determined framework. Taking up the technique of timbre composition he had developed not only in electronic works but also in orchestral pieces from *Spiel* to *Gruppen*, Stockhausen assembles sounds from the three principal instruments, using additional percussion instruments and vocal enunciations to colour attacks and resonances. The vocal interventions, in particular, give to the piece the aura of a ritual enactment, while the resonant sound-world and the long suspensions additionally make the piece a striking prefiguration of the direction in which Stockhausen would travel after his first visit to Japan, in 1965–6. This is the framework. The chance element concerns the placing of the 'refrain' material, with its clusters, its glissandos, and its far more dynamic feel. On the single-page score, this music is notated on a transparent strip that can be revolved to different positions against the six 'verses', which are therefore printed partly (where the 'refrain' can fall) in concentric circles. Thus the score itself—a typical European reinjection of intention into a Cage prototype (the kit score of *Fontana Mix*)—displays that 'curvi-linear' form[8] which Stockhausen was hoping to achieve by combining the stasis of randomness with the dynamism of goal-orientation.

The intimacy of *Refrain* is unusual for Stockhausen; so is the brevity. Its technique of composing timbres from vocal and instrumental sounds he transferred to a more typical scale in *Carré*, whose similarity to *Gruppen*, in being a work for spaced groups, is deceptive. *Gruppen*, like Piano Piece XI and *Zyklus*, was a magnified image of sound's behaviour; *Carré* and *Refrain* return to more direct concerns with making sounds. They mark a change from the speculative to the empirical, and from variety to a concentration on static events. Stockhausen has recalled how the idea of *Carré* came to him during his first tour of the United States, when he spent a lot of time in aeroplanes, and 'I was always leaning my ear . . . against the window, like listening with earphones directly to the inner vibrations. And though a physicist would have said that the engine sound doesn't change, it changed all the time

[7] Stravinsky and Craft, *Memories and Commentaries*, 118.
[8] Note by the composer in Wörner, *Stockhausen*, 42.

because I was listening to all the partials within the spectrum.'[9] Here was another, and important, discovery about musical time: that listening—the movement of aural attention within the sound—could be a dynamic activity.

Carré accordingly became Stockhausen's purest and most comprehensive essay in timbre composition with conventional resources: music which, like the second movement of *Spiel*, calls for active contemplation of sounds which succeed one another without any strong sense of logical connection. But the work does not rely entirely on the dynamism of listening, for its sounds generally have built-in gradual change in the form, for example, of a slow glissando or the layering of more precisely figured detail on to a smooth surface, and the work's tranquil unfolding is several times interrupted by the insertion of episodes which vigorously exploit the possibility, as at the climax of *Gruppen*, of having sounds spin in the centrifuge of the separated ensembles.

One other innovation in *Carré* is significant. Having planned the work, Stockhausen handed over much of the task of realization to Cardew,[10] which suggests a mode of working more characteristic of the architectural practice than of the composer's desk. No doubt Stockhausen had got used to working with associates in the electronic studio; there was also the point that he was pressed for time, since while *Carré* was in progress he was simultaneously at work in the studio on *Kontakte*. But the practical circumstances are less important than the assumptions that made them possible—the assumption, in particular, that one could separate the plan (Stockhausen's term, which he has used when speaking of many of his works, is 'form scheme') from the detail, with the implication that the plan is paramount. Serialism had supposed a method of working from the small to the large; Stockhausen had substituted a reverse process, and at the same time indicated that the essence of composition is in the setting-up of musical situations, whose particular conduct is relatively unimportant: whole sections of *Carré* can be omitted.

Kontakte belongs with *Carré* in being for four sound sources at compass points (but now loudspeakers), in its slowly changing sonorities, and in its swirling of sounds through space. But at the same time it capitalizes on properties unique to the electronic medium, as Stockhausen firmly asserted in a radio talk on the piece.[11] He draws attention to four 'criteria' that distinguish electronic from instrumental music—or that, one might rather say (since all four had been interests of his instrumental compositions), presuppose an electronic, analytic experience of sound and correspondingly lend themselves to electronic creativity. For example, two of them are old concerns of his—the composition and 'de-composition' of timbres, the making of scales between pitched tone and noise—that can be more easily and thoroughly pursued in a medium where smooth transitions between dissimilar states can be engineered. A third criterion is the possibility of scales of loudness, which had been a rather unconvincing postulate of total serialism, and

[9] Cott, *Stockhausen*, 31.

[10] See Cardew's article 'Report on Stockhausen's "Carré" ', *Musical Times*, 102 (1961), 619–22, 698–700.

[11] 'Die Einheit der musikalischen Zeite', *Texte*, i. 211–21.

which Stockhausen now uses, in a characteristic move from theoretical integrity to display, for illusions of depth. By carefully regulating volume and reverberation, he creates in *Kontakte* the effect of distinct screens of sound receding from the listener, screens which may be transparent to the ear, or which may be drawn back to reveal others 'behind' them. In this artificial space, as important to the work as the real space separating the loudspeakers, sounds may appear to come out of the distance and then, dropping in pitch to imitate the Doppler effect, fly past the listener, irresistibly suggesting the aeroplane engines that stimulated *Carré*.

But the most significant special feature of electronic music, and the one Stockhausen places first, is the opportunity it provides to show and use the coherent unity of the three parameters of timbre, pitch, and duration, or—as Stockhausen preferred to call them, his emphasis shifting from the atomic, written note to the substantial, heard sound—'coloristic composition, harmonic–melodic composition and metrical–rhythmic composition'. The continuity of the parameters, their common basis in the phenomenon of vibration, had of course been a primary subject of the preceding group of works associated with the essay '. . . how time passes . . .'. But *Kontakte*, typically for this period, makes the whole business more concrete. Example 31 shows a clear instance—clear even in the graphic representation of the electronic music—where a complex sound is progressively stripped of its components, each of which appears to float away and degenerate into the basic material from which the work was made: single impulses. Progressive deceleration of the constituents takes them smoothly from the realm of timbre to that of pitched sound and so to that of rhythm.

The 'contacts' of the title may thus be understood as happening among the parameters, and also between the domains of pitched sound and noise, since the slowing components slip not just from pitch to rhythm but from pitch to rhythmic noise. But there are also metaphorical contacts between sounds that appear familiar, because they resemble sounds we meet in life (including music, especially the music of percussion instruments—though everything here is artificially synthesized), and sounds that are unknown, that we cannot immediately categorize. In the alternative version, with pianist and percussionist contributing a new level of 'contacts' with the tape, the electronic images of instrumental sounds create the opportunity for a dramatic interplay: the performers may seem to capture sounds from out of the ether, or the tape may appear to hijack instrumental material and develop it way beyond instrumental possibility. Or to quote the composer's description: 'The known sounds give orientation, perspective to the listening experience; they function as traffic signs in the unbounded space of the newly discovered electronic world.'[12] There is a case of instrumental–electronic contact in the final segment of Example 31, where both players join the tape in blobs of sound in the upper register.

[12] Note with Vox STGBY 638.

Ex. 31. Stockhausen, *Kontakte* (1958–60)

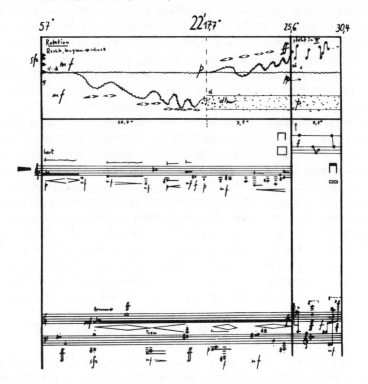

Example 31 may also suggest how *Kontakte* is a bundle of processes, a matter more of forming than of form, going further in the composer's characteristic direction. The processes come to a suitable conclusion, in a spinning swish of sound that disappears into the far distance and so makes an effective withdrawal, but Stockhausen has said that this ending is arbitrary.[13] In both *Kontakte* and *Carré* he sought alternatives to directional music, but left behind the mobile-form option of Piano Piece XI, *Zyklus*, and *Refrain*. His new means were long duration (*Kontakte* lasts for more than thirty minutes, and *Carré* can take almost an hour, both works playing continuously: now unremarkable, such expanses of sound were quite exceptional at the time) and a diminishment of causal connection between segments. As he said of *Kontakte*: 'The musical events do not take a fixed course between a determined beginning and an inevitable ending, and the moments are not merely consequents of what precedes them and antecedents of what follows; rather the concentration on the Now—on every Now—as if it were a vertical slice dominating over any horizontal conception of time and reaching into timelessness,

---

[13] See Wörner, *Stockhausen*, 110.

which I call eternity: an eternity which does not begin at the end of time, but is attainable at every *moment*.'[14]

This is the first and basic statement of Stockhausen's concept of 'moment form',[15] a kind of musical structure in which the 'moments', each with its distinctive character and way, are to be heard as individual, as implicit eternities, rather than as stations on a journey. Where Schoenberg in his serial works had attempted to find forces to compensate for the loss of the directed thrust of diatonic harmony, Stockhausen and his colleagues were moving along without. Barraqué found in Hermann Broch's novel *The Death of Virgil* an embedding of his own conclusion that now there could be no conclusion, that music's dynamic must be one of striving for unreachable attainment. Boulez explicitly contrasted the old universe of tonal gravitation with the new universe 'in constant expansion'. And Stockhausen arrived at moment form, soon grandly celebrated in *Momente* for soprano, four choral groups, brass octet, two electronic organs, and three percussion players. (The highly irregular formation is a testament to the optimism and the funding that still buoyed up the key players in the European musical vanguard. From Stockhausen's point of view, the choice of resources was an essential creative idea, and ought to be unrepeatable.)

Momente may well have been meant, like *Punkte* and *Gruppen*, as the apotheosis and the exemplary instance of its declared technique (Stockhausen cannot have been unaware of the function each new piece would have as a teaching instrument at the next Darmstadt session), and the individuality of the moments is made manifest in an unusual return to mobile form.[16] However, the score's variability is greatly circumscribed by the composer's care for mediation, and also, in the final version of 1972, by the sense of occasion which infuses a long, exhilarating section that could never be anything but an opening.[17] In neither version are the moments freely interchangeable; rather they must be organized like planets around the three suns that each concentrate on one of the fundamental parameters, which are again those that Stockhausen's acoustic studies had taught him were fundamentally unified: duration, melody and timbre. The planetary moments mix these categories in different combinations, or else ignore them, and the permissible forms are governed by associations of similarity and contrast. Moreover, Stockhausen sprinkles the work with foretastes of moments to come or reminiscences of moments past, so that, characteristically, ideology is not immune to the claims of drama.

As a result, *Momente* is impressive not as a haphazard succession of isolated events but as a spectacle and a grand synthesis.[18] It follows on from *Gesang der Jünglinge* in ignoring any boundary between speech and music, the solo soprano and the choirs enjoying a vast Kagelian repertory of modes of vocal and non-vocal

---

[14] Ibid. 46–7.   [15] See also his 'Momentform', *Texte*, i. 189–210.

[16] Sketches for the work have been published as *Ein Schlüssel für 'Momente'* (Kassel, Boczkowski, 1971).

[17] On the two versions see Maconie, *The Works of Karlheinz Stockhausen*, 137.

[18] See Stockhausen's note on the work in Wörner, *Stockhausen*, 48–53, for insights into the philosophical thinking on which the synthesis was partly based.

behaviour. With *Kontakte* it shares a refusal to acknowledge any division between the pitched and the unpitched, and it also ranks with that work as a crowning achievement in timbre composition, using its superficially limited but in effect very versatile ensemble (an ensemble which of course holds the speech–music and pitched–unpitched mediations implicit) to create a wealth of complex sonorities, often dark and enclosed in the music of 1961–4, more extrovert and brighter in the sections written later. (The early 1960s found Stockhausen unusually recoiled both personally and professionally. His invention of moment form was symbolic at a time when the unified thrust of the 1950s seemed to have gone from music, and his affair with the American visual artist Mary Bauermeister forced him to rethink himself.)

The Last Concert: Nono and Boulez

Momente became a momentous public statement only in the later stages of its development, but even while Stockhausen was working on the earlier version several of his colleagues were starting to concern themselves with music directed beyond the circuit of specialist festivals that was by now giving them perhaps too comfortable a time. For Nono, the existence of a new-music culture was artistic and political death: he was interested in disrupting bourgeois conventions, not in creating a new one. For Boulez too, the lapse from engaged attack into ordinary life seems to have been dispiriting. Since 1945 he had been able to see himself as the leader of a group in determined opposition; now there was no group, and nothing to oppose. The works he had begun in 1956–7—the Third Piano Sonata, the second book of *Structures, Figures–Doubles–Prismes* and *Pli selon pli*—remained the last new pieces he brought to performance for almost a decade, and he entered that long period during which most of his creative work has been refashioning.

Nono found an alternative to that in continuing the attack on other fronts. His *Intolleranza* (1960–1) was the first opera by one who had not fled the ranks of the avant garde, and in it he projected on to the stage that spirit of contra-bourgeois feeling and thinking which he had seen as inherent in postwar musical practice. The work is a protest against capitalist society's heartless treatment of an immigrant, a protest made as a sequence of short scenes which encapsulate incidents of inhumanity and, through the almost constant presence of the chorus, both universalize them and teach from them. All the most broad and vigorous features of Nono's previous output are brought to a culmination: the strident handling of orchestral sonorities out of *Diario polacco* and *Incontri*, the range of choral disposition from keenly divided, extenuated textures to powerful massings, the solo melodic lines of fierce expressive insistence. But for the first time these are combined with electronic sounds of a penetrating force. Nono had made a belated acquisition of studio techniques in Milan, producing his *Omaggio a Emilio Vedova* in 1960 (Vedova was the painter whose stark images were projected during the first performances of *Intolleranza*), and he began to realize that electronic music could provide him with both the musical material and the forum for continuing his offensive against bourgeois society. After two more sets of songs for voices and instruments, the *Canti di vita e d'amore* (1962) and the *Canciones a Guiomar* (1962–3), he turned his back on the resources of normal concert life.

PART II. SIX WAVES AND FIVE MASTERS: THE 1960s AND 1970s

In music, as in other areas of life, 'the sixties' began in 1965, and soon blew apart the orderliness of the postwar world. As far as new music was concerned, the success of the various avant gardes—those who had their spiritual homes in Darmstadt, in Princeton, or in the nowhere and everywhere of Cage—was bringing about their dissolution, since composers of a new generation, reacting to their elders (whether positively or negatively), were going off in different directions. But still there were directions to go off in. Progress remained as much an ideal as it had been for Boulez twenty years before, except that it was much harder in this increasingly various world to find a uniform historical imperative, and progress without need provided the recipe for fashion. Even in the mid-1950s, the newest works of Boulez and Stockhausen, in particular, had been rapidly imitated by younger composers, as if those works provided the key to the future: *Gruppen* was followed by numerous scores for spaced orchestral groups, *Le marteau* by a host of adamantine ensembles. By the middle of the next decade, the pursuit of fashion and the splintering of factions had together created a turmoil of trends, among which those explored below were particularly conspicuous. Something else that mattered was the increasing seriousness, range, and appeal of popular music. The simultaneity, say, of Babbitt's *Semi-Simple Variations* with Elvis Presley's *Blue Suede Shoes* seems— and surely seemed at the time—devoid of meaning, but ten years later the Beatles' album *Revolver* (1966) was just one symptom of rock musicians' urge to develop their language, and to do so, in part, by looking over the wall: the Beatles' next release, *Sgt. Pepper's Lonely Hearts Club Band* (1967) enshrines Stockhausen among the gurus on its cover. Meanwhile, classically trained composers were reciprocating the interest, and so fuelling or following new fashions: minimalism, live electronic music. Meanwhile, the possibility of the lone genius remained.

Of Elsewhen and Elsewhere

Though the passage of time irrevocably obscures novelty of any kind, one of the most striking features of the avant-garde music of the 1950s remains its isolation, in so many respects of aim and technique, from any immediate precedent. Separation from the past became an item of belief: every feature cherished in the great western tradition was now to be abandoned, whether by destruction, in Boulez, by blithe disregard, in Cage, or by intensive searching elsewhere, in Stockhausen. Of course, the extreme apartness of 1951–2—the period of Cage's *4′ 33″*, Stockhausen's *Kreuzspiel*, and Boulez's first book of *Structures*—was soon compromised in all kinds of ways, and rapprochements were made: Cage returned to writing music, and Boulez and Stockhausen found themselves caught up in more continuous ways of moving through time. But making things new was still the ideal.

Boulez has consistently been the most vociferous spokesman for this position, for all his vigorous conducting activity, especially during the 1970s, within the museum of musical tradition. Writing in the middle of that decade, fanfaring the foundation of his Institut de Recherche et de Coordination Acoustique/Musique (IRCAM) in Paris, he insisted that: 'Our age is one of persistent, relentless, almost unbearable inquiry. In its exaltation it cuts off all retreats and bans all sanctuaries; its passion is contagious, its thirst for the unknown projects us forcefully, violently into the future . . . Despite the skilful ruses we have cultivated in our desperate effort to make the world of the past serve our present-day needs, we can no longer elude the essential trial: that of becoming an absolute part of the present, of forsaking all memory to forge a perception without precedent, of renouncing the legacies of the past, to discover yet undreamed-of territories.'[1]

But this is perhaps too lyrical to be true, even allowing for the fact that Boulez was hoping to justify the considerable state expenditure involved in establishing and maintaining his institution. The position is—given the replacement of a thirty-year-old's abruptness by a fifty-year-old's more mannered discourse—little changed since the days of *Le marteau sans maître*, except that where Boulez in the mid-1950s could plausibly feel himself to be spearheading a great musical movement, by the mid-1970s this was no longer the case, and the adherence to an old revolutionary rhetoric was to stymie both IRCAM and Boulez's own creative endeavours. For by 1974 it had become very clear that 'renouncing the legacies of the past' was no simple matter. What about the revolutionary asceticism that was itself a legacy of the past? Amnesia is the privilege of the young, and even by the later 1960s the new

[1] IRCAM press brochure (Paris, 1974), 6–7.

wave was growing up. As that wave broke up, as the arrow of determined progress splintered, so the possibilities multiplied of touching back to what had been.

The Distant Past

The achievement of the eighteenth and nineteenth centuries remains the great sun of the musical solar system: the repertory that dominates performance and recording. Composers who approach it must either maintain their ironic distance, as Stravinsky did, and as Ligeti more recently has done, or else be content (and here the examples are legion) to turn into its orbit, adopt its premises and its modes of thought. The further past offers less gravitational pull—partly just because it is further off, but also partly because its forces seem to be complemented by, rather than at war with, those of our own age. Pertinent here is Stravinsky's progress during the 1950s: forward to Webern and Boulez, but at the same time backward to Gesualdo and to pre-Renaissance music. The more general growth of interest in 'early music', following behind Stravinsky by a decade or so, may be evidence of a community of thought and feeling; it has also made it possible for composers to write for instruments that had been extinct for centuries, as Kagel did in his quite un-Renaissance-sounding *Musik für Renaissance-Instrumente* (1965). As for matters of compositional technique rather than instrumental means, the medieval view of rhythm as number suggests comparison with the attitudes of Messiaen and of those composers who, influenced by him, developed rhythmic serialization in Europe: Barraqué drew attention to that in an article on rhythm, where, with no sense of incongruity, he moves directly from Machaut's *Messe de Notre Dame* to *The Rite of Spring*.[2] Also, as Charles Wuorinen pointed out, the rhythmic complexities cultivated by composers of the post-Machaut generation are such as to make *Le marteau sans maître* appear quite normal.[3]

But these are instances of correspondence rather than influence. For examples of the latter, English music of the 1950s and 1960s provides the richest field, perhaps for various reasons: the fact that English musicians and musicologists were taking a leading part in the rediscovery of early music, the fact that composers of an older generation, such as Britten and Tippett, had interested themselves in Tudor music and Purcell, the fact that English musical culture had last been actively progressive in the age of Dunstable. Three composers who were fellow students in Manchester during the early 1950s—Peter Maxwell Davies (b. 1934), Harrison Birtwistle (b. 1934), and Alexander Goehr (b. 1932)—were quite aware that what they were learning from the recent music of Boulez and Nono had its parallels in what they could find in the pages of *Musica Britannica*.

Davies's concern with the further past has stayed intense, and the role of pre-Baroque music in his work has been various and profound. A great many of his

---

[2] 'Rythme et développement', *Polyphonie*, 9–10 (1954), 47–73.

[3] 'Notes on the Performance of Contemporary Music', *Perspectives of New Music*, 3/1 (1964), 10–21.

works are founded—as the music of the medieval and Renaissance polyphonists was founded—on fragments of plainsong, but his processes of transformation usually leave little kinship between the music and its seed: even in his transcriptions—and he has made many, of works by Machaut, Dunstable, Purcell, Buxtehude, and others—the original is often twisted into alien, and sometimes perversely alien, harmonic or instrumental territory. At the simplest level, a plainsong theme may be subjected to octave displacement of its pitches, melodic alteration and a very unchant-like rhythmic presentation, combining sixteenth-century techniques of parody with nineteenth-century variation and twentieth-century serialism: Example 32 shows an instance of this in a comparison of the opening of the Easter sequence *Victimae paschali laudes*, transposed up a semitone (Example 32*a*), with the cello solo from the final scene of Davies's opera *Taverner* of 1962–70 (Example 32*b*), the plainsong here serving, as Stephen Arnold has pointed out,[4] not only as a musical source but as a symbol of resurrection by virtue of its text. (For Taverner, the Catholic composer who turns himself into a zealous despoiler of his heritage, it is a deceptive resurrection he acquires for himself in putting to death the White Abbot in the opera's closing scene.) The use of plainsong themes at once for their musical qualities and for their associated meanings is common in Davies's music, though normally the relationship between chant and variant is more complex.

Ex. 32*a*. *Victimae paschali laudes*

Ex. 32*b*. Davies, *Taverner* (1962–70): final scene

A counter-example is provided in Messiaen's music. Like Davies, Messiaen was alive to the textual connotations of the melodies he used, and when he returned to explicitly religious subject matter, in *Couleurs de la Cité Céleste* for piano, wind and percussion (1963), he began bringing appropriate chant melodies into his music. One instance is the alleluia for the eighth Sunday after Pentecost, *Magnus Dominus*, which Messiaen accepts without melodic change and integrates into his musical world by means of harmonization (in this case using his fourth mode of limited transpositions) and orchestration (for wind and bells). Because his music is essentially modal, rather than, like Davies's, essentially chromatic, this acceptance is musically possible. But it is also spiritually essential in the music of a man whose

---

[4] 'The Music of *Taverner*', *Tempo*, 101 (1972), 20–39.

first creative effort, as he said, was 'to highlight the theological truths of the Catholic faith'.[5]

Davies has another standpoint. His is a music not of exposition but of questioning, even to the extent of negation—negation which can be musically effected by the gradual melodic transformation of a melody into its precise inversion,[6] and which stands behind his abiding concern with themes of betrayal. In his dramatic works, betrayal is staged: Taverner betrays himself in extinguishing what was good and creative in his personality; the solo dancer in *Vesalii icones* betrays the image of Christ he was presented by turning, finally, into a vision of Antichrist, cavorting to a foxtrot. Outside the theatrical context, music itself can be betrayed by means of this sort of parody—the parody of distortion and mockery, rather than the expressively neutral parody of elaboration conducted in Renaissance masses (though Davies's music has also implied what so many popes suspected, that polyphonic settings can destroy what they purport to adorn).

Many of Davies's earlier works are parodies of parodies, in that they are based on polyphonic pieces themselves based on plainsongs: examples include the wind sextet *Alma redemptoris mater* (1957) after a Dunstable motet, the String Quartet (1961) and other works linked in some way to the Monteverdi Vespers, and a larger family of compositions derived from the Benedictus of Taverner's *Gloria Tibi Trinitas* mass—a family including not only the opera *Taverner* but also two orchestral fantasias (1962 and 1964) and the *Seven In Nomine* for chamber ensemble (1963–5). In these works Davies's parody is to a large degree secret and, for that reason, not expressed, though the music in other respects may be fiercely expressive, in ways that strike back to Mahler and Schoenberg. In pieces from the late 1960s, however, parody becomes overt and takes on its modern sense, dramatized in the theatre works (such as *Taverner* and *Vesalii icones*), but no less disturbing in orchestral and chamber works, where it may be felt to infect the whole substance of the music.

Davies has described his 'foxtrot for orchestra' *St Thomas Wake* (1969) as being based on 'three levels of musical experience—that of the original sixteenth century "St Thomas Wake" pavan, played on the harp, the level of the foxtrots derived from this, played by a foxtrot band, and the level of my "real" music, also derived from the pavan, played by the symphony orchestra.'[7] But there remain the questions—as evidently Davies is aware, when he makes the word 'real' creep inside quotation marks—as to how 'real' music can be, and why we should accept one level of music as being more 'real' than the foxtrots that crop up in so many of his works of this period (see also, besides *Vesalii icones*, the *Fantasia on a Ground and Two Pavans* after Purcell), and that may even be felt to identify those works. There is no obvious reason why his post-Schoenberg style of endless development should be presumed to have a 'reality' not shared with the other guises his music was capable of taking—

---

[5] *Music and Color*, 176.   [6] See Arnold, 'The Music of *Taverner*'.
[7] Programme note for the first performance of *Vesalii icones*, at the Queen Elizabeth Hall, London, on 9 December 1969; the note is reprinted in Paul Griffiths, *Peter Maxwell Davies* (London, 1981), 152–4.

or why, to look at it the other way, that style should not also be interpreted as a manner of pastiche. These uncertainties Davies seemed to be recognizing himself in concluding his Second Taverner Fantasia—which powerfully enshrines the Schoenbergian weight and drift of argumentation—with a woodwind dispatch that swiftly and grotesquely parodies half an hour of searching, string-led music. The pathos and musical tension accumulated through a long and troubled development are simply cast aside, and at the same time redoubled by being cast aside, because now the foundations are under attack: the music is questioning its own assumptions, even its own honesty.

His bigger orchestral work of this period, *Worldes Blis* (1966–9), Davies has presented as a recuperation, 'a conscious attempt to reintegrate the shattered and scattered fragments of my creative persona'.[8] This is again an immense musical edifice founded on given material—a medieval monody—but now there is no separation of levels and no blatant autodestruction: the quest for reintegration imposes rather a steady progress in which constant self-interrogation answers itself. As Stephen Pruslin has observed: 'The main allegro pays only lip-service to closure and after the transition the music careens through a whole series of sections, all of them unclosed. The effect is that of amassing a series of left-hand parentheses without bothering about the corresponding right-hand ones, so that one builds up a large "structural overdraft".'[9] Where the Second Taverner Fantasia had presented a process of growth whose premises were alarmingly shaken at the end, *Worldes Blis* advances in momentous instability, and only in conclusion comes overwhelmingly to affirmation. Its thirteenth-century source, speaking of bitter resignation to the vanity of the world, seems to have offered not only musical stimulus but also a poetic metaphor for this harsh vision.

Davies's later adherence to traditional genres, in the sequence of symphonies, concertos, and sonatas he began with his First Symphony of 1973–6, seems an almost inevitable development from the quasi-symphonic manner of the Second Taverner Fantasia and *Worldes Blis*. Here was a paradox. Medieval material provided Davies with a mechanism of return not to medieval modes of thought and musical practice but rather to the musical–psychological crises of Vienna in the late Romantic and early modern periods: in points of style and motivation, the connections are with Mahler and Schoenberg, not Machaut—hence the possibility that Davies, among composers of his generation, should have been one of the first to write a symphony. (Even so, there was shock at the time, when postmodern avenues to the recent past were still so little worn.) Two decades after his earliest works, Davies had developed ways of using plainsong melodies that paralleled Schoenberg's ways with twelve-note rows, and the evolution of his style—from an 'expressionist' period in the 1960s to re-found classicism—may have come about in more or less conscious emulation of Schoenberg.

At the same time, Davies makes a deeply traditional insistence—explicitly in his

---

[8] Griffiths, *Peter Maxwell Davies*, 150.

[9] 'Returns and Departures: Recent Maxwell Davies', *Tempo*, 113 (1975), 22–8.

writings and implicitly in everything he has composed—on music as linear argument and as expressive correlative. In a note on his chamber symphony *A Mirror of Whitening Light* (1976–7), for example, he remarks how he has tried to create 'functional harmony operating over and relating large spans of time',[10] and from this point onwards his analyses of his own pieces make free with such terms as 'introduction' and 'recapitulation' (though in place of 'development' he prefers 'transformation processes'), or 'dominant'.[11] The note on *A Mirror* is also remarkably clear about the music's connotations: it is 'the great cliff-bound bay before my window where the Atlantic and the North Sea meet [off Hoy], . . . at all times a miracle of ever-changing reflected light, . . . which is the physical mirror of the title', a title whose reference is also alchemical, 'to the purification of "whitening" process, by which a base metal may be transformed into gold, and, by extension, to the purification of the human soul'. Davies's prodigious output since the mid-1970s is, in itself, proof of the success of his self-reintegration, though the earlier music—music of doubt, disquiet and duplicity—has justly commanded wider and intenser admiration.

The Distant or not so Distant East

Davies's engagement with medieval and Renaissance music, and with techniques of parody, may perhaps be a legitimation (a legitimation according to Boulezian criteria that structure be articulable but not articulate) for a composer whose musical business is essentially modern and Romantic: the violence with which he has treated his source material (most dramatically in the arrangements of his 'expressionist' period, such as the *Seven In Nomine* and the *Fantasia on a Ground and Two Pavans*) may almost suggest as much, since the effect is not so much to cherish as to dismember. It is from a modern, even modernist, viewpoint that retroversion becomes a cause for anxiety; those who are determined to move forward have most to lose by looking back.

Composers disinclined to progress, though, risk nothing: found materials for them are objects requiring placement, not subjects demanding consideration. Hence the very different tone of Messiaen's appropriation of medieval material, and his ability to make use of materials from other places, as well as other times, with the same combination of care and detachment: the Indian rhythmic figures he found in an encyclopaedia, or the gamelan-like metallophone section he incorporated in the orchestra of *Turangalîla* and many later scores, or the complete tradition copied into the 'Gagaku' of the *Sept haïkaï*. Messiaen's imitations regard Asian music (and also avian music) as closer to the timelessness of paradise, and it is

---

[10] Griffiths, *Peter Maxwell Davies*, 164. For analytical comments on the work see David Roberts's review in *Contact*, 19 (1978), 26–9.

[11] See e.g. his note on his Second Symphony in Griffiths, *Peter Maxwell Davies*, 171–4, and other notes printed with recordings.

perhaps the lack in such music of post-Renaissance Europe's manifold dynamisms (harmonic, metric, formal) that is responsible for its claim on so many composers since the abandonment or destruction of those dynamic principles became an aim around 1945. It was no accident that Messiaen, open to non-European music, should have been the most prestigious European composition teacher from the 1950s to the 1980s, nor that non-western composers should then have begun to contribute significantly to what had hitherto been a predominantly western tradition.

In Japan, Tōru Takemitsu (b. 1930) showed quite explicitly how close European and American composers had come, in the late 1950s and early 1960s, to oriental ways of considering time as unthrusted blank space, of accommodating the unpredictable, and of attuning art to nature. His solo piece *Piano Distance* (1961), for example, has connections with Boulez's Third Sonata and second book of *Structures* in its feeling for resonance, and with Cage in its inscription of sound calligrams on silence. Other works of this radical period include *Ring* for flute, guitar, and lute (also 1961), whose four movements can be played in any order, with a graphically scored improvisation interpolated, several electronic pieces, and—following a meeting with Cage in 1964—happenings. *November Steps* (1967) combined a western orchestra with eastern soloists (on shakuhachi and biwa), but marked a withdrawal from experiment back to developing the francophone style of Takemitsu's earliest works. Much of his later music is close to Messiaen, though with a gentler, more yielding character.

Takemitsu's acceptance in the west—where his music has been performed far more than that of any other Asian musician—may have to do not only with his music's quality but also with western expectations of Asian art as serene, passive, decorative and subsidiary, since it remains difficult for even the most sympathetic western observers to separate a real appreciation of Asian art from an idolization of stereotype, or for even the most sympathetic western composers to accept Asian music on equal terms rather than draw it into contexts of their own. The ideas, ever prone to wishful interpretation, have flown faster than any deep acquaintance with traditions and instruments, and fusions, whether made by western or non-western composers, have had to take place on western territory, using western media. The point was made satirically in reverse by Kagel in his *Exotica* (1971), which depends precisely on the lack of familiarity and expertise that six European musicians will bring to a collection of at least sixty non-European instruments. When Boulez and Stockhausen took up ideals of instrumentation from Asian or African music, they did so, like Messiaen, with European ensembles, as in the former's *Le marteau sans maître* and *Improvisations sur Mallarmé* or the latter's *Kreuzspiel* and *Refrain*.

The possibility that oriental artistic practices and philosophies will unsettle western music more profoundly remains for the future, however much noise there has been. Even Cage, in his pursuit of a zen music of non-intention, could not escape western conditions of musical communication (the score, the rehearsal, the concert, the recording), let alone western notions of artist and oeuvre. With other composers, even the attempt is doubtful. Boulez, for example, has recorded that, when he first heard examples of Asian and African music on records, he was struck not only by their beauty but also 'by the concepts behind these elaborate works of art. Nothing, I found, was based on the "masterpiece", on the closed cycle, on passive contemplation or narrowly aesthetic pleasure. In these civilizations music is a way of existence in the world of which it forms an integral part and with which it is indissolubly linked—an ethical rather than simply an aesthetic category.'[12] This insistence on music as an active mode of being in the world is arguably a legacy more from Artaud than from Messiaen, but by this point in Boulez's career (the article was first published in 1960) there was a contradiction, or at least a tension, between such inflammatory pronouncements and the man's musical routines. (That contradiction or tension was most famously exposed in 1967, when in an interview with *Der Spiegel*[13] he called for opera houses to be blown up, while at the same time he must have been preparing to conduct *Parsifal* at Bayreuth the next summer and *Pelléas* at Covent Garden the following year.) The Third Piano Sonata, which provided the occasion for this article, surely was intended as a 'masterpiece', and a masterpiece indeed by virtue of—not despite—its innovation in respecting 'the "finite" quality of western art, with its closed circle, . . . while introducing the element of "chance" from the open circle of oriental art'.[14] Besides, this talk of chance and openness suggests that Boulez was really talking about Cage rather than about anything directly from the east, which might explain the bleak decisiveness of his last statements on eastern music, in another interview of 1967: 'The music of Asia and India is to be admired because it has reached a stage of perfection, and it is this perfection that interests me. But otherwise the music is dead.'[15]

Quite apart from the problem that Cage appeared to have taken out rights in music east of the Indus, Boulez seems to have been caught between a fascination with oriental art and a horror of imitation or even conspicuous reference. The things that captivated him in music from outside the cultivated European tradition were sounds and the sense of time: suppleness and fluidity of pulse, hospitality to improvisation, slowness and length, a comparative unimportance of the end. In publicly introducing his second *Improvisation sur Mallarmé* in 1960, for instance, he remarked how he had 'heard Andean peasants in Peru playing harps with a most extraordinary sonority and learned from them the use of the instrument's highest notes and a variety of "dampings" ',[16] while the third *Improvisation*—at least in the version that was current between 1959 and the mid-1980s—clearly shows both kinds of indebtedness: to exotic sounds in its clattering heterophonies for homogeneous percussion ensembles (of two xylophones, three harps, etc.) and its immense opening soprano melisma delicately inflected with quarter-tones, and to new temporalities in its long suspensions, its offering of alternatives, and its loose coordination of overlapping blocks. But that was as far as Boulez was prepared to go.

[12] ' "Sonate, que me veux-tu?" ', *Orientations*, 145.

[13] In issue 40 of that year.

[14] 'Alea', *Stocktakings*, 35.

[15] *Orientations*, 421.

[16] Ibid. 158.

He praised Messiaen for providing the lesson 'that *all* can become music',[17] but in his own work he could never have accepted the extraneous allusions of Indian rhythms, plainsong melodies or imitation gagaku: the need—as in learning from Debussy or Webern—was to analyse, and then to construct from basic particles whose origins would be as deeply buried as the worldwide music in *Le marteau*.

So it was with Stockhausen until, in the early months of 1966, he made an extended visit to Japan in order to compose an electronic work in the Tokyo radio studios. Michael Kurtz has suggested that dislocation—an experience confined before the present age to refugees and immigrants, who have other problems—elicited a new outlook. 'Could he compose exactly the same kind of piece in Tokyo as in Cologne? If so, why travel to Tokyo?'[18] Stockhausen's own accounts confirm that it was being in Japan that made it possible for him 'to take a step further in the direction of composing not "my" music, but a music of the whole world'.[19] This was *Telemusik*. Here exotic music is not analysed but accepted, in the form of recordings, and only afterwards submitted to electronic techniques of modulation and integration. As Stockhausen has explained, the work contains '"electronic" passages, which are of today, together with tape recordings of music, for example from the south Sahara, from the Shipibo of the Amazon, from a Spanish village festival, Hungarian, Balinese music, recordings from temple ceremonies in Japan, . . . music of the highland dwellers of Vietnam, etc.'[20] He has also insisted that the piece is not a collage but rather 'an untrammelled spiritual encounter',[21] because the different kinds of music are both carefully assembled and made to affect one another. The stage is provided by purely electronic sounds—often piercing high frequencies, which introduce what was to be for several years in Stockhausen's music a common image of listening to shortwave broadcasts: in such works as *Kurzwellen* (1968) shortwave receivers are used in performance, so that the 'music of the whole world' becomes part of the live piece. The meetings of musics in *Telemusik* are engineered by studio procedures that the composer has also explained: 'I modulate the rhythm of one event with the dynamic curve of another. Or I modulate electronic chords, regulated by myself, with the dynamic curve of a priestly chant, then this with the monotonous song (therefore the pitch line) of a Shipibo song, and so on.'[22] This technique of 'intermodulation', to use Stockhausen's own term, generates complex textures and dense events in which the original recordings, when they can be distinguished at all, sound as if they are being jammed by interference—the interference of other recordings that collide with and obscure them.

The use of Japanese percussion instruments to signal each new section is a nice gesture of deference to the composer's hosts, but in dedicating *Telemusik* to the Japanese people Stockhausen was concerned with deeper issues. 'I have learnt', he wrote, '—especially in Japan—that tradition does not simply exist, but that it must be created anew every day . . . Let us not forget that everything we do and say must

[17] Programme note for a concert at Severance Hall, Cleveland, on 5 December 1970.
[18] *Stockhausen*, 142.   [19] *Texte*, iii (Cologne, 1971), 75.   [20] Ibid. 79.
[21] Ibid. 76.   [22] Ibid. 80.

be considered as a moment in a continuing tradition.'[23] Hitherto Stockhausen had written about his music as if each work were a pure thought experiment, dependent only on methods and ideals chosen for that work. From now on, as Robin Maconie has observed, he 'is eager to discover parallels between his own and other music (especially traditional music of oral cultures) as proof that his personal intuitions are in tune with universal forms of musical expression'.[24] And in beginning to search out roots and linkages he was, not for the first time, thinking and acting for his generation.

Quotation

Telemusik also belongs with the best of early Stockhausen—with *Kontra-Punkte*, *Gesang der Jünglinge*, *Kontakte*, and the Piano Pieces—in making a composition out of a solution to a problem, and so in achieving a compelling unity of material and design. Only this material—ethnic music which would provide abundant variety without triggering immediate recognitions and responses in any likely listener—was suitable for intermodulation; only intermodulation could unify this material. But around the same time other composers were starting to use found ideas that would, on the contrary, be recognized, and that would by intention create a disparity between material and design—that would appear as quotations in alien contexts.

The rediscovery of Ives may have played some part in this, though more probably Ives arrived as confirmation rather than influence. The reasons for the tide of quotations in music of the mid-1960s are likely to be deeper, and to include a wish to engage with aspects of the governing culture from which postwar composers had held themselves apart (a wish growing as musicians born in the 1920s now entered middle age), a desire to make contact with audiences for that governing culture, and a hope that music might mirror the multiple and simultaneous sensory bombardment in a world where, during the 1950s and 1960s, most western homes had acquired television sets and record players.

Cage, in particular, was struck by this change, and by Marshall McLuhan's analysis of its meaning in *The Gutenberg Galaxy* (1962) and later books and articles. McLuhan, he wrote, 'has given a dramatic cause (the effect of electronics as opposed to the effect of print on sense perceptions) for the present social change . . . New art and music do not communicate an individual's conceptions in ordered structures, but they implement processes which are, as are our daily lives, opportunities for perception (observation and listening). McLuhan emphasises this shift from life done for us to life that we do for ourselves.'[25] But though these words come from a short article entitled 'McLuhan's Influence', again the case was more one of confirmation. Cage's production of unordered, multifarious music went back a

---

[23] *Texte*, iii (Cologne, 1971), 76.   [24] *The Works of Karlheinz Stockhausen* (London, 1976), 210.
[25] Kostelanetz (ed.), *John Cage*, 170.

decade before *The Gutenberg Galaxy* to *Williams Mix*, and a further decade before that he had composed a collage of a simpler sort in *Credo in Us* (1942), where a gramophone record provides one voice in a counterpoint otherwise for piano and percussion (Cage suggests the use of something by Beethoven, Dvořak, Sibelius or Shostakovich—music, therefore, from a wholly alien world of harmonic–symphonic form).

Nevertheless, the contact with McLuhan—and with another prophet of optimistic millenarianism, Buckminster Fuller—came at a time of change in Cage's work, the time when he had almost abandoned composition in favour of writing and lecturing. The texts of 1961–7 collected in his second volume, *A Year from Monday*, resonate with the joy he felt in his new status as a cultural phenomenon—joy that did not imply diminished responsibility; joy that was responsibility. In *0′ 0″* (1962) he overstepped his usual proscription of improvisation, and at the same time inscribed himself in his new status into the piece. What is presented here is not Cage's music but Cage himself, since he was the first and designated performer of the score's single instruction: 'In a situation provided with maximum amplification (no feedback) perform a disciplined action'. Like *Telemusik*, the work was a product of its composer's first visit to Japan: at the première, in Tokyo, Cage's disciplined action was the writing-out of the score. Like *Telemusik*, too, it marked its composer's awareness of himself as a global figure. On the world stage, and at a time of rapid, widespread social transformation, composing perhaps began to seem inconsequential—even evasive, too much a matter of 'an individual's conceptions'—and both Cage and Stockhausen returned from Tokyo to devote themselves more completely to group endeavours (especially in live electronic music) and to regroupings of music other than their own.

For example, most of Cage's rather few published compositions of 1963–8 belong to the *Variations* series and propose a multiplicity of activities: the sanctioned recordings of *Variations V* (1963), performed by Cage and Tudor, present vast sweeps of musical excerpts and other sound detritus. *HPSCHD* (1967–9), on which Cage collaborated with Lejaren Hiller as computer programmer, became in its public stagings a carnival of live musicians (up to seven harpsichordists playing music from Mozart to the present), tapes (up to fifty-one of them, each in its own temperament), slides, and films. Other 'works', never published, were perhaps only intended to happen once, like the *Musicircus* (1967) to which Cage invited various composers and performers, and the music went on along with films and slides in a large space with floating balloons and refreshment stalls.

These things were temporary—as temporary as the balloons and the hamburgers—and Cage's failure to publish *Musicircus* or the next year's *Reunion* may be taken as an acknowledgement of that. To revive those works now could only be an exercise in 1960s nostalgia; anarchy—as Cage's subsequent output so magnificently demonstrated—constantly has to be reinvented, for otherwise it is form and custom. Less obviously inevitable, perhaps, is the datedness of other music in which existing music was used not in a tumult of diversity but with deliberation, by the bar—the music, for instance, of George Crumb (b. 1929), whose works were conspicuously successful in the years around 1970. Crumb described himself as having 'an urge to fuse unrelated elements and juxtapose the seemingly incongruous',[26] as in his *Night of the Four Moons* for contralto and four players (1969), of which Richard Steinitz has remarked that: 'The direct quotations from Bach, Schubert or Chopin, heard through Crumb's strange and unworldly soundscape, acquire an amazing aura of distance both cultural and temporal. Surrealist museum exhibits, their mummified beauty seems utterly remote, like a childhood memory of warm, homely security.'[27] It worked. But it worked only as long as tonal and atonal were strictly separate categories, implying a similarly strict separation between ancient and modern. Once composers began re-establishing tonality, and working again in traditional genres (and Davies was doing both from the mid-1970s), such quotations as Crumb's lost the shock, the inadmissibility, on which their sentimental effect depended.

The problem of integrating quotations into a foreign musical substance—a problem that barely arises in the otherwise very different works from this period by Cage and Crumb—is tackled in most of what Bernd Alois Zimmermann (1918–70) wrote during his last decade. A few years older than most of his Darmstadt colleagues, Zimmermann had always been less adamant about the need, or the feasibility, of a completely fresh start, and alongside post-Webernian essays, such as his *Perspektiven* for two pianos (1955–6), he had written works with deeper roots in common practice, like his trumpet concerto *Nobody knows the trouble I see* (1954). (Two generations of German composers, from Hindemith and Krenek to Zimmermann and Henze, saw in jazz and blues at once a challenge and a solace, an instance of music being vigorously new and popular.) His resolution of this divergence was a doctrine of 'pluralism', first put into practice in his opera *Die Soldaten* (1958–64), which not only uses the full panoply of musical means—speech, song and *Sprechgesang*, a vivid score for large orchestra, and electronic sounds on tape—but also introduces quotations from Bach and other composers. Zimmermann's technique here evidently derives from that of the Violin Concerto of Berg, whose *Wozzeck* is a major influence on the opera as a whole, in the measure that Jakob Michael Reinhold Lenz, on whose play of 1776 the work is based, was an influence on Büchner.

Zimmermann's 'pluralism' was stimulated by his view of the musical world in which he found himself: the claims of the future and of the past—the claims of *Perspektiven* and of *Nobody knows the trouble I see*—could be reconciled only by accepting both, at the cost of stylistic unity. 'We should have the courage to admit that, in the light of musical reality, style is simply an anachronism.'[28] Hence the deliberate oppositions of his *Antiphonen* (1962)—not only between the viola soloist and the orchestra, as in any concerto (and he returned again and again to this most combative of forms), but also between recalled and original materials, and between

---

[26] Note with Nonesuch H 71255.   [27] 'The Music of George Crumb', *Contact*, 11 (1975), 14–22.
[28] From *Intervall und Zeit*, quoted in note with Teldec 9031 72775.

instrumental sound and speech from the players. Work on *Die Soldaten* appears to have released several other pieces in which confrontations between new and old are worked out, including *Monologe* for two pianos (1960–4), with its overlay of, and commentary on, quotations from Bach and Messiaen, or *Présence* for piano trio (1961), in which the three players are cast as literary characters—Don Quixote (violin), Molly Bloom (cello), and Ubu (piano)—whom the music leads through diverse encounters sharpened by quotations from Bach, Prokofiev, and others. The orchestral *Musique pour les soupers du roi Ubu* (1967) again takes Jarry's character as presiding genius for an unruly banquet of musical memories.

Unlike Davies, Zimmermann did not take the view that the music he composed was more real than the music he quoted: both were necessary to his works, and therefore equally integral and authentic. Bach in Zimmermann, or Bach in Berg, is not the same as Bach in Bach: something has happened, and it is the later composer who, responding to his musical situation, has made it happen. At least, this seems to be the position from which Zimmermann set out. 'One cannot avoid observing that we live in harmony with a huge diversity of culture from the most varied periods; that we exist simultaneously on many different levels of time and experience, most of which are neither connected with one another, nor do they appear to derive from one another. And yet, let's be quite honest—we feel at home in this network of countless tangled threads.'[29] Quite soon, though, the quotations in his music began to take on a more ominous resonance. In his orchestral *Photoptosis* (1968), there is no longer the attempt to conjure citations out of original music; instead Beethoven, Wagner, and the rest gather to observe the passing of a tradition, framed and supported by brilliant but empty rhetoric. Zimmermann's last works, before he committed suicide, are bleak essays on the death of art and the extinction of hope: the *Requiem für einem jungen Dichter* (1967–9) and the 'ecclesiastical action' *Ich wandte mich und sah an alles Unrecht, das geschah unter der Sonne* (1970).

The curve of Zimmermann's career suggests a gradual collapse of the ability, or perhaps even the wish, to control the material and affective power of the music of the past: his output seems to tell a story of ghosts who return. Kagel never lets them come so close. As an ironic observer of the musical world, he took the opportunity of the vogue for quotation—which usefully coincided with the Beethoven bicentenary—to ask questions about the phenomenon of the great composer. His chamber orchestral version of his multi-purpose *Ludwig van* (1969) reduces Beethoven themes to banality by empty repetition and distortion, and so provides an image of how music in western culture has its meaning changed in similar ways, through the endless repetition of the standard repertory and the distortions of performers. As with several other works of this period, Kagel also made a film version, in which the same points are made more explicit by the use, again ironic, of modes characteristic of 'serious' television, such as the historical documentary and the panel discussion.

[29] Ibid.

Other composers besides Kagel were prompted by the Beethoven anniversary to subject 'Ludwig van' to some scrutiny. Stockhausen, for example, created in *Opus 1970* a realization of his *Kurzwellen* in which Beethoven material on tape (fragments from the works and readings from the Heiligenstadt Testament) replaced the original shortwave radios as sources of ideas for intuitive elaboration by live electronic ensemble. According to the composer, the performers should be able 'to hear familiar, old, pre-formed musical material with new ears, to penetrate and transform it with a musical consciousness of today',[30] so that the music is explicitly removed from the musical and social contexts with which Kagel was concerned, and by which Zimmermann found himself oppressed. At least, that was perhaps the intention. Because of the tightness with which contexts are bound into Beethoven's music—the fact that just a bar, maybe even a chord, is enough to summon all kinds of images way beyond the structural effects and implications of the notes—irony is far more difficult to escape than had been the case in *Telemusik*. Stockhausen, lacking a sense of irony (as witness his jokes, or, more positively, the unashamed grandiosity of his visions), could not be satisfied, and *Opus 1970* had no life and no progeny after the occasion for which it had been made.

Meta-music

The chatter of quotations in new music became noisiest at some time close to the Beethoven year, and then subsided. It indicated what was perhaps the sharpest crisis in music since the eruption immediately before the First World War, a crisis that was again a crisis of confidence, productive in some cases of creative collapse or hysteria. Few composers were untouched. Apart from those already mentioned— musicians as diverse as Cage and Davies, Stockhausen and Zimmermann—composers who introduced quotations into their works included several established figures: Shostakovich cited excerpts from Wagner and Rossini's *William Tell* overture in his Fifteenth Symphony (1971); Michael Tippett (b. 1905) came back to the *Schreckensfanfare* from Beethoven's Ninth Symphony in his own Third (1972). Resistance to the trend was generally restricted to the categories of those who fell silent (such as Boulez, silence being another response to crisis) and of those who quoted not the substance of past music but its basic vocabulary in repetitive minimalism. The ending of the avant-garde thrusts had left a musical world with no great project, no direction ahead. A music of quotations could either celebrate that freedom from history, as in Cage, or else react savagely or sombrely to deracination.

However, either-ors are commoner in criticism than in art, and it was perfectly possible for works to be jubilant and monitory at the same time: the judgement belongs in any case, more or less, to the listener. There was also, as so often, a third alternative, which was neither to glory in confusion nor to let quotations worry and

---

[30] Note with DG 139 461.

disturb an intendedly original linear discourse, but rather to create new forms in which quotation was a necessity: meta-forms for meta-music. In such forms, old music is not set against new music, because the two are not present on the same level of action; the old music can work both on its own terms, and on the terms of its participation in new music. All that is required is the irony unexpectable from Stockhausen reworking Beethoven. All that was required was the irony Berio had shown in self-consciously using different musical languages, in creating solo pieces as performances, or in making new arrangements of his own and other music (an art of which he is the greatest master since another of music's chief ironists, Ravel).

The middle movement of Berio's *Sinfonia* for vocal octet and orchestra (1968–9) achieves a complex irony, since not only is it a wash of quotations, but that wash is contained within what is itself a quotation: the scherzo from Mahler's 'Resurrection' Symphony, a movement whose meandering river-like progress is found now to be carrying an abundant flotsam of memories. What was form in Mahler (music made of notes) becomes meta-form in Berio (music made of other music)— though this is not a complete change, since there is evidence of deliberate allusion in the original (the form was already meta-form),[31] and since, too, Berio's treatment may be just the virtuoso actualization of associations any listener might bring to an experience of the Mahler (form becomes meta-form in the way that it is received). Berio's task was not to compose so much as to decompose (to block out more or less of the Mahler movement as it went along), to assemble (to select at each moment the elements that could take their places on the Mahler stream), and to comment, largely in the vocal parts, which keep up their own current of cross-references impinging on a recitation from Beckett's *The Unnamable*.

Example 33 shows the opening of the movement, where the first discernible quotations come from the start of the 'Jeux de vagues' from Debussy's *La mer* (bars 4–5: reeds and strings, plus figure in glockenspiel and harp) and from the beginning of Mahler's Fourth Symphony (bars 2–7: flutes and snare drum, with men humorously adding directions from the score). These citations are duly recognized by the two sopranos, but the second contralto has noticed also the arrival of the wholesale borrowing of the Mahler scherzo in something close to its original scoring (bars 7 ff: woodwind and timpani). The connections, already, are of various kinds: connections of oeuvre (Mahler's), of rhythmic character (elements of ostinato in both the Mahler samplings, and of scherzo in both the Debussy and the gathering Mahler matrix), of harmony (the G major of the Fourth Symphony lighting the approach of C minor with the Second), of verbal association (the Mahler scherzo started out as a song, 'Des Antonius von Padua Fischpredigt', and so has a watery link to the Debussy). In its gentle reminder of the many varieties of musical understanding, the movement stands out against the 1950s–Boulezian insistence on material structure alone. It also has a superbness of public effect that the status of the erstwhile avant garde was beginning to make possible: the ultimate version of Stockhausen's

---

[31] See David Osmond-Smith, *Playing on Words: a Guide to Luciano Berio's Sinfonia* (London, 1985), 41–3, which provides an Ariadne's thread through the whole work.

Ex. 33. Berio, *Sinfonia* (1968–9): III

Momente is another witness to this brief time when it seemed that modern music was on the verge of reaching large audiences—the large audiences who had recently participated in the rediscovery of Mahler.

However it may have been planned, the rest of the work seems to lead towards and then depart from the centrepiece, whose strong presence created problems of containment not settled until Berio added a fifth movement to the original four. The other movements could hardly be simulacra of the Mahler reworking, but nor could they ignore it. Continuity of sound was provided by the webbing of amplified voices and instrumental drifts (the work was conceived for the Swingle Singers, whose speciality was scat-singing Bach); continuity of manner came from the absorption throughout in processes of generation and reworking. For example, the finale is, Berio has said, at once the first movement's completion and a further commentary on everything that has gone before: 'The first four parts of *Sinfonia* are to the fifth as Mahler's scherzo is to the third.'[32] The work ends, then, in self-quotation, in meta-meta-music.

Crossing great swathes of time, seeming to evoke the origins of music in the burgeoning cries and calls of the first movement, the *Sinfonia* is yet very much a work of its age, packed with its age's hope that the analysis of underlying structures would reveal similarities between the apparently dissimilar, and carrying the fresh-found voices of its world: Mahler, Lévi-Strauss on the beginnings of myth (quoted in the first movement), Martin Luther King (for whom the second movement is an elegy). As a work of reportage, it takes its imagery, as *Telemusik* did, from radio, from tuning in. Radio had given composers of Berio's generation their main opportunities, both in presenting concerts and in providing facilities for electronic music (Berio and Maderna had been joint directors of an Italian radio electronic studio in Milan in the late 1950s and early 1960s); radio also, by placing the knob-turning listener in seemingly immediate control, provided a positive experience of contemporary confusion. Hence the importance of radio as a metaphor for composers as they moved away from the search for a new language to the discovery of the many languages already existing.

For Berio, the many languages included not only those from the history of western music he placed in the middle movement of the *Sinfonia*, but also the languages of folk music from around the world. In *Folk Songs* (1964), written for Berberian, he fashioned a cycle of sophisticated arrangements not so distant from those of Stravinsky, Ravel, and Falla, but later works place ethnic materials in much larger and more complex structures of cherishing and analysis. *Coro* for forty singers and forty instrumentalists (1975–7), for example, takes up not particular tunes but models of musical language and behaviour from different traditions—the art song of western Europe, the heterophony of central Africa, the shape of Yugoslav melody—in 'an anthology of different modes of "setting to music" '.[33] But where the *Sinfonia*, even in its lament over King, had held out the prospect of a new dawn of jostling

<hr>

[32] Rosanna Dalmonte and Bálint András Varga, *Luciano Berio: Two Interviews* (London, 1985), 108.

[33] Berio's note with DG 423 902.

multiplicity, *Coro* is more commemorative than celebratory, repeatedly gathering its many performers and many cultures into clustered monoliths on a line of Neruda: 'Come and see the blood in the streets.' The mood of 1968 had changed.

That change can be heard, too, in Stockhausen's music, in the shift from the optimistic universality of his electronic *Hymnen* (1966–7) to the autobiographical dreams of *Sirius* (1975–7) and the works beyond. *Hymnen* repeats the intermodulatory techniques of *Telemusik*, though on a much larger scale (*Telemusik*, at seventeen and a half minutes, is an item, whereas *Hymnen* has the two-hour span of an entire concert) and to quite different effect, since now the raw materials are chosen to be recognizable and to elicit associations: they are the national anthems of numerous countries, sampled from recordings. Another difference is in the variety that spaciousness makes possible, for where *Telemusik* was quick and electric, *Hymnen* is grandly loose. It voyages from what sounds like poor reception (again the radio experience) into the clear exposure of an anthem, or from passages which take up the methods of *Kontakte* (operating, before the listener's ears, processes of transformation and decomposition on the recordings) to purely verbal sequences, like the multi-lingual litany on the word 'red' or the ominous calls of a croupier. And the scale and the range of the material are matched by the versatility of the work, which is, Stockhausen has said, 'composed in such a way that various screenplays or librettos for films, operas and ballets can be written to the music'.[34] Not only that, but 'the order of the characteristic sections and the total duration are variable. Depending on the dramatic requirements, regions may be extended, added or omitted.' The work can therefore, by design, preserve its character through deformation; it has that amplitude and that resilience. Stockhausen had moved from the kind of locking process at work in *Kreuzspiel* through moment form to a libertarianism that *Hymnen* exemplifies in both structure and content. His own radical alterations to the original tape include a version with a live electronic ensemble to imitate what they hear and forge connections between anthems, and one in which, additionally, an orchestra plays along in the third of the four 'regions'. (This last version was, like Berio's *Sinfonia*, written for the New York Philharmonic. Both composers had spent long periods in the region of San Francisco—Berio, based in America between 1963 and 1972, taught at Mills College in Oakland, besides the Juilliard School in New York, and Stockhausen was at the University of California at Davis in 1966–7—and so both were close to the source of the new anarchy as it began to emerge.)

A couple of the processes at work in the original tape are suggested in Example 34, which follows the simplified notation of the 'listening score' devised to guide the ear, not to show, as the published version of *Studie II* had shown, how the piece was made. Here the German anthem is torn between a unison chorus (downward stems) and an orchestral accompaniment (upward stems), with jolting internal repetitions; then the choral and orchestral sound is magically sustained, gradually

---

[34] Preface to the score.

Ex. 34. Stockhausen, *Hymnen* (1966–7)

pulled towards opposite extremes of pitch as if by giant magnets, and finally allowed to continue when the octave interval has been reached. As so often in the work, these electronic transformations, operating on known material, bring about temporal dislocations: the choral and orchestral recordings, for instance, are two streams of unfolding time subject to the new time scheme of the piece. *Hymnen* not only mimics but also deconstructs radio experience, to show the difference between time as in the recording (time which can be edited or frozen) and time as in the broadcast (time which goes on). Like Berio's *Sinfonia*, it is a meta-world, a window into other worlds, but with the crucial difference that the music viewed here is music devoid of musical meaning—music which is all symbol, and so can be manipulated without irony. *Hymnen* is even a window into itself, for later in the second region the development of German and African anthems is cut off for the insertion of a conversation between the composer and his assistant recorded during the composition of the piece.

Stockhausen gave a simpler explanation of how his particular material allowed him to work in this meta-realm, where the music is what happens to the constituent music: 'If one integrates familiar music into the composition of unfamiliar, new music,' he wrote, 'the listener can hear particularly clearly how it has been integrated: untransformed, more or less transformed, transposed, modulated, etc.'[35] But here again was a change from *Kreuzspiel* and *Kontra-Punkte*, and one in keeping with the time: the composer's activity was to be apparent to the listener as the music proceeded. (The same hope seems to have helped prompt minimalism, at least for Steve Reich.) National anthems offered 'the most familiar music imaginable'; they were also, in a radio studio, readily available. But Stockhausen has not wanted to disguise the importance to him also of their associations, and thereby the importance of his work as having to do not only with music and meta-music but with nationhood and supra-nationhood. For the ending, the recorded bands and choirs are cleared away to leave, floated over the sounds of the composer's breathing, a manufactured anthem 'which belongs to the utopian realm of *Hymnunion* in *Harmondy* under *Pluramon*'. Such babbling puns were to become characteristic of him when conscious of himself as prophet or lover, and the ending of *Hymnen* is perhaps the first portent—promise or warning as one may take it to be—of his awareness of a divine mission. What was tested and learned through the art of quotation was music's capacity to mean. Stockhausen, always more extreme than his colleagues, discovered himself as a mouthpiece.

[35] Preface to the score.

Music Theatre

In the 1950s, when attention generally was fixed on musical fundamentals, few young composers wanted to work in the theatre. Indeed, to express that want was almost enough, as in the case of Henze, self-consciously to separate oneself from the avant garde: Boulez, while earning his living as a theatre musician, kept his creative work almost entirely separate until near the end of his time with Jean-Louis Barrault, when he wrote a score for a production of the *Oresteia* (1955), and even that work he never published or otherwise accepted into his official oeuvre. Things began to change on both sides of the Atlantic around 1960, the year when Cage produced his *Theatre Piece* and Nono began *Intolleranza*, the first opera from inside the Darmstadt circle. However, opportunities to present new operas remained rare: even in Germany, where there were dozens of theatres producing opera, and where the new operas of the 1920s had found support, the Hamburg State Opera, under the direction of Rolf Liebermann from 1959 to 1973, was unusual in commissioning works from Penderecki, Kagel, and others. Also, most composers who had lived through the analytical 1950s were suspicious of standard genres, wanting new musical–theatrical forms that sprang from new material rather than from what appeared a long-moribund tradition. (It was already a truism that no opera since *Turandot* had joined the regular international repertory. What was not realized until the late 1970s was that there could be a living operatic culture based on rapid obsolescence.) Both from institutions and from artists, therefore, there was a pressure to invent new unions of music and theatre, while Cage's work—especially the piano pieces he had written for Tudor in the 1950s—had shown that no 'new union' was necessary, that all music is by nature theatre, that all performance is drama.

Opera and 'Opera'

Ligeti no doubt spoke for most of his colleagues in the late 1960s and early 1970s when he declared that 'I cannot, will not compose a traditional "opera"; for me the operatic genre is irrelevant today—it belongs to a historical period utterly different from the present compositional situation.' No doubt he spoke for many, too, in going on to say that, nevertheless, 'I do not mean at all that I cannot compose a work for the facilities an opera house offers.'[1] (At this point he had written *Aventures* and its sequel *Nouvelles aventures*, two pieces for three singers and ensemble that

---

[1] Ursula Stürzbecher, *Werkstattgespräche mit Komponisten* (Cologne 1971), 43.

can be staged, though their flux of minuscule wordless dramas, careering from comedy to pathos, is freer and more immediate without theatrical trappings. They show how he was able to profit from his position as a mature student of the western European avant garde: by following his models—in this case, Kagel—while at the same time exaggerating them, and bringing to them his own charm and perfectionism.) But by the time he came to write his 'Opernhaus-Stück', *Le Grand Macabre* (1975–6), there had been a change in his view, and a change too in the musical climate. The age of anti-opera had passed; the new work would have to be, as he said, an 'anti-anti-opera'.

During the decade or so before *Le Grand Macabre* opera had been the preserve of composers willing and able to deal in some way with the genre's traditions, whether by following them (Henze and Zimmermann), by analysing them (Berio), by countering them (Kagel), or by seizing on the single truth that opera gives music a tongue with which to speak (Nono). Nono's was a rare escape. Why the power of tradition should have been felt so much more strongly in opera than in, say, orchestral or piano music (there are no operatic equivalents to *Gruppen* or the sonatas of Boulez and Barraqué) is a complex matter, having to do, perhaps, with the rigidity and smallness of the standard opera repertory, and therefore with the costs of experiment (financial and aesthetic costs) and the pressure to conform. The great lesson of the standard repertory is that the story is paramount, that the music should be in synchrony with the story's narrative flow. Diatonic music, with its progressive narratives of harmonic movement and thematic transformation, is very good at that, which is why opera flourished during the era of diatonic music's supremacy, from Monteverdi to Puccini and Strauss. Atonal opera is opera in crisis: *Erwartung*, *Wozzeck*. And crisis is hard to perpetuate. Hence the need for later composers either to acknowledge tradition in writing operas, or else to find new forms and new kinds of narrative, whether in oriental theatre, in folklore, in contemporary western drama, or in unstructured 'happenings' of the kind enabled by Cage and the Fluxus composers.

Henze, the most prolific and most performed opera composer since Britten, is so by virtue of his warm, thorough-going acceptance of opera's history and conditions. Where Berg in *Wozzeck* wrote a symphony at some ironic remove from the action, as if to suggest how the normal world of diatonic–thematic narrative was now broken and suspended, Henze's symphony in *The Bassarids* (1965)—a reworking of the *Bacchae* of Euripides, for which W. H. Auden and Chester Kallman wrote the libretto—is plushly in the foreground. As he has explained, the first movement is a sonata which establishes the conflict between the principals, Dionysus and Pentheus, as a musical conflict between fluid, unmeasured, ululating voice (the call of Dionysus, a tenor) and staccato trumpet fanfare.[2] The second movement is a scherzo in the form of a suite of Dionysian dances; the third, incorporating Dionysus's hypnotizing of Pentheus, is an adagio succeeded by a fugue; and the finale is a passacaglia.

[2] See 'The Bassarids: Hans Werner Henze talks to Paul Griffiths', *Musical Times*, 115 (1974), 831–2.

The Bassarids was the culmination of the sensuous, unashamedly nostalgic style Henze had pursued since moving to Italy a decade before. The symphonic structure, recalling not so much Berg as Mahler, is ample enough to include gestures made in diverse directions, from the knowing, deliberately vulgarized pastiche of Baroque French cantata style in the intermezzo interrupting the slow movement to quotations from Bach, both as an earlier master of the siciliana rhythm on which the opera floats (Henze belongs squarely, even self-consciously, in the line of German artists rhapsodizing the Mediterranean) and as a source of references to support a parallel between the Crucifixion and the sacrifice of Adonis. (What are here treated as separate waves—historicism, theatre, politics—were flowing together.) The integration of varied materials and opposed themes, as displayed in the opera, is in Henze's view a characteristic of the 'segregated' artist, the 'outlaw'. Undoubtedly he sees himself in this role, at odds with conventional society by virtue of his homosexuality (for him, as for Britten, writing opera is a way to express both apartness and the wish for acceptance), and artistically contrary both to tradition (though ever less so) and (ever more so) to the avant garde, since he turned aside from the tentative approach to total serialism he had essayed in his Second Quartet (1952). His inclusion in 1958 in the issue of *Die Reihe* devoted to 'young composers'—along with Stockhausen, Boulez, Nono, and the rest—had already been an anachronism; by the time of *The Bassarids* the divide was absolute: *Momente* had already been written. 'Never would he aim at an accord with the basic tendencies of his time', Henze writes of his chosen type; instead he must devote himself to a minority 'which merits his sympathy and which excites his sensual and spiritual substance'.[3]

Henze's concern with the individual as a feeling being—even with himself as a feeling being—is part of his grand Romantic inheritance, and it has inclined him, as it did the Romantics, to another genre in which these relationships with sympathetic minorities and uncomprehending masses could be played out: the concerto. *The Bassarids* was followed by a rush of such works: chamber concertos for double bass and for oboe and harp (several such works were written by various composers for the marital duo of Heinz and Ursula Holliger), and the determinedly autobiographical Second Piano Concerto. But then this absorption in his own personal and artistic situation was joined by a commitment to the interests of all those ignored or oppressed by bourgeois society. The darling of the Salzburg Festival, for which *The Bassarids* had been written, became a revolutionary; the poet of the soul began to shout about social iniquities. It was 1968.

In the quasi-operatic oratorio *Das Floss der 'Medusa'* of that year, dedicated to Che Guevara, Henze dealt with the historical episode in which a group of shipwrecked men were abandoned to a raft by their officers, and left to face the perils of drowning and starvation. After the experience of its abortive Berlin première, lost amid struggles between police and left-wing students, Henze spent a year in Cuba,

---

[3] *Essays* (Mainz, 1964), 32.

writing his Sixth Symphony, and expressing in that score his delight in the sonorities and rhythms of Cuban music, as well as reaffirming his alignment with socialism by including in the elaborate polyphony quotations from Vietnamese and Greek protest songs.

But apart from the appearance of a new edge and anger in the music, and a partial, momentary relinquishment of continuity, not so much had changed. The Caribbean was a new Mediterranean: a new south, a new sensuality, a new escape. And the revolutionary activist—whether appearing as a character in the works or writing them—was a new guise for the Romantic hero. Henze's awareness of this is perhaps signalled by his preoccupation not so much with revolution as with the problems of being a revolutionary artist—problems he addressed in his first post-1968 piece designed for stage presentation, the 'show' *Das langwierige Weg in die Wohnung der Natascha Ungeheuer* (1971), scored for baritone and several ensembles. How, this work asks, can the left-wing intellectual justify the part-way commitment of pushing for revolution in his work but taking no active part in the class struggle? The music, like much that Henze wrote during this period, abounds in quotations and opportunities for more or less directed improvisation, as well as in broader references of cultural type, these bringing out the nature and force of the alternative siren songs by which the artist hero is beset. A *Pierrot* quintet, dressed in hospital overalls, represents the sick bourgeoisie (as so often for composers of this generation—not least Boulez—Schoenberg is a Freudian–Oedipal father). A brass quintet, with police helmets, are the agents of the oppressive state machine, just as the brass in *The Bassarids* perform for Pentheus. A rock group provides the voice of the underground. And there are two instrumental soloists: a percussionist, whose violent, physical activity is a metaphor for the complete engagement from which the hero withholds himself, and a Hammond organist as plutocrat.

Henze took up the contradictions exposed in this perhaps necessarily confused score in another concerto—his Second Violin Concerto of the same year—and dealt with them on a more abstract level, though still theatrically. The soloist is here cast, in a dramatization of what had been the case in Henze's earlier concertos, as the self-willed Romantic virtuoso, trying at once to relate to the system (the orchestra) and to prove his independence: his quixotic condition (and a male soloist does seem to be necessarily implied) is displayed in his being costumed as the Baron von Munchhausen of German story. He plays; he speaks. And the music unwinds around a poetic commentary by Hans Magnus Enzensberger on Gödel's theorem, the theorem that any complex system contains propositions which, within that system, can be neither proved nor refuted. From this the work conjures the extrapolation that any system—especially any musical or social system, one is led to infer—must destroy itself.

Undoubtedly Henze's own system of political expression was doing so. The allurements he felt were, perhaps beyond those of *Natascha Ungeheuer*, the dreams and fantasies and pleasures of his earlier music—things he had carried with him, as he had carried his southern attachments to the New World. His Cuba, as sung in his

Sixth Symphony, in his dramatic 'recital' *El Cimarrón* (1969–70), and in his 'vaude-ville' *La Cubana* (1973), is not that of Castro and the struggle to build a socialist soci-ety but that of the tropical forest, of plantations lying under the beating sun, of seedy urban night life and exotic dance rhythms. His sympathies, as expressed in *Das Floss der 'Medusa', El Cimarrón, Natascha Ungeheuer, La Cubana*, and the Second Violin Concerto, are with the individual rather than the mass, which is cus-tomarily presented, Romantically, as wanting to have a restraining influence on the flood of life and love in the individual's breast (*Der Prinz von Homburg*) or else as following blindly in the charismatic leader's wake (*The Bassarids*). Henze's personal and artistic apartnesses remain, of course, relevant.

The single striking difference in his explicitly revolutionary output is the absence of opera, as if that most bourgeois of musical institutions had to be spurned, and replaced by the alternative concert-hall theatrical forms of such works as *El Cimarrón, Natascha Ungeheuer*, and the Second Violin Concerto. Only a decade after *The Bassarids* did Henze return to opera with *We Come to the River* (1974–6), which nominally carries the torch of revolution into the precincts of sedate culture: the libretto, by Edward Bond, makes the point fervently and forcefully. Henze, though, prevaricates. The casting of the Emperor as a mezzo role seems to be meant to indicate effeteness, but the allusion is to a modern tradition of entrusting Handel's castrato parts to women singers, and thereby to a world of vibrant sensu-ousness and heroism. Also, the Emperor's aria has enough weight and seductive-ness to outbalance any intended irony. No other character is so roundly presented: the sympathy for the common soldier is as generalized as the contempt for upper-class ladies is shrill.

We Come to the River marks a point in Henze's career where his desire to be polit-ically on the side of rebel angels is finally being routed by the return of innate musi-cal impulses that place him firmly among the conservatives. Soon he was to give up the struggle, and to accept the rewards and the limitations of his eminence and expertise within mainstream musical culture. Opera returned to the centre of his world, and his decisive, if still uneasy, rapprochement with the German tradition was marked by a new batch of string quartets in 1975–6 and, notably, by his Seventh Symphony (1983–4).

For Henze, opera became a problematic medium at the time of his political engagement; for Nono and Berio, it was the proper arena for controversy and provocation. Nono's commitment seems to have led him to opera even at a time when the genre seemed most outmoded: *Intolleranza* was a spurt of energy against the nature of the medium, doing away with story and display, insisting on the pow-erful presence of the chorus, and introducing into the theatre the brutally new sound-world of electronic music. In the case of Berio, his theatre works of the 1960s are more overtly political than anything else in his output, even if the message gets more complexly overlaid along the line from *Passaggio* to *Laborintus II* (1965) to *Opera* (1970).

Laborintus II is a double labyrinth of words and music, one in which the Ariadne's thread is a spoken narration written by Edoardo Sanguineti around phrases and images from Dante's *Inferno*. As this line of text unwinds, so it triggers music from an ensemble of voices and instruments covering a broad spectrum of styles from madrigalian euphony to contemporary jazz: we hear the voice of a lover, of a mob, of a flute, a trumpet or a harp, of the electronic constructs on tape. The ranging is typical of the time, but where Henze in *Natascha Ungeheuer*, for instance, used different styles as distinct social tokens, Berio's purpose is to tease out musical connections: what most distinguishes the score is the fluid movement from one situation to another, the hazy in-between rather than the specific reference. The work lies also in between music and language, in an area Berio had already explored in such works as *Thema*, *Circles*, and *Epifanie*. As in his *Chemins* series, where a previously composed instrumental solo is surrounded by music for ensemble, the voices and instruments of *Laborintus II* provide an oblique commentary on the spoken text, while at the same time the text is an oblique commentary on the music—a kind of running poetic programme note. Yet another in-betweenness of this opalescent score is its midway status between concert hall and theatre. It has no explicit action, but in concert it tends to sound like an unstaged opera. Perhaps its home is in the medium for which it was written, and to which so much of this period's music appeals, in grateful thanks: radio.

The maze structure of *Laborintus II*—another constant of the time, as witness Boulez's Third Sonata or Stockhausen's *Momente*—is also a feature of Berio's first opera, whose title is a signal that its concern is with the genre itself. Berio probably would have echoed Ligeti's statement about the impossibility of writing just another opera, a contribution to a history. His answer was to take that history as his subject, both by self-consciously creating operatic forms, as Berg had done in *Lulu*, and by searching back to the origins of opera, beginning each act with an 'Air' to a text from Striggio's libretto for Monteverdi's *Orfeo*. *Opera* is a celebration of opera, and also—because it refuses to abide by the rules it entertains—an implicit criticism. The history of opera is to be seen as a history of dissolution and decline, going on in parallel with other sliding catastrophes the work presents: the history of western capitalism and the sinking of the *Titanic*.

Music theatre

If opera in the mid-1960s seemed in its dotage, there appeared to be new possibilities in smaller, more flexible combinations of music and drama, often denoted as 'music theatre'. There was a sporadic history of such works: *Pierrot lunaire* and *Histoire du soldat* were the classic twentieth-century examples ubiquitously cited; Monteverdi's *Combattimento* was a distant ancestor. But there was no precedent for the sudden and brief flowering that happened now, and that could be seen in the work of composers as removed from the avant garde as Britten (in his church parables).

The explosion of music theatre out of opera was more than a metaphor in the case of the new genre's most active proponent, Davies, whose work on his opera *Taverner* sparked off an interrupting succession of dramatic pieces for smaller forces, beginning with *Revelation and Fall* for soprano and sixteen players (1965–6). His model was decisively Schoenberg rather than Stravinsky or Monteverdi, and he was instrumental in founding a performing ensemble—originally called the Pierrot Players, later the Fires of London—based on the *Pierrot* line-up, for which all his later music-theatre pieces were composed. *Revelation and Fall*, though scored for a larger group, makes musical reference to Schoenberg, and also enters that Viennese period by way of its Trakl text and its allusion also to Lehár, in a characteristic love–hate embrace of light music. It is also typical of Davies in taking the expression of extreme emotion as by itself dramatic. He is a dramatist of the individual (and especially of the individual under stress), not of relationships, and all his best theatre pieces are for soloists: the scarlet-habited nun of *Revelation and Fall*, screaming into a megaphone at the moment of crisis, the even more unhinged male vocalist of *Eight Songs for a Mad King* (1969), the nude male dancer of *Vesalii icones* (also 1969).

Based on a story that King George III in his madness tried to teach birds to sing, *Eight Songs* places its instrumentalists in giant cages to witness and suffer the manic ravings of the soloist, whose part calls for a huge range, both in pitch and in vocal colour. If this is the most spectacular of Davies's dramatic inventions, *Vesalii icones* is the most intense. The dancer, whose gestures mirror both the engravings in the sixteenth-century anatomy text by Vesalius and the Stations of the Cross, lays bare the agonies of Christ, while the instruments—among which the cello has the principal role as the dancer's shadow, partner, or ideal—add further layers of analysis and distortion, in which Davies's characteristic use of hidden and overt parody keeps the music on the disquieting border between commitment and mockery.[4] At the eighth station, for instance, there is a complex masquerade of musical images stimulated by the episode in which St Veronica wipes Christ's face and receives the imprint of his features on her cloth. The opening of this section has the cello declaiming a theme from Davies's *Ecce manus tradentis* for soloists, chorus and instruments (1965), a work itself based on the plainsong setting of those words: the chant of betrayal is thus doubly betrayed by the time it reaches *Vesalii icones*. At the same time the piano decorates a second plainsong theme in the style of a nineteenth-century salon piece. Subsequently the material is bent to allude to the scherzos of two Beethoven symphonies, to de la Rue's *L'homme armé* Mass, and to Davies's own *Missa super L'homme armé*. There are also more flagrant, even exhibitionist parodies, as at the sixth Station, where the mocking of Christ is the occasion for twisting the *L'homme armé* tune into a comfortable Victorian-style hymn (that style itself a sort of blasphemy, the music insists) and later into a foxtrot, which the dancer is to play on a honky-tonk piano. Parody and drama in this work spring

---

[4] See Michael Taylor, 'Maxwell Davies's *Vesalii icones*', *Tempo*, 92 (1970), 22–7.

from the same source: the violence shown on stage is a violence which the music is doing to itself.

Davies's dependence on Schoenberg is paralleled by the relation to Stravinsky in the work of his colleague Birtwistle—to the clear-cut forms of such works as the Symphonies of Wind Instruments and *Agon*, and to the rustic theatre of *Renard* and *Histoire du soldat*. (The composers continued their association after Manchester: the Pierrot Players were founded under their joint direction.) Birtwistle's first major theatre work was the chamber opera *Punch and Judy* (1966), which is based on the old puppet shows, and which presents a gallery of characters who are part clown, part monster, all of them still puppet-like in their abrupt and grotesque behaviour, their appalling passions, and their murderous savagery. Parody is part of Birtwistle's arsenal too, but more important is a pure fury of gesture: for example, the high woodwind chords of screeching alarm that entered his music in *Tragœdia* for ensemble (1965). The Schoenberg–Davies violence is a violence of strain within culture, whereas the Stravinsky–Birtwistle violence is a violence of unassimilated disparities.

Punch and Judy is, like Stravinsky's *Renard*, closed and cyclic: a rite of death and resurrection, night and day, winter and summer. Its highly symmetrical structure includes, for example, four 'Melodramas' in which Punch traps his victims in word-play, each followed by a 'Murder Ensemble' which is the celebration of a ritual exe-cution; and these larger sections are filled with tiny, compact forms, often strung together in patterns of verse and refrain. Though the work is nominally an opera, it relates to the music-theatre tradition not only in its links with *Renard* but also in its reduced scale and its dramatic style. The action is to be presented as if from a pup-pet booth, in which the characters go through their motions and in which also a wind quintet is seated, the pit orchestra consisting of just ten further players. As for dramatic style, the cyclic ceremonial necessarily discards narrative continuity, and the characters are sharp-featured, bright-coloured figures in formal patterns of ferocious hate and consuming lust.

Instrumental Theatre

The antiphony in *Punch and Judy* between the stage quintet and the pit band is one signal that Birtwistle's drama belongs to the instrumentalists as well as to the singers. Accordingly, the work's progeny includes not only his subsequent theatri-cal output—beginning with the magical-humorous *Down by the Greenwood Side*, which is another ceremony of killing and rebirth, another touch with English folk art, and another assembly of zesty fragments—but also his *Verses for Ensembles* (1969, see Example 35), a drama enacted by instrumentalists, and played out on dif-ferent platforms. The three percussionists have one level for their noise instru-ments and another for their xylophones and glockenspiels; the five woodwind players are seated at the left when playing high instruments and at the right when

Ex. 35. Birtwistle, *Verses for Ensembles* (1969)

Ex. 36. Kagel, *Match* (1964)

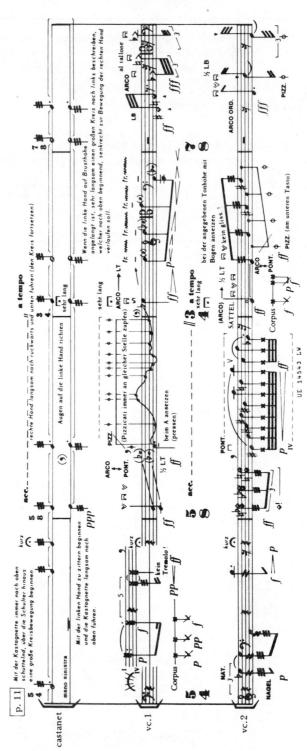

using their lower equivalents; the brass quintet has its own station; and there are also antiphonally separated desks for trumpet duets and for woodwind solos accompanied by the horn. Example 35 shows the opening of the first of two climactic sections of echoing and answer placed within the sequence of 'verses' for different groupings—sections which in their severe pulsation look forward to the time-measuring that underlies many of Birtwistle's works of the next decade. The arresting quality of the music in performance can be imagined.

The idea of musicians in movement was another cherished notion of the 1960s and early 1970s: it was put into effect, for instance, by Berio in *Circles* (perhaps the first such work), by Boulez in his *Domaines* for a clarinettist strolling among six ensembles, and by Stockhausen in his *Harlekin* for dancing solo clarinettist (1975), a work that perhaps instigated his projection of instrumentalists as characters in his operatic cycle *Licht*. But the more fundamental idea, which perhaps come out of the music that Cage composed for David Tudor, was that musical performance is by nature dramatic, and that a soloist in concert dress, playing on a platform, is an actor. The drama of performance is a current in all of Birtwistle and in all of Berio, even where it is not emphasized by movement or by unusual orchestral layouts. It is a current, too, in all of Kagel, though in his case what is on show is not only musical expertise. His *Match* (1964), for example, is a musical contest between rival cellists, refereed by a percussionist: the extreme difficulty of the cello parts may be judged from Example 36, and if the calculated absurdity of the enterprise is not evident from the score, it is abundantly clear in the composer's film version. (*Match* is one of several Kagel pieces that seem to demand the close-up, deadpan inspection of the camera, and that belong to a cinematic tradition of wordless comic shorts.)

Another Kagel piece, *Der Atem* (1970), is one of many works by him concerned with the pathology of performance and with performance as pathology. According to his description: 'A retired wind player devotes himself to the continual repetition of the same thing: maintaining his instruments. At each moment he goes to the cupboard, takes out the instruments and puts them back, oils them, blows into them, wipes the saliva traps, warms the reeds and the mouthpieces, silently does some exercises; often he talks to himself while polishing away all the time. Occasionally he happens to play, properly speaking.'

It was Kagel, almost inevitably, who created the anti-opera that Ligeti had anticipated and been obliged to go beyond, for Kagel's amused, ironic eye could hardly fail to turn the opera house inside out. His *Staatstheater* (1967–70) uses all the resources of such an institution—principals, chorus, orchestra, corps de ballet, scenery, costumes—in activities that satirize, ignore or contravene customary purpose, the soloists being brought together in a crazy sixteen-part ensemble, the dancers put through their paces in gymnastic exercises. But not all Kagel's theatre works of the period were so absurd or so loosely structured. In *Tremens* (1963–5) he considered the effect of hallucinogenic drugs on aural experience: the subject was presented in a hospital cubicle, forcibly encouraged by a doctor to listen to tapes of music which a live ensemble distorted, as if projecting the subjects's imagined versions. And in *Mare nostrum* (1973–5) he played with the idea of a party of Amazonians trying to make sense of Mediterranean culture, so that the work displays the relativity of norms, musical and social, and the danger of condescension in anthropology.

Stockhausen, though close to Kagel in developing instrumental theatre, is emphatically not an ironist: dramatic action in his works is deliberate, even portentous, and the intention is not to make sceptical comments about the dominant culture but rather to introduce revelations of a new one. Stockhausen is also an exemplary figure in the context of post-1945 opera and music theatre, and its history of neglect followed by abundance, since until 1968 he had composed almost nothing with a theatrical component (the single exception was *Originale*, a 1961 version of *Kontakte* that took the form of a regulated happening, with contributions from Cologne artists and other 'originals'), whereas since 1971 almost all his works have been determinedly dramatic: even '*Atem gibt das Leben . . .*', conceived in 1974 as a simple piece for amateur choir, was later revised as a 'choral opera'. Of course, the composer of *Gruppen*, of *Kontakte*, of *Momente* was always a dramatist in his handling of sound and in his set-up of sounding resources: even the tape pieces are dramas, if invisible ones. But the later works attempt to dramatize material coming from beyond the concert hall: events in the composer's life, views of the nature and purpose of sound, and, most especially, a mythology of extra-terrestrial beings and universal spirits.

Two orchestral works of the early seventies, *Trans* (1971) and *Inori* (1973–4), show Stockhausen's dramatic imagination in unusual focus. *Trans* presents its audience with the awesome spectacle of a string orchestra seated in close rows behind a magenta-lit gauze, solemnly unfolding a sequence of still, dense harmonies. From behind come the amplified but indistinct sounds of wind and percussion groups in marching chords or swirling melodies, this music impervious to the implacable crashes of a weaving shuttle (heard at irregular intervals from loudspeakers), to which the strings respond each time with a change of chord. All this, like Kagel's *Match*, came to its composer in a dream, and there is a further connection with Kagel in the four moments of surreal comedy that are superimposed on the rest: the first of these has a viola player performing a virtuoso cadenza, 'like a little wound-up toy instrument'[5] switched on by a marching drummer. But what is particularly Stockhausen's in the present age is the majesty of the conception, and the way its execution is at once bold and tacky: it is a great work by the Berlioz or the Liszt of our time.

The larger *Inori* is comparable in this respect, and in its massive orchestral sonorities, which map out the development of a melody through a two-hour span in phases concentrating on rhythm, dynamics, melody, harmony, and polyphony, as if in a resumé of musical history. But where *Trans* made theatre out of orchestral performance, *Inori* adds the actions of a mime, or pair of mimes, in attitudes of wor-

[5] Cott, *Stockhausen*, 63.

ship taken from many different cultures, these actions of prayer seeming to be amplified by the orchestra: the Japanese title has the meaning of 'Adorations'. Or at least this is how the work was first presented. The solo part is simply marked for 'Beter' (worshipper or worshippers) in the score, and is notated as a melodic line which could be sung or played on an instrument. However, mimed performance, interpreting each pitch as a basic gesture, would seem essential to the work's ceremonial character. Example 37 shows a simplified extract in which the solo part comprises the third of the fundamental melody's five sections; the part's dynamics are notated numerically on a scale of increasing loudness. The extreme differentiation of dynamics is one of the tasks Stockhausen has repeatedly set himself since the mid-1970s.

Ex. 37. Stockhausen, *Inori* (1973–4)

Inori is typical of Stockhausen's later music too in that its drama is a metaphysical one, a drama of sound as contact with the spiritual. His *Alphabet für Liège* (1972)—not so much a work as an occasion, in the manner of Cage's music circuses of the 1960s (though with considerably more control), or of the site-specific installations of contemporary visual artists—was an exhibition of the effects of acoustic vibrations on fish, on fine powder scattered on metal plates (Chladni's experiment), on the yeast in dough, and on the physical and mental faculties of human beings. 'Sounds can do anything', Stockhausen remarked at the time: 'They can kill. The whole Indian mantric tradition knows that with sounds you can concentrate on any part of the body and calm it down, excite it, even hurt it in the extreme.'[6] In *Musik im Bauch* (1974–5), a children's tale played and mimed by six percussionists, he

---

[6] Ibid. 59.

showed this discovery of acoustic powers being made by three brothers who find the secret of ordered sound in some music boxes, hidden in the stomach of a giant dummy and programmed with choices from *Tierkreis*, a book of twelve melodies for the signs of the zodiac. And in *Licht* the main characters are all musicians, and can appear on stage as either singers or instrumentalists or both. The cycle's cosmic combat is fought out among musical forces—essentially among melodies—and opera and instrumental theatre are one.

Politics

The Passion of Cornelius Cardew

'The ideology of a ruling class is present in its art implicitly; the ideology of a revolutionary class must be expressed in its art explicitly. Progressive ideas must shine like a bright light into the dusty cobwebs of bourgeois ideology in the avantgarde, so that any genuinely progressive spirits working in the avantgarde find their way out, take a stand on the side of the people and set about making a positive contribution to the revolutionary movement.'[1]

The words of Cornelius Cardew express a hope shared by several composers of his generation in the early 1970s, as it became clear both that political establishments in the west were retreating from the apparent idealism of the early 1960s (Kennedy had been the friend of liberal intellectuals; Nixon found his allies elsewhere) and that, on a more local level, the musical avant garde had been compromised in its opposition to the dominant culture. Boulez, who had been a firebrand as a young man in Paris, was now conducting Brahms in London and New York. The most iconoclastic music of Cage had been embraced by the publishing, recording and broadcasting industries. The early works of Stockhausen were being taught in colleges and conservatories. Now, at the time of the Vietnam war, of the evident failure of postwar liberalism to efface social divisions, and of increasing agitation for the rights of minorities, younger composers were bound to feel uneasy at the prospect of being assimilated into the controlling system. If, as it seemed, any kind of music could become acceptable, then the most emphatic political expression seemed to many to provide the only way of being unacceptable.

Cardew had gone on from his work with Stockhausen to align himself more with Cage, and to produce in his *Treatise* (1963–7) a magnum opus of music as graphic design, as game without instructions, map without key: Example 38 shows a representative extract. The work was, by intention, both triumph and disaster. 'Psychologically', Cardew wrote, 'the existence of *Treatise* is fully explained by the situation of the composer who is not in a position to make music.'[2] The only music he could make at this time was improvised music, as a member of the London performing group AMM, who worked with conventional instruments and electronics, and who sought, through communal concentration and discipline, to exceed their individual boundaries as musicians trained in jazz or classical traditions. For Cardew, and for other musicians, the experience of improvisation was a politically

---

[1] *Stockhausen Serves Imperialism* (London, 1974), 86.   [2] *Treatise Handbook.*

Ex. 38. Cardew, *Treatise* (1963–7)

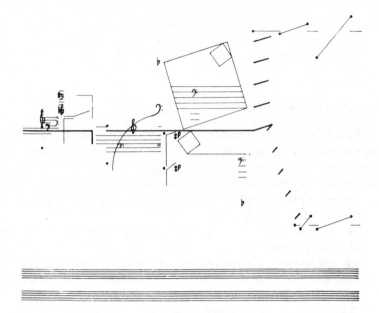

radicalizing influence, for its lessons of fruitful co-operation and productive free-dom seemed ready for application to the wider world.

First they might be applied to the wider musical world. Cardew went on from *Treatise* to make settings in *The Great Learning* (1968–70) of the first seven para-graphs from a classic Confucian text—settings which might bring professional musicians and amateurs together. *Paragraph 2*, for instance, simply offers twenty-six drum rhythms and twenty-five rudimentary melodies of five or six notes. The performers are divided into several groups, each consisting of a drummer and singers. The drummer chooses one of the rhythms and repeats it continuously, while the singers, following a leader, proceed slowly through one of the melodies. Then all move on.

Work on this piece led to the formation in 1969 of the Scratch Orchestra, a group of composers, musicians, and non-musicians who joined together idealistically to continue to break down barriers between professional and amateur. A musical training provided no special privileges and might even be a handicap; the atmos-phere was one of benign anarchy. Scratch Orchestra programmes included com-positions from the new generation of American experimental musicians—La Monte Young, Terry Riley, Frederic Rzewski (b.1938)—and by members of the group, as well as scratch performances of popular classics and 'improvisation rites', which were designed so that they did not 'attempt to influence the music that will be played' but rather tried to 'establish a community of feeling, or a communal starting-point, through ritual'.[3]

Like a revolutionary cadre, the Scratch Orchestra was from the first to be alert to its own evolution, and almost inevitably that evolution led it from the modelling of egalitarian relationships in music to active political engagement. News of the Cultural Revolution in China was welcomed as showing the way forward—a way that led through subjection to public criticism (or at least to criticism within the group) and a horrifying willingness to abandon anything but the slogan of the moment. For a performance of the first two paragraphs of *The Great Learning* in 1972, Cardew made a new translation of the characters, so that the call for keen introspection in the Ezra Pound version—'*The Great Learning* takes root in clarifying the way wherein intelligence increases through the process of looking straight into one's own heart and acting on the result; it is rooted in watching with affection the way people grow'—took on a ruthless political cast: '*The Great Learning* means raising your level of consciousness by getting right to the heart of the matter and acting on your conclusions. *The Great Learning* is rooted in love for the broad masses of the people.' It was also at this point that he began to attack his erstwhile mentors Cage and Stockhausen, and to repudiate his own earlier works, as politically irrelevant if not downright pernicious. He began to write simple didactic songs, to make arrangements of equally impoverished material from Beijing, and to produce piano transcriptions of Chinese and Irish revolutionary ballads in the manner of nineteenth-century salon music. The opening of one of the songs, 'Soon' (1971), shown in Example 39, may indicate how far Cardew had travelled in the few years since *Treatise*.

Ex. 39. Cardew, 'Soon' (1971)

The musical quality of 'Soon' is not the point, any more than the musical quality of *Treatise*, being inaudible, could possibly be the point—or any more than the musical quality of *Structures Ia* is the point. Each is a victory of ideology, but with the difference that whereas *Structures Ia* and *Treatise* alike are expressions of musical ideology, 'Soon' says nothing about music. Thereby it marks the moment—as surely as such other phenomena of the period as minimalism and historicism—when the idea of musical progress was abandoned, or perhaps had to be abandoned. Progress now, for Cardew and composers who thought like him, could only

---

[3] Cardew, 'A Scratch Orchestra: Draft Constitution', *Musical Times*, 10 (1969), 617.

be political progress, and music must relinquish all its own hopes and histories in order to serve that cause.[4]

Among those who shared Cardew's view were composers from the United States, including Rzewski and Wolff, both of whom, like Cardew, had roots in the classic avant garde: Wolff as a pupil of Cage, Rzewski sharing Cardew's own background as an associate of Stockhausen's. In the mid-1960s Rzewski, with other American musicians in Rome, founded one of the first live electronic ensembles, Musica Elettronica Viva, whose broad interests are suggested by one of their publicity statements: 'Tapes, complex electronics—Moog synthesizer, brainwave amplifiers, photocell mixers for movement of sound in space—are combined with traditional instruments, everyday objects and the environment itself, amplified by means of contact mikes, or not. Sounds may originate both inside and outside the performing–listening space and may move freely within and around it. Jazz, rock, primitive and Oriental musics, Western classical tradition, verbal and organic sound both individual and collective may all be present.'[5]

MEV began by playing determined compositions by members, but soon turned rather more to improvisatory pieces, following the example of jazz and rock groups, and following too the nature of the medium. This was not music for standard instrumental line-ups that could be reproduced around the world and for decades to come; it was music made for what was to hand, music for the moment. That temporariness was an invitation to deal with issues of the moment, be they musical or political; there was also the evidence from improvisation, as with AMM at the same time, that musical issues were political issues in microcosm. *Spacecraft*, performed by MEV on numerous occasions in 1967–8, had the programme of leading each player from an 'occupied space' of personal inclination to 'a new space which was neither his nor another's but everybody's'.[6] Then in *Free Soup* (1968) Rzewski asked that the audience should play with the ensemble, who were 'to relate to each other and to people and act as naturally and free as possible, without the odious role-playing ceremony of traditional concerts'.[7]

Rzewski's first outspokenly political works, *Coming Together* and *Attica* (both 1972), call for an unspecified instrumental ensemble to give cumulative force to a repeating melody, rather as in his earlier improvisation piece *Les moutons de Panurge* (1969), and along the lines of the early music of Philip Glass. But the 1972 pieces also include spoken texts, taken from moving and noble statements made by prisoners involved in the Attica revolt of September 1971, and now it seems that the driving music is driving home the words. Of Rzewski's later works, two big piano compositions—a set of thirty-six variations on the Chilean protest song '¡El pueblo unido jamás será vencido!' ('The People United Will Never Be Defeated!', 1973) and the Four North American Ballads (1978–9)—express their political message not

---

[4] For a conspectus of Cardew's musical and political development, see Richard Barrett, 'Cornelius Cardew', in Michael Finnissy and Roger Wright (eds.), *New Music 87* (Oxford, 1987), 20–33.

[5] Quoted in Nyman, *Experimental Music*, 110.   [6] Rzewski, quoted ibid. 110.

[7] Ibid. 111.

only by choice of tune but also by diversity of treatment, in the line of Liszt and Busoni. The adaptation of past styles to present political needs becomes, perhaps, a way of rescuing those styles from their bourgeois origins. It also demonstrates that the composer has refused the role of artistic pacemaker, the historical role which bourgeois culture had neatly assigned the avant garde.

The Composer in the Factory

Nono's response to the music of Cardew and Rzewski may be imagined. Like them, he was very aware of the power of the dominant culture to appropriate musical innovation; like them he was struggling—and for much longer had been struggling—with that power. But he could never accept that the answer was to forsake all hope of musical advance, since for him political and musical revolutions went hand in hand. 'I see no reason', he wrote, 'why music today should not take part in the discovery, the formation of new dimensions—human, technical, virtual and real—which exhibit and express the fundamental historical movement of our time: the fight by the international working class for socialist liberty.'[8] Revolutionary thought demanded revolutionary means, and the way to avoid assimilation was to move entirely out of the official arena, by rejecting the network of institutions—concert halls, festivals, modern music ensembles, recording companies—through which capitalist culture had domesticated the avant garde. Accordingly Nono began to present his music in factories—especially *La fabbrica illuminata* for soprano and tape (1964), which uses the words of factory workers and the noises of factory machinery—and to write for new media. Most of his works from this point on use electronics, for reasons both musical and, on several levels, ideological. Studio composition made the composer himself into a worker: using his hands, having responsibilities to colleagues, dealing with actual material rather than with mental figments. Also, the use of recorded factory noises—not only in *La fabbrica illuminata* but in several succeeding works—helped place the music within the experience of workers, and estranged it from the experience of bourgeois concert-goers. Finally, through tape it was possible to bring into the music direct signals of political involvement: the sounds of street demonstrations in *Contrappunto dialettico alla mente* (1967-8) or of Castro reading a letter from Che Guevara in *Y entonces comprendió* (1969-70).

The sounds of actuality give Nono's works of this period vividness, but they also contribute to a broadening of detail. Though the music still makes use of abstract constructive techniques the composer had developed in works leading up to *Il canto sospeso*, especially in the handling of rhythm, the pitch realm is less differentiated—partly because of the recorded material, partly for artistic reasons in which Nono's electronic experience may have played a part. Strident, anguished sounds

[8] 'Der Musiker in der Fabrik', *Mitteilungen der Deutschen Akademie der Künste*, 5 (1967), 6–8.

are very much to the fore in his first tape piece, *Omaggio a Emilio Vedova* (1960), and in another, *Ricorda cosa ti hanno fatto in Auschwitz* (1966). But then of course such sounds are proper both to his voicing of protest and to the urban, mechanized world which he wanted his music to echo, and they are instrumentally embodied in the clusters and sustained, searing sonorities of his orchestral writing from *Incontri* onwards. The essential difference in the later music is that the expressive urgency of such sounds makes it impossible to hear them as merely a by-product of compositional research. In *Per Bastiana—Tai-yang cheng* for orchestra and tape (1967)— a work dedicated to the composer's second daughter, and takings its subtitle from the Chinese revolutionary song 'The East is Red', which is immersed in the music— the fury swerves into the foreground. Nothing could more forcibly demonstrate Nono's distance from the China-watching songs of Cardew and Wolff.

Per Bastiana is unusual among his works of this period in returning to the concert hall, but such a return was inevitable in order to work with large forces, and the compromise was reduced when he could work with musicians who, like Claudio Abbado and Maurizio Pollini, sympathized with his musical and political ideals. For them he wrote *Como una ola de fuerza y luz* (1971–2), a memorial to South American freedom fighters; it was also Abbado who facilitated his return to opera. Like Berio, he had been fascinated by the new techniques introduced by American theatre companies: he had used part of the Living Theatre's Vietnam war protest play *Escalation* in *A floresta è jovem e cheja de vida* for voices, clarinet, bell plates, and tape (1966), and the experience left an impression on the open structure of his second opera, *Al gran sole carico d'amore* (1972–4), which is not so much a narrative as it is a documentary anthology focused on the plight of the lone principal character, an unnamed Mother. Like *Intolleranza*, the work is boldly and blockily scored for soloists, chorus, orchestra, and tape, but it also takes advantage of the more direct methods Nono had discovered in the intervening compositions—not least in its projection of the solo female voice against orchestral or electronic backcloths as a 'symbol of life, of love, and of freedom from all new forms of oppression'.[9]

[9] Nono's note with Wego 60067.

Virtuosity and Improvisation

The history of music is a history of performers continuously transcending what were thought to be limits, and maybe the simple existence of such challenging scores as *Le marteau sans maître* and *Zeitmasze* was enough to encourage a new race of modern virtuosos, who detected in postwar music an invitation to extend the possibilities of performance. This was something new. Virtuosity in previous ages had been the domain of the composer–performer, and where performers and composers were tied in personal and professional relationships, as with Brahms and Mühlfeld or Stravinsky and Dushkin, the result was not a wild extrapolation of technique. But music now was in an extreme situation, and the new music of the 1960s, especially, was often a music of extreme and unprecedented demands. The rapid turnover in compositional technique was paralleled by rapid extensions of what could be expected from instruments and voices—extensions which eventually took on a life of their own, as instrumentalists began to feel that composers were not necessary, that virtuosity had its best display as improvisation.

The Virtuoso

The revolution in performance practice, at its height in the mid-1960s, had effects which defy easy summary. Woodwind players found it possible to produce 'multi-phonics' (i.e. chords), either by using particular fingers or by singing into their instruments; they could also make percussive noises (by tapping on parts of the instrument), microtones, and unusual sounds created by means of more or less severe alterations to the embouchure and mouthpiece. Many of these devices were also found possible on brass instruments. On strings, new sounds could be obtained by unconventional bowing pressures, by bowing on unconventional parts of the instrument, by striking the instrument in various ways, and so on. Changes in piano technique have tended to be more straightforward tightenings of traditional demands in terms of dexterity, but percussionists have found vastly wider scope, in terms of their instrumentaria, their techniques, and their musical importance. It is enough to note that a virtuoso percussionist could hardly have existed in western music before the 1950s—Stockhausen had to write *Zyklus* because no test pieces for the species existed—whereas percussion ensembles and soloists are now a normal part of musical life.

The simplest possible response to these new riches is to use them as extensions of timbral resource, without letting them influence the premises of creative thought. This is often what happens in Henze's music, as for instance in his *Heliogabalus Imperator* (1971–2), where woodwind multiphonics create effects of festering decadence within what is a conventional symphonic poem. The case is quite different in Berio's music. Each of his many works for soloists, whether unaccompanied or concertante, seems to arise in a very direct manner from the instrument or voice concerned: from the physical exercise of playing it, and from the history and repertory it has. What follows is that technical effects—and new technical effects all the more so—are engrained in how the music is: they are not embellishments, nor are they curlicues of adventitious difficulty. The works of his *Sequenza* series are showpieces, certainly, but the showiness is not an extra. In *Sequenza VI* for viola (1967), frenetic tremolo chords are the substance of the piece. *Sequenza V* for trombone (1966) could not exist without the new effects of the period, especially singing into the instrument. *Sequenza III* for female voice (1965–6) is not a song with new vocal techniques, but new vocal techniques that make a song. If later members of the series tend to withdraw from these new sounds, that is partly because music as a whole has done so, and partly because Berio has become more concerned with the histories of instruments than with their practicalities. *Sequenza IX* (1978), for example, is for a clarinet which remembers it is also the instrument of Mozart, Weber, Mühlfeld–Brahms, and Benny Goodman, and the melodic looping, as in the works for violin and trumpet, requires a different kind of virtuosity. Another difference is that the earlier members of the series were written for a rather narrow band of new-music practitioners, including Severino Gazzelloni (*Sequenza I* for flute, 1958), Cathy Berberian (*Sequenza III*), Vinko Globokar (*Sequenza V*), and Heinz Holliger (*Sequenza VII* for oboe, 1969), whereas the later pieces have entered a world far more densely populated with ready performers.

All the *Sequenze* are composed performances; what also distinguishes the earlier pieces, especially those for voice and for trombone, is that the performances are theatre as much as music—that they belong with the music theatre of the time. *Sequenza III* is a setting of a short poem by Markus Kutter, but the main concern, as in the earlier electronic pieces *Thema* and *Visage*, is with vocal behaviour rather than verbal meaning: the words, deliberately elementary, are there to be confused. Example 40, from near the opening of the piece, shows something of the variety of vocal styles required, and shows too Berio's characteristic use of psychological cues ('tense', 'giddy' and so on) without any justification in the text. The music does not express a dramatic situation; it is that situation. So the work belongs with others in Berio's output, such as *Circles* and *Epifanie*, which, written with Berberian's many voices in mind, make music the generative force of theatre. The composer's later operas can be seen as successive attempts to create much larger musical forms which would have the same autonomy, the same supremacy over words and action.

If *Sequenza III* is typical of Berio in its dramatic nature and in its dwelling at the frontiers between music and language, it also displays, like all its companions in the series, his command of hectic activity within closely defined harmonic limits, his obsession with repeated return, redefinition, and re-elaboration. *Sequenza VII*, for example, is a flurry of escapes from, decorations of, and rejoinings to a note sustained throughout the piece as a drone. (An abiding characteristic of the composer is his fascination with the musical world in which he finds himself—even with the popular musical world, as witness his arrangements of Beatles numbers—and his response to the advent of minimalism was typically alert.) Often the urge to re-elaborate cannot be confined within the piece, and produces richer versions, as in the case of *Sequenza II* for harp, which, in *Chemins I* (1965), was embedded in an orchestral tissue developing its ideas in diverging directions. Writing of this work Berio has remarked that: 'A thing done is never finished. The "completed" work is the ritual and the commentary of another work which preceded it, of another work which will follow it. The question does not provoke a response but rather a commentary and new questions . . .'[1]

Ex. 40. Berio, *Sequenza III* (1965–6)

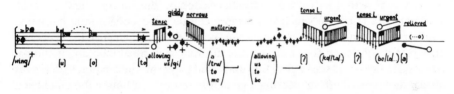

Sequenza VI was a particularly fruitful source of proliferating avenues. Berio first wrapped the viola solo in music for an instrumental nonet to create *Chemins II* (1967), and then surrounded this work with orchestral divagations to make *Chemins III* (1968). A further, oblique route from *Chemins II* is taken in *Chemins IIb* (1970), an orchestral commentary from which the solo part has been removed, and this in turn gave rise to *Chemins IIc* (1972), which adds back the solo thread but now allots it to a bass clarinet. The three directly linked works—*Sequenza VI*, *Chemins II*, and *Chemins III*—are related to each other, Berio has said, 'like the layers of an onion: distinct, separate, yet intimately contoured on each other: each new layer creates a new, though related surface, and each older layer assumes a new function as soon as it is covered.'[2] There is thus a two-way flow of musical thought, outwards from the original solo to the orchestra, and inwards to the centre. The process may be one of unfolding, as when latent harmonies in the solo are explicitly stated by the nonet or the orchestra, but it is more likely to be one of development and change.

The principle of commentary, enshrined in these three works in exemplary fashion, belonged to the age. Composers of Berio's generation had learned that the ideal of the immediate postwar years, that of starting music again from scratch, could not so easily be accomplished, or at least that it could not be repeatedly accomplished. Stockhausen had spoken of the limitless availability of new systems, waiting to be

[1] Programme note for a concert at the Palais des Beaux-Arts, Brussels, on 18 December 1966.
[2] Note with RCA LSC 3168.

discovered, but the experience of the 1960s was that history remained, even if it was only the history of each composer's own works. Composition was not pure invention; it was adaptation. And the consciousness of that seems to have led composers to make adaptation the point. Berio, whose *Sinfonia* is the great classic of music as commentary, has produced not only expanding versions of his own scores but also orchestral treatments of works by Brahms, Mahler, and Verdi.

His leaning towards commentary has naturally led him to two genres in which the text–commentary duality is inherent: settings of words, and concertos, the latter including not only the *Chemins* series but also other recompositions—such as *Corale* for violin and ensemble (1980–1), based on *Sequenze VIII* for violin—and new works created immediately in concertante format, such as *Points on the Curve to Find . . .* (1973–4), in which a small orchestra fills out the harmonic potential in an almost exclusively monodic solo piano part consisting mostly of rapid trills and tremolos, and in which the brass, by providing sustained pitches and chords in what is otherwise an excited polyphony, underpin a nervous movement towards the resolution of the final unison D. Another example is the Concerto for two pianos and orchestra (1972–3), which has a more complex but equally sure harmonic groundplan, beginning over an E pedal, and coming in its second half to an increasingly firm definition of G as tonal centre, this finally affirmed by G major chords. Here again, Berio was sensitive to the time—and to his own inclination to deal with history, not write it off—in seeking a greater harmonic continuity than had been characteristic of music in the 1950s and early 1960s. However, the harmonic statements and processes in his music are unambiguous only on the largest scale: at any moment they may be surrounded by alternatives which nudge at the music's basic principles, and keep it in the world of questions rather than answers. Berio's Concerto—the only one of his many concertante works to have that title until *Concerto II* (1988–90), subtitled *Echoing Curves*, the echoed curves being those of *Points . . .*—is by implication and by deed a commentary on the whole concerto form, as much as his *Sinfonia* is a commentary on the symphony. And just as the *Sinfonia* tries at moments to escape from being a symphony, so the Concerto at times evades concerto-ness, as when the nominal soloists begin to become accompanists to members of the orchestra.

The notion of music as commentary, so fecund for Berio, seems to have been for Boulez—previously so insistent on innovation—a cause at once of excitement and despair. 'When I have in front of me', he has said, in terms which call to mind his *Trope*, 'a musical idea or a kind of musical expression to be given to a particular text of my own invention, I discover in the text, when submitting it to my own kind of analysis and looking at it from every possible angle, more and more possible ways of varying it, transforming it, augmenting it and making it proliferate.'[3] Much of his output since 1960 has consisted of reworkings, and his biggest project of this period, *Pli selon pli*, exists in so many versions that perhaps one should consider it

---

[3] *Conversations with Célestin Deliège*, 15.

less a work than a nexus of possibilities, which, 'fold by fold', have multiplied. Other examples include the orchestral *Notations*, begun in 1977 as vast amplifications of piano miniatures from 1945, and *Eclat/Multiples*, in which the proliferation of musical ideas and ensembles is the modus operandi. So it is too on a more compact scale in *Domaines*, which, like so many of Berio's works, finds the commentary idea at home in concertante form, and which is Boulez's sole contribution to the virtuosity of display. (His piano sonatas, though certainly hugely demanding, do not make a point of virtuosity, and though his orchestral scores, developed through his performing experience, require a virtuoso conductor, their virtuosity virtually eliminates showmanship.)

In its version for clarinet and six ensembles (it may also be done as a clarinet solo), *Domaines* presents a sequence of antiphonal exchanges between the soloist's simple ideas and the more developed music of the ensembles, each of which is drawn in turn into a dialogue with the clarinet. First the clarinettist makes a tour of the ensembles, and offers to each a chain of six fragments that can be combined and proliferated. Example 41 gives some indication of how one of the clarinet's 'domains', taken from 'Cahier E' of the solo part, is developed by the relevant ensemble. The horn projects the clarinet's opening note (the middle-register E♭ which centres also . . . *explosante-fixe* . . . and that work's dependent *Rituel*), the electric guitar its opening interval, while the oboe's music is much more intimately and intricately implied by the original: it is characteristic of the work that the dialogue should be closer the closer the resemblance between the conversing

Ex. 41. Boulez, *Domaines* (1961–8)

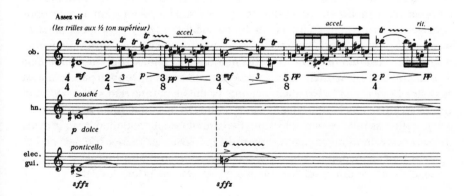

instruments, so that the trombone quartet gives the most peremptory response and the lone bass clarinet (the six ensembles cover a scale of size, from soloist to sextet) the most comprehensive. The second half of the work reverses the antiphonal layout of the first, so that the ensemble pieces now elicit replies from the soloist, but the techniques of liaison remain the same. Altogether, therefore, the piece has a rather bald form, as the composer seems to have recognized in promising to reconceive it. As left so far, it gives the impression of being a demonstration of compositional method, another testimony to Boulez's awareness of his role as teacher.

One reflection of his doubts about virtuosity, even here, is the lack of interest in new instrumental techniques: he offers his clarinettist the option of including multiphonics, but specifies only the principal note, which seems less an advancing of aleatory freedom than an admission that marginal sounds are only decorative. It was not so for Berio, at least in his works of the mid-1960s, and it was not so for composers who were themselves instrumentalists, such as two for whom Berio wrote *Sequenze*: Globokar and Holliger. The latter studied with Boulez, whose influence is evident in the orchestration of his oboe concerto *Siebengesang* (1966–7), and also in the work's transposition into instrumental music of the form and feeling of a Trakl poem, 'Siebengesang des Todes'. But in writing for the oboe Holliger was writing for his own voice, and he seems to have put into the work everything he then knew about playing.

This is a 'seven song' in being divided into seven sections, in having orchestral groupings in sevens (to a total of seven-squared players), in using sevenfold divisions of time, and in concluding with a seven-part female chorus to vocalize on syllables from the poem's last line. But the response is to the imagery as well as the numerology of the poem—to the image of death as a beautiful voyage, with the oboist riding 'shimmering torrents, full of purple stars' as he calls on different orchestral ensembles to serve him either as foils (glockenspiel, celesta, and two harps, in the second section) or as assemblies of colleagues (alto flute, cor anglais, horn, and viola, in the fourth). The solo part requires multiphonics—as shown in Example 42, from the virtuoso utterance with which the work opens (not shown is the complex, delicate arpeggio of cymbals, celesta and violin harmonics at the first bar)—as well as, at the end, the ability to sustain a soft high A for about fifty seconds (Holliger's own method of 'circular breathing' made this feasible), while in the sixth section, to great dramatic effect, the player has to take up an instrument with a microphone inserted into it, and use techniques which make this amplified oboe able to imitate almost anything the orchestra can come up with, from disruptive staccatos in the brass to woodwind chords or the highest jitterings of the violins. Holliger's immediately subsequent works tended to push the exploration of virtuosity—rather as in Kagel's music—into denatured terrain, and thereby to provide the virtuoso with more ambiguous rewards. In his String Quartet (1973–4) he not only asks for all manner of new playing techniques but also (the wind player's revenge) demands unnatural breathing exercises and waits for the effects.

Ex. 42. Holliger, *Siebengesang* (1966–7)

Virtuosity in Question

Much of the music considered above not only celebrates virtuosity but is circumspect about it: that was the nature of the analytical age in which these works were composed, and of the analytical composers who created them. But there are composers who, like Berio, relish artistry, and others who, like Kagel, want to look behind at mechanics and motivations, at the psychological, physiological and cultural nature of improvisation, its requirements and its costs. *Match*, for instance, is, in addition to a display piece, an essay on the competitiveness of our musical culture, and on the closeness of the concert to the sports event. In later works the questions tend to take over, and Kagel turns virtuosity against itself, either by asking players to take part in musical situations which inevitably deflate the strenuous efforts they demand, or by asking them to devote their skills to quite unaccustomed activities. *Unter Strom* (1969) begins with its three players performing on an electric fan, to which is attached a strip of cloth that strikes the strings of a guitar at each rotation, three children's sirens amplified by a megaphone, and a hard rubber ball in an electric coffee grinder. As so often in Kagel's music, the ridiculousness is partnered by a strange beauty—a beauty all the stranger for being, so it seems, by the way—and a highly formal presentation, not only in the score but in the performance, forbids the piece being dismissed as a joke, or as only a joke. Writing about *Der Schall*, which is similarly scored for a small group using a variety of musical and non-musical instruments, Dieter Schnebel has noted that 'the debilitated or run-down or worn-out sounds, the notes of strange instruments and the noises of non-instruments are employed in a musical progression that radiates the aura of the great classical repertory; a symphony, composed as it were from the wreckage of the old symphonic school'.[4]

As Kagel himself has remarked, an essential aspect of his work is 'strict composition with elements which are not themselves pure'.[5] The music is strict in that it is exactly prescribed, as has already been shown in Example 36, from *Match*. Kagel, like Cage, was not in the business of improvisation. But he found his material in phenomena that had been overlooked, viewed as secondary, or even spurned: unusual instrumental resources (non-instruments in *Unter Strom*, unaccustomed instruments in *Musik für Renaissance-Instrumente* and *Exotica*), players' gestures,

---

[4] *Mauricio Kagel, Musik, Theater, Film* (Cologne, 1970).
[5] Quoted by Josef Häusler in his article on Kagel for *The New Grove*.

routines of practising. His works of the later 1960s and early 1970s carried thereby a critical charge as much as the contemporary works of politically motivated composers, but with the criticism operating on the cultural plane, and with the object not so much of pointing to a better world as of demonstrating the failures and assumptions of the old one. In Germany, where the power of Adorno's thought was still immense, his works were highly valued and highly influential, and music's ability to express its own deterioration—as well as to structure the ashes, and perhaps thereby claim survival, if not hope—was tested too by Helmut Lachenmann (b. 1935), in a whole series of works initiated by the remarkable *temA* for flute, mezzo-soprano, and cello (1968).

For Lachenmann, a pupil of Nono, the challenge was to reach beyond models of musical practice that were not only outworn but also compromised, in that they had been taken over by bourgeois culture. The business of composers was to reclaim their materials: to discover new and unsuspected beauty in what, by traditional canons, would be regarded as malformed and inadmissible. *Pression* for solo cellist (1969) is typical of Lachenmann's work of this period in its insistence on irregular techniques, and thereby on the physical mechanism by which the sounds are produced. The score is, as in Cage's prepared piano music, a programme for action. At the start of the piece, shown in Example 43, the directions indicate how the bow is to be held in the fist while the fingers produce whispering glissandos of quasi-harmonics. A further removal from the norm is the scordatura: Ab–G–Db–F. Lachenmann referred to such pieces as 'instrumental *musique concrète*', and remarked how the listening experience becomes concrete because 'one hears under what conditions, with what materials, with what energies, and against what (mechanical) resistances each sound or noise is produced'.[6]

The sophistication and self-denial in his thinking are met by simplicity and hedonism, for the eschewal of convention (in *temA*, as in *Pression*, normal techniques are almost permanently avoided) provides access to moments of intense, new brilliance, lighting an atmosphere of frigidity and exile, where—particularly in works of the 1970s, such as *Schwankungen am Rand* for brass and strings (1974–5)—the possibilities of musical discourse are shrunk to an inert repetition. Lachenmann's works after *temA* are fully aware of the culture into which they come: of its tastes, of its abuses, and of its needs. They offer no refuge in wit, unlike comparable works by Kagel and Ligeti, or in the more sensuous irony of Berio. They accept from tradition the duties of seriousness and weight: the orchestral works are un-symphonies, *Gran Torso* (1971–2) stands, for all the abraded variety of its string effects, knowingly in the line of quartets.

But the challenge to virtuosity also came from other sides. Much of Xenakis's music of the 1960s and 1970s makes exceptional demands on instrumental soloists, either alone or in combination, and—in extreme contrast with Berio's works of the time—there is rather little concern either with practicality or with history. Xenakis

---

[6] Note with Col Legno WWE 31863.

Ex. 43. Lachenmann, *Pression* (1969)

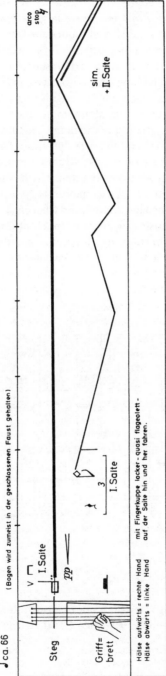

had concluded from his analysis of serial music that detail was lost and could therefore be discounted; what mattered were larger effects which could be composed with the help of mathematical techniques for handling complexities. A notable example is the solo piano piece *Evryali* (1974), which is one of the first works in which Xenakis created branching 'arborescences' of his 'non-octaving' scales (scales in which the repeating unit is some other interval than the octave), and which presents itself as a torrent of sound, as might be suggested by Example 44.[7] Virtuosity here is dexterity—the ability to get the notes—without anything to be communicated beyond the fact of the notes. There is nothing for the performer to understand: the player is as mindless as the weather in throwing down a hail storm, in which regard Xenakis's music, like Kagel's, connects with Cage. Moreover, the performer is presented with material that may be judged impossible. The pianist Peter Hill has suggested that in such pieces as *Evryali* the player must decide what can be achieved, what can be omitted, and what can be altered without severe detriment.[8] The printed music—again as in much of Cage—is a kit inviting the performer to be involved in choosing the sounds, and then to disappear, leaving only the sounds in the air.

Ex. 44. Xenakis, *Evryali* (1973)

The Electric Musician

Holliger's *Siebengesang* was a dramatic demonstration of how the virtuoso can find through electronic means a new voice, but the arrival of live electronic music had

---

[7] A page from the composer's graphic representation of the piece, clearly showing the branching scales, is reproduced in the booklet with Montaigne 782 005.

[8] 'Xenakis and the Performer', *Tempo*, 112 (1975), 17–22.

more profound effects on the nature of performance. Being difficult to predict, because subject to the particularities of the equipment and to fine subleties of adjustment, live electronic music welcomed indeterminacy and improvisation. The medium seemed almost to demand an empirical choice of means, which in the 1960s and early 1970s would have included conventional instruments or voices with electronic extensions, adapted or invented instruments, and standard electronic devices. Exploration—of timbre, of ensemble relationships, of the interface between composition and interpretation—was crucial, largely because the electrification of performance took musicians into a world in which nothing had been standardized. Since little could be foreseen, conditions of performance outweighed what could be written down in advance, and so performing ensembles quickly established their own practices, and normally created their own material. (Something similar was happening in popular music at the time.)

Cage's *Cartridge Music* (1960) has already been noted as first in the field; several of his subsequent pieces were prone to electronic performance, even if this was not specifically stated in the score. That of his *Variations II* (1961), for example, develops the principle of Example 22 from the *Concert*, being an assortment of straight lines and points printed on eleven transparent sheets, which may be overlaid in any manner; the performer, or performers, must then draw perpendiculars from each point to each line, and measure the lengths to determine, for each musical event, values for the parameters of pitch, volume, duration, timbre, point of occurrence, and structure. Tudor, whose interests were moving from the piano towards electronic means, made a version which applied to the piano—as to other objects in *Cartridge Music*—gramophone cartridges and contact microphones, so that the instrument became a reservoir of sounds ranging from the most fragile resonances to the ugliest scrapes. Cage and Tudor together, and independently, also made live electronic performances in the 1960s with dances by Merce Cunningham's company.

Stockhausen's first live electronic works—*Mikrophonie I* for six explorers of the sounds of a tam-tam (1964), *Mixtur* for ring-modulated orchestra (1964), and *Mikrophonie II* for small ring-modulated chorus with Hammond organ and tape (1965)—reveal, not coincidentally, a new experimental feel in his music. According to his own account, he created *Mixtur* as an improvisation: the piece is basically a sequence of textures to be obtained by modulating different orchestral ensembles with different sine tones. (Ring modulation, one of the fundamental techniques of live electronic music in the 1960s and 1970s, took two inputs and produced sum and difference frequencies from them—an effect somewhat like that of a slightly off-tune radio signal.) One result of the new approach was that works could be achieved very much more quickly, without the long labour on paper that had been necessary to bring about new sounds in *Gruppen*, *Carré*, and *Momente*.

Mikrophonie I also was developed by trial. Here a large tam-tam is activated by two performers using a variety of objects, while two others pick up the resulting vibrations with microphones and a further pair operate filters and volume controls.

The score specifies the kind of sound to be made ('whispering', 'grunting', 'trumpeting', and so on), the means of production, the rhythm, the loudness, and the electronic controls to be applied. Moreover, the work is formally determined, for though 'the order of structures may vary considerably from version to version' (and *Mixtur* is similarly a late example of mobile structure), 'a strong and directional form' is guaranteed, the composer asserted, by a scheme of permitted connections among the structures.[9]

Clearly we are some way from the direction taken by MEV and by other American groups, such as the Sonic Arts Union, founded by Robert Ashley, David Behrman, Alvin Lucier, and Gordon Mumma. Stockhausen's group, formed in the first place to give *Mikrophonie I*, was thoroughly dominated by him both as composer (very rarely was anyone else's music played) and as performer (seated at a console to control the final outcome). His work was not about self-projection for the performers, still less about enfranchising the audience; it was about realizing sounds he had imagined, or to which he would in performance give his imprimatur, and it was about generating musical form. In *Mikrophonie I* that form is enforced not only by the composer's written scheme but also, more fundamentally, by the use of a single instrument, and hence of a connected, if extremely wide, net of resonances. As Robin Maconie has observed, 'the process of articulation actually resembles the mechanics of speech, the tam-tam representing the vocal cavity, the various modes of excitation consonants and vowels, and the filters and potentiometers shaping diphthongs and envelope curves',[10] so that there is still here an inheritance from Meyer-Eppler's courses. Heard in this way, the piece is the tam-tam's song or lecture, in which it shows off its vocal repertory.

Most of Stockhausen's later music has required electronic equipment of some kind in performance, even when the means have been relatively conventional: electronic technology is, for him, just a normal part of the composer's means. His orchestral works *Trans* and *Inori*, for instance, need amplification for balance, and *Stimmung* (1968) requires its six singers to use microphones so that particular resonances in the vocal cavity can be heard. In such works live electronic music ceases to be a distinct medium. But Stockhausen still cultivated it as such in the pieces he wrote for the performing group he had assembled for *Mikrophonie I*, a group whose members included Aloys Kontarsky, Christoph Caskel, Harald Bojé, and Peter Eötvös. In those pieces he pursued a principle he had introduced with his *Plus–Minus* of 1963: that of providing in the score only the skeletal indication of a process to be applied to materials chosen or discovered by the performers. The essential difference from the open, graphic notations of Brown and Cage was that in Stockhausen's scores a process in time was laid down. Another difference—perhaps equally essential, though not stated—was that the composer would be present to rehearse and control performances. It is a moot point whether a performance given without his participation could be considered a Stockhausen performance at

⁹ Note with CBS 72647.   ¹⁰ *The Works of Karlheinz Stockhausen*, 142.

all. Cage's scores allowed, and allow, anyone to make Cage; the music's transparency is its guarantee against maltreatment, which will be revealed of itself.
Stockhausen's practice—publicly expressed in his authorization of definitive
recordings—suggests more restriction, and thereby more intention, though he has
seemed to smile on the possibility of being surprised, at least in the case of
Plus–Minus.[11]

Where the symbols of *Plus–Minus* detail sounds and processes quite precisely,
those of later pieces are much freer, because the composer was now working with a
familiar ensemble. *Prozession* (1967) and *Kurzwellen* (1968), for example, are
notated largely in plus, minus, and equals signs. In Example 45, from the tam-tam
part of *Prozession*, the player must follow the lead of the electronium (an instrument constructed by Bojé) in register ('R') and duration ('D') for eight changes of
event; the mathematical symbols are to be applied to the parameters of register,
duration, volume, and complexity (number of subsidiary sections), so that, for
instance, the fourth event here may be louder and longer (or higher and longer, or
louder and more subdivided, or any other combination) than the third; the sign
'Per' indicates an alteration towards greater periodicity. *Prozession* is thus an invitation to 'chain reactions of imitation, transformation and mutation',[12] starting out
from the players' memories of earlier Stockhausen works. The inclusion in
Mikrophonie II of taped 'windows' on to *Gesang der Jünglinge*, *Carré*, and *Momente*
had been perhaps the nearest thing in Stockhausen to irony: a reviewing of grand,
public occasions from within a dark, inward-pointed work. The appeal to performers' reminiscences in *Prozession* comes, quite differently, from the composer's
sureness that he has created his own musical culture.

Ex. 45. Stockhausen, *Prozession* (1967)

Kurzwellen, with characteristic confidence, goes on to show how this culture has
no need of explicit mementoes: now the basic material comes from shortwaves
(hence the title), each player using a shortwave receiver as well as an instrument.
Stockhausen had been working in radio for fifteen years, and had often used the
imagery of radio, but this was his first work with radios as sound sources, and his
opening to quite unpredictable sound material—material which even he could not
steer in rehearsal or develop in performance—coincided with a development in his

[11] See *Texte*, iii. 42–3.   [12] Stockhausen's note in Wörner, *Stockhausen*, 64.

musical metaphysics. Instead of trying to embrace the 'music of the world', as he had in *Telemusik* and *Hymnen*, he asked the players of *Kurzwellen* to be always alert to the call of the unknown. This is a work not of integration but of listening; its poise is not to gather but to receive; it is a voyage, in the composer's words, 'to the edge of a world which offers us the limits of the accessible'.[13] The improvisatory *Spacecraft* developed by MEV at the same time was devised for similar ends, but where Rzewski and his colleagues seem to have been interested in a social journey from self-absorption to group commitment—and where the 'free improvisations' of Globokar's New Phonic Art Ensemble, and of other such groups at the time, were being undertaken partly in liberation from the dictatorship of composers—Stockhausen's intentions for *Kurzwellen* were that it might effect a spiritual unloosening, for both players and listeners. Bringing the unknown into dialogue was to be more than a musical procedure.

From this point onwards Stockhausen became readier to see his music as having metaphysical properties and functions—or at least readier to declare such to be the case. *Stimmung* is a 'winged vehicle voyaging to the cosmos and the divine';[14] *Alphabet für Liège* was an exhibition of spiritual sound; and the collections *Aus den sieben Tagen* (1968) and *Für kommende Zeiten* (1968–70), both intended for the composer's live electronic group, consisted of prose poems, couched in oracular language and suggesting meditative exercises in improvisation, or, to use Stockhausen's preferred term, 'intuitive music'.

Improvisation

The nature of improvisation (musical freedom) is as hard to pin down as the nature of socialism (political freedom), with which it has had several points of linkage through twentieth-century cultural history—not least in 1968. For Cardew and Rzewski, as was suggested in the last chapter, the linkage was strong; for other composers less so. The impetus to improvise might come out of more general or more specifically musical considerations: for example, Franco Evangelisti (1926–80)—who had been among those at the Darmstadt core, there every year from 1952 to 1961—determined in 1962 that to continue composing would be to repeat himself, and from 1965 onwards his public activity consisted only of improvising, with the variable ensemble he founded in Rome under the name 'Nuova Consonanza'. Nevertheless, the heyday of this organisation came at the end of the 1960s, and the further coincidence of the May events in Paris and of street demonstrations (especially of students hostile to the Vietnam War) with *Kurzwellen*, and with the most libertarian music of Berio, Kagel, Globokar, and others, is too striking to be thought accidental. Improvisation was liberation. Virtuoso performers, having taken into themselves the exceptional variousness and the extreme techniques of the music of the last two decades, could now use that stock on their own accounts.

[13] Stockhausen's note in Wörner, *Stockhausen*, 69.   [14] Ibid. 67.

Globokar, who had worked closely with Stockhausen, Berio, and Kagel, enumerated the reasons why performers should engage in free improvisation, and began precisely with 'a need for liberation', followed by 'a search for a new musical aesthetic, a provocation, a wish to work collectively, to develop their instruments, to amuse themselves, a political or social engagement, the wish to belong to an élite capable of improvising, a way of evaluating themselves, a way of expressing themselves not only through sounds but through physical comportment [perhaps because musicians improvising can feel more completely that their instruments are extensions of their bodies, since there is no need for conscious analysis to keep track of the score], a need to create a contact (and the most direct possible) with the audience, a need to give free rein to his imagination (without being obliged to spend hours of reflection at a worktable), and many other things'.[15]

This makes a fine manifesto, but most of its points could all too easily be reversed. For example, musicians might consider themselves freer in front of a score than when faced with the fearsome demand to be themselves. Collective work is as much a feature of a traditional orchestra, choir or string quartet as of an improvising ensemble. Evaluation is easier against the standard of a written part. Audiences can be brought into closer contact when there is some shared framework of discourse—and indeed the survival of improvisation (and, like almost everything in music since 1945, it has survived) appears to have depended on the evolution of attunements within ensembles and between ensembles and audiences. Correspondingly the eclipse of improvisation (and every survival implies an eclipse) may have come from the recognition that its promises were over-optimistic.

Stockhausen surmounted the problem of the lapsed framework by outlining processes of response, whether to his own earlier music in *Prozession*, specifically to his *Hymnen* in the version of that work with ensemble, or to shortwave signals in *Kurzwellen*, but in the two sets of text pieces he abandoned such moment-to-moment guidance. For example, *Verbindung*, from *Aus den sieben Tagen* (so called because the texts were written during a week-long retreat[16]), asks each musician to 'play a vibration in the rhythm of' his or her body, heart, breathing, thinking, intuition, enlightenment, and of the universe. The resulting music, according to the composer, 'comes virtually unhindered from the intuition', through 'joint concentration on a written text of mine which provokes the intuitive faculty in a clearly defined manner'.[17] Where improvisation, in Globokar's terms, is about self-discovery and self-assertion, Stockhausen's stated concern was with finding music outside the self: it is the difference between autobiography and prayer.

His action, therefore, in overseeing and authorizing performances of *Aus den sieben Tagen*—in claiming ownership not only of the prayer text but of the praying—was bound to cause difficulties. During the few years when *Aus den sieben Tagen* was in regular currency, he preferred to give performances with musicians who had had long practice in playing his music; a rare exception was a performance

---

[15] 'Ils improvisent . . . improvisez . . . improvisons', *Musique en jeu*, 6 (1972), 14.
[16] See Kurtz, *Stockhausen*, 160–2. [17] *Texte*, iii. 123–4.

of *Setz die Segel zur Sonne* with the BBC Symphony Orchestra in 1970, but that too was 'rehearsed by the composer'.[18] Moreover, comparisons of different certified performances of the same text suggest that the composer in rehearsal stipulated rather more than is contained in the lines of the score, and this supposition is borne out by evidence from performers.[19] The gulf between improvisation and his brand of directed intuition produced its emblematic conflict when Globokar disavowed his participation in recordings of *Aus den sieben Tagen*.[20]

But the vulgar interpretation of Stockhausen's motives as megalomaniac is insufficient. There were real problems of formal sameness in improvisation, as Globokar was aware: 'Movements between action–reaction, simple–complex, tension–relaxation are made progressively, rarely in an abrupt manner. The form is often sinusoidal, each situation lasting until it has been exhausted. For the same reason it goes slowly to extinction; brutal conclusions are rare.'[21] Many of these features can be observed in the recordings of *Aus den sieben Tagen* and *Für kommende Zeiten* validated by the composer—especially the slow growths and slow decays. Yet there is variety of structure, gesture and atmosphere, and the pieces sound different from one another. To that extent they rescue what Globokar's free improvisation had hoped to obliterate: identity, repeatability.

Free improvisation, as an ideal if not in practice, was a model of the ending of history—the ending that was being expressed simultaneously in the explosion of quotation, in the collapse of the avant garde, in Cage's virtual abandonment of composition, and in minimalism's reversion to fundamentals. Nothing inherited or learned was to matter, and if traditional instruments too were abandoned or surpassed—as they were by live electronic groups such as Stockhausen's—then each improvisation was a new beginning and a new end, a loop in time that belonged to no continuity. Such nowness had been Stockhausen's explicit aim since *Momente*, and *Aus den sieben Tagen* was, as a project, part of a development that began with Piano Piece XI. But the final move, into complete creative abdication, might still be sidestepped by the closet guidance involved in intuitive music. History then could continue. Stockhausen had always seen his role more as an initiator of processes than as a maker of works; *Aus den sieben Tagen* was a particular demonstration of that, and a doorway into a liberation not so much for the performers as for the composer. It gave him permission to trust his own intuition.

---

[18] See *Texte*, iv (Cologne, 1978), 126.

[19] See Paul Griffiths, *A Guide to Electronic Music*, 81, for a comparison of two versions of *Verbindung*, and Harald Bojé, 'Aus den sieben Tagen: "Text"-Interpretation', *Feedback Papers*, 16 (1978), 10–14, for performance notes by musicians closely associated with Stockhausen.

[20] He is mentioned in *Texte*, iii. 113–28, as having taken part in a sequence of recordings made in the summer of 1969 by members of the Stockhausen group and of New Phonic Art , but the leaflet published with the DG set refers only—and several times—to 'a trombonist (who wishes to remain anonymous)'. See also Kurtz, *Stockhausen*, 174.

[21] 'Ils improvisent . . .'

Computer Music

A great deal in music since 1945 seems, if perhaps only in retrospect, to have been leaning towards cybernetics: the idea of music as sounding numbers, the importance of rules and algorithms in composition, the development of electronic sound synthesis, the concept of the work as a temporary equilibrium of possibilities that could be otherwise realized. Images of the composing mind during this period, as evidenced not only in music but in writing about music, tend to suppose rational selection and combination rather than inspiration. Music created with computers is, therefore, part of a much wider concurrence of music and computing.

As in the early days of *musique concrète*, the first computer pieces tended to be acclaimed more for primacy than for aesthetic quality, and correspondingly they now figure more in histories, as here, than in performance. The *Illiac Suite* for string quartet (1955–6), programmed by Lejaren Hiller and Leonard Isaacson at the University of Illinois, is widely cited as the pioneer achievement. Xenakis used a computer to handle the manifold calculations that his stochastic music had previously required him to make by hand: an early example is his *ST4–1,080262* (1955–62), also for string quartet. And Xenakis's stochastic music, more generally, shows the advent of digital thinking in, for example, the down-grading of the individual event and of moment-to-moment continuity; musical data were now to be assessed globally. Where traditional tonal music had offered time lines hospitable to the listener—lines along which musical processes could be followed—Xenakis was presenting states and unpredictable changes of state. He was not alone: Stockhausen's moment form was explicitly a venture in the same direction. Indeed, the movement towards a new kind of time—a time without reasons and purposes— is the most general and perhaps the most fundamental feature of music since 1945. Reasons and purposes have been displaced into other areas—into the compositional process (which, as in much serial music, may not be laid out for the listening ear), or into political or aesthetic ideology—or else they have been made frankly apparent: not leading the ear but presented to it for monitoring; not communication but structure, as in the early music of Steve Reich. Like the ideals of composing, the ideals too of listening were, in the mid-1960s, becoming objective and combinatorial.

This was when the first steps made in using computers to determine not notes that would be played by natural instruments (as in the *Illiac Suite* and *ST4*) but sounds that would be synthesized electronically. Programs for sound synthesis were developed by Max Mathews at the Bell Telephone Laboratories in Murray Hill,

New Jersey, in the late 1950s and 1960s; those programs were then adapted by composers, among whom both John Chowning at Stanford University and James K. Randall at Princeton produced their first computer pieces in 1964. As explained by Charles Dodge, another early in the field, anyone composing with computer music programs 'must typically provide: (1) *Stored functions* which will reside in the computer's memory representing waveforms to be used by the *unit generators* of the program. (2) "Instruments" of his own design which logically interconnect these *unit generators*. (*Unit generators* are subprograms that simulate all the sound generation, modification, and storage devices of the ideal electronic music studio.) The computer "instruments" play the *notes* of the composition. (3) *Notes* may correspond to the familiar "pitch in time" or, alternatively, may represent some convenient way of dividing the time continuum.'[1]

Early computer composers naturally fastened on elementary ideas that would have been difficult or impossible to realize without the computer's resources of calculation and control, such as the creation of quasi-instruments which could function over very wide pitch ranges (Randall's *Quartets in Pairs*, 1964), or of a process by which irregularly placed chords affect the timbres of continuing contrapuntal lines (Dodge's *Changes*, 1970), or of a harmonic system in which the Golden mean ratio of 1 : 1.618 governs the octave relationship, with timbres made to produce the effect of consonance (Chowning's *Stria*, 1977). But American composers were also impressed—as Babbitt had been when working with the RCA Synthesizer a few years earlier—by the possibility of making complex music that resisted the performance conditions of the time. (This was another symptom of the age, that so much music should be designed for mechanical, definable performance, though of course there were also economic reasons why university composers—and most professional composers in the United States in the 1960s and 1970s were attached to universities—would find time a commodity easier to obtain on computers than at orchestral rehearsals.) For example, Benjamin Boretz—like Randall and Dodge, a Babbitt pupil, and editor of *Perspectives of New Music*—rescored his chamber orchestral *Group Variations* (1964–7) as a computer-generated tape in 1968–71.

In Europe, computer techniques were introduced at various private and public electronic-music studios in the late 1960s and early 1970s: Birtwistle created *Chronometer* (1971–2), with clock sounds, at Peter Zinovieff's studio in London. But from the late 1970s onwards the main European centre for computer music was IRCAM.

---

[1] Note with Nonesuch H 71245, a record of early pieces by Randall, Dodge, and Barry Vercoe.

Minimalism and Melody

'Minimalism' is a term that no composer likes for a phenomenon that almost no composer working since the late 1960s has avoided. Its essential qualities are two: an extreme reduction and simplicity of means, and repetition. Put in that way, it is nothing new: the introduction to Handel's *Zadok the Priest*, for example, provides an instance of repetitive arpeggiation almost a quarter of a millennium before that became the norm in the music of Philip Glass. But where the function of minimalism in the Handel is preparatory—to provide a stretch of empty time, of non-music, in order to intensify anticipation of the music to come (*Das Rheingold* offers another such case)—in Glass this is all there is. And minimalism as total, and as all-pervasive, was indeed new in the 1960s; odd earlier examples (Satie's *Vexations*, Cage's *Music for Marcel Duchamp*, and other pieces) had not been widely followed, and seem to have been rediscovered in the 1960s rather than to have been influential. The starting points (allowing that so strong a thrust is unlikely to have had just one) are more likely to be found in the music of La Monte Young.

New York Minimalism

In 1962, after his early pieces based on few, long notes and his Fluxus text scores, Young founded his own performing group, the Theatre of Eternal Music, to give performances of highly repetitive, drone-based music using carefully chosen frequencies in simple ratios.[1] Ideally, his 'dream music' was intended for continuous performance in 'dream houses' as a 'total environmental set of frequency structures in the media of sound and light'.[2] The frequencies could just be electronically generated sine tones, drifting very slowly in phase relationship and hence in perceived volume (*Drift Studies*), or there could be live performers adding further frequencies, while the visual complement would be the 'ornamental lightyears tracery' of patterned slides and coloured lights designed by the composer's wife, Marian Zazeela.

In 1964 Young began to concentrate his attention on two projects: *The Well-Tuned Piano*, given as a solo improvisation through various themes and chords on a piano tuned to particular ratios,[3] and *The Tortoise, His Dreams and Journeys* (so

[1] See Dave Smith, 'Following a Straight Line: La Monte Young', *Contact*, 18 (1977–8), 4–9.

[2] Note with Shandar 83 510.

[3] See Kyle Gann: 'La Monte Young's *The Well-Tuned Piano*', *Perspectives of New Music*, 31/1 (1993), 134–62.

called in honour of a creature having Youngian virtues of longevity and slowness), of which excerpts were presented by the Theatre of Eternal Music. The members of the ensemble—who included rock musicians, such as John Cale, and others who were to become leading minimalist composers, such as Terry Riley (b. 1935)—had to be expert in attuning their contributions to the frequency structure in use and, in the case of vocalists, employing different parts of the vocal cavity to bring forward different harmonics. Young studied the Indian *kirana* style with Pandit Pran Nath, which perhaps encouraged a deeper confluence with Indian thought in his conception of music as environment to be lived in rather than message to be understood, and in his association of frequency structures with moods. At the same time, as with Partch, his insistence on just intonation and on his own performing forces had the effect of displacing his music wholesale from the western tradition. Example 46, from the five-hour recorded version of *The Well-Tuned Piano*,[4] can only hint at his way of working with variation in an ambience that is, almost as far as possible, stationary. The example can only hint also at the tuning. At it affects the notes in play here, Young's system has the F♯ and the B, in just intonation, rather below their positions in the equal-tempered scale, but the G, D, A, and E belong to a different cycle of just fifths, and are all conspicuously raised with respect to equal temperament, the G being above the equal-tempered G♯. So, for instance, the intervals B–D and F♯–A in the example are close to major thirds, the G–A is narrowed, and the F♯–G is almost a minor tenth.

Ex. 46. Young, *The Well-Tuned Piano* (1964–)

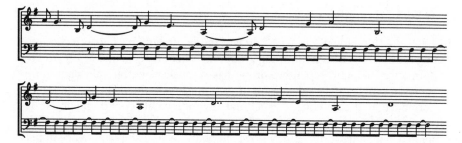

Because Young's music required his presence to tune and play (so that most performances took place in New York), and because no commercial recordings were available until the 1970s, the dissemination of repetitive music was largely in the hands of others. Stockhausen's *Stimmung* for six vocalists (1968)—which, like Young's music, requires singing on resonances and adjustment to a pure consonant harmony, in this case made up of overtones on a low B♭—provided a minimalist experience that was more user-friendly (in that it lasted for little more than

---

[4] As transcribed in the article by Kyle Gann, to whom, and to *Perspectives*, I am most grateful for permission to reproduce it.

an hour), that presented itself more traditionally as a work (having a fixed shape and strong compositorial intentions, in the form both of love poems grafted into it and of statements about its metaphysical purpose as an instrument of meditation), and that was readily available as a score and on record. Riley's *In C* (1964), whose performers play to the same beat while making their own choices from fifty-three different motifs in C major, was another momentarily successful simplification of Young's practice and purpose.

Around the same time, Steve Reich (b. 1936) and Philip Glass (b. 1937) began to combine repetition with process. Both of them, like Young, were influenced by non-western musical traditions: Glass worked with Ravi Shankar while pursuing more orthodox studies with Nadia Boulanger in Paris, and also studied the tabla with Alla Rakha before composing any of his acknowledged works, while Reich studied African drumming in Accra and Balinese gamelan in Seattle, though only after he had embarked on his career as a composer and performer. In neither case, though, did world-music exploration lead to an abandonment of western notions of the art work or western instrumentation and tuning, any more than it did for Stockhausen. As Reich put it: 'One can study the rhythmic structure of non-Western music, and let that study lead one where it will while continuing to use the instruments, scales, and any other sound one has grown up with.'[5]

In Glass's early music the basic principle of rhythmic structure was the simplest possible: that of adding, repeating or removing units in a context of repetition and harmonic stasis. Example 47 shows four bars from his *Music in Similar Motion* (1969): each bar is repeated over and over again until the composer gives the signal to move on to the next; instrumentation is not specified, as was usual, for Glass was not interested in having his music played by ensembles other than his own, which generally consisted—during the late 1960s and the 1970s, when they were regularly on tour—of half a dozen players on electronic keyboards and woodwind instruments. Experience together was needed if the method of signalling was to work—especially when the music was designed for high speeds and high volume levels, together producing an effect of forward motion at high pressure, jolted by changes of figure and density.

The simple parallel harmony of Example 47 is characteristic of Glass's 1969 pieces: *Two Pages* is in unison; *Music in Fifths*, again in two parts, is self-explanatory. Later works, including *Music with Changing Parts* (1970) and *Music in Twelve Parts* (1971–4), are much richer, more harmonically varied, and, in performance, much longer, with the original rather severe rhythmic processes joined by sustained chordal progressions, so that there are layered textures of musical planes in different but meshing tempos, sometimes very much as in Balinese gamelan music. The nature of the harmony, though, is western, and has to be in order that, through repetition, a state of estrangement may be generated. In *Another Look at Harmony* (1975) Glass 'took a VI–II–IV–V–I cadence with some altered things in it', and made

[5] *Writings about Music* (Halifax, 1974), 40.

Ex. 47. Glass, *Music in Similar Motion* (1969)

it so that 'you start hearing this cadence that you've heard all your life in a very different way'.[6] In his opera *Einstein on the Beach* (1975), written to a scenario by its producer Robert Wilson, he used similar techniques, and proved the value—and the appeal—of his estranged simplicity and repetitiveness in underpinning a stage spectacle of slow enigma.

Reich's first works, like Glass's, have the clarity of a totally fresh approach to musical fundamentals; the two composers were even associated in the beginning as performers, and shared other musicians in their ensembles. But Reich had already set out his own independent areas of interest before Glass established himself: in particular, he fixed the scoring of his pieces, because matters of timbre and texture were always integral, and he concerned himself with continuous processes of change. 'I want', he said, 'to be able to hear the process happening through the sounding music.'[7]

This is rather a remarkable statement. For though music from Bach to Boulez might also seem to expose process, it does so, as experience shows, in ways that are ambiguous and that allow other possibilities of interpretation having nothing to do with process, whereas for Reich, at least at the start of his career, the process was the music. The music was self-disclosing and even self-analysing; there was no meaning beyond the movement of sounds. As he explained in the case of one of his first compositions, the tape piece *It's Gonna Rain* (1965), created from tape loops of recorded speech: 'Two loops are lined up in unison and then gradually move out of phase with each other, and then back into unison. The experience of that musical process is, above all else, impersonal: *it* just goes *its* way. Another aspect is its precision; there is nothing left to chance whatsoever. Once the process has been set up it inexorably works itself out.'[8] For Reich, therefore, minimalism was an escape from the embarrassments and unjustifiabilities of choice, just as chance procedures had been for Cage. And in the same way, by what is only a seeming paradox, it opened up a new and personal world.

Reich went on to use 'phasing' processes in another tape piece, *Come Out* (1966), and then the next year adapted them to live performance in *Piano Phase* for two pianos and *Violin Phase* for four violins, of which the latter revealed to him 'the

[6] Keith Potter and Dave Smith, 'Interview with Philip Glass', *Contact*, 13 (1976), 25–30.
[7] *Writings*, 9.   [8] Ibid. 50.

many melodic patterns resulting from the combination of two or more identical instruments playing the same repeating pattern one or more bars out of phase with each other'.[9] In Example 48 the phase shifting has reached a point where the second violin is two crotchet beats ahead of the first and the third is two crotchet beats ahead of the second (therefore two crotchet beats behind the first); the fourth violin picks out resulting patterns, such as the one shown (three others are also to be projected during the repetitions of this bar). However, from the combination of all four violins the listener may deduce other patterns. The single, objective process is therefore, once again, constantly susceptible to adventitious interpretations, but these are now in the mind not of the composer but of the listener: the music is made by the ear. 'When I say there is more in my music than what I put there, I primarily mean these resulting patterns.'[10]

Ex. 48. Reich, *Violin Phase* (1967)

Similar processes of phasing and pattern enhancement are involved in *Phase Patterns* for four electronic organs (1970), while in another work for the same combination, written the same year and called *Four Organs*, a different sort of process is allowed to run its course: a nine-note chord, jabbed by the organs, has its notes extended one at a time, so that melodic patterns emerge from it and are then obscured again as the notes grow to fill all the available time. *Drumming* (1971) was a synthesis of these and other processes, and also a grander public statement, both in its ninety-minute duration and in its scoring for percussion ensemble with piccolo and with female vocalists imitating instrumental sounds. After this came other works for larger, mixed formations, such as *Music for Mallet Instruments, Voices and Organ* (1973) and *Music for Eighteen Musicians* (1974–6), whose breadth and glamour perhaps reflected the success the composer had come to enjoy. With these

---

[9] Ibid. 53.   [10] Ibid.

works, and with Glass's *Einstein on the Beach,* minimalism had moved from a fringe existence in the SoHo area of New York to international acclaim and imitation.

Melody

The fact that Ligeti in 1971 could give the title *Melodien* to an orchestral piece is a signal that minimalism was part of a wider recuperation of simplicity and definition in music—a recuperation noticeable even in the work of composers explicitly hostile to minimalism, such as Boulez. In *Le marteau sans maître* there is little opportunity to identify cross-references—so that those which exist in the finale, however oblique they may be, reach out dramatically—and manipulative techniques with cells of notes and intervals can only be uncovered at the slower pace of analysis. But in his few works of the 1960s, Boulez began to make connections more unitary and hence more identifiable; he began to speak of working, if not with themes, at least with figures—a development expressed and announced in the evolution of the orchestral piece *Doubles* (1957) into *Figures–Doubles–Prismes* during the next decade.[11]

His next orchestral work—*Eclat/multiples,* begun in 1965—goes further, even if his own descriptions of it have tended to fasten on matters of timbre and time rather than melody and harmony. The scoring is based on an opposition between a concertante group of nine playing on tuned percussion instruments (an enlargement of the ensemble used in the first two *Improvisations sur Mallarmé*) and an orchestra of sustaining instruments—winds and strings—which, according to the plan of the piece, should gradually grow. In the first section, which has a separate existence as *Eclat* and was the seed, this orchestra has just six members (alto flute and cor anglais, viola and cello, trumpet and trombone); the second section adds a basset horn and nine more violas, and so continues the typically Boulezian emphasis of the alto register. With the play between resonators and non-resonators, Boulez creates what he calls 'a kind of "suspended" musical space in opposition to very dynamic ideas', and hence develops a contrast between 'a contemplative attitude towards the phenomenon of sonority—demanding a different way of listening, attentive to what is happening within the resonance itself—and active effort of thought occupying itself still more with the thought connecting the musical events and which makes them take a determined direction'.[12] The contrast is, on the rhythmic level, clear. Throughout much of *Eclat* the percussion group is heard alone in events following one another in a tempo felt to be slow, however rapid the internal detail: chords, with or without grace-notes; trills; random assemblies of spurts (random in that ordering and co-ordination can be improvised by the con-

---

[11] See Allen Edwards, 'Boulez's "Doubles" and "Figures Doubles Prismes": A Preliminary Study', *Tempo,* 185 (1993), 6–17.

[12] Programme note for the first performance of *Eclat/multiples,* at the Royal Festival Hall, London, on 21 October 1970.

Ex. 49. Boulez, *Eclat* (1965)

ductor: like much of Boulez's later music, the work is designed for the skills of sharp, multiple focus he had cultivated as a performer).[13] Contrary to this 'smooth time', to use the composer's terminology,[14] the sustaining sextet live in 'striated time'—especially at the end of *Eclat*, where they jerk Stravinskianly against a rapid pulse. In smooth time the ear can wander through something stationary or unformed, exploring resonances and catching ideas; in striated time it is directed.

However, the pitch construction of the piece rather modifies this opposition. Once again drawing attention to his new concern with figure, Boulez describes *Eclat/multiples* as: 'a succession of mirror images in which developments reflect each other, or, so to speak, the multiple reflections of the original musical images interfere with each other and create divergent perspectives'.[15] At the slow speed of smooth time, such reflections of image are more readily noticed than in the rush of striation, and so the former, for all its seductive invitations to dwell in the moment, may come to seem purposeful, while the latter may, in pitch terms, bewilder. This characteristic modification of an initial contrast can be observed, for instance, in the slow central portion of *Eclat*, where the composer–conductor plays on his percussion ensemble as on a giant keyboard, calling on different groupings to colour each suspended resonance. Example 49 shows just the pitches from the opening of this passage; each chord is played by one or more of the nine percussionists, and has a long duration determined partly by the conductor. The first sequence divides the total chromatic into five units; the second then repeats these in rotated order, beginning with the second, and, as it were, rotates each one through different transpositions and octave placements. One pitch class alone, C, remains fixed in register and is always played on a tubular bell; its importance is further brought out by the fact that it arrives to complete the opening twelve-note set. It therefore has an almost motivic function, in that it is an identity that seems to make sense. And other events in this sequence, because they relate to near or distant neighbours, similarly begin to set up skeins of connectedness. The music does not invite prediction: it retains its improvisatory freedom. But the listener can begin to make a pattern from its past.

[13] See Robert Piencikowski, ' "Assez lent, suspendu, comme imprévisible": Quelques aperçus sur les travaux d'approche d'*Eclat*', *Genesis*, 4 (1993), 51–67.

[14] *Boulez on Music Today*, 89.   [15] Programme note.

The constructive techniques of *Eclat/multiples* were not new: registral fixing went back to the Second Piano Sonata, and chord multiplication (used to generate much of the material from the five units of Example 49) to *Le marteau*. What was new was the openness to view, which is a feature too of *Domaines*. And Boulez went further. In *Rituel* (1974–5) he based an orchestral work not on a vast network of cells and their products but on a single seven-note set, and not on ensembles of darting figures but on melody and chorale. The piece is a litany of verses and refrains for eight homogeneous gatherings ranging in size from a solo oboe to a fourteen-piece brass group, each accompanied by a percussionist beating out time on an unpitched instrument. (The sumptuous resonances of *Eclat/multiples* are thus replaced by a complex clockwork.) Example 50 shows the first verse, and so the first statement of the tritone-rich source set in its melodic form. In succeeding verses, which bring more and more of the groups into heterophonic combination (so that there is at least some link with *Eclat/multiples* in this additive kind of orchestration, as if, in keeping with the new transparency in Boulez's mode of operation, the music had to demonstrate its resources and its need for those resources), the melody is extended, reordered and transposed, but its stable rhythmic character and its limitation to seven notes keep its identity sure. Nor is there any doubt, because of this paucity of intervals, that the same set, though inverted, governs the chordal refrains. The awesome grandeur of the result—its march through time so contrasting with Boulez's normal fluidities, complexities, and ambiguities—appear a curious throwback to the world of Messiaen, and especially to that of *Et exspecto resurrectionem mortuorum*, Messiaen's own liturgy of solos and ensembles with percussion. It also offers a coincidence with current developments in Ligeti and, most strikingly, Stockhausen. But it is neither a celebration of resurrection nor a venturing into new worlds: it is a memorial. In paying tribute to Bruno Maderna, the first of the central

Ex. 50. Boulez, *Rituel* (1974–5)

Darmstadt band to have died, it seems to throw a wreath over the whole enterprise of the 1950s and 1960s.

Ligeti's recovery of melody was more gradual, and its tone more positive. In several works of the 1960s, including the large-scale Requiem, the unaccompanied *Lux aeterna*, and the orchestral *Lontano*, he continued his 'micropolyphonic' style, in which, as in *Atmosphères*, clusters glide and slowly evolve. However, there are also more defined features in, for instance, the exaggeratedly dramatic 'Dies irae' from the Requiem, or in *Lontano*, which conveys the sense of a harmonic undercurrent occasionally revealed when the chords thin out towards octaves.[16] Ligeti has seemed to confirm this in writing about the harmony of his music from the mid-1960s to the mid-1970s: 'There are specific predominant arrangements of intervals, which determine the course of the music and the development of the form. The complex polyphony . . . is embodied in a harmonic–musical flow, in which the harmonies . . . do not change suddenly, but merge into one another; one clearly discernible interval combination is gradually blurred, and from this cloudiness it is possible to discern a new interval combination taking shape.' As in Boulez's *Figures–Doubles–Prismes* and *Eclat/multiples*, the restoration of definition was a restoration of flow.

But of course flow can also erode definition in other areas, and the two textural types of the first pieces Ligeti wrote in the west—the static coloured clusters and the precise, puppet-like movements characteristic of *Aventures* and *Nouvelles aventures*—began to intermingle. Not always. The two are separately presented in his Cello Concerto (1966), where he follows his compatriot Bartók in treating the same material in quite different ways (a characteristic trait found also in his Second String Quartet, for example), first as stillness, then as abstract comedy. In many later scores, however, the two kinds of music are made to combine and to grow out of one another: this is particularly the case in *Clocks and Clouds* for orchestra with female chorus (1972–3), whose title draws attention to the antinomy it will both display and undermine, and in the Double Concerto for flute and oboe (1972). From the interaction seems to come the possibility of a music of notes rather than textures: a music of melody glimpsed first in the last movement of the Chamber Concerto (1969–70).[17]

This work and the Double Concerto also develop those tremulous repeating patterns that Ligeti had introduced in *Continuum* for harpsichord (1968) and *Coulée* for organ (1969),[18] and whose proximity to the world of Reich and Riley is acknowledged in the title of the centrepiece of the two-piano triptych of 1976: 'Self portrait with Reich and Riley (and Chopin is there too)'. The incessant repetition of small

[16] See Helmut Lachenmann, 'Beedingungen des Materials', *Darmstädter Beiträge*, 17 (1978), 93–9.

[17] See Michael Searby, 'Ligeti's Chamber Concerto: Summation or Turning Point?', *Tempo*, 168 (1988), 30–4. See also Robert Piencikowski, 'Le Concert de chambre de Ligeti', *Inharmoniques*, 2 (1987), 211–16.

[18] For convergent–divergent analyses of these pieces see Richard Toop, 'L'Illusion de la surface', *Contrechamps*, 12–13 (1990), 61–93; Michael Hicks, 'Interval and Form in Ligeti's *Continuum* and *Coulée*, *Perspectives of New Music*, 31/1 (1993), 172–90; and Jane Piper Clendinning, 'The Pattern-Meccanico Compositions of György Ligeti', *Perspectives of New Music*, 31/1 (1993), 192–234.

fragments brings about a blurring , within which Ligeti's processes of gradual harmonic change can accomplish themselves. An alternative resource is that of microtonal deviation to momentarily confuse the harmony, as in the Second Quartet, *Ramifications* for two string groups tuned a quarter-tone apart, and again in the Double Concerto, where 'normal' and 'abnormal' harmonies shimmer and merge in glassy brilliance.

All these techniques—the clouding of harmony into cluster, the repetition that obscures, the microtones that infiltrate doubt—are exquisitely calculated to veil the music's underlying processes. Similarly, the bundles of melodies in *Melodien* or *San Francisco Polyphony* (1973–4) defy the effort to take note of them all. Some of Ligeti's works suggest directly that they are portions of things larger: *Lontano* is one that seems not to end but to withdraw beyond hearing, and if the movements of a concerto or a quartet are all variations on each other, then there could notionally be more. But complexity is also a way of showing, within a work's span, how any idea necessarily entails alternatives, variations, and commentaries, that would—were they all present—obliterate it in their concourse. Like Boulez and Berio at the same time, Ligeti was following though the implications of serialism's combinatorial grammar, the limitless possibilities of proliferation and prevarication. What was his alone was the interpretation of musical process as machine. A machine does not sing melodies; a machine manufactures them. And Ligeti was happy to reacquaint himself with melody, harmony, and counterpoint as manufactured composites, as part of the weave.

As with Stravinsky's, his musical mechanisms are sharpest when they come from mechanized instruments: the harpsichord, the organ, the piano. The two-piano work with the self portrait, *Monument–Selbstportrait–Bewegung*, ends with a chorale in the form of 'an eight-voice mirror canon which contracts like a telescope' and which is 'the common coda of all three pieces'.[19] As far as *Bewegung* is concerned, it has that role because it is the apotheosis of the canonic workings trapped amid the earlier lustrous figuration, as in Example 51, where the accented notes sound out canons: one of two voices, joined up by the dashed lines, in rhythmic unison (F–E–G–C–A . . . plus its inversion beginning a fifth below), another of two staggered voices. As with Reich's phasing pieces, the cascade of detail gives rise to something simpler, but at the same time the cascade seems to be a rippling out from the simpler feature. Reich provides a ground out of which we derive a figure; Ligeti provides both ground and figure, and leaves us uncertain as to which is primary.

Melody in the context of repetitive figuration was a marked feature of the sound world of the early 1970s, as composers began to respond to New York minimalism: there are examples in Berio's music, for instance in his *Agnus* for two sopranos, three clarinets, and drone (1970–1), included in later versions of *Opera*. In Birtwistle's music of this period, however, melody starts to exert itself unques-

[19] Programme note for the first British performance, at the Queen Elizabeth Hall, London, on 8 May 1977.

Ex. 51. Ligeti, *Bewegung* (1976)

tioned, retrieving its primitive force as declamation. With reference to his orchestral work *The Triumph of Time* (1972) he has mentioned his interest in working with different rates of change, drawing attention to a cor anglais melody that never alters, and to a soprano saxophone signal that is similarly fixed and insistent until it suddenly flowers near the end of the piece.[20] His melodies often given prominence to groups of neighbouring pitch classes, whether in meandering through small intervals or leaping jaggedly, and often too they unfold as if emerging, in somewhat Varèsian fashion, from a sustained or reiterated note: thus in *Melencolia I* for clarinet, harp, and two string orchestras (1976), the wind instrument seems to summon the music out of a held A, drawing forth both its own fearsome pronouncements and the intricate network of the strings. Example 52 shows the start of the piece, where melody is gradually made possible as the pitch repertory grows out from the initial A, with the addition of G in the falling gesture from the harp, and then of G♯ and A♯ from the low strings, while the harp works over another conjunct chromatic space (from B♯ to F♭). Eventually the clarinet picks up the harp's A–G, and sets out on its own melodic path, which will be interrupted, but never properly concluded. Such a conception of melody as continuing growth, rather than as completed statement, is one of the sources of Birtwistle's continuity, and of the strong sense in each piece that it is creating itself out of the rudiments of sound.

The rhythmic equivalent to this procedure is the evolution of the most complex

---

[20] Note with Argo ZRG 790.

Ex. 52. Birtwistle, *Melencolia I* (1976)

patterns from a regular pulse, or more usually, from a geared machinery of inter-locking pulses. In Example 52, the harp's quintuplet quavers prepare—rather in the manner of Carter's metric modulation—the new pulse that enters at crotchet = 112, and every stream in the music proceeds at an even or slightly uneven pulse (the lat-ter in the case of the strings in the crotchet = 44 music, where successive entries fol-low after intervals of eleven, ten, and eleven triplet quavers). Just as the introduction of a new note is an invitation to melody, so the introduction of a new pulse (quintuplet quavers at crotchet = 44, equivalent to crotchets at crotchet = 112) enables the arrival of others (crotchets tied to semiquavers or to triplet quavers in the faster tempo, in the low string chords which are shown only in rhythmic nota-tion in the example). In this way the music discovers its 'pulse labyrinth', to take up the term Birtwistle used in relation to his *Silbury Air* for chamber orchestra (1977), whose score prints the labyrinth in operation.

Birtwistle's concern with origins and fundamentals is also at the heart of his opera *The Mask of Orpheus*, to which many of his works of the 1970s relate as stud-ies or pendants. It is highly characteristic of him that not only should each work grow of itself but that his output as a whole should do so, with poetic ideas and musical objects repeated from work to work, fulfilling the same function in differ-ent contexts, or finding other ways to develop. The first of his Orphic works, *Nenia: the Death of Orpheus* for soprano and five players (1970), was also the first to display a centring in melody, as the voice's invocation of Orpheus at the start cues a long clarinet line. And the prominence of the clarinet in Birtwistle's music of this period seems to be not only an autobiographical remnant (this was his own instrument), and not only the fruit of a creative association with the clarinettist Alan Hacker, but also determined by the instrument's powers of vocal forthrightness and flexibility.

But Stockhausen was the composer whose restoration of melody was most sur-prising, most systematic, and most self-conscious. Having steadily opened his notation (if only that) in his works of the later 1960s, he abruptly presented a fully notated score in his *Mantra* for two pianists with ring modulators (1970). Everything in the hour-long work is derived from a melody—or 'formula', to use Stockhausen's term—subjected to variation and to rhythmic expansion and con-traction. Example 53 shows the formula as it first appears: the right hand plays its four 'limbs', as the composer calls them,[21] while the left hand plays an inverted vari-ant with the limbs crossed over (i.e. in the order 2–1–4–3). The rhythmic alteration of the formula by regular augmentation or diminution is straightforwardly classical; more unusual is Stockhausen's kind of melodic variation, by which the formula is played in one or other of twelve artificial scales, ranging from the normal chromatic to one in which all the intervals are major or minor thirds, and in which the for-mula's intervals are correspondingly enlarged, as if it were a design on an inflated balloon. In this maximal expansion, the upward sixth in the first bar of the formula becomes a leap of nearly three octaves.

---

[21] Note with recording, Stockhausen 16.

Ex. 53. Stockhausen, *Mantra* (1970)

The formula also rules the large form of the composition, in that there are thir-teen principal sections, based on the skeleton notes of the formula in turn. Each note of the formula has a different character, as shown in Example 53 (rapid repeti-tion for the first, sharp final attack for the second, and so on), and the character dominates the respective phase of the work, while the note itself is presented by a sine-wave generator, one for each pianist. Since the piano sounds are ring modu-lated with these sine tones, the latter serve as omnipresent tonics. At the start, for instance, both sine-tone generators are tuned to A = 220Hz, the pitch with which the formula begins and ends; the initial and final notes will, therefore, produce a relatively simple ring-modulated product. In practice the case is more complicated, owing to the inharmonicity of piano sounds; and the effect of ring-modulation to brighten consonant notes (such as those that end each limb) and darken dissonant ones is compromised by equal temperament. Flutes in just intonation might have been a sounder choice on both grounds.

But the effectiveness of the electronically applied tonality is not really the point. The formula is already tonal in itself, with its strong opening suggestion of A minor: it instances the return of the twelve-note modality that Stockhausen had aban-doned with *Formel* nearly twenty years before, and hardly needs electronic enhancement. Perhaps Stockhausen needed the ring-modulation system partly to bring the piece (which it must have been an extraordinary experience to write, after several years away from staves) into a more familiar world, partly to assure himself of formal integrity, and partly for the sheer joy of new sounds—sounds which often suggest Cage's prepared piano.

It is the joy that seems to propel the music—more powerfully than the sine-tone cantus firmus and the electronic harmony—through its diverse musical phases and through its moments of characteristic humour and wonderment: the moment when both pianists scan massive chords with sweeping glissandos in their sine-wave generators; the moment when they fight for possession of a motif (bars 218–28); the moment when they stand to call to each other in the manner of noh percussionists (bar 639); the moment when the composition breaks off in its final phase for a résumé of all the formula's melodic transmutations in flurries of even semiquavers. These are exceptional moments, and the work has more typically a ceremonial continuity; but it is music of moments rather than of symphonic growth, as the composer recognizes in his image of it as a galaxy of different shapes.[22]

Nearly all Stockhausen's works since *Mantra* have been based on formula melodies of a similar kind. *Inori* offers a close parallel to *Mantra* in being almost a demonstration of formula composition and transformation: at this point in his career, Stockhausen was widely acclaimed as the outstanding composer of his generation, and the formula style fitted him in its declamatory authority and its impression of clarity and logic, its declaration of its way of proceeding. Music here draws near to the nature of lecture, and indeed Stockhausen composed a chanted lecture for soprano to preface *Inori*: a lecture on the lecture. His awareness of his status is also revealed in a sequence of works devoted to music as cosmic message. *Musik im Bauch* and *Harlekin* both concerned themselves with the figure of the musician as educator–joker, a thinly disguised self-projection. Then in 1975–6 Stockhausen used four of the zodiac melodies from the former work to create a ninety-minute enactment, *Sirius*, in which four virtuosos—a soprano, a bass, a trumpeter, and a bass clarinettist—arrive from outer space to instruct the inhabitants of earth, against a continuous electronic soundtrack. Similar music resources—and similar dramatic materials, drawn from autobiography, world mythology, science fiction, and a certain sort of humour—lie behind *Licht*, the week of operas, on which the composer began work in 1977, and which is founded on three formulae, one for each of the three principal characters.

Formula composition gave Stockhausen's music something it had barely had in the 1950s and 1960s: a style. Especially during the decade that began in 1952, he had been able, as he remarked at the time, to devise a new compositional system for each piece, over a range from *Kontra-Punkte* to *Kontakte*, from *Momente* to *Refrain*. Of course, there are constancies, such as the home-made approach to orchestration and the concerns—technical, aesthetic, spiritual—with music as voice, but the differences are still astonishing. By contrast, the post-1970 output is all of a piece, and distinct (not only in that regard) from what went before. For the composer,

---

[22] Note with DG 2530 208.

however, the operatic projection of his later music grew out of a sense of drama that had, undeniably, been strong in his earlier music, and formula composition was a natural outcome of serialism,[23] not part of the return to tonality that had been one of the chief features of this muddled period.

---

[23] 'Zur Situation', *Darmstädter Beiträge*, 14 (1974), 19–23.

Five Masters

As wave succeeded wave during the 1960s and early 1970s, some composers retained, or reacquired, the ability to stay firmly on their own paths. And where stability in the 1950s had been a strategy of avoiding the freeing of music (a strategy imposed on composers in eastern Europe, chosen by others elsewhere), now the terms were changed, and stability began to become a mechanism of creative survival in the face of the meaningless alteration of fashion. This was a hinge moment, between the era when composers summoned themselves and each other to extend and develop music's possibilities, and the time, beginning in the late 1970s, when the programme began to become more one of self-discovery, of finding an individual music.

It was also a critical time for the concept of the great composer. If to be a composer is to be in search of an individual music, then composers cease to be comparable, and notions of greatness, of historical importance, become groundless. Among the composers considered below, Stravinsky, Shostakovich, and Messiaen were perhaps the last to whom the words 'great composer' can be applied without doubt, wariness or embarrassment: they fulfilled the criteria in terms not only of achievement (which can never be demonstrated) but of influence and acclaim (which can be). The case of Barraqué is crucial in the history of the great composer. 'I know', he wrote, 'that today there is room for only *one* great musician.'[1] He composed in that conviction, in the conviction that greatness was required of him. But he composed in the conviction too that greatness now would have to be besieged, dangerous, going into extinction.

Stravinsky and Shostakovich

With the dispersal of the avant-garde endeavour in the mid-1960s, musical history as a history of progress seemed to come to an end, and for some composers the death of music became the only subject. In the case of composers themselves nearing death, there were obviously also immediate personal reasons for writing about it. To Messiaen it was not a problem: death was the gate to the afterlife, to which he looked forward jubilantly in his music, particularly his late music. Stravinsky's late works stay rather with those on earth, in ceremonies of mourning and memorial,

---

[1] 'Propos impromptu', *Le courrier musical de France*, 26 (1969), 75–80.

while Shostakovich, taking and feeling a more personal view, saw death as pathos and macabre joke.

Stravinsky's music had been monumentalizing, self-petrifying, at least since *Les noces*, but the final stage of the process happened quite fast: *Movements* was followed by two short tributes written in 1959, *Epitaphium* and the Double Canon for string quartet, and then by a transcription of Gesualdo madrigals, *Monumentum*, written on the occasion of the composer's quatercentenary. The speed of the compact piano concerto was gone; so were its tumbling rhythms and flickering colour. The later works tend to be in severe block forms, often with conspicuous symmetry, and to be scored for instruments and voices in choirs, though there is an exception in *Abraham and Isaac* (1962–3), where the baritone's narration of the Bible story in Hebrew is accompanied by a thin but mobile and tensile orchestral accompaniment. After this piece, nearly all Stravinsky's compositions were stelae: the Variations for orchestra (1963–4), a litany of tiny ensembles and choruses inscribed to the memory of Aldous Huxley; the *Elegy for J.F.K.* for baritone and three clarinets (1964); the unusually sombre-voiced *Introitus* for men's voices with low percussion and low strings (1965), written in memory of T. S. Eliot; the *Requiem Canticles* (1965–6), a compact mass for the dead; and, last of all, the arrangement of two sacred songs by Hugo Wolf, a kind of creative death into the music of a tradition— that of the Romantic Lied—from which the composer might have been thought most distant.

Apart, of course, from this final piece and the other late transcriptions of music by Gesualdo, Sibelius, and himself, all Stravinsky's last works are serial, and serial in ways that have much more to do with the severe twelve-note unfoldings of *Threni* than with the ramifications of *Movements*. Example 54 shows the opening of *Introitus*, where a row in the voices is accompanied by its retrograde in the instruments, prefaced by tetrachords in the harp and piano: the utterance could hardly be plainer or more severe. There is none of the comradely liveliness of *Movements*, and indeed the composer in his last references to the European avant garde distanced himself from what he had earlier admired, emulated, and perhaps surpassed. 'I seldom listen to new music any more', he said in an interview recorded shortly before his death; 'so much of it seems arbitrary to me, which all true art is, of course, but by my lights—dim as they are by Day-Glo—must not *seem* to be.'[2] Serialism, as practised in *Introitus* and other works of this period, provided just the sort of arbitrariness he wanted: a choice (the series) which, once installed, became a law. Death is a law too, and the unswerving movement of Stravinsky's late music seems to represent an acceptance without rancour.

It is otherwise in late Shostakovich. Some of his works, beginning with the Twelfth String Quartet (1968), contain twelve-note ideas, but these are set within diatonic flows, and exist not as sequences of items to be pronounced but as melodies, with all the rich traditional means of harmony and metre to make them

---

[2] Igor Stravinsky and Robert Craft, *Themes and Conclusions* (London, 1972), 182.

Ex. 54. Stravinsky, *Introitus* (1965)

so. The Twelfth Quartet begins with a twelve-note melody which increasingly recognizes its final note as a tonal goal, from which point the music begins to develop
through characteristic textures of ostinato and wandering line. This twelve-note
theme is unusual for Shostakovich only in the speed and certainty with which it
finds a base: more typically, his melodies travel on in search of a home they never
can find. (There is a bleak example at the end of the Thirteenth Quartet, where the
only accompaniment consists of percussive raps of bow on tailpiece.) Such
melody—lonely, alienated—provides one of the composer's images of bereave-
ment; his preference for slow tempos is also germane. In his last quartet, No. 15
(1974), all of the six movements are slow, and when the music is fast, it is ironically
fast—especially in the unsettling last symphony, also No. 15 (1971), with its quotations from Rossini's *William Tell* overture and from Wagner. Shostakovich also
made the subject of his late music explicit by setting poems having to do with death,
especially in his Fourteenth Symphony (1969), an anthology song cycle. Where
Stravinsky looked at death through choral ritual, he was repeatedly led to the more
subjective medium of song. (One of the extraordinary features of *Abraham and*

Isaac is that it is Stravinsky's only sustained work for solo singer after the very early and quite uncharacteristic erotic scena *The Faun and the Shepherdess*—though subjectivity is cauterized by the language.)

Viewed within a wider context, Shostakovich's late elegies convey a pessimism within musical culture that typified the late 1960s as much as did the optimism of *Sinfonia, Hymnen,* and early New York minimalism. A spirit—that of the creative individual, alone responsible for originating and conveying a unique, unambiguous, and public message—was going down. Barraqué and Shostakovich, perhaps the two last true Romantics in musical history, felt the waning of the composer's authority. Barraqué protested, and amassed in his support all the means that the immediate postwar revolution had made available—all the means, that is, whose implications were being discovered to undermine the composer's place as sole source. Shostakovich had only limited access to those means—after the brief late-Khrushchev thaw that had made possible his Thirteenth Symphony, which sets Yevtushenko's denouncement of anti-Semitism—and expressed embattlement in the awkwardness, irony, emptiness, and frustration of his music.

Messiaen

In 1964, the year of his *Couleurs de la Cité Céleste,* Messiaen also wrote *Et exspecto resurrectionem mortuorum* for symphonic wind and percussion—a rather special case, in that it was intended for large church acoustics (and also, the composer suggested, for outdoors; the ideal performance, on a peak in the French alps he loved, perhaps has to remain a wonderful imagining). Those two works marked a turning point: they were his first explicitly sacred compositions for the concert hall since the *Trois petites liturgies,* and they heralded a sequence of large-scale sacred concert pieces that resumed contact with everything in his music since the 1930s. To some extent this move was a withdrawal from the avant garde, though it could equally be read as a recognition that there was no longer an avant garde to withdraw from. With experiment over, what was left was the possibility of immensity, in the oratorio–liturgy *Transfiguration de Notre Seigneur Jésus-Christ* (1965–9), the organ cycle *Méditations sur le mystère de la Sainte Trinité* (1969), *Des canyons aux étoiles . . .* for piano and orchestra (1971–4), the opera *Saint François d'Assise* (1975–83), *Le livre du Saint Sacrement,* a last book of organ pieces (1984), and the orchestral *Eclairs sur l'Au-delà . . .* (1987–92).

Messiaen's spiritual themes were what they always had been: the presence of God on earth, both in the life of Christ (*La Transfiguration*) and in the communion sacrament (*Le livre du Saint Sacrement*), the Trinity as a further sign of human affiliation to the divine (*Méditations*), the promise of paradise as the fulfilment of that affiliation (*Des canyons, Eclairs*), and all through the joy that comes with certainty in such a vision. There is, of course, a mutuality between these themes and the composer's musical ideas and practices. For example, birdsong provided material uncontaminated by human failing. The expression of joy entailed brightness of sound, high registers, and often exuberant speed; the certainty implied the single, undeviable perspectives of modality. Most of all, Messiaen's appeal to divine time took him away from the continuity of human self-representation to chronic fragments and eternities. These late pieces need to be long; they also need to be chopped into quite dissimilar, unconnected sections, whose internal forms will generally be either seamless or else themselves sectional, often following some kind of verse–refrain pattern.

The segmented and eternal rhythms of Messiaen's music had perhaps been at the root of his closeness to the avant garde during the 1950s. When younger composers began to concern themselves again more with continuity—both with continuity of process within pieces, and with continuity through musical history—they inevitably peeled away from Messiaen's path, and left him to follow it more or less alone. But there remained points of contact. *Saint François* was Messiaen's wholly unexpected and remarkable contribution to the operatic revival of the time—though it is a work whose liturgical plan and rhythm are suggestive more of non-European traditions of theatre. Each of the eight scenes is like a panel in a stained-glass window: there may be a narrative image (for example, Francis's curing a leper by kissing him), but this is taken up into a design of space and colour that almost dazzles out the picture. The vocal style is also quite particular, as is the relationship between the soloists and the huge choir and orchestra. As he had for the choir in *La Transfiguration*, Messiaen used a kind of flexible modal chant that came out of his songs of the 1930s and 1940s. Often in the opera this is unaccompanied, and interspersed with orchestral refrains made up of signals (a small number, for the major characters and for ideas such as 'decision' and 'joy') and birdsongs. In the great birdsong chorus that comes in the scene of the sermon to the birds, Messiaen moved gently into aleatory waters (otherwise so alien to an artist of his certainty) by allowing instrumental soloists to proceed at their own tempos. He also responded to his juniors' exploration of sound: in *Des canyons* he used the sound of blowing through a horn mouthpiece, and in *Éclairs* he achieved what was, even for him, a special radiance that may have been stimulated in part by younger French composers' work with orchestral timbre. Where his writing for orchestra had previously been choric, this final work has phrases that turn in colour, and chords that blend wind and percussion tones. Otherwise, form, materials, and subject are unchanged: the work is especially close in all these ways to the *Quatuor pour la fin du temps*. It is, however, that work raised to an apotheosis.

Barraqué

In 1956, the year after he had completed *Séquence*, Barraqué was introduced by Michel Foucault to Herman Broch's novel *The Death of Virgil*, in which he discovered a sympathetic demand for a philosophically aware art, a sympathetic grand reach through whatever fragmentation, and sympathetic material, in the book's dense web of meditations on death, on the act and purposes of creation, and on the inevitability of failure and incompletion. 'All dies, all goes', the composer later wrote. 'Every trustee of creation must accept that, as he accepts his own death. Even on the technical level his art must evolve towards death; it must be completed within "incessant incompletion".'[3] The hungering for evolution, the self-motivated drive to complete what could not be completed, did not by any means lead Barraqué to join any of the revolutionary musical movements of his time: to the contrary, one of the most remarkable features of his art is its consistency.

La mort de Virgile was planned as a universe of works in five books, one for each part of the novel, and a fifth of commentary. Of course, commentary is inherent all through, in that Barraqué created texts around quotations from Broch, and in that his whole project was a commentary on the novel. However, there is a deep difference between *La mort de Virgile* and such contemporary works of musical commentary as Boulez's *Pli selon pli*: a difference of voice. Barraqué's voice, whether in vocal or in instrumental lines, is desperately engaged; this is the voice of a consciousness uttering the words for itself, not commenting upon them, as may be suggested by Example 55, from . . . *au delà du hasard* for four instrumental groups and one of voices (1958–9). The moment is characteristic of Barraqué in its richly figured and strongly dynamic polyphony, which is a real polyphony of individual but interlaced lines, and not a Boulezian heterophony of similar but unconnected parts. Where Boulez's technique of chord multiplication rationalized static harmony, Barraqué kept to the principle of the twelve-note sequence, which he made contribute to his music's linear force. The perpetual circulation of pitch classes is the rule, the force that drives the wind; reiterations, within and between lines, stand against the rule, like trees in the wind. There are numerous instances in Example 55: both linear repetitions, especially in the vocal part, and network repetitions, emphasized by registral locking (for example, of B and F♯ in the second and third bars)—another technique that has a static effect in Boulez and a dynamic one in Barraqué.

Possibilities are widened in . . . *au delà du hasard* by the music's layout as a polyphony of polyphonies, an assembly of five groups which tend to be contrapuntally—as they are timbrally—relatively homogeneous: the first is of brass, saxophones, and vibraphone, the second of tuned percussion, the third of untuned percussion, the fourth a quartet of clarinets, the fifth a female chorus with solo soprano. The solo soprano voice is the chief bearer of the music's voice here—as in *Séquence*, and as in the other two parts of *La mort de Virgile* that were completed: *Le temps restitué* with chorus and orchestra (1956–68) and *Chant après chant* with piano and percussion ensemble (1965–6)—though there is almost as much a sense of vocal utterance—linear, dynamic, phrased—in Barraqué's instrumental writing. Fluid but intensely pressured, and maintaining a rhythmic drive despite—or

---

[3] 'Propos impromptu'.

because of—flickerings in the basic pulse, these instrumental voices may contain an echo of modern jazz, which is also suggested by the line-up of . . . *au delà du hasard* in particular.

The grand rhetoric of this work—evident on the small scale in Example 55 in, for instance, the setting of 'volonté', the graphic clarinet image at 'chûte', and the emphatic rush throughout—comes to a head in the tenth of the thirteen sections, the one which sets a quotation from Broch: 'Blinded by the dream and made by the dream to see, I know your death, I know the limit which is fixed for you, the limit of the dream, which you deny. Do you know it yourself? Do you want it so?' A long orchestral passage is suddenly cut off, and the music stops for fifteen seconds; there is then an immense orchestral crescendo in two phases, followed by a further fifteen-second silence, before the untuned percussion loudly usher in the sibylline utterance of Broch's words. Such magniloquence, arising from a context of impatient and despairing rapidity, is characteristic of Barraqué, and unique in the period.

All three completed parts of *La mort de Virgile* use a technique of 'proliferating series', which would seem to have been a pitch-class adaptation of Messiaen's method of rhythmic interversion. Two serial forms are taken, and one is regarded as a permutation of the other; a third form is then obtained by applying the same permutational process to the one. For instance, if the basic series of . . . *au delà du hasard* (C–Ab–G–Db–E–D–Bb–Eb–B–F–F#–A) is understood as a permutation of its retrograde inversion (A–C–C#–G–D#–G#–E–D–F–B–A#–F#), then repeating the permutation and ignoring enharmonic differences (A goes to C, C goes to Ab/G#, C#/Db goes to G, etc.) will produce a new series that is not related in any classical way to the others two: Ab–D–Db–G–Bb–Eb–F#–E–F–B–A–C. By constantly changing the interval sequence within twelve-note successions, the technique eradicated one remnant of stability in classic serialism, and contributed to the sense of perpetual and turbulent self-renewal in much of Barraqué's music. Serial proliferation also ensured that, as he wished, derivations could never be unambiguously unravelled, despite the fact that—as in Example 55 and so often in his music—serial forms are clearly presented.[4] 'Analysis', he wrote, 'must concern itself with the final result: that is, with the work as part of history . . . The composer's thinking remains his marvellous secret.'[5] And though he was thinking here of Debussy, Debussy was his great model of renovation, just as Beethoven was his great model of development.

Barraqué's proliferating series matched the poetic proliferation inherent in the Broch project, which was to have embraced works on different scales (sketches exist for a piece for eighteen voices a cappella; there was also to have been an opera), and

[4] For further details of Barraqué's serial practice see Bill Hopkins, 'Barraqué and the Serial Idea', *Proceedings of the Royal Musical Association*, 105 (1978–9), 13–24; François Nicolas, 'Le souci du développement chez Barraqué', *Entretemps*, 5 (1987), 7–24; André Riotte, 'Les séries proliférantes selon Barraqué: approche formelle', *Entretemps*, 5 (1987), 65–74; and Andrew Fathers, *Jean Barraqué and L'inachèvement sans cesse* (diss., Oxford, 1993).

[5] 'Debussy ou la naissance d'une forme ouverte', quoted in François Nicolas: 'Le souci du développement chez Barraqué', 13.

Ex. 55. Barraqué, . . . *au delá du hasard* (1958–9)

which the composer surely cannot have expected to complete. Incompletion was written into the artistic contract; *La mort de Virgile* was his response not only to Beethoven's dynamism and Debussy's fluidity,[6] but also to the work that had set him on his course as a composer: Schubert's 'Unfinished' Symphony.[7] Each part that he did achieve is a protest against the dissolution and hopelessness inherent in the project: that is one source of the music's energy, to be always fighting itself into existence. It is music of becoming, which Barraqué registers in leaving off double barlines (his works do not end, but rather fade into an acceptance of silence), in the complexity of his polyphony, in his constant interplay of sound with silence and with noise, and in his impatience with anything stable or achieved.

[6] See, besides his book on Debussy, his analysis of *La mer*, edited by Alain Poirier as 'La mer de Debussy ou la naissance des formes ouvertes', *Analyse musicale*, 12 (1988), 15–62.

[7] See 'Propos impromptu'.

Hopkins

Bill Hopkins (1943–81) went to Paris in 1964 in order principally to meet Barraqué, to whose Piano Sonata, in Yvonne Loriod's recording, he 'had listened repeatedly, intently, and with an overwhelming apprehension of living greatness. If music meant anything today, only here was that meaning fully grasped, and it was to a like ideal that my own work falteringly aspired.'[8] What Barraqué's work demonstrated, and implicitly demanded of successors, was 'the meaningful interrelatedness of each single musical decision' within a world where nothing could be taken for granted: 'no witnesses are called, no charades acted out, no authorities invoked,

---

[8] 'Portrait of a Sonata', *Tempo*, 186 (1993), 13–14. Nicolas Hodges's essay 'The Music of Bill Hopkins' in the same issue, 4–12, provides an admirable and sympathetic introduction to the composer.

and no restrictive assumptions made'.[9] Pursuing these ideals of total coherence and total independence condemned Hopkins to a creative life less of production than of preparation, dissatisfaction, and waiting, which duly became the subject and manner of his music. An extraordinary command of musical resources—especially of harmonic resources—could only begin to operate beyond, around, and in consciousness of an immense blockage compounded of rigour and responsibility.

Under Barraqué's tutelage Hopkins wrote *Sensation* for soprano and four players (1965), a work slightly modelled on his teacher's *Séquence*, but going its own way from ecstasy in setting Rimbaud to bleakness in setting Beckett, who was the other great influence on him—an influence that reinforced Barraqué's in demanding ruthless artistic conscientiousness, while also according with a concision, an intermittent simplicity, a fumbling, an irresolution, and a grim humour that separate his music from Barraqué's. Barraqué's music never ends; Hopkins's is ending all the time. His principal achievement after *Sensation* was the set of nine piano pieces, *Etudes en série* (1965–72), which reveal how he was able to develop out of Barraqué a much quieter rhetoric. The music is richly detailed and sonorous in its harmony, and surely propelled by unstable rhythm in a Barraqué-like way, though its movement is much less likely to be towards climax than towards exhaustion and evaporation. Two further pieces came out of the long process that produced the *Etudes*: *Pendant* for violin and the *Nouvelle étude hors série* for organ, of which the opening of the former, shown in Example 56, may indicate how Hopkins's music finds a fine trail through scattered fragments, and maybe how the music seems to include an awareness which inspects and rejects what comes to it before moving on. The microtonal inflections were apparently suggested by the ideal of birdsong[10] and contribute to the music's freedom, which is the freedom not so much of song as of ruminating thought. The only stability arrives at the centre of the piece in a strange dumb tune, which is at once pitifully inadequate and, by virtue of its inadequacy, bang on. It suggests that Hopkins was already seeing in the mentally subnormal a metaphor for the creative artist at a point in history where language seemed to have stopped working.

Hopkins came out of the *Etudes* with two projects in hand, both of them unfinishable and even unstartable. One was for a dramatic piece centred on a mentally subnormal boy; the other, *Voix privée*, was for an unaccompanied voice never meant to be heard outside the composer's head. The fact that he did begin *Voix privée* many times is evidence that he also discarded it many times, and that it could never be really begun at all. As usual with him, the title was a pun, to be interpreted not only as 'private voice' but also as 'deprived voice' and as 'no entry' ('voie privée'). Had he lived, he might have emerged from this period of hopelessness: a chamber piece achieved in 1976–7, *En attendant*, was perhaps only a holding operation, but other compositions were under way when he died. Nevertheless, *Voix privée*, the impossible notation of a composer's self-communing, marks out the

[9] Review of the Claude Helffer recording in *Tempo*, 95 (1970–1), reprinted in *Tempo*, 186 (1993), 2–3.
[10] See Patrick Ozzard-Low's review of the recording in *Tempo*, 188 (1994), 38.

Ex. 56. Hopkins, *Pendant* (1968–9, rev. 1973)

difficulties besetting the discovery and communication of an interior voice, even if it is one's own.

PART III. MANY RIVERS: THE 1980s
AND 1990s

The abundance of music now being written makes it hard to see the wood for the trees, the currents for the water. Perhaps in time the view will become clearer. But, as has been mentioned, the current great number of professional composers is a new phenomenon, and one that may alter—may already have altered—the way history could extract a deposit of contemporary work for permanence. Also, time's winnowing no longer seems to be happening as it used to. Since the arrival of the compact disc, in 1982, the available repertory in all periods has vastly increased, and trends in criticism have questioned the criteria and even the value of selecting an agreed canon of masterpieces. We live now with many musical histories, and many musical presents.

This may be a problem for musical institutions—orchestras, festivals, publishing companies—based on the idea of finding and fostering the great composer. It may be a problem too for composers, if their notions of success are based on the kind of career enjoyed by a Ligeti or a Berio: greater numbers are likely to mean narrower reputations. And it is a problem for listeners simply to find ways around the great archipelago of contemporary music.

It is, finally, a problem also for this book, whose pretences to comprehensiveness have already worn thin and must now be abandoned. What follows is a sampling of some composers and some topics in recent music—strings and knots, inevitably limited by my own experiences and interests, as well as by some concern to register diversity without a superabundance of examples. Some of these examples could, no doubt, have been different. Most could not. If we are indeed moving out of the era of the great composer, this is an interesting twilight.

Strings and Knots

Iannis Xenakis

One of the odd things about music in the late twentieth century is the continuing prestige, throughout the period, of composers born in the 1920s (Boulez, Berio, Nono, Feldman, Stockhausen, Xenakis, Ligeti), with a few from the next decade (Birtwistle, Reich, Glass) or the previous dozen years (Messiaen, Cage, Shostakovich, Carter, Babbitt). Most of these people were well established internationally by 1960; the 1930s generation became so during the next decade; and composers who have claimed great attention subsequently have still tended to be of this favoured epoch: Scelsi, Schnittke, Gubaydulina, Donatoni. One looks in vain for musicians born in the 1960s or 1970s who are changing the art at the century's end as much as Cage and Boulez were at its midpoint. The age of revolution seems to have passed—which has been a problem, underneath the eminence, for those who felt themselves born to command it.

Among those peace-time generals, Xenakis stands out for remaining as raw in the 1990s as he was in the 1950s and 1960s. He seems not to have introduced any completely new technique since the early 1970s (in which he is by no means alone), but neither has he developed those he had. The change in the mid-1970s—with his use of 'non-octaving' scales to make not long ribbons but abrupt motifs, and his corresponding reduction of rhythm to regular pulsation—was rather an anti-development that enabled him to regress to evocations of folk music (perhaps the folk music of his Balkan childhood), or of folk music as mediated by Stravinsky. His orchestral piece *Jonchaies* (1977) vividly recalls *The Rite of Spring*; *Ikhoor* for string trio (1978) begins by almost quoting the 'The Augurs of Spring' from that work. When he introduces elements from the central tradition—an E♭ major chord suddenly in *Echange* for bass clarinet and ensemble (1989), some struggling polyphonic imitation in *Akea* for piano quintet (1986), and of course the conventional chamber media of this and several other pieces—the effect is to emphasize difference rather than assimilation. By traditional criteria, the harmony is unmotivated, the counterpoint primitive, the scoring brutal. Example 57, from *Tetora* for string quartet (1990), illustrates this distance from canonical respectability in the most canonical form. By means of his prolonged notes, non-vibrato requirement and close harmonies the composer creates a quite new quartet sound, one suggestive more of the wheeze of a mouth organ.

Xenakis—rather magnificently, given the omnipresence in the arts of allusion and retrieval—has learned nothing from the music around him. Nor has he learned

Ex. 57. Xenakis, *Tetora* (1990)

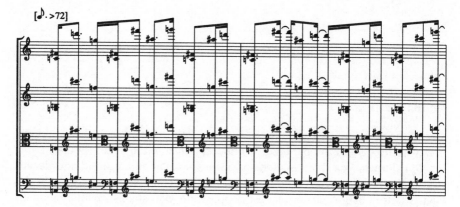

anything from his own practice, except maybe fluency. For though his output since 1970 has been formidable—nearly always in instrumental genres, with particular preferences for concertos and mixed-ensemble pieces (yet one should be cautious about interpreting as preference what might be merely opportunity: composers work to commission, and solo instrumentalists and modern-music ensembles are among the keenest commissioners)—his instrumentation is forcibly blunt. From the mismatch of timbres, the abrasiveness of the sound, comes his music's power— from that and from the paring of materials to the bare essentials of pulsation, insistent note repetition, and textural contrast.

Judith Weir

Postmodernism, to come to that, is many other things. It may be a matter of composing as before, of continuing or restoring the forms, genres, and rhetoric of earlier music, if not the ethics. (Also, the choice of earlier music seems to be forced, oddly, between, on the one hand, the symphonic tradition of the late nineteenth and early twentieth centuries, and on the other, Bach-cum-Pérotin.) It may be all jumbled quotation. Or it may be a question of irony—in the case of Judith Weir (b. 1954),[1] of amused disbelief. Weir's sense of a friendly apartness from the rules, formulae, standards, and instruments of western music may have to do with her own double-outsider status as a Scot and a woman (there is not much music in the old tradition from Scots; not much from women), as well as by her admiration for Stravinsky and by her Stravinskian offbeam way of building music from the ground—the folk-music ground-up. She has written pieces treating of Scottish folk culture, such as the song cycle *Scotch Minstrelsy* (1982) or the opera *The Vanishing*

---

[1] For a discussion of Weir's early work, with plentiful music examples, see Tom Morgan, 'Judith Weir', in Michael Finnissy, Malcolm Hayes and Roger Wright (eds.), *New Music 88* (Oxford, 1988), 22–50.

Bridegroom (1990), which is a neat nesting of three traditional tales; more widely in her work can be sensed a Scottish modality and the drone-plus-decoration of the pipes. She has also made imaginary folk-musical occasions: *A Serbian Cabaret* (1984), and *A Night at the Chinese Opera* (1987).

Example 58 shows a passage from this latter work, and illustrates features that are typical of Weir's style: the treble texture, which helps keep the harmony in the air; the use, then, of simple chords in an environment where they can float; the chop of melody into brief bursts and spills; the clear instrumentation, by families; the corresponding short formal blocks; the absence of counterpoint—except for the counterpoint between what is said and what is not said. Weir delights in the inappropriate. *King Harald's Saga* (1979) is a grand opera told in ten minutes by a solo soprano, who takes on all the roles, including that of the Norwegian army. (The piece is only a squib, but in giving a concrete reason of mimicry for the vocal alternations of Cage's *Aria* or Berio's *Sequenza III*, it shows how Weir's scepticism extends to the immortals of the previous generation.) In later works, subterfuge and dismantling are achieved by subtler means: by—as may be seen in the example—the placing of tonal chords contrary to conventional practice (a Ligetian tactic), or the use of a deliberately flat vocal style, or the doubling of voice and instrument, which makes a display of unpretentiousness. Weir's works are beautiful things that cannot be trusted, and her operas have tended to exploit this unreliability of narrative as a dramatic theme. In *A Night at the Chinese Opera*, the hero finds his life reflected in a play, but the discovery does not help him avoid his fate. In *The Vanishing Bridegroom*, a thief reveals himself by his response to a story. In *Blond Eckbert* (1993), the whole progress of the drama is riven with doubts and paradoxes, and eventually the piece collapses back into its beginning. As often with illustrations in books of fairytales, Weir's pieces contrive a fresh, vivid, and colourful presentation of what may be sinister and macabre.

Ex. 58. Weir, *A Night at the Chinese Opera*, Act I, scene I (1987)

Tan Dun

One striking development in music since the early 1980s has been the arrival of a generation of composers who trained at the Beijing Conservatory in the years immediately after the Cultural Revolution in China, and who took from that experience a lasting sense of composition as exploration—as breaking bounds. The excitement of fresh information and fresh discovery was perhaps comparable with what was felt in Europe immediately after the war, except that the young Chinese composers saw what they needed in the west rather than in the past. A visit to Beijing by Alexander Goehr in 1980 was of the highest importance for these composers, among them Tan Dun (b. 1957), but by then Tan and his colleagues had already been exposed to two other powerful influences. One, of course, was that of Chinese music (Tan had played the violin for a Beijing Opera company during the time he was living with his grandmother in Hunan, before going to the conservatory in 1978); the other was that of Shostakovich, as transmitted by the Soviet-trained teachers at the conservatory. The new music they discovered through Goehr made it possible for them to bring these disparate parts of their backgrounds—a Chinese savouring of the moment, and therefore of the unprecedented (Taoist immediacy being more important to them than Confucian respect for tradition), and a commitment to long line and passionate subjectivity inherited from Shostakovich—into a powerful dialogue.

One of Tan's first works to achieve this appears to have been *On Taoism* for voice and orchestra (1985), which was among the last pieces he wrote before leaving for New York in 1986. (His large preceding output—including symphonies and string quartets as well as the prototype of Chinese electronic music—has not been published in the west.) Attending his grandmother's traditional funeral had awakened memories of Chinese ritual, folk, and theatre music—memories predating his conservatory professionalism—and he let them find expression in a voice part that can suggest a shaman or a Beijing Opera performer; two instrumental soloists, on bassoon and bass clarinet, are intermediaries between the vocalist and the orchestra: Example 59 shows how these elements are engaged in vivid interplay. Partly because he wrote it for himself to perform, *On Taoism* is hyper-subjective: it slices through that great Gordian knot of aesthetics, the identifiability of the composer's voice. It also opened the way to further fusions of Chinese and western, of vocal and instrumental, and of ritual and concert.

In composing his next large-scale work, *Orchestral Theatre I: Xun* (1990), Tan began by asking himself 'if a classical orchestra could sound not classical; could it convey the sense of another culture, a ritual of instruments and vocalization?'[2] Hence not only his combination here of conventional western instruments with *xun* (Chinese ocarina-like instruments, played by a soloist and by the orchestral woodwind), but his requirement for the orchestral musicians to use their voices. A

---

[2] Note with Fontec 3276.

Ex. 59. Tan, *On Taoism* (1985)

taboo is broken; the concert hall becomes a more unsettling place. In later works, *Circle with Four Trios, Conductor and Audience* (1992) and *Orchestral Theatre II: Re* (1993), the audience, too, has to vocalize at certain moments. What matters most, though, to the ritual effect is the drama we witness: an orchestra that hums or chants or shouts; solo instruments taking on the sliding, narrow-register lines of Beijing Opera; long melodies, as notably in *Snow in June* for cello and percussion quartet (1991); sudden eruptions, equally characteristic of *Orchedstral Theatre II*, which counterparts Scelsi by offering a monotone (as the subtitle indicates) of violent exchanges between orchestral groups, or between sound and silence.

Karlheinz Stockhausen

Stockhausen's status as an originator, from the early 1950s to the early 1970s, has been amply documented in the first two parts of this book. Then things changed. There was the general lapse of belief in origination, and as a result the composer's self-belief—never in any doubt, to judge from all appearances[3]—increasingly had to express itself in a personal mythology, and by personal means: he became his own publisher and his own record producer, and, continuing as his own performer, he began to concentrate his attention on a group consisting of his children and regular members of his household. Since 1975 much of his music has featured his sons Markus (trumpet) and Simon (saxophone and synthesizer), his daughter Majella (piano), and his companion Suzanne Stephens (bass clarinet); the flautist Kathinka Pasveer joined the central team in 1983.

To some extent this resort to the composer's intimate circle was a continuation of the group work he had undertaken in the late 1960s and early 1970s; it was also a practical solution to the problem of rehearsing complex music—music which generally demands a partly mimed presentation, often in costume, and which therefore has to be played from memory. Close contact with these players resulted, too, in unlikely encounters with music of the classical period, in a sequence of cadenzas which treat themes by Haydn and Mozart as post-*Mantra* formulae,[4] and which have a singular tone by virtue of the humour, craziness, and awesomeness characteristic of *Licht*. However, the Stockhausen 'family' has served to isolate the composer from wider musical culture—or perhaps rather to compensate for an isolation he would have found anyway. Avant gardes are out of style: avant-garde leaders even more so.

The seven-opera project *Licht* can be seen as a strategy of creative survival in an age sceptical of the forging genius and inimical to innovation. Begun in 1977, the

---

[3] See e.g. *Texte* v and vi (both Cologne, 1989), which cover the first three *Licht* operas, and the material published with the recordings.

[4] For a discussion of these cadenzas, especially those for Haydn's Trumpet Concerto, see Glenn Watkins, *Pyramids at the Louvre: Music, Culture, and Collage from Stravinsky to the Postmodernists* (Cambridge, Mass., 1994), 433–8.

work effectively released Stockhausen from the need to have any new ideas for the next quarter century. As he put it himself, after twenty-five years of discovery would come twenty-five years of integrating what had been discovered,[5] and, indeed, most of his earlier preoccupations continue on into *Licht*: setting music in space; finding new timbres, both electronic and instrumental; mixing vocal and instrumental categories; creating images of divine order; making the concert a ritual act. *Licht* can be understood too as a response, in shallow times, to the call to greatness—a call coming not only from the composer himself but from his public.

While the scale of the enterprise would appear to imply the highest ambitions (Wagner's *Ring* provides the inevitable comparison), the working-out seems designed, by its deficiency, its comedy, and its inconsistency, to contradict any such claims. By offering individual scenes as responses to commissions, the composer ensures that each opera is a ragbag: *Montag* (1984–8), for example, includes a girls' chorus, a keyboard intervention (Piano Piece XIV), trios for sopranos and tenors, a ballet of perambulators, various solos and ensembles for wind instruments (especially Stephens's basset horn and Pasveer's flute), an enactment of the Pied Piper legend, and much else washing in on tides of sound from synthesizers and percussion, which Stockhausen uses as a 'modern orchestra', a replacement for the standard orchestra, with which he has not worked since *Donnerstag* (1978–80), the first *Licht* opera to be composed. Of course, the multifarious elements of *Montag* are connected by their dependence on the three ground formulae of *Licht*—one for each of the principal characters—but the elaboration of those formulae into multi-layered textures produces, in almost all cases, an extremely slow harmonic rhythm, and Stockhausen's formal ideal remains that of *Momente*: not an impelled continuity but a succession of diverse moments.

Example 60*a* presents one of the formulae in its basic state, and Example 60*b* shows an extract from one of the moments: *Pietà*, from the second act of *Dienstag*[6] (1987–91, but incorporating *Der Jahreslauf*, which was written in 1977 for Japan, where Stockhausen formed the plan for *Licht*). The formula, as usual with Stockhausen, includes all twelve notes, parcelled into strikingly characteristized motifs that by no means eschew tonal echoes. Among the motifs here, several are recalled by the soprano, whose main preoccupation is with the fifth bar of the formula. At the same time, both lines are locked into formula expositions proceeding at much slower tempos: Stockhausen's basic scheme for the piece[7] shows seven simultaneous, slow-motion formulae.

A short example cannot communicate the immensity of *Pietà* as a flugelhorn showpiece, covering a range of almost five octaves, continuing for almost half an hour, requiring the production of quarter-tones and approximate eight-tones by

---

[5] See Tim Nevill (ed.), *Towards a Cosmic Music: Texts by Karlheinz Stockhausen* (London, 1989), 102.

[6] For a note on the tape which runs through this act, together with six pages from the score, see Karlheinz Stockhausen, '*Octophony*: Electronic Music from *Tuesday from Light*', *Perspectives of New Music*, 31/2 (1993), 150–70.

[7] Reproduced with the recording on Stockhausen 43.

Ex. 60a. Stockhausen, nuclear formula for Eva

Ex. 60b. Stockhausen, *Pietà* from *Dienstag* (1990)

means of chosen fingers and rustling breath (notated by a diagonal stroke through the notehead), and introducing 'vowel sounds and vowel transitions . . . which sometimes resemble a movingly "weeping" human voice . . . , kissing-noises into the mouthpiece, new kinds of tremoli, tongue-trills, soft tonguing technique, use of plunger mute'.[8] The piece is, on this level, a testimony to Markus Stockhausen's prowess. Nor can the example adequately convey the power of one of the most affecting episodes in *Licht*, where, during the course of a combat between Michael trumpeters and Luzifer trombonists, one of the former is wounded. 'A woman—the soprano—appears, and sits down. The trumpeter is laid across her lap in a way similar to that in which Christ is seen on the lap of his mother Mary in Pietà paintings and sculptures. The soul of the trumpeter then rises out of his body, hovers behind the soprano, stands very large as a spirit behind her and plays—on flugelhorn—the duet with her, while she constantly looks at the body on her lap or sings upwards to Heaven.'[9] However, even three bars may be enough to show how Stockhausen's *Licht* music is a constant, fluid reiteration of selected notes and patterns.

The prevalent musical qualities—the slowness, the lack of dynamism, and the stasis and repetitiveness implicit in the formula method—are appropriate to the ritual nature of the work, given that Stockhausen's conception of ritual is conditioned by his European background and by his keen response to Japanese temple practice. *Donnerstags Abschied*, for five trumpets sounding from high positions as the audience leaves the first opera, belongs to a German tradition of tower music, and *Mädchenprozession*, a *Montag* episode for girls singing and bearing candles, has parallels in Catholic liturgy, while the final scene of *Samstag* (1981–3), *Luzifers Abschied*, recalls the composer's reminiscences of the Omizutori ceremony, which he witnessed during his 1966 visit to Japan.[10] And then, besides reproducing other rituals, *Licht* is a ritual itself. One normal feature of rituals, however, is that they present beliefs and actions in which there is a common consent, and this cannot be imagined to be so of *Licht*. Just as each opera is a collection of assorted musical items, so the heptalogy's myth is a synthetic mix of occult lore, science fiction, Christianity, and autobiography. Miscellaneity, though, need not disqualify. On the contrary, the variety is a remarkable achievement, when so many of the musical numbers are scored for similar ensembles, with trumpet, basset horn, flute, piano, and synthesizer at the nucleus, and when everything is guided by the three generative formulae. *Licht* may be regarded, too, as a creative contribution to the questioning of wholeness that was going on at the same time in—to pursue the obvious analogy—stagings of Wagner's operas and the revival of piano transcriptions of episodes from them. Stockhausen's work positively embraces contradiction and variation, and disputes the primacy of the whole by proving the self-sufficiency and mutability of the elements. Moreover, the deliquescence has increased.

Donnerstag has a certain integrity of means and subject matter, marked by its steady accumulation of musical resources (the first act is for vocal and instrumental

---

[8] Note, reproduced with the recording on Stockhausen 43.   [9] Ibid.

[10] See *Texte*, iv. 443–7.

soloists plus tape; the second is a concerto for stage trumpeter and pit orchestra, with occasional secondary soloists; the third brings on full choral and orchestral forces) and by its portrayal of the hero's formation, journey around the earth, and return to the heavens. This hero is Michael—part angel, part Christ, part cosmic messenger, part self-image on the part of the composer—who is represented in this opera by a trumpeter, a tenor, and a male dancer. His father–antagonist, Luzifer, also has three embodiments, as trombonist, bass, and male dancer; so does the third main character, Eva, who is the eternal female, Michael's mother, guardian, and consort, appearing as basset hornist, soprano, and female dancer. In later operas these associations have been somewhat modified: in *Montag*, for instance, the manifestations are often tripled, and the arrival of Pasveer encouraged the composer to create large roles for flautist as Eva figure in *Samstag*, *Montag*, and *Freitag*. Also, the partial but real wholeness of *Donnerstag* has disintegrated by the time of *Samstag*, which is a sequence of four quite separate acts, and disintegrated further in *Montag*, where the unit is the scene within an act. (The order of composition has been logical, beginning with the three operas spotlighting the central characters in turn, and continuing with the three concerned with pairs of characters—Michael and Luzifer in *Dienstag*, the day of war; Luzifer and Eva in *Freitag*; and Eva and Michael in *Mittwoch*—before coming finally to the concelebration of all three in *Sonntag*.) Since the time of *Montag*, too, Stockhausen has often gone back to earlier parts of the cycle in what is a potentially limitless process of rearrangement. For example, whole scenes and acts of *Donnerstag* and *Samstag* have been adapted for different formations, sometimes more than once, or quarried for new smaller pieces, as when a soprano–bass duet from the first act of *Donnerstag* emerged in 1993 as *Bijou* for alto flute and bass clarinet with tape. Just as Stockhausen's librettos ululate with metamorphosis ('fraitak mahakdak mähäkdok frakfrik frigga venusik nikkelfik a-haintselfrik venuspik fridach venuschelmuschel frigigapuschel', to quote from *Montag*) so *Licht* is a perpetually self-generating, self-regenerating network.

The grandeur of the project is inseparable from its bathos. By its absurdity and by its mess, the work testifies to the impossibility of a real drama of the world and time being achieved at the end of the twentieth century. Its destiny is to be at once magnificent and ridiculous.

Spectral Music

Concern with timbre—with what has often been called, by analogy with light, the 'spectrum' of sound—is one of the few immediate postwar topics to have remained alive half a century later. Among composers working with computer sound synthesis, whether at Stanford, at IRCAM or elsewhere, timbre is obviously of paramount importance by reason of the complexity of factors on which it depends: the contributions of different frequency components with different points of onset, different amplitudes, different phase relationships, and different envelopes. But the fine structure of sound, as something which can be created, is crucial too for many composers of instrumental music, whether in working with the colours obtainable from individual players, as in the many solo and duo pieces that have come out of Stockhausen's *Licht*, or in assembling timbres by assembling orchestral masses, as in the music of Tristan Murail (b. 1947) and other French musicians, with whom the term 'spectral music' is particularly associated.

A remarkable exponent of this latter kind of timbre composition is the Romanian-born composer Horatiu Radulescu (b. 1942), who moved to Paris in 1969, in which year he also began to work with sound spectra. Five years later he found an instrument ideal for his purposes: the 'sound icon', which is his term for a grand piano lying on its side, so that the strings may be bowed, producing complexes of bowed tone and resonance depending on the tuning of the strings and the bowing technique. In, for example, *Clepsydra* for sixteen sound icons placed around the audience (1982), the result is a 'sound plasma': 'living sound that can only be comprehended from a global perspective, resembling the blue image of earth as viewed from outer space.'[11] As this image suggests, the sound is tremulous with inner life while being broadly static, moving in a slow process from a dense mass to a single pitch (though one still with a rich spectrum of its own) and back again. By means of such slow processes—and by centring itself on a single sound, which it explores—Radulescu's music achieves the awesomeness of a thing both scientific (dependent on knowledge, on precision of measurement in matters of tuning, on clarity of method) and sacred (geared to singleness, presenting all phenomena as aspects of that singleness, as also in the music of Scelsi, whose rise to prominence coincided with the growth of spectral music). In *Inner Time II* for seven carefully tuned clarinets (1993), where the more definite medium makes for a greater definition of spectra, the effect of highly articulate strangeness is even more pronounced.

Sex and Sexuality

The great rotation that occurred in music around 1970, from issues of language and general practice to matters of individual sensibility, was something like a sex change. Musical conditions that may be seen as heterosexual male by traditional standards—authority, vested solely in the composer and descending lineally from composer to composer; the concomitant view of history as a chain of originators, and of performers and listeners as receivers; the veneration of conception as the prime moment, and therefore of creative intention as meaning—had come under threat during the 1950s and 1960s, with the arrival of indeterminacy and improvisation, but it was the collapse of modernism that brought the possibility of an eclipse. Modernism had been straight male: the writings of the great modernist pioneers, from Varèse to Boulez, are full of sexual imagery of a traditionally male

[11] Note with Edition RZ 1007.

cast—the imagery of action, seizure, impregnation. After modernism the way was opened to more fluid and ambiguous relationships: among composers, performers, and listeners, and between musicians and history.

Because music could now admit the personal, the assertion of female and homosexual identities might have become easier. But there are problems here, since the demasculinization of music made the previously heterodox normal. Qualities of camp—ironic inversion of values, collage, quotation, display—have become endemic since the end of modernism. And the appearance on the operatic stage of sexually ambivalent voices (notably the counter-tenor) and cross-dressers is no more a particularly homosexual phenomenon than it was in the eighteenth century. In many instances the construction of artificial or equivocal sexualities may have a strong homosexual charge—as in the counter-tenor Oberon of Britten's *A Midsummer Night's Dream* (1960), or the principal character of *The Intelligence Park* (1981-8) by Gerald Barry (b. 1952), or the Joan of Arc, again a counter-tenor role, in *Arms and the Maid* (1993) by Luke Stoneham—but the possibility of such characters seems to be in the nature of the art as much as in that of the composer. Explicit treatments of homosexual feeling have been remarkably few in opera: the examples include Lou Harrison's puppet opera *Young Caesar* (1971) and Britten's *Death in Venice* (1973). Also, since male homosexuals have, in all probability, contributed more than proportionately as composers during the last century and a half, music is perhaps subcutaneously gay already, for all the straight male character it projected until quite recently. And the relaxing of penal and social sanctions, similarly taking place in most western countries around 1970, may have reduced the particularity of homosexual expression by removing its necessary covertness and likely guilt—the covertness and the guilt that find themselves in Britten's operas.

The case is different with women composers, who were in a minuscule minority, and remain in a small one. Yet if there is necessarily something female in a female composer's music, the distinctiveness is not easy to see in the work of some outstanding examples. Weir's sly comedy, for instance, bears comparison with Donatoni's; Gubaydulina's religious intensity has parallels in Schnittke; Saariaho's exploration of timbre is not uncommon among composers of her generation. Others, though, have felt that women's music would have to go another way, which might have to mean rejecting the dominant culture: the issues have been considered by Susan McClary[12] and—over a longer period, in creative work—by Pauline Oliveros (b. 1932), whose music has tended to be open to improvisation and participation. Elaine Barkin (b. 1932) has wanted to follow this line while distancing herself from Oliveros in holding on to the achievements and experiences of previous western music and musical analysis at its most sophisticated: she emerged as a composer and scholar from the school of Babbitt. What she would avoid, or transcend, is the maleness of music, the composer's exertion of authority and power. 'The original concern was not to compose music but to find a way to be an inhabi-

---

[12] See her *Feminine Endings* (Minneapolis: University of Minnesota Press, 1991).

tant in a world of music that could be done and made and shared with others within a non-competitive, nonhierarchical, and non-authoritarian environment . . . We meed at home, at school, out-of-doors; a participant suggests an idea, a working hypothesis, a strategy, a thought; we listen, we sound, we make our time, we shape ourselves.'[13]

The difference between Oliveros and Barkin perhaps has to do with different aims. Where Oliveros would seem to be in search of music that is female, for Barkin the projection of sexuality is less important than the need within music itself to continue its sexual transition. And this is something which male composers too may serve. For example, Barkin's colleague Benjamin Boretz has denigrated as 'masterpiece culture' the male nature of the art. As he put it in a 1987 lecture: 'In masterpiece culture, musical behavior is strictly the symbolic behavior of abstract Ideas, idealized Figures, and schematized structures of quantified sonic particles. Music History, the official record of musical phenomena within masterpiece culture, is merely the recorded chronology and taxonomy of these idealized behaviors. It is only when music is seen as something that is done by and among *people*, as a form of *people's* behavior among other forms of behavior, that real-time, people-size circumstances of history, culture, and experience become indispensably relevant, both as input to and as output from, our conceptions and practices of music.'[14]

For Boretz, this has meant abandoning the idea of fixing sounds for all time—the abandonment is perhaps taking place during the course of his *Group Variations II* for computer (1968–71), as the music moves away from bristling informativeness— and dedicating himself instead to improvisation by himself or with friends. 'A long time ago', he said in 1990, 'I would have felt that a valuable outcome of my ideas would be that they would be appropriated widely by other people . . . But now I believe . . . that the main value of my ideas is rather to create a space within which I, perhaps, can survive, alongside of everyone else working out their survival in their own ways.'[15] Recordings of Boretz's improvisations, though he has made them public, cannot be more than relics. 'In music, as in everything, the disappearing moment of experience is the firmest reality.'[16]

But Boretz's self-denial, though convincing as a response to the musical present and honourable in itself, leaves no possibility of conveying information, thought, and feeling from person to person across much wider times and spaces than those of the private room at some particular time. In his work, the much-vaunted ending of history is real.

---

[13] Quoted in Janice Mowery Frey, 'Elaine Barkin: Active Participant', *Perspectives of New Music*, 31/2 (1993), 252–63.

[14] 'Interface Part III: Relevance. Liberation', in John Rahn (ed.), *Perspectives on Musical Aesthetics* (New York, 1994), 125–8.

[15] 'Interface Part V: The Inner Studio (Strategies for Retrieving Reality in Music Experience and Practice)', ibid. 134–42.

[16] 'Interface Part II: Thoughts in Reply to Boulez/Foucault: "Contemporary Music and the Public"', ibid. 121–4.

Alfred Schnittke

Since the death of Shostakovich, in 1975, Alfred Schnittke (b. 1934) has been regularly pronounced his heir, for reasons that surely have to do not just with his pursuit of standard genres (symphony, concerto, quartet, sonata) but also with his esclation of the most distinctive modes of post-1936 Shostakovich: anxiety (when we might feel we are hearing the composer's voice directly), irony (when we know we are not), and anxious irony or ironic anxiousness (when we cannot be sure). That Schnittke is aware of this musical paternity is evident from his use of the DSCH motif in, for example, his Third String Quartet (1983) and Seventh Symphony (1993).[17] It may even be that a sense of writing someone else's music is part of the desperation his works convey, and in which they seem to have been created—a desperation whose symptoms include a startling productivity, especially since the mid-1980s. The sources of that desperation must include the composer's persistent ill-health, but they would also have to involve his artistic alarms: panic at the collapse of history into a meaningless simultaneity, and the trepidations of a man belonging to and reporting from a culture passing from tight constraint into unchecked freedom.

The moderated freedom of the late Khrushchev years, and the resultant visit of Nono to the Soviet Union in 1962, brought for many Russian composers a feeling of fresh opportunity, and Schnittke too travelled the serial road a while. But by the end of the 1960s he had come to the conclusion that serialism did not offer the means to command big, continuous forms, and so he began to work with combinations of tonal and atonal elements. Also, Nono's visit had perhaps opened a Pandora's box. If style was not vouchsafed by a tradition, if one could pick and choose, then the possibility of creative integrity—of music arising and presented without artifice or manipulation—was over. This might be a cause for joy (creativity no longer being encumbered with Romantic ideology) or gloom (the guidelines of artistic morality having disappeared). In Schnittke's case, a wild hilarity in much of his music of the 1970s seems to hold despondency implicit, while many of his later works are simply and appallingly bleak. As in the music of his contemporary Davies, overt, exuberant parody subsequently receded, but what has been left behind, in Schnittke's case, is often a disconcerting skeleton. Long stretches of the opening allegro of the Sixth Symphony (1992), for example, are occupied by just a few brass instruments, or by the low strings, and much of the material is abrupt: idea, silence, idea. The absence of phrasing marks and dynamic gradations also suggests something bare.

Schnittke's first major expression of what he called 'poly-stylistics' was his First Symphony (1969–72), which includes quotations from Haydn, Beethoven, Chopin, Johann Strauss, Tchaikovsky, and Grieg, as well as jazz episodes in its hour-long continuous stream. The breakdown of unity is demonstrated, too, theatrically, in that the work starts out with just three musicians on the platform; the rest then

---

[17] See Paul Griffiths, 'Schnittke's Seventh', *The New Yorker* (7 Mar. 1994), 91–3.

enter, in a chaos of improvisation to which the conductor has to call a halt. In mirror fashion, most of the players go off before the end, leaving just a violinist, whose reminiscences of Haydn's 'Farewell' Symphony bring them back. Other works to show a rampageous and partly humorous, partly despairing medley of historical references include the Concerto Grosso No. 1 for two violins, harpsichord, prepared piano, and strings (1977), which includes 'formulae and forms of Baroque music; free chromaticism and micro-intervals; and banal popular music which enters as it were from the outside with a disruptive effect'.[18]

The Third Quartet begins with three quotations marked as such in the score: a double cadence from Lassus's *Stabat mater*, the head theme of Beethoven's *Grosse Fuge*, and the DSCH motif. As the slow first movement continues, it remembers these ideas fairly closely, though there are interpolations that seem to be foreign, and that sometimes enter to dramatic effect, as well as passages that seem to grow from general features of the opening material, including a long stretch of what is initially white-note canon (though the disturbing vision of innocence soon characteristically clouds and distorts). The second, scherzo-like movement has an obsessive first theme that looks back to the canon, and through that to the Lassus and the Beethoven, both of which are soon recalled more directly. Like Hamlet rushing from place to place in order to escape his spectral father, the scherzo theme keeps being rattled by the ghosts of Lassus and Beethoven, and jumping from one harmonic position to another: Example 61 shows a passage in which a Lassus variation introduces a counterpoint between the scherzo theme in the viola and the Beethoven in the first violin. The movement continues into fierce drama and parody, and is followed by a slow march finale. Here the conflict is not resolved: it ends in exhaustion.[19]

Schnittke's vivid expressivity demands a traditional musical milieu of means and form, for it makes its points through contortion, parody, and extremity: bizarre thematic transformation, guying by misappropriation, a venturing towards the far edges of register or dynamic. The traditional role of string instruments as expressive agents is also strongly implicated. In his comparatively few vocal works—comparatively few, that is, until the flood of operas from him in the nineties—the singers often seem, in contrast, generalized, taking part in some ceremonial. The ceremonial may be explicitly Christian, as in the Second Symphony (1979), based on the composer's visit to Bruckner's church of St Florian and incorporating an 'invisible mass', or in the Concerto for chorus (1984–5), with its radiant restorations of traditional Orthodox music. Alternatively, in the Fourth Symphony for four singers and orchestra (1984), the music is based on four different styles of chant: Russian Orthodox, Gregorian, Lutheran, and Jewish, all sung wordlessly. There is also often an atmosphere of chant in the dislocated litanies of the Sixth Symphony. In both the vocal symphonies, the Second and the Fourth, the muted voices suggest a mummed worship. Part of the point may have been to make a protest against the

[18] Preface to the score. See also Ivan Moody, 'The Music of Alfred Schnittke', *Tempo*, 168 (1989), 4–11.
[19] On this work see also Hugh Collins Rice, 'Further Thoughts on Schnittke', *Tempo*, 168 (1989), 12–14.

Ex. 61. Schnittke, String Quartet No. 3 (1983): II

persecution of religion in the Soviet Union, but equally the music laments the loss of divine community, of the social order that sustained the individuality which all Schnittke's music pursues through labyrinths of intensity, disaffection, and black comedy.

Giacinto Scelsi

By age, Giacinto Scelsi (1905–88) belonged to the generation of Messiaen and Carter, and most of his work had been done by the mid-1970s, so that if date of composition were to be the criterion, his music would have been covered much earlier in this book. By renown, though, he is a figure of the 1980s and after. Most of his larger works lay unheard until the very last years of his life, and the spate of recordings began at the same time. Other senior composers also became more widely known in the age of the compact disc, including Nancarrow and Lou Harrison, but Scelsi's provides the most striking case of the great revaluation of recent history that overtook music then. Where earlier he had been a marginal figure, by the mid-1990s his music was far more widely disseminated and admired than that of his Italian contemporaries Luigi Dallapiccola (1904–75) and Goffredo Petrassi (b. 1904).

Perhaps because of his belief in music's transcendence—a belief that unfitted him for the positivism of the 1950s and 1960s, but then became so much more generally congenial—he avoided autobiography. He apparently travelled through India and Nepal, and suffered some kind of mental breakdown before re-establishing himself as a composer in Rome in the early 1950s. Concentration and singleness became his purposes. At first his music was essentially monodic and modal, often with an Indian flavour. This occasionally resurfaced in the melodic protraction and decoration of his later pieces, though from the late 1950s onwards his music became much more thoroughly itself, investigating sound as if from within. Whole movements would be based on a very slow drift through the pitch spectrum, or on an antagonism between two notes, or even on just a single note, as in the two works that opened this mature period: the String Trio (1958) and the *Quattro pezzi* for chamber orchestra (1959). With pitch held static, or almost so, there was the opportunity to work with microtonal fluctuations and with timbre, and Scelsi's writing for string instruments, in particular, became intensively exploratory.

Example 62 shows a passage from his Fourth Quartet (1964), a work which traces a single slow curve throughout its ten-minute duration. At this point the glide up from the opening C is reaching A♭ (typically blurred by quarter-tone dissonances, with G half sharp and A half flat) and then, briefly, A. Scelsi writes for the four strings of each instrument separately, which helps him create a fabric that is continuously in change but also continuously the same. His own term, the 'sphericity' of sound, aptly describes the effect, which is of an invisible object turning to reveal new parts of itself—especially new harmonics, which may be actually played or else sounded as a result of strained performing techniques (including the use of special mutes in such works as the Second Quartet and *Khoom*), as if from a fundamental that remains in place or slowly shifts. A true bass in his music is rare: the cello's third string is seldom used in this quartet, its fourth never. The octaves and estranged octaves (estranged by dissonant inflection, as in gagaku and other Asian traditions with which the composer could have been familiar), here on three registral levels, relate to an imaginary hum. Something close to motionlessness is combined with fizzing activity in the trills and tremolandos that Scelsi characteristically uses to make his glissandos as imperceptible as may be.

String instruments, allowing fine tuning of pitch and adjustment of timbre, suited him well, and he wrote much for them. But he also favoured low brass for their weight of sound, and again for their adaptability, through the use of mutes, while the voice, generally wordless, could powerfully transmit the incantatory character of his music, whether in unaccompanied vocalises (*Wo Ma* for bass, the *Canti del Capricorno* for soprano) or in abstract narratives of solitary tragedy (*Khoom* for soprano, string quartet, horn and percussion) and corporate upheaval (*Uaxactum* for chorus and orchestra). Just as his music seems to be at once very slow and very fast, so its microtonal dissonances can be felt as simultaneously ferocious and calm, in dispute and (because found on the same sphere of sound) in accord. However, there does seem to have been a development in his work from tumult towards

Ex. 62. Scelsi, String Quartet No. 4 (1964)

simplicity and luminosity, with the increasing reappearance in the 1970s of modal melody and the arrival of compositions—like the Fifth Quartet and its relative *Aitsi* for amplified piano—based on slow reiteration.

Scale

At a time when everything is permitted, time scale provides a dimension in which music can still remove itself into a time all its own. The need for a removal may have been behind Stockhausen's scaling up of his music in the late 1960s: if a work lasts for two hours or so, it becomes legitimately the sole substance of a performance. Part of the subsequent attraction of opera to so many composers may have come from its permission to work on this scale—a scale on which the composer can control how a work is presented and heard, not leave it to the hazards of concert programming.

Full-evening scale need not mean continuous length, as witness Kurtág's *Kafka-Fragmente*, where it is the collective power of so many fragments that blots out the possibility of anything else. An alternative is to build your own programme, as Ferneyhough did in his *Carceri d'invenzione* cycle, or as Reich, Glass, and again Stockhausen have done with their touring ensembles, almost never performing anything but their own music. Of course, where electronic equipment is involved, self-determination is a practical as well as an aesthetic solution, and one of Boulez's problems with *Répons* was that the work needed to be, for reasons of practicality, much longer than its material could happily sustain.

The swivel in dissemination from the concert, or broadcast concert, to the compact disc does not change the scale very much: one wonders what effect it might have had if records could comfortably accommodate three hours of music, or if they had never got beyond the length of a 78 rpm side. As it is, music on such extremes of scale becomes, by that fact alone, particular. Working on a large scale may imply a grandeur which has to be achieved or deliberately not achieved: both seem to be happening in the unbroken hundred-minute orchestral *Odyssey* (1972–85) by Nicholas Maw (b. 1935). Or the music may just be there for that long—without anyone seeming to be intending it so, or to be worried that it is so: such is the case in the long works of Young and the later Feldman.

Brevity is another world. The bagatelle is often either a joke (Ligeti) or a sigh (Webern); it may be both, as in Kurtág. Reduction of scale is just as much a characteristic of recent music as expansion: what has been vacated has been the middle ground of twenty or thirty minutes, except in works meant for traditional contexts. This may have to do with the much-bruited shortening of attention span. It must also have to do with composers' increasing tastes for humour (Donatoni's entertainments, for example, are aptly scaled at around ten minutes), for fine detail (as in Ferneyhough), and for conditions of extremity. Much of the music of Oliver Knussen (b. 1952)—and not only that of his two operas made out of children's books: *Where the Wild Things are* (1979–83) and *Higglety Pigglety Pop!* (1984–90)—shows a Ravelian fascination with working in the small. The compositions of Hans Abrahamsen (b. 1952) are re-creations of the early Romantic miniature, but done quite freshly. In the music of Stefano Gervasoni (b. 1962) there is an exquisiteness of the only just possible, where the addition of a new note becomes a major event and the effort to articulate cannot go on for long.

Wolfgang Rihm

A quick starter and prolific, Wolfgang Rihm (b. 1952) began to gain attention in Germany and even beyond when he was still in his early twenties. The first performance of his orchestral piece *Morphonie–Sektor IV* at the 1974 Donaueschingen Festival seems to have been crucial, for reasons similar to those that had made Ligeti a talking point after the première of *Atmosphères* at the same place fourteen years before: here was something new. At that time, and for some years afterward, Rihm was lumped with other German composers of his generation as manifesting a revolt against the ageing avant garde (though he had studied with Stockhausen) in favour of a return to traditional genres and traditional notions of gesture and expressivity. It was not an unjust view. Rihm rapidly produced three symphonies, and his music emphatically asserted an expressive immediacy and power rare in music since Mahler and the expressionist Schoenberg.

However, his message was not comfortable. His choice of song texts from the work of madmen—Hölderlin, Ernst Herbeck, Adolf Wölffli (also a favourite of the Danish composer Per Nørgård at the same time)—suggested that musical expression now was in an extreme situation, that the direct voice was necessarily a deranged voice, if a voice more dislocated and infantile than hysterical in the manner of Davies. The spokesmen of Rihm's early songs and operas (two genres not so separate in his output, since each of the song cycles is voiced by a character: the poet) have a madman's licence to transgress: 'I loved you once! I love you no more. I shit in your eyes!' begins the *Wölffli-Liederbuch* (1980–1). The violence done on musical language is fierce and cold. Often it is a matter of abrupt shift, or of dismantling models of simpler, more innocent musical times: Schubertian Lied or nursery rhyme. The freedom to quote and imitate was something Rihm took from his age, but there is nothing playful in his practice, and nostalgia is more a waking nightmare than a dream, for always the gap between past model and present reality is evident and disquieting. The second movement of his Third String Quartet (1976), for example, settles into a Mahlerian adagio, but one tugged and strained, so that it appears to be unfolding both in its own time frame, coherently, and in a new one, incoherently.

Whether as cause or effect of his music of ruination, Rihm conjured the ruined mind not only in his songs but also in his widely performed chamber opera *Jakob Lenz* (1977–8). His subsequent theatre works have absorbed ruin, showing it not as a protagonist's condition but as the nature of the world. Of *Die Hamletmaschine* (1983–6), based on Heiner Müller's simultaneous deconstruction and reconstruction of the play, he wrote that 'the whole thing sings of extensive destruction', and noted that the action takes place 'in front of the "ruins of Europe" whose dust is still the best nourishment for anyone who wants to confront things or wants to know where we come from'.[20] However, he has also said that he is interested less in where he has come from than in where he is going,[21] less in connection and memory than in breakage and freedom. 'Freedom must be *seized*. . . This is only possible through free *displacements*—initially in breaks and interruptions (on the stylistic level as well)—which can crowd themselves together to create a total consistency of sound activity. The connecting potential of music is enormous and often a bother for me, since I would like to break out of general contexts . . . I and my work are animated

[20] Note with Wergo 6195.
[21] See Dieter Rexroth (ed.), *Der Komponist Wolfgang Rihm* (Mainz, 1985).

by the search for "dis-connection" (parataxis as a form of thought and imagination).'[22]

It is perhaps because 'dis-connection' implies connection (in that there has to be an evident something that has been broken, or—better—that is in the process of being broken) that Rihm's music maintains a hold on pitch, and especially on the precarious extreme high treble. A tenuous, pressured progress from one dangerous high note to another, with fallings into noise, the equally extreme bass, or the banality of more ordinary registers, is a characteristic of his later works, and one that reflects his admiration for Nono: the 1988 ensemble piece *Kein Firmament*, of which an excerpt is shown in Example 63, provides a remarkably sustained example of fragility become force. The far treble is perhaps for Rihm the last wilderness of music, the last place where there are no maps, and where it might be possible to depart, to quote the last line of the brief Rimbaud illumination he set in *Départ* for chorus and small orchestra (1988), 'in affection and noises that are new'. 'Dis-connection' is often projected, too, through space, with instruments placed at distant points in the auditorium, as when two trumpets sound out from behind the audience in the piano concerto *sphere* (1992–4). As he has recalled, his experience of singing in oratorio performances as a boy gave him this feeling of sound as happening all around.[23]

Music that is, in all senses, spaced out has tended to displace the more heavyweight wreckage on which much of the power of *Die Hamletmaschine* was based: the wreckage of Beethoven–Wagner funeral march, of Handel aria, of dramatic-soprano scena, of the expressionist music dramas (*Erwartung*, *Die glückliche Hand*, *Wozzeck*) Rihm had needed in order to discover that piece. His later opera *Die Eroberung von Mexiko* (1987–91) finds destruction imminent rather than achieved: the work's essential point is the moment of confrontation between Montezuma and Cortez, which—repeating and intensifying one of the themes of *Die Hamletmaschine*—is a confrontation between female (Montezuma is a soprano) and male. Accordingly, the text is not a catastrophic 'afterwards', like Heiner Müller's treatment of *Hamlet*, but a tense 'not yet': Rihm adapted his libretto from a dramatic project by Artaud.

That Artaud should have returned to relevance (Rihm had already based his full-length ballet *Tutuguri* on Artaud) is a signal of how composers in the 1980s wanted to draw again on a spontaneity and a nakedness that had been Boulez's in the late 1940s, and that subsequent European modernism had compromised by system. For Rihm, system is anathema. Words can be too binding: he has done without them in several works, including the music-theatre piece *Séraphin* (1994). The only syntax is internal need. 'The whole thing free, without scaffolding. The grid work which arises has not been knitted together previously or painted on afterwards. It exists in what happens. The consistency, when it arises, belongs to the music as

---

[22] Note with Wergo 6195.   [23] See *Der Komponist Wolfgang Rihm*.

Ex. 63. Rihm, *Kein Firmament* (1988)

something entirely its own and not the result of an analogy, a reference to some level of planning. What is—is.'[24]

Steve Reich

Reich's works have followed, over the years, a path as steady and rigorous as any of them takes during its course—though, on certain levels, with jump cuts that are

24 Note with Wergo 6195.

equally characteristic of the way the music behaves. His expansion of his scoring—normally with his own percussion ensemble at the centre, or at least as an element—went on through *Music for Eighteen Musicians* (1974–6), *Music for a Large Ensemble* (1978), and *Variations for Winds, Strings and Keyboards* (1979) to the full orchestra of *The Four Sections* (1987). In another line of pieces he brought voices to the fore: in *Tehillim* (1981) he set psalm texts in Hebrew; in *The Desert Music* (1982–3) the words came from William Carlos Williams. Both these works, like *Variations* and *The Four Sections*, use an orchestra that is an ensemble of ensembles, but in another set of 1980s pieces, all with 'counterpoint' in the title, Reich went back to the *Violin Phase* model of an instrumental soloist playing against a multi-tracked recording, albeit with the more complex patterning of his later music.

Though more complicated and multi-layered than it was in the 1960s (*Vermont Counterpoint*, for instance, is for flute plus ten recorded flutes), Reich's music has never lost its roots in repetition and process. If he has, nevertheless, insisted that *Tehillim* 'is not composed of short repeating patterns' but rather of melodies whose 'flexible changing metres' (another departure) were dictated by the texts, because the melodies are composed of chains of motifs, and because they are frequently heard in strict unison canon, the effect is often of patterns circling at an insistent pulse. Indeed, the ambivalence between simple reiteration (reasonless) and canonic order (reasoned) is essential to the music's dwelling on the border between magic and lucidity—a border along which Reich can bend towards joyful exuberance (as in *Tehillim*) or a grimmer inexorability (as in *The Four Sections*). The grid of regular pulse is always there, but it can be more or less densely overlaid with conflicting rhythms: rhythms of different pace, as in the gamelan-like stratification of the orchestra in *The Four Sections*, where the strings are normally slow-moving and the tuned percussion rapid, or rhythms of different metre or alignment. 'Very often,' Reich has said, 'I'll find myself working in 12-beat phrases, which can divide up in very different ways; and that ambiguity as to whether you're in duple or triple time is, in fact, the rhythmic life-blood of much of my music.'[25] In rather the same way, on the melodic–harmonic plane, there may be uncertainty about which note is the tonic, and therefore about which mode the music is in: from *Tehillim* onwards the texture is often not only more complex but also more chromatic, allowing for suggestions of oriental modes as well as of Coplandesque pure diatonicism.

Sprung in rhythm and mode, Reich's music had always conveyed freshness too in its self-demonstrative character, its way of building itself from simple basic elements as it went along. *Tehillim* seems to have brought a realization that those elements were not freely invented—that they had histories in the composer's Jewish and American heritages. Among later works, *Different Trains* for string quartet and tape (1988) and *The Cave* for voices, ensemble, and videotapes (1990–3) go further in Reich's exploration of his cultural genes; they also move on from the plateau his

---

[25] Interview with Jonathan Cott included with Elektra Nonesuch 979 101.

music had reached in the mid-1980s. It is symptomatic of this re-girding that *Different Trains* should, at last, have taken up an idea considered and rejected during the composition of *The Desert Music*: the idea of using recorded speech in a musical composition.[26]

For the new piece Reich collected verbal testimony about train journeys in the United States—from his governess, with whom he made transcontinental trips as a child, and from a retired porter—and, from survivors, about the other trains that were taking Jews across Europe at the same time. He then notated excerpts as speech melodies, and produced a score in which these melodies are imitated by both recorded and live string quartets (four quartets all told in the first movement, three in the other two)—or rather, as shown in Example 64, the speech melodies enter as if to musical prompting, and then the music can take them on by itself. In this case, the motif is first heard from a recorded cello, then repeated by the live viola, and at the second repetition doubled by the voice on tape. Filling alternate units of seven semiquavers, the motif progressively moves against the eight-semiquaver grid in a simple example of a Reichian rhythmic process; the next repetition will bring it back to the start of the bar, and then it will be extended. The tape component of the piece also includes train sounds (rattles of wheels and carriages that accord with the moto perpetuo, whistlings that similarly go with the sustained chords), so that the piece, besides being a description of train journeys, seems to enact one, as it shuttles along the tracks of repetition and shifts—across points made by metric or tonal modulation—from one speech melody to another.

Ex. 64. Reich, *Different Trains* (1988)

---

[26] Note, interview with Jonathan Cott included with Elektra Nonesuch 979 101.

Making music out of reiterating speech was not new: Reich had done that in two of his earliest pieces. And perhaps all opera composers have, to some degree, found music by following the patterns of speech—music that might then become instrumental. (There are also cases, notably in Hindemith and Henze, of instrumental melody founded on silent lines of poetry.) What was, however, new in *Different Trains*—and characteristically Reichian in showing the works—was the presentation of instrumental product and vocal source together. The discovery set Reich on a new track, which led directly on to *The Cave* and to *City Life* for ensemble and samplers (1994–5), the former using much fuller means to expose different understandings—Israeli, Palestinian, and American—of the stories concerning the forefather who is Abraham for Jews and Ibrahim in Islamic tradition.[27]

Postmodernism

What is extraordinary, in retrospect, is how the modernist project of perpetual revolution so dominated an epoch. No doubt, as mentioned above, there was some feeling among musicians of wanting to participate in the great events of the age: postwar rebuilding, the worldwide success of movements for socialism and nationhood, the spread of free education, the mechanization of farming and industry, and all the time the threat (if a threat can be allowed as a protracted event) of nuclear war. As these imperatives of and for change variously spent themselves in the 1970s and 1980s, so musical revolution lost its adherents. Even those who had been its outstanding architects, Boulez and Stockhausen, had to accept that they were not, as they had thought, making possible the art of the future but rather contributing, in circumscribed, personal ways, to that of the present.

Because the lapsing of modernism was a failure of confidence, once it had happened it could not be gainsaid: the belief of believers is changed in a world of unbelievers, and to the extent that, say, Brian Ferneyhough may be seen as a continuing modernist, his modernism is necessarily of a different kind from that of Boulez in the mid-1950s. The doubt Boulez faced was about whether his was the right way forward; the doubt Ferneyhough faces is that there may be no way forward at all. Ferneyhough's solutions to the musical exigencies of his times may be unusually powerful, but they do not seem to be long-range strategies: the needs of the moment are, perhaps, too pressing for that to be possible. Similarly, Ferneyhough, unlike Boulez, has rarely called the achievements of the past to witness to the necessities of the present: his writings and interviews contain remarkably few attempts to justify his works with reference to the past, or to stake any claim in history. Nor has he seemed much concerned with public standing, which was so essential to the modernist. (Not—or at lest, not just—for reasons of vanity: you cannot be leading the advance if your works and your ideas are unknown.) Indeed,

[27] For a review of the first performance see Paul Griffiths, 'Abraham and Ibrahim', *The New Yorker* (31 May 1993), 155–8.

apart from George Benjamin (b. 1960), few composers of the post-Darmstadt generation have followed Boulez's example in taking up the modernist challenge to create and educate audiences. In the postmodern world, music no longer belongs to society but separately to each individual, and its location is not in the concert hall but in the record store.

Similarly, the individual composer is no longer a partner in the grand enterprise of music, adding a cornice or a floor to a constantly growing edifice. The building now seems complete; the composer stands outside, as observer rather than participant. As a result, new works no longer have to be subject to planning requirements and the laws of materials. Where, for example, *Le marteau sans maître* could claim validity as a logical extension from predecessors (Messiaen, Schoenberg, Debussy, Webern, Stravinsky) and as an apt marriage of aims to means, the postmodern work has nothing to verify it. (Cage, in seeking an escape from the arbitrary arbitrations of taste in the early 1950s, was probably the first to recognize the postmodern condition—though one might want to say it is something more than taste that convinces one of the value of Kurtág or Birtwistle: their music might even ask for an overcoming of taste.) Even the need for novelty seems no longer to apply, in that it has been perfectly possible, since the early 1980s, to make a career out of pastiche—whether the camp pastiche of deliberately varied and wayward styles, or the earnest pastiche of symphonies patterned after Bruckner. The former—exemplified in much of the music of William Bolcom (b. 1938)— has the virtue of an irony that admits the old game is up; it may also be funny. But even the most supine imitation may have something to say about questions of musical valuation and individuality—about, for instance, the difference between a newly discovered Haydn sonata and a newly invented one.

Returns to the past have been recurrent in western music, and the post-1980 wave of style imitation, self-consciousness, and unashamed spuriousness has much in common with the neoclassicism of the 1920s and 1930s. What is different this time around is that the antithesis has changed. Where neoclassicism was seen as an alternative to serialism—but still as an alternative way forward—'postmodernism' (not a style, nor a movement, but only a statement of where we are) has been taken as an answer to modernism. The postmodern composer is free to make use of everything except the most advanced music of the last hundred years, as if modernism were the enemy: hence Ferneyhough's rarity as what might be called a postmodern modernist, or Lachenmann's as one who has kept faith with the modernist imperative to respond to the specialness of the present, even while he has, in works since the late 1970s, entered into dialogue with the past. His *Tanzsuite mit Deutschlandlied* for string quartet and orchestra (1979–80), for example, includes blistered remnants of old music; his fifty-minute piano concerto *Ausklang* (1984–5) contains tonal chords and arpeggios, along with a plethora of stuttering monotones, but so far from representing visions of stability, these features are fractured and issueless. Lachenmann has spoken wryly of a need to 'deny denial', and declared more solidly that his pursuit of a new way of hearing—a way of hearing alert to the means by which sounds are produced—had to be shown to function with familiar, central sounds as well as with the marginalia of *temA* or *Pression*.[28] By focusing on reverberation (which is one meaning of the title)—especially on the reverberation of the solo piano, which the orchestra so often extends, transforms, colours or abuses—*Ausklang* deprives itself of the fiction that music can reinvigorate itself by returning to methods and principles of the past. Every gesture here is fading. But the rich variety of fadings becomes a new kind of musical optimism, a demonstration of the possibility of re-creating, out of an entirely modern sensibility, music on the grand scale, for *Tanzsuite* and *Ausklang* are both quasi-symphonies in matters of extent, density, and (concealed) multi-movement form.

In other works—such as his second string quartet, *Reigen seliger Geister* (1989)—Lachenmann seems concerned with a nearer past, as he revisits sites of earlier catastrophes within his own output. This may be, perhaps, a necessary third stage, a denial of the denial of denial, or it may indicate how conscientious modernists face a precarious task: that of not looking back, and yet of remembering where they have come from and why they are here. Modernism—which insists (and not only to such a scrupulous artist as Lachenmann) that music has far wider responsibilities and opportunities, social and historical, than those of self-assertion—is the enemy of recycling, but then so is Bruckner, to the extent that his music was created as a response to a historical moment.

However, apostles of postmodernist restitution have tended to situate their quarrel with modernism on a different ground, that of unbridled fancy and audience appeal. Music whose pleasure may require an acknowledgement of otherness—a category that would have to include Avignon motets and gagaku as well as Barraqué—is, by the ruthless laws of the market, less productive and therefore unjustifiable. If the only judgement is one of taste, then, so the argument goes, the only marker of success is commercial, and the alignment of this exiguous aesthetics with the interests of the record industry may perhaps be cause for concern. There can be no pretending that the failure of confidence in modernism has not happened—or even that it was not bound to happen sooner or later, since there are limits, as even Stockhausen found, to the ways in which music can be reinvented (or if not that, then certainly the meaning of reinvention changes once it has happened a dozen times). But equally there can be no pretending that the failure of confidence in modernism might make possible a replacement of confidence in the nineteenth-century symphony, or whatever. The challenge of the postmodern age—for composers, for performers and for listeners—is to search out what seems to be necessary, even if it may only be necessary for the moment. The opportunity of the postmodern age is that there need be no limitations to this search—least of all a limitation by canons of the past. A freedom only to quote and re-enact is a limp sort of freedom.

---

[28] See note with Col Legno WWE 31862.

Arvo Pärt

Ex. 65. Pärt, *Passio Domini Nostri Jesu Christi secundum Joannem* (1982)

Opera

There are not many conclusions to be drawn about opera since 1980, except those concerning abundance, and the evidence which abundance conveys of the deep alteration in music since the 1950s, when opportunities to write operas were few, and when correspondingly few composers were ready to write them. Lots of factors are involved here: the wish of many more composers to engage their music, if not with the world, then at least with the makeshift world of character and action that can be conjured inside a theatre; the comparative commercial success of several composers; a feeling perhaps that the energy—in terms of creativity and staging—has shifted from the spoken theatre to opera; and a lapsing of the purely aural in western culture (though of course many composers have been active against that, notably Nono, whose *Prometeo* was resolutely a non-opera: an opera-length work, on an opera-style subject, but made to be performed for the ear alone, and in a specially constructed chamber that would rule out the escape of supposing it to be a real opera heard in concert).

Yet there are rather few pieces that have scored more than one production: Stockhausen's *Donnerstag*, Messiaen's *Saint François d'Assise*, Henze's *The English Cat*, and the operas of Rihm, von Bose, Weir, and Berio are the miscellaneous works among this small group, and nearly all of them have been lost to sight and hearing within a few years of appearing. (Perhaps only the operas of Messiaen, Berio, Birtwistle, Stockhausen,and Rihm are destined to last.) As a rule, a new opera will be played only by the company or companies which commissioned it; the notion of making a permanent addition to the repertory has become so unthinkable as no longer to be a matter of attention. This has freed composers to create works which fall outside the regularities a repertory imposes: works with a strong electronic component, like Birtwistle's *The Mask of Orpheus* or Stockhausen's operas, or works requiring unusually large forces, like *Saint François*. Also, if a work is to be presented in only one production, then the work of the stage director becomes perhaps more important than that of the librettist, as, for example, in the two operas created by the team of John Adams as composer, Alice Goodman as librettist, and Peter Sellars as director.

(Even so, the music and words alone of *Nixon in China*, in their combination, have a touching quality that seems to come out of an imbalance between the great international events and the small homely music—an imbalance that might express the diminishment of heroism in the television age. Nixon, arriving at Beijing in the first scene, exults in having 'made history', while his music is ruthlessly commonplace. 'Trivial things are not for me', sings his wife Pat; but they are, in what she sings. These characters provide Adams with the opportunity, found also in some of his concert works, to treat minimalism's deficit of meaning—so much made of so little—as an irony. Only Chou En-lai, in the aria that closes the opera, appears to perceive that irony while being contained in it, his music entering, as shown in Example 66, over a Holstian ostinato.)

Ex. 66. Adams, *Nixon in China*: Act III (1987)

The exclusion of contemporary opera from hopes of joining the repertory—and therefore its unappealable posteriority—has inevitably been reflected in subject matter and treatment. Where, for example, Berio's *Opera* (1970) was partly about the death of opera, his later—as it were, posthumous—operas have been interviews of the ghost, with brilliant efforts to renew and reanimate going along with a profound philosophic gloom about the continuing value and legitimacy of the form. *La vera storia* is 'the real story' of *Il trovatore*, which is dismantled into its components in the first part, where it is also subjected by Brechtian songs (perhaps the culmination of Berio's several essays in inventing the vernacular) to implicit criticism on grounds of evasion, and then reassembled, or scrambled, to make a tragic fresco in the second part. 'The real story' is not the story but the story of the story, as it is in all of Berio's stage music, and in much of Birtwistle's. In the work that Berio and his literary collaborator Italo Calvino produced soon after *La vera storia*, *Un re in ascolto*, the 'listening king' is in charge of an empire which is falling out of his grasp: he is Prospero in an enactment of *The Tempest*; he is the impresario of the theatre in which the play is taking place; and he is the modern creator, whose art strains to touch, but cannot, the revolution going on outside.[29]

Other composers have taken the almost unavoidable futility of opera—the hopelessness of creating lasting value—less seriously. If we are all going to die, then let us at least have fun while we last: that was the moral of Ligeti's *Le Grand Macabre*—but Ligeti meant it ironically, whereas the alleviation of all responsibilities is played for all it is worth in such works as *Marilyn* by Lorenzo Ferrero (b. 1951), whose music exults in cheapness, glamour, and stylistic reference. Still others have refused to accept that greatness is now unattainable. In Messiaen's case one can hardly speak of refusal, since it would never have occurred to him that his task was other than to make great works—and works which stake their claim not for their human author but for the universe of divine creation, as witness the fact that so much of the orchestral score of *Saint François* consists of imitated birdsong. Stockhausen's operas, on the other hand, are dramatizations of himself as great composer.

Birtwistle's are not, but nor are their rituals those of a creed in which the composer can, Messiaen-like, lose himself. In *The Mask of Orpheus*, the myth is placed at a remove, and the work sifts through different versions of the story, by means of a complex system in which the central characters are each present in three incarnations (as human being, as mythic figure, as hero), and in which other Greek myths of death and metamorphosis are mimed to electronic windows in the score. In *Gawain*, based on the Middle English poem of *Sir Gawain and the Green Knight*, the composer found a story in which he could place a greater investment. The uneasy interlacing of Christian motifs with images drawn from nature's cycles of regeneration—a characteristically English compromise—had been a powerful element in earlier works, such as the music-theatre piece *Down by the Greenwood Side*, and he had set a passage from the poem in a choral piece, *Narration: a Description of the Passing of a Year* (1963). The setting in a remote antiquity, too, could profit from the musical poetics of barbarism—slow pulse, a thunderous bass of low brass and percussion—he had developed in *The Mask of Orpheus* and more recently in *Earth Dances*. And the work provided the occasion for rituals in repetitive forms that had again recurred in his output: the vesting of Gawain in his armour, a masque of the seasons while he is on his journey, and the threefold trials, hunts, and tests of his time in the Green Knight's domain. But the essence of the work—new in the opera, not found in the poem—is that Gawain returns to a hero's welcome he finds meaningless. Arthur and his court want something to celebrate, something to be proud of. Gawain keeps insisting he is 'not that hero', just as his composer has insisted that 'I'm part of the establishment in some way, but I don't think what I do is part of the establishment. I don't think they'd recognize it if they fell over it.'[30] The world of opera wants heroes. They will not come.

---

[29] The programme for the 1989 Covent Garden production includes interviews with the composer by Umberto Eco and by himself, and a delightful and distinguished essay by Massimo Mila.

[30] *Musical Times*, 135 (1994), 336.

Luigi Nono

According to Nono's own account, he was set on a new path in the wake of his second opera, *Al gran sole carico d'amore*: 'After that complexity I felt the need to begin again from the beginning, to put myself back to study, starting out just with the most constrictive and demanding of instruments, the piano.'[31] The result was a solo piece for Maurizio Pollini, . . . *sofferte onde serene* . . .(1974–6), which again exploits the strong bass of Pollini's style that had been prominent in the concerto-like *Como una ola de fuerza y luz* just a few years before, but now without political explicitness, and with a lessening of the drive that had been just as much a Nono characteristic. Tape, hitherto a resource for documentary realism or sonic power, becomes a medium of exploration, as the pianist plays against manipulated recordings of chords and of the instrument's mechanism. 'Sometimes I cut off the attack, so that the sound manifests itself as resonance without time . . . It's like listening to the wind, you listen to something that passes, but you don't hear the start, you don't hear the end: you perceive a continuity of distances, of presences, of undefinable essences.'[32]

The wafting passage of the piece seems bound up with its means, with the slow movement of reality (the live performance) over memory (the recording)—or perhaps of memory (innate) over reality (external). All is echo. The pianist echoes events on tape, turns chords that emerge from the recording; the tape, with its reverberation, places the music in a widened space. The piece also finds the composer attending not to global events but to his immediate location and tradition—and then through them to the distance. At a time when media of communication have become subject to the interests of profit, direct sensual experience offers the only guarantee of truth, and from this moment onwards the composer is first of all a listener, listening to the sounds he puts on paper, listening to other sounds in the electronic studio, listening to the world. 'In my house on the Giudecca in Venice, one constantly hears the sound of bells, coming day and night, through the mist and with the sun, with different resonances, different meanings. They are signs of life on the lagoon, on the sea. Invitations to work, to meditate; announcements. And life goes in the suffered and serene necessity of "the balance at the bottom of our being", as Kafka says. Pollini on live piano is amplified with Pollini on piano elaborated and composed on tape. No contrast, no counterpoint . . . Between these two planes there is the study of the formative relationships of the sound, notably in the use of the vibrations of pedal strikes, which are perhaps the particular resonances "at the bottom of our being". These are not "episodes" which expend themselves in succession, but "memories" and "presences" that superimpose themselves on each other.'[33]

After this there was, mot unusually, a gap in Nono's output. He revised *Al gran sole* for return performances at La Scala in 1978, in which year was broached the

---

[31] *Ecrits*, 104.   [32] Ibid.   [33] Note with DG 2531 004.

prospect of a third opera, after Aeschylus' *Prometheus*. But there was nothing new until 1979, when he wrote *Con Luigi Dallapiccola* for six percussionists with electronics and began *Fragmente–Stille, an Diotima* for string quartet. Still no voices; still muffled sound-worlds, for *Con Luigi Dallapiccola* has the alert quietude of a piece whose musicians must listen to their instruments as much as play them, and *Fragmente–Stille* unfolds on the edge of sense, being, as the title indicates, a sequence of fragments and silences.

The address of the piece 'to Diotima' is explained by the presence throughout the score of quotations from Hölderlin, and especially of phrases from his poem to Diotima. These quotations are meant as stimuli and indications for the performers; they are, according to the composer, 'diverse moments, thoughts, silences, "songs", from other spaces, other heavens, for rediscovering in other ways the possibility of not "decisively bidding farewell to hope" ',[34] this last phrase coming from a letter Hölderlin wrote to Susette Gontard in 1799. Hope is always in Nono the hope for a just society: the political intention in *Fragmente–Stille* is as vital and actual as it was in the revolutionary frescos of a decade before. But the manner has changed from rhetoric to silence, from persuasion to listening. Good listening was, for Nono in this last decade, a political act—good listening that would be searching for the other, and not only for echoes of the self. As he said in a lecture in 1983: 'When one comes to listen, one often tries to rediscover oneself in others. To rediscover one's own mechanisms, system, rationalism, in the other. And that: that's a violence that's thoroughly conservative.'[35] By its use of quarter tones, of high registers, and of silence, *Fragmente–Stille* invites the minutest observation—the kind of observation that must go into its performance and that went into its making, for Nono seems to have written the piece as a kind of diary, waiting for time alone to tell him what to place next.[36] Occasionally there are coded messages, as in the viola's quotation, towards the end, of the tenor from a song, 'Maleur me bat', that was printed in Venice with an attribution to Ockeghem, and that Nono had studied with Maderna. (The Hölderlin fragment here is 'Wenn ich traurend versank . . . das zweifelnde Haupt': 'When I grieving went down . . . the doubting head'.) Messages of regret, then, exist along with the push of hope, but the hope is unsparing and transpersonal.

Playing continuously for around forty minutes (the duration is unspecifiable because there are so many variable pauses), the quartet has its players for the most part in rhythmic unison. Once more there is 'no contrast, no counterpoint', but rather a single slow line that travels through quarter-tone discrepancies and is perfused, melodically and harmonically, by tritones. These tritones—and the fragmentary presentation, one breath or one chord at a time—give the work its consistency, while the journey presses on from the opening unsupported treble through the gains of the lower register, of quarter tones and eventually of harmonics.

---

[34] Preface to the score.　　　　　　　　　　[35] 'L'Erreur comme nécessité', *Ecrits*, 256.
[36] See Wolfgang Rihm's reminiscence of a conversation with the composer, in Josef Häusler (ed.), *Brennpunkt Nono* (Salzburg, 1993), 55–6.

Where ... *sofferte onde serene* ... had been residually dramatic, and thereby effective in quite a conventional way, the quartet appears to shun overt success: central to its hope is the hope for something that is not yet available, that cannot yet be heard, that goes on being searched for—the hope for another world. In its fragmentation and its stillness (stillness of dynamic and stillness of motion), as well as in its intimate appeal to the intent ear and in its turn from the all-interval series to the 'scala enigmatica' of Verdi's *Ave Maria* (C–D♯–E–F♯–G♯–A♯–B–C, returning downwards C–B–B♭–A♭–F–E–D♭–C, and so providing three of the six possible tritones), the work announced what were to be the dominant features of Nono's abundant last decade, and in particular prepared the way for *Prometeo* (1981–5), which emerged not as an opera but as a 'tragedy of listening', in which the drama takes place between sound and ear. There is no staging, no action. Instead, everyone concerned, whether musician or auditor, has a place in a wooden boat-like construction designed for the piece by Renzo Piano. This provided Nono with something on which he repeatedly insisted during his last years: space—the space, the emptiness, to which music could bring a purpose, if sound sources were to be dispersed within it, and if the sound were to be such as would explore and vivify what it came into. At the Südwestfunk studios in Freiburg he worked, during the period of *Prometeo*, on techniques of sound modification and projection with Hans Peter Haller (with whom Boulez had worked on early versions of ... *explosante-fixe* ...) and on instrumental possibilities with a circle of dedicated musicians, among them the flautist Roberto Fabbriciani, the clarinettist Ciro Scarponi, and the tuba player Giancarlo Schiaffini. He was particularly interested in sounds which do not disclose their origins, as he had been in *Fragmente–Stille*, where violin, viola, and cello are so seldom heard as distinct voices; in the new pieces he worked with tones from registers in which the instruments produce almost pure frequencies, and also with unusually low and unusually high registers, and with sounds achieved by irregular playing techniques. Often his material would, too, be microintervallically inflected, representing by other means another world. Such sounds would, for the listener, slip out of the carapace of timbral and harmonic taxonomy: unnameable, they would be invitations to think in new terms.

The first tentatives towards *Prometeo* came in *Das atmende Klarsein* for small chorus, bass flute, and electronics (1980–1), and *Io* for three sopranos, small chorus, bass flute, contrabass clarinet, and electronics (1981), both of which formed part of the full work when it had its first performances, in the disused church of San Lorenzo in Venice in 1984. Another step came in 1982, when Nono wrote a second 'Polish diary' in answer to a commission from the Warsaw Autumn festival, which in the event did not take place that year, because of the imposition of martial law and the country's economic catastrophe. *Quando stanno morendo*—not a big orchestral piece as the first *Diario polacco* had been at the time of the late 1950s thaw, but small and quiescent—takes its title from the words by Velemir Chlebnikov with which its anthology of eastern European poetry ends: 'When they are dying men sing.' Once again, hope has to be realized out of a context of despair, voiced here for the most part in a slow interweaving of four female singers over flute, cello, and electronics. By this point in history it was time to sing requiems over the revolution; resistance and progress, both human and musical, demanded a departure—and it would have to be a sorrowful departure—from cherished systems, Marxist and Schoenbergian, that had outlived their usefulness as beacons of a better world.

The circle of works around *Prometeo* includes not only preparations (*Omaggio a György Kurtág*, too, was one) but re-echoings, as in the pieces Nono went on composing with and for Fabbriciani, Scarponi, and Schiaffini, such as *A Pierre* (written for Boulez's sixtieth birthday, in 1985, and renewing the friendship that had been broken when, as Nono saw it, Boulez had failed to take up the political implications of radical music: in an echo of Beethoven's gesture, he had withdrawn the dedication of *Canti per tredici* to 'Pierre Boulez, for his humanity'). The *Prometeo* sound-world—rarely assertive, much more usually slow, quiet and invitatory—is one of keening high voices (the solo singers are the same quartet as in *Quando stanno morendo*, with the single addition of a tenor), of electronically modulated instruments often going further into the as-if-underwater reverberations of . . . *sofferte onde serene* . . . , and of orchestral textures made strange by quarter tones. This last aspect of *Prometeo* took on separate life in the short orchestra piece *A Carlo Scarpa* (1984–5), whose prickling near-unisons and near-octaves suggest Scelsi, though in a context not of steady movement but, as in *Fragmente–Stille*, of event laid after event.

After *Prometeo* had been revised, for its 1985 revival, Nono moved on to a group of works written under the sign of an inscription found on a cloister wall in Toledo: 'Caminantes, no hay caminos, hay que caminar' ('Wayfarers, there are no ways, only faring on'). This had been the belief enshrined in his music at least since *Fragmente–Stille*: the belief, as musically expressed, that what absorbs all importance is the next step, not some hoped-for destination—the belief, as much political as musical, that freedom moving under contract is freedom limited. But the belief in freedom—in a pure freedom under which liberty of individual thought and action would be boundless—had always guided him, and his creative life had repeatedly shown a willingness to jettison what he had learned for what was unknown, the 'caminos' for the 'caminar'. (*Il canto sospeso* and *Intolleranza* were watersheds as critical as *Al gran sole*.) In these last works, however, the intimation of freedom—the hope—is even more than before expressed by musical means which are themselves intimations, pointers, and trajectories: the use of space, looking towards a potential omnipresence of sound; the soaring into an extreme high treble; the involvement of the performer as a companion traveller, presaging a collectivity of creative endeavour.

The last two large-scale works, *Caminantes* . . . (1986–7) and *No hay caminos, hay que caminar* . . . (1987), both require orchestral musicians to be disposed in various groups: *Caminantes* . . . was written for the Munich Gasteig, one of the modern halls the composer approved as extrapolations from San Marco in terms of polychoral possibility (once more the composer listens out in his music from his home base in Venice); *No hay caminos*, which is, with *Fragmente–Stille* and *A Carlo Scarpa*, one of his few works since the early 1960s without electronics, extends the sound-searching manner of the quartet to a collection of seven groups. During the busy time of these two works he also formed a plan for a series of small pieces with electronics, still exploring space. For example in *Post-prae-ludium No. 3* for piccolo, the player was to walk around the hall, sometimes drawing near to one or other of four microphones that would capture the sound for different kinds of electronic treatment. But the idea was never fully developed: at the only performance, in 1988, 'Fabbriciani and his piccolo "walked"—guided by Nono's gestures—through the hall, freely improvising, with live electronics but no written score'.[37] To some degree, opening the work to the performer was a way of freeing it, or at least of showing how it might be free. As Nono wrote of *Post-prae-ludium No. 1*, for tuba, of which he did produce a final score: 'The course of this composition is fixed in all its details, but the score is intended only to be a basic guide for the performer . . . The given notation, new performing techniques, and live electronics all unite to supplant any interpretation on my part.'[38] Nevertheless, there had to be something to interpret. In the 1950s Nono had reacted violently against Cage, in whose music he saw an image of the disconnected individuals of a failed society. And though the fragmentation and the looseness of his late music might seem implicitly to rescind that dispraise, what stays is the quite un-Cageian onward and outward urge: from sound to sound, from place to place, from notation to realization. However disintegrated, the music is looking for another harmony.

In his last two years Nono found a new collaborator in Gidon Kremer, who was for him perhaps not just a supreme violinist but also a representative of Russian culture—the culture in which, for Nono, the political and artistic questions of the twentieth century had been felt and fought most intensely. (In *Al gran sole* he had worked with the stage director Yuri Lyubimov; *No hay caminos* was a memorial to the film director Andrey Tarkovsky; and Russian texts are sprinkled through many of his works.) The departure was not new: the title '*Hay que caminar' soñando* indicates the link Nono's last composition, for two violins, has with preceding works, and *La lontananza nostalgica utopica futura* for violin and tapes (1988–9) takes up the live-recorded interplay of . . . *sofferte onde serene* . . . , under a title suggesting how, for Nono, utopia was both a long way ahead ('the future utopian distance') and, in feeling, a long way behind ('nostalgic'). Also, both pieces continue the idea of the ambulant musician, moving between music desks in different parts of the hall. But these final works are distinguished from their immediate predecessors by the colour and, in particular, the range of the violin, from open strings (recurrent, rooting the sound in the nature of the violin) to notes way above the treble staff, as shown in Example 67. The music can look back, perhaps

---

[37] Hans Peter Haller, in *A proposito di* Découvrir la subversion: Hommage à Edmond Jabès *e* Post-praeludium n.3 'Baab-arr' *di Luigi Nono* (Milan: Ricordi, 1993).

[38] Note with Ricordi CRMCD 1003.

Ex. 67. Nono, *La lontananza nostalgica utopica futura* (1988)

nostalgically, to *Fragmente–Stille* by way of string scoring, tritones and changes of colour (nostalgically, for the years between 1980 and 1988 had seen the hardening of an everyman's capitalism in the west and a repudiation of socialism in eastern Europe), and at the same time, however slowly and laboriously, onward and upward.

Minimalism

There are at least two great paradoxes at the heart of minimalism. One is that an extreme reduction of means—to regular pulsation, to homogeneity of sound, to simple modes and chords—by no means eliminates personal style, as was already evident in the 1960s, in the different directions taken by Young, Reich, and Glass, or even in the 1930s, in the proto-minimalist music of Orff and Cage. Indeed, a bar of Glass may be more immediately identifiable as such than a bar of Ferneyhough, for all that the latter would contain so much more information—though perhaps this is not a paradox at all, since minimalism is by nature a flaunting of style over content, which is devalued by simplicity and repetition. Though seeming to exercise a new communality by its return to what is instinctual, minimalism has made possible a belated triumph of the individual, which minimalist composers have had to combat or use. As examples of the former, Young, by the sheer length of his pieces, removes them from the status of art objects, implying a creator, to that of environments, implying a listener (there is a parallel in late Feldman), while Reich's concentration on patent process excites the fiction of music in possession of itself, proceeding according to audible rules with apparently no help from its human originator. On the other hand, Adams's concern has been with the troubling frailties by which individuality is imagined and projected, and Glass's reworkings of Cocteau films, in *Orphée* (1993) and *La Belle et la Bête* (1994), can be read as either defiant or self-questioning identifications with a man for whom art could only be found in the mirror of showmanship.

Being so variously interpretable, minimalism has been one of the great growth areas in music, especially since the mid-1970s consummation represented by *Einstein on the Beach*. In the United States, Meredith Monk (b. 1943) had begun a few years before to develop a minimalism of voices—her own and those of a small group of performers trained by her—singing in her best work without accompaniment, vibrato-free, and on simple intervals and motifs, as if singing had only just been discovered. (One of the delights at minimalism's disposal is this joy in recovered origins: in Reich it is more sophisticated.) Also in the United States, David Lang (b. 1957) and Michael Torke (b. 1961) have been among the most successful second-generation minimalists. In Europe, minimalism has had most influence—always excepting Ligeti's early brush—on composers in Great Britain and the Netherlands, which may have to do with the lack of a language barrier to American English, or, perhaps more likely, with a certain apartness in these countries from any weight of tradition. To be a British composer or a Dutch composer means by itself rather little; to be a German composer a great deal. And certainly minimalism in both Britain and the Netherlands had most appeal to composers who had least time for musical institutions—whether the institutions of traditional musical life or the new institutions of the Darmstadt-gazing avant garde. So the influence of Cage, as great anarch, was followed by that of Reich and Riley.

Michael Nyman (b. 1944), later a minimalist composer himself, identified this strand in British–American composition as 'experimental music', in contrast with the avant garde,[39] and to some extent the distinction has continued to hold. Being a protest movement (in Budapest, the composers of the New Music Studio took this line in the late 1960s to mark themselves off from government-condoned new music), and having close connections with rock, minimalism in the Netherlands, especially, became political. Louis Andriessen (b. 1939), like Rzewski around 1970, began constructing musical systems in order to create metaphors—in the system or in the construction—of new forms of social order, and his amplified ensemble Hoketus, active in the 1970s and 1980s, used the aggressive sound world of heavy-metal to put the message across. Other Dutch ensembles, notably the wind band De Volharding, similarly set out on a course away from the sites and styles of 'classical' music for a populism of the street, rather as Weill had done in the 1920s and 1930s, and with similar intentions. For many Dutch composers, however, the great exemplar is Stravinsky, with his sources in folk music, his overturning of traditional functions, and his jointure of construction with carnival.

Perhaps more British composers, at least in the 1970s, took their bearings instead from Satie, as Cage had done. For Gavin Bryars (b. 1943), born on the same day as Brian Ferneyhough, Satie's lesson was a lesson in irony: in the wise handling of inappropriate materials, in the relishing of the banal, commonplace, and aesthetically disreputable. Minimalism—potentially implying an ironic distance between duration and value (though not in Reich), and sanctioned by Satie's *Vexations*[40]—naturally joined Bryars's stock of resources, and at an early point. In *The Sinking of the Titanic* (1969)—where the essence of the work is its unfulfilled idea, as in the 'conceptual art' of the period, so that the score is a body of verbal instructions—the

---

[39] See his *Experimental Music*.

[40] See Gavin Bryars, ' "Vexations" and its Performers', *Contact*, 26 (1983), 12–19; and also his 'Satie and the British', *Contact*, 25 (1982), 4–14.

aim was to recover the sound of the band on the sinking liner playing a hymntune as they went down with their vessel; authorized performances, of which three have been recorded, have strongly featured a slow chordal descent, from the tune 'Autumn', in minimalist repetition. In *Jesus' Blood Never Failed Me Yet* (1971), the repetition is that of voice recorded on a tape loop, as in Reich's early pieces, except that the voice (of an emphysematic tramp) is singing, and the variation comes in the accompaniment. As the repetitions go on, so sentimentality gives way to nobility: the tramp's nobility in defying his circumstances (for here, surely, is one who has been 'failed' by the world), the band's nobility in staying with him.[41]

Bryars's use of hymns in both these works is empty of religious meaning. Indeed, all his work questions the assumption of a psychological continuity between an artist's work and his self—hence his penchants for what could not be believed: for the sentimental, for the manifestly constructed (as in minimalism), for meaningless coincidence, for fantasy novels. Faced with the appearance, in the late 1980s, of music which claimed to convey a spiritual message by minimalist means, his response was to open the question again, and to write pieces which approximate to the sound worlds of Arvo Pärt and John Tavener—pieces such as *Glorious Hill* for four male voices (1988) and *Incipit vita nuova* for male alto and string trio (1989)—but which leave religious commitment in abeyance.

And this is the second paradox inherent in minimalism, that its twin origins—in rock and in the sacred musics of Asia and Africa—have resulted in a bizarre alliance of spirituality and commerce. There is of course no reason why spiritual art should not be popular and therefore commercially successful. The question that Bryars's works pose is whether minimalist spirituality may not be just style, and it is a question on which history has something to say, since there have repeatedly been calls for music to denude itself in order to attain a spirituality that, in retrospect, is questionable: the nineteenth-century Cecilian movement provides one example. A further question is simply whether music can be divided at all into the spiritual and the non-spiritual, or whether spirituality does not rather reside in the music's texts (Pärt and Taverner, for instance, have almost exclusively set sacred texts, often in sacred languages) and—this most of all—in how the music is heard.

György Ligeti

Dates are crude utensils with which to dismember the careers of artists, but at least in the case of Ligeti there was a pronounced change around 1980, occasioned partly by the fact that *Le Grand Macabre*, his biggest work, had ended one period and opened another, and partly by the illness which meant that he composed very little between the completion of the opera, in 1977, and 1982, when his Trio for violin,

[41] On Bryars, see Keith Potter, 'Just the Tip of the Iceberg: Some Aspects of Gavin Bryars' Music', *Contact*, 22 (1981), 4–15; and Richard Bernas, 'Three Works by Gavin Bryars', in Michael Finnissy and Roger Wright (eds.), *New Music 87*, 34–46.

horn, and piano appeared. Since then he has been composing steadily, but relatively slowly, for reasons that have to do not only with his health but perhaps also with the complexity—and the increasing complexity—of his music. His entire output since the trio consists of a few sets of choral pieces, a sequence of études for piano (begun in 1985), concertos for piano (1985–8), and violin (1989–93), and a sonata for solo viola (1991–4).

The complexity of this music is, on one level, the inevitable end result of his gathering recovery, since *Atmosphères*, of elements of definition—the crystallization, to use one of his own metaphors (and he is a master of musical metaphors), of what had been a super-saturated solution, where rhythm, pitch, and individual timbre were all melded into continuity. But it is also a response to two great discoveries he made in the 1980s: 'first of all the complex polymetres of Conlon Nancarrow's Studies for Player Piano, and secondly the great diversity of non-European musical cultures',[42] among which he mentions Caribbean music, to which he was introduced in 1980 by a pupil, Roberto Sierra, and the choral polyphony of the Banda Linda people of the Central African Republic, which came to his notice in 1982–3. Beyond that, as he has again acknowledged, he was led to complexity by the computer, not used as a tool (he gave up electronic music after his early experiments in Cologne, and would have no use—being so fascinated by compositional handiwork, as his busily inscribed scores indicate—for computer aids in calculation) but interpreted as a key to new ways of thinking. 'It's a question of adopting a "generative" kind of compositional thinking, where basic principles function in the manner of genetic codes in the unfolding of "vegetal" musical forms . . . A final scientific pursuit, whose engrossing results have a decisive effect on my musical conceptions, is the world of fractal geometry, developed by Benoît Mandelbrot, and quite particularly the graphic representation of complex limits.'[43]

A further stimulus to Ligeti's music since *Le Grand Macabre* has been a passionate contrariness to the postmodern restoration of a late Romantic rhetoric ('I hate neo-Expressionism and I can't stand the neo-Mahlerite and the neo-Bergian affectations'[44]), perhaps intensified by his awareness that his own development was becoming recuperative. But he found ways to stay at a distance from the comfortable confidence of nineteenth-century music—particularly its confidence in the composer as expressive agent—even while reclaiming tonal harmony, metre, and traditional genres. One way was through analysis and construction. He has approached traditional music as if he had no idea what it was for, but was fascinated by how it is put together. The Horn Trio, which unashamedly repeats a Brahmsian model, is a kind of golem Brahms, made with great virtuosity, but with deliberately unsuitable materials. And this was another way in which Ligeti dissociated himself from traditional music, and even more so from neo-traditional music. The trio goes on from the dislocated tonal harmony that had arrived in parts of *Le*

---

[42] 'Ma position comme compositeur aujourd'hui', *Contrechamps*, 12–13 (1990), 8–10.
[43] Ibid.
[44] Tünde Szitha, 'A Conversation with György Ligeti', *Hungarian Music Quarterly*, 3/1 (1992), 13–17.

Grand Macabre and then been considered, perhaps with some surprise, in the harpsichord pieces that had followed: the harmony in which simple consonances return, but not in the right order, producing a disturbing or comic effect which, as in any clown act, depends on a precise knowledge of the customary, and of how it may be tilted. Further tilting comes in his use of non-tempered tunings, which in such earlier pieces as *Ramifications* and the Double Concerto had been introduced for rather broad effects of harmonic colour and fuzziness, but which now had a quite particular function in setting up rivalries and tensions with normal tuning. In the case of the trio, it is by recourse to the horn's natural overtones, slightly 'mistuned', that these effects are obtained.

But Ligeti may have felt he had opened too many possibilities all at once, which would explain his subsequent concentration on the piano, in the first six Etudes (1985). Now there could be no microtonal inflections, but on the other hand the new possibilities of broken consonance and polymetre could be explored lucidly, without the confusion of different instrumental colours. The first Etude, 'Désordre', offers, as Denys Bouliane has shown,[45] an exemplary demonstration of polymetric process, of synthesis from elements drawn out of different musical cultures, and of 'vegetal' growth from a set of ad hoc ideas and rules, most of which are stated or implicit in the opening bars, reproduced in Example 68. The principal idea (one might even say 'theme', except that it is an object which, in keeping with the 'generative' ideal, just goes on repeating itself in different circumstances—in circumstances which it has helped to make different) is a melody in three segments, of four, four, and six bars, as indicated by the phrasing. Among the rules are the following. The melody keeps changing its mind about whether there are three-plus-five or five-plus-three quavers in each bar. Unused quaver beats are filled with scale patterns, so that the melody, initially going at a quick but not immoderate pace, is placed in a hectic moto perpetuo. Where the right hand plays only on the white keys, the left plays only on the black. The left hand doubles the right, but because it is working in a five-note mode rather than a seven-note one, its intervals are larger. (Rider: This rule is subject to a lot of exceptions, which perhaps have to do with other aims Ligeti has for his harmony. For example, the interval between the two hands in the first segment of the melody is always a minor sixth, tritone or major third, whereas in the second segment the minor third replaces the minor sixth. However, one of the sources of 'disorder' in the piece is the lack of agreement between harmony and rhythm: see the next rule.) The two hands slip out of synchrony in a manner that is at first organized—the right hand jumps a quaver every fourth bar—but later becomes more chaotic (as, indeed, so much in the music becomes more chaotic as it makes its journey upwards and offwards). The melody is repeated fourteen times, moving up a scale degree each time. From the fourth repetition to the tenth, a process of compression sets in, until by the tenth the notes of the melody are almost indistinguishable from those of the scalar infill.

[45] ' "Six Etudes pour piano" de György Ligeti', *Contrechamps*, 12–13 (1990), 98–132.

Ex. 68. Ligeti, Etude No. 1 'Désordre' (1985)

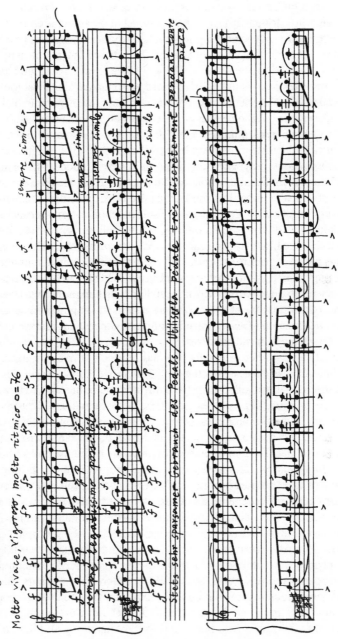

Many of the features of this study—the withdrawal of figure into ground, the swirling but precisely mechanical activity, the intimations of processes which are never fully revealed, or which go astray (an essential point of difference from Reich)—can be traced back quite clearly to *Monument–Selbstportrait–Bewegung*, and even, a little less clearly, to *Continuum*. What is new is the retrieval of some sort of tonal harmony out of undifferentiated chromaticism, and the exactly analogous retrieval of some sort of metre out of undifferentiated pulsation. Or at least the systematic organization of these things is new: since so much of Ligeti has always been about aural illusions—illusions of distance, say, created by the fashioning of sonorities in *Lontano*, or of sustained pitch and harmony made by rapid flickerings in the Double Concerto—it is never easy to be sure whether some new feature of his music has not in fact been produced by feint before. The harmonic retrieval is helped by the nature of the instrument, and by Bartók's example of a total chromaticism created by two hands playing on the piano in different modes. (In the seventh Etude the hands play in meshing whole-tone modes.) But the retrieval is not assumed: it has to be wrested anew in each bar, as the music's disordered trajectory keeps changing the situation. Certainties about tonic or mode are perpetually having to be redefined. Is the right-hand melody in the Aeolian mode on A or in the Locrian on B? Unable to make up its mind, it takes a step upwards. In just the same way—and this may be easier to appreciate in a short extract—certainties about accent or metre keep changing too, and the influence of Nancarrow is evident not just in the mad-machine sound world (which Ligeti had long had as his own) but in the liveliness and awkwardness of the polymetre and in the engineered acceleration. The music is in a marvellously organized confusion, which it has made inevitable, seemingly of itself, by its basic premises.

Of the twelve studies originally planned, thirteen have so far been written, and they share the basic features of the first: 'generative' construction from simple elements, imprints from folk music, harmony and metre in states of bewilderment or veiling, novel musical processes that come from the nature of the instrument—as in the third, 'Touches bloquées', where a moto perpetuo in the right hand moves over keys silently depressed by the left, so that gapped rhythms are made automatically. The titles of the pieces may, as in this case, be indications of how they were made, or they may be salutes to other musical cultures (the whole-tone piece has an Indonesian title, 'Galamb borong'), or they may be metaphors of effect: 'Désordre', 'Fanfares' for the fourth piece, a study in sixths, fifths, and thirds, 'Vertige'. Not only the titles but the iridescent uncertainties of harmony and rhythm place the studies within the ambit of Debussy.

Ligeti's Piano Concerto is, in a sense, a set of five more studies with the addition of an orchestra, which made it possible for the composer to take up the matter of non-tempered tunings again. In the odd-numbered movements the piano plays almost continuously, throwing up ideas that then take on lives of their own in the orchestra, as if, in congenial substrates, they could express the genetic material contained within them. The piano here is the originating and directing machine, whereas in the second movement—and again in the startling fourth, which the composer has described as 'a fractal piece', 'a geometric vortex' in which 'the ever-decreasing rhythmical values produce the sensation of a kind of acceleration'[46]—it seems that both piano and orchestra are worked by a machine existing elsewhere, in the composer's imagination.

The Violin Concerto—Ligeti's first instrumental work without a major keyboard component since *San Francisco Polyphony*, nearly twenty years before—takes off into the stratosphere of treble register and aerated tuning to which the Piano Concerto had pointed. Its first movement looks back to such works of the 1960s as the Cello Concerto and the Second Quartet in the way it evolves melodies and machines from trills, but within a new-Ligeti style of elaborate polymetres and fine-spun textures of harmonics, of which the latter determine what the composer has called the 'glassy-shimmering character of the movement', their uncertainty engendering 'the expression of fragility and danger'. Two instruments in the orchestra—a violin and a viola—are tuned throughout the work to natural harmonics played by the double bass, so that the haze of intonation is further complicated; in the score this gives a forbidding look to what sounds, by contrast, clear and weird. The ensemble is a small one, smaller than in the Piano Concerto, in order that niceties of tuning will not be lost. According to Ligeti's own account, he had begun by exploring possibilities of retuning a harp and a harpsichord ('glassy-shimmering' indeed), but realized he was 'entering a harmonic labyrinth so complicated that I was getting lost in it'.[47] Hence the scordatura, the natural harmonics (on brass instruments as well as the double bass), and the introduction later in the work of instruments of wayward intonation: pairs of ocarinas and recorders. From the trembling of tunings comes extraordinariness: a brass chorale mouldering with 'mistuned' harmonics, a melody for the soloist that appears to arise as a rainbow from the interference between the light of sustained tones and the showering of chromatic scales, a ground bass winding slowly upwards through the orchestra, with ocarinas and recorders enhancing the hazardousness as it arrives in the high treble.

György Kurtág

György Ligeti and György Kurtág (b. 1926), fellow students in Budapest immediately after the war, form a neat pair of opposites: the one wild-white-haired (at least since his late forties), articulate, productive, international, the other almost shaven-headed, almost silent, almost non-productive (at least until his late forties), and spending his life teaching chamber music at the academy where the two had met. At that first encounter, in 1945, Ligeti had been impressed by 'Kurtág's timidity, his introverted attitude and his total lack of vanity or presumption. He was intelligent,

---

[46] Szitha interview, 17.   [47] Ibid. 16.

sincere, and simple in a highly complex way. Later he told me that he, for his part, had taken me for a student of Protestant theology.'[48]

Both Ligeti and Kurtág had gone to Budapest in search of the spirit of Bartók; both of them later found also the spirit of Webern, though in Kurtág's case this seems not to have happened until 1957–8, when he was in Paris for a year, attending Milhaud's and Messiaen's classes, receiving psychological therapy from Marianne Stein (to whom he dedicated his Op. 1, a string quartet, and much later his *Kafka-Fragmente*), and copying out by hand Webern's entire works.[49] During this year he was at rock bottom: 'I realized to the point of despair that nothing I had believed to constitute the world was true . . . I was staying with another pupil of Marianne Stein, an American actress, and instead of paying rent I would walk her two children in the park. The park in question was the Parc Montsouris—a magnificent place, with fantastic trees. The impression made on me by these trees in winter was maybe then my first reality. That lasted until spring, and the appearance of my second reality: birds.'[50]

This anecdote—almost a Kurtág composition itself in how it opens a world of feeling with a few quick strokes—suggests what became the manner of his creativity: to start with nothing, to take nothing for certain, and then to make something utterly simple, utterly trustworthy. When he began to compose again, it was for some years exclusively in small instrumental forms: miniatures on a Webernesque scale—where a three-minute movement is Brucknerian and the average is the sixty-second spurt or flagging—but combining the imitative counterpoint of serial Webern with the rare timbres and the ostinatos of atonal Webern, and introducing personal qualities: bleak humour, scrawniness, sometimes moments of intense light. 'The cockroach in search of the way towards the light' was to have been the programme of the first movement of the quartet, with light 'symbolized by the chord in harmonics with all that filth in between'.[51]

By 1963, when he was thirty-seven, Kurtág had only five works ready for publication: about a minute of music for each year of his age, and with a wind quintet the largest ensemble.[52] During the next five years he produced about as much music again, all towards one piece, *The Sayings of Péter Bornemisza*, a 'concerto' for soprano and piano, whose four sections are made up once more of fragments. Bornemisza was a writer and Protestant preacher of the sixteenth century, and his

[48] 'Begegnung mit Kurtág im Nachkriegs-Budapest', in Friedrich Spangemacher (ed.), *György Kurtág* (Bonn, 1989), 14–17.

[49] See Peter Szendy, 'Musique et texte dans l'œuvre de György Kurtág', *Contrechamps*, 12–13 (1990), 266–84.

[50] Bálint András Varga, *Három kérdés—Nyolcvankét zeneszerző* (Budapest, Editio Musica, 1986), 202–13. There is a French translation of the interview—the only one the composer has sanctioned—in *Contrechamps*, 12–13 (1990), 175–83. I am grateful to the author for correcting my translation of the French text.

[51] Varga interview.

[52] For an excellent introduction to Kurtág's music, see Stephen Walsh, 'György Kurtág: an Outline Study', *Tempo*, 140 (1982), 11–21, and 141 (1982), 10–19. A postscript is provided by his 'A Brief Office for György Kurtág', *Musical Times*, 130 (1989), 525–6.

'sayings', assembled by the composer, cut to the quick. A new doctrine of personal accountability makes its demands. The text also has the newness of being couched in what was then an emergent language, lusty and rugged, with some sniff of the plough still among the biblical phrases. Tone and style were right for a composer who was, similarly, cutting himself a new language, and for whom the liberty to do so imposed a need for unflinching self-observation and self-criticism in the act of composing. The words also encouraged him, in his first vocal work apart from an early chorus, to push the voice to its limits of expression (the piano too: Barraqué's Sonata provides the work's lonely company in points of strength, freedom from precedent, and certainty—and it is a tantalizing coincidence that both composers should have been set on their paths by hearing Schubert's 'Unfinished' when they were children[53]), those limits including not only violent declamation and almost deranged, jubilatory savagery, as if the voice were intoxicated with the horrors of which it sings, but also a breathtaking lyrical nakedness—more breathtaking and more naked because it requires the singer to be absolutely on target. Example 69 shows such a passage.

Ex. 69. Kurtág, *The Sayings of Péter Bornemisza* (1963–8)

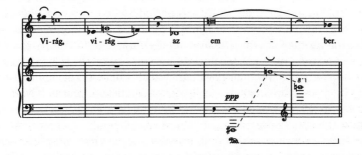

Kurtág's assignment of this voice to a soprano effectively removes the work from the realm of operatic vignette, since a singing Bornemisza would surely have to be a bass-baritone. Adrienne Csengery, the singer who worked with Kurtág intensively in the 1980s, has suggested that all his works are dramas, 'camouflaged operas',[54] which is certainly true in respect of their expressive quickness. Yet often they are operas with words but no characters. Because nobody is pretending to be Bornemisza, we are all—composer, singer, audience—in franker and more intimate contact with the words. There is no hiding from what they say, no palliative of understanding them as the language of a character. We may not be living in the fiery dawn of the Reformation, but we know sin and we know death, and we may hope for the luminous spring that is the subject of the work's third main section. These

---

[53] See Varga interview; and Barraqué's 'Propos impromptu'.

[54] István Balázs, 'Portrait eines Komponisten aus der Sicht einer Sängerin', in Spangemacher (ed.), *György Kurtág*; French translation in *Contrechamps*, 12–13 (1990), 184–94.

are realities. Quite how the music forces them on us when its means are often so simple is hard to say. There could hardly be less in Example 69 and still be something. On the other hand, there could be more and nothing at all.

One might venture that Kurtág's achievement—well established by this point—was so to particularize the momentary gesture that it released itself from musical syntax. This is what we mean by realism, whether in Monteverdi or in Musorgsky, but Kurtág is able to go further (as each realist must go further than the last), in that his miniature forms can virtually preclude syntax, and in that the disintegrated state of musical language extends the freedom of the gesture, as with Webern. No less crucial, to a realist, is the ability to invent gestures which are almost onomatopoeic, caught up in what they connote: the slow, soft, wide span of the voice in Example 69, or the piano glissando rising like a wisp of smoke, or the hunchbacked ostinato of the violin part in the 'Rondo' of *Scenes from a Novel* (1981–2)—a line that not only evokes obsession but seems desperately to be living it, as if the music were reporting on its own feelings, and not on those of the composer or some imagined subject. Again, a character would make the directness impossible.

Chronology would place Kurtág's Op. 7 in a previous part of this book, though, like Scelsi's music, it has a fair position here in terms of when it entered musical history, since the composer was little known outside Hungary until the 1980s. An important role in his wider discovery was played by Boulez, who came upon the score of *The Sayings of Péter Bornemisza* and commissioned a work for the Ensemble InterContemporain, *Messages of the Late Miss R. V. Trusova* for soprano and thirteen players (1976–80). Meanwhile, the completion of the Bornemisza concerto (perhaps so called by analogy with the sacred concertos of Schütz) had been followed by two shorter song sets, a failed orchestra project (*Twenty-Four Antiphonae* Op. 10 for diverse groups—though the failure may not be permanent, since other remnants have eventually found completion, sometimes after many years) and then a further period of dumbness, relieved by Kurtág's recognition, prompted by the younger composers of the New Music Studio,[55] that silence might be broached through serious playfulness. Like Stravinsky and Bartók at points of crisis, he tested a new way forward in music for children, and in 1973 began writing pieces for what were to become five volumes of piano pieces: *Játékok*, or *Games*—games played with notes, whether games of formal and technical device, or games of imitation. From this point onwards his music is full of arrangements and homages, covering the repertory from Machaut to the present, in every mood except the nostalgic, and including reworkings of his own discoveries: Example 69 has its derivatives in *Játékok*. The many works that have come since Kurtág began his piano games might be considered *Játékok* for grown-ups: the significantly titled *Twelve Microludes* for string quartet (1977–8)—fragments, as always with Kurtág—provide an example. Like Bartók's *Mikrokosmos*, *Játékok* is educational music in the widest sense, in that it provides an education in a composer's sources, sympathies, and techniques, an education valid for large further areas of his output.

[55] See Varga interview.

One great difference, however, between *Játékok* and the 'adult' music of 1973–87 is that nearly all the latter is vocal, and much of it, following their work together on *Trusova*, was written for Csengery, whose reminiscences provide abundant testimony to the intensity of their preparations and rehearsals: the composer's experience in teaching chamber music was not, after all, peripheral, but central to his ideal of making musical communication maximally responsive and responsible. It may be that the comparative dearth of instrumental works during this period, by contrast with the pattern of his output before the Bornemisza piece, came from a need he felt to discover, in composition and rehearsal, another person, whether the person of a singer or of a poet. In *Trusova* and two companion works, *Omaggio a Luigi Nono* for chorus (1979) and *Scenes from a Novel*, that poet was Rimma Dalosh, a Russian writer living in Hungary. During this time Russian became for him 'almost a sacred language'[56]—sacred, perhaps, in having been rescued, in Dalosh's compact and highly charged poems, from the laxness and cynicism of its daily use during the dying years of Soviet hegemony. Towards the end of his 'Dalosh' period, in 1981, Kurtág returned to twentieth-century Hungarian poetry, but his work with Csengery continued: indeed, almost everything he completed between 1980 and 1987 was written for her, the main exception being a second choral set, to poems by an inventor of verbal 'játékok', Dezsö Tandori.

The two Dalosh compositions for Csengery, *Trusova* and *Scenes from a Novel*, are unusual among Kurtág's works in projecting a character who reports past and present feelings: a woman at the end of a passionate affair, a woman in the lull between meetings with her lover. But still the composer avoids making his music seem merely illustrative. All that we know of the heroine of *Scenes from a Novel* is provided by the music; we cannot imagine how she would sound if she did not sound like this. Such an effect is possible partly because Dalosh's texts are so simple as well as so intense, partly because the music, catching the intensity in its quasi-onomatopoeia, cannot be thought secondary: one might well think that the words are describing what the music is saying, rather than the other way around. In *Trusova* Kurtág wrote for a larger ensemble than hitherto: an expansion of the twangy formations of the Four Capriccios and Four Pilinszky Songs, and curiously —perhaps deliberately—close to the instrumentation of Boulez's *Eclat*, though sounding so different. Kurtág's music proceeds in spidery counterpoint, exerted at every turn, rather than in waves and splashes, and normally it uses just a small number of the available forces, focusing increasingly on the combination of voice and solo string instrument that had been a recurrent ideal since *In Memory of a Winter Sunset* (1969). Not only did this combination provide a model of the interaction of music and verbal language, but it made possible a close interdependence and a fluidity of roles: the voice may seem to accompany the instrument.

It was for soprano and violin that Kurtág wrote his longest work so far, the *Kafka-Fragmente* (1985–6), in which forty extracts—chosen chiefly from the letters and

---

[56] As quoted in István Balázs, 'Dans la prison de la vie privée', *Contrechamps*, 12–13 (1990), 198–210.

diaries, and ranging from apophthegm to anecdote—are assembled in four sequences, lasting altogether for seventy minutes. Kafka's paradoxical edges—between irony and anxiety, between withdrawal and explosion, between creative potency and indecision—are Kurtág's too, and in this collaboration the composer was perhaps closest to standing before a mirror, of challenging clarity. The work was a culmination, and after it came just two small collections for soprano and piano before a return to instrumental composition, for larger forces than hitherto, in . . .*quasi una fantasia* . . . for piano and instrumental groups (1987–8).

By dispersing the instruments—in a way perhaps opened to him by Nono—Kurtág discovered a fragmented orchestra suited to his fragmented form. Ideally the pianist is to be on stage with only timpani and drums; other percussion—an unpitched metal group of cymbals, gongs, and triangles, a smaller 'echo' ensemble of them, and a number of tuned instruments including the composer's much-favoured cimbalom—are to be on a middle gallery, with mouth organs; teams of five woodwind, four brass, and five strings are then to be placed on the highest level. Drama, which had previously been justified and described in the music by words, was now implicit in the resources, and the composer's relationship with a poet became the relationships his music could build in space: relationships of echo, non-relationships of concurrent dissimilarities (especially in the third of the four short movements, a wild 'Presto minaccioso e lamentoso'). The work also echoes earlier pieces, in a way by now characteristic: once a reality had been built, it remained a reality for other circumstances. Example 70*a* shows the ending of the fifth of the *Microludes*, and Example 70*b* the corresponding passage from the finale of . . . *quasi una fantasia* . . . . The material is expanded in time, by echoing, as well as in texture, but it is arguably also intensified, particularly when the tonic E is repeatedly undershot. Once again, with the simplest materials—hardly more than a descending scale—Kurtág creates an original and unforgettable gesture.

This vestige of a piano concerto was followed by a third work for string quartet, the *Officium breve in memoriam Andreae Szervánszky* (1988–9), which is a voiceless requiem in fifteen movements ranging from the merest wisps to an arrangement of the chorale-canon from Webern's Second Cantata: the work is an ellipse around foci that are this Webern composition and a serenade for strings by Endre

Ex. 70*a*. Kurtág, *Twelve Microludes*: V (1977–8)

Ex. 70b. Kurtág, . . . *quasi una fantasia* . . . : IV (1987–8)

Szervánszky (1911–77). Kurtág then returned to the splintered orchestra for *Grabstein für Stephan* with solo guitar (1989), *Op. 27 No. 2* (... *quasi una fantasia* ... had been Op. 27) with solo piano and cello (1989–90), and *Samuel Beckett: What is the Word* for contralto, voices, and ensembles (1991). This last astonishing piece is not so much a setting as a dramatic production of Beckett's last published text, a production in which the soloist struggles to make and then hold on to vocal expression as it evaporates from her into the distant groups of musicians. Kurtág's international reputation had brought him the means and perhaps also the confidence to work on the large scale, but the Beckett work, like each of its purely instrumental predecessors, shows how real fullness comes from deprivation. The most remarkable demonstration of the composer's consistency, however, is his *Rückblick* (1993), a collection of forty-six pieces for four players (trumpet, double bass, pianos, and keyboards) that incorporates new compositions and arrangements of pieces from as far back as his Op. 3; Example 69 has its place here, as one of the realities which, once found, remain valid.

Humour

The 1980s resurgence of musical humour (not a prodigious category in the 1950s and 1960s) may have come about because comedy in music seems to require a certain duplicity, a countering of expectation, whether that expectation has been aroused by promises couched in a discursive musical language or by more general norms and proprieties—all of which implies that there indeed are discourses, norms or proprieties. Music committed to constant change, as modernism was by design, could not be funny: a joke in Varèse is unthinkable. But postmodernism, so rippled with ironies, is almost a joke in itself, and the postmodern empowerment of music to reflect, on itself and on the past, opens a mirrorscape of levels on which what happens may deceive.

The music of Ligeti and Kagel—latecomers to the Darmstadt avant garde, and therefore able to come to it with a distinct ironic detachment—introduced into new music the occasional possibility of comedy in the late 1950s: Ligeti's *Artikulation* is a rare, possibly unique, example of funny electronic music, and much of his later music shows the same ability to use precisely made gestures as vocables in comic scenes, dialogues, and monologues (hence his fascination with the concerto, as a particularly opportune occasion for the projection of characters who, like the heroes and heroines of silent film comedy, courageously take on enormous demands, under the duress of a form that makes epics into miniatures). Nancarrow's adventures in comedy also go back to the 1950s. But where these were rather isolated instances, a lot of music since the late 1970s has had humour as an option: not only Ligeti's but that of Kurtág, Donatoni, Weir, Heinz Karl Gruber (b. 1943)—author of the horror comedy *Frankenstein!!* for his own eldritch *Sprechgesang* narration with orchestra (1976–7)—and others. The advent of postmodernism also made it easier to recognize the comedy inherent in neoclassicism: Weir's essay on *Oedipus rex*[57] is an interesting document in this regard.

What is perhaps most remarkable is how, with the rising tide, comedy in the late 1980s and 1990s began to enter the music of composers one might have thought immune or incapable: the solo of the Supreme Lyre-Bird in Messiaen's *Eclairs sur l'Au-delà*, or the boyish game of military combat played out by platoons of musicians in Stockhausen's *Dienstag* (the work of a composer whose previous idea of humour had been represented by the disporting lozenged-tights-clad clarinettist of *Harlekin*). In other music, where the composer's expression is concealed by a mask of objectivity, comedy may be more difficult to discern—as seems to have been the case with Stravinsky's *Apollo*, Capriccio or indeed *Oedipus rex* when those works were new. There is certainly benignity in Cage, for example, and his laughing face became one of the photographic icons of the 1970s and 1980s; but do we laugh too? Also, the comic potential of repetition (and even more so of slipped repetition) does not appear to have been noted by many minimalist and ex-minimalist composers, with the exception of Adams in what may be his best pieces—pieces such as *Grand Pianola Music*, *The Chairman Dances*, and *Nixon in China*, in all of which the glorying in vulgar music, the exuberance, and the glamour have the poignancy that goes along with hilarity.

Heinz Holliger

Already in the early 1970s Holliger's exploration of extreme possibilities, in his work as a performer, had become crucial also to his creative activity, when writing for himself and for others. Extreme possibilities suggest that language is being expanded, through the addition of non-standard timbres, microtones, far registers—and the thrill of discovery is there in such early works as *Siebengesang*. But Holliger's later music reveals another implication in radicalism, of minimization and constraint, as in Nono, Kurtág, and Rihm. Music seems destined to move on to what had been neglected as unpromising wasteland: this is the imperative if one is to avoid quoting the styles and materials of past music, and if one is to avoid—as may be a still more commanding injunction—the rhetoric of certainty. Holliger's music breathes uncertainty in its choice of marginal vocal and instrumental techniques, and refuses the directive first-person-singular of the composer's voice by dealing with materials and forms that are so simple as to be impersonal.

Taking his way along this arduous but fruitful path, Holliger has since the mid-1970s gone with the help of two guide-books. One was provided by the late dramas of Beckett, which supported him in his attention to tight structure, bareness, and a sense of the performer as a body and a voice: out of this collaboration came settings of *Come and Go* for three trios of female singers with trios of flutes, clarinets, and

[57] In Nicholas John (ed.): *Igor Stravinsky: The Rake's Progress, Oedipus Rex* (ENO Opera Guide 43, London: John Calder, 1991), pp. 17–21.

violas (1976–7), *Not I* for soprano with a tape created at IRCAM (1978–80), and *What Where* for four male singers with four trombones and percussion (1988). Holliger's other vade-mecum was Hölderlin, whose poetry has challenged and fascinated composers throughout this period, so that one might almost write a history of music since 1945 in which all the examples were from responses to Hölderlin, by Nono, Britten, Henze, Maderna, Kurtág, Ligeti, Rihm, and others.

The attractions of Hölderlin must include the musicality of his syllables and images, as well as his evocation of another world, created by sound almost before it is created by words, and the fragmentary nature of much of his work, apt to a time and a musical climate in which the definitive statement is hard to sustain. But Holliger, like Rihm, was drawn also by the late poetry written under the pseudonym 'Scardanelli'—the 'mad' poetry, whose escape from rules of sense, taste, and cultural nobility makes it unusually relevant in a musical world similarly loosened from agreed ideals. Between 1975 and 1979 came three seasonal cycles of settings for sixteen voices, to which the composer then added instrumental paraphrases, commentaries, and interludes—*Übungen zu Scardanelli* for small orchestra and tape (1978–85), *(t)air(e)* for solo flute (1980–3) and *Ostinato funebre* for small orchestra (1991)—to make an entire concert.

That Holliger should have made his Hölderlin settings for chorus rather than for solo singer may have to do with his wish for an impersonal voicing, with the relationship he had formed with Clytus Gottwald and the Schola Cantorum Stuttgart (who had performed his earlier *Dona nobis pacem* and Celan setting *Psalm*), and perhaps also with a certain Swiss veneration of Bach: the *Scardanelli-Zyklus* is a secular Passion, slowly oscillating between homophonic and canonic movements, and inviting contemplation of a solitary and exemplary figure, that of the poet, confined in his tower at Tübingen but with his mind wandering.

The chorus is not, though, the unified community it was in eighteenth-century Leipzig, and Holliger's choral writing takes traces through disintegration. In 'Der Frühling (I)', for example, the singers have to deliver root-position triads breathily, or with almost emptied lungs, or humming. 'Der Winter (III)' is a four-part mirror canon in triads moving through intervals between a tone and a quarter-tone. 'Der Winter (II)', also a four-part canon, has all the performers singing *ppp* in a narrow 'dummy bass' register (between A and E♭ at the bottom of the treble stave for the sopranos, for instance). The soprano, alto, and tenor parts of 'Der Herbst (I)' have sudden shifts of register from chord to chord, sometimes by more than two and a half octaves, as these singers project dissonant overtones on a bass line plummeting to A below the stave. 'Der Sommer (III)' is a chain of three canons for seven female voices (number symbolism recurs here as in *Siebengesang*, and indeed as in Bach: the tempos of 37 and 73 in 'Der Herbst (II)' relate to Hölderlin's age when he entered the tower and his age when he died), the first canon in semitones, the second reducing each interval by a half, and the third halving the intervals again. Example 71 shows the melody of this last canon; the arrows on the accidentals indicate a quarter-tone rise, and those on the note heads on eighth-tone rise. As in the

Ex. 71. Holliger, 'Der Sommer (III)' (1979)

other two summer pieces, each singer sings to the tempo of her pulse, which not only manifests the physiology of performance, as in earlier Holliger pieces, but makes the chorus—even in a unison canon—into a collection of errant individuals. One of the *Übungen*, 'Sommerkanon IV', is an orchestral version of the same piece; others are images that relate more tangentially and metaphorically to Hölderlin: 'Eisblumen', or 'Ice Flowers', a string septet in harmonics; 'Schaufelrad', or 'Paddlewheel', in two slowly rotating six-note chords; 'Ad marginem', where the instruments move towards, but do not reach, the extreme registers represented on tape throughout.

Sofya Gubaydulina

Belonging to the same time and place as Schnittke, Sofya Gubaydulina (b. 1931) similarly emerged from the school of Shostakovich, through serialism, to create works whose intensities depend on multifarious references. She has not, though, embedded those references in standard genres, except in her string quartets. Her single symphony, '*Stimmen . . . Verstummen*' (1986), has twelve movements; her violin concerto *Offertorium* (1980), plays continuously. Many more of her works set up conditions which pertain to them alone: *The Hour of the Soul* (1974), in which a percussionist stirs up an orchestra, out of which a mezzo-soprano eventually arises; other works that place percussion instruments to the fore; still others with a prominent part for the bayan, a kind of accordion; *Perception* for soprano, baritone, string septet, and tape (1983), which is one of several pieces concerned with an antinomy between female and male sensibilities. (*The Hour of the Soul* was written for a male percussionist, Marek Pekarski, and in the composer's words: 'only at the end does the truly feminine nature appear'.[58])

This femaleness is, however, a theme subsidiary in most of her music to matters of spirituality and belief. As with Skryabin and some of his followers, such as Nikolay Obukhov, she works with musical events and processes as symbols. In *Offertorium*, for instance, the subject from Bach's *Musical Offering*, which is first dismembered in the manner of Webern's orchestration, stands for the composers 'who have produced . . . the greatest impression on me'; more importantly, its progressive curtailment, lopped from both ends, is the realization of her germinal idea that 'the theme would offer itself up as a sacrifice'.[59] No material which could be

---

[58] Claire Polin, 'Conversations in Leningrad, 1988', *Tempo*, 168 (1989), 19.

[59] Quoted in note with DG 427 336.

used in such a symbolic drama is ruled out, and since the music has its meaning through representation, through a language in which mental states and transformations are to be understood as figured in sound hieroglyphs, a purely musical integrity is beside the point, and might even be misleading, if it were to divert attention from the symbolism. This is where Gubaydulina differs from Messiaen, whose proclamatory harmonies her music sometimes encounters. In her work there is no commitment to *écriture*, or to symmetry. The characteristics are instead abrupt, ripped change, a finish that is often rough, raw, and ragged, and a variety equalling Schnittke's. A further Skryabinesque feature, is some of her music of the 1990s, is the use of light as well as sound.

Gubaydulina, again like Schnittke, earned her living during the Soviet years as a composer for films, though in her case for animated films, and her concert works may suggest—because their intention is always towards something beyond what is heard—a cartoon music of the soul. '*Stimmen . . . Verstummen*' is a case in point. The angelic rapture with which it begins, and to which it keeps returning, is a fibrility of high D major triads—an image of childlike simplicity. Another such image is threaded through the Second Quartet in the form of a unison G. In asking us to accept the elementary as part of a vastly ranging soundscape—and not only as part but by implication as the highest part—Gubaydulina offers no intrinsically musical motivation but only an invitation to stay the course.

Folk music

With the demise of modernism, music lost its absolutes. There was no single past (Boulez had provided the extreme example of modernist historical selectivity, disparaging large parts of the outputs even of the composers he most admires) and no certain future. As for the present, there was no agreement on principles or practices. The renewal of interest in folk music—coming about, as it did, just when modernism was petering out, in the early 1970s—may be interpreted as a search for something certain, for some sure foundation, for a re-rooting of the science of music in its natural history. (What was also to be regained, as in Cage's *Roaratorio*, was a music of saturnalia.) To the extent that minimalism, for instance, was a re-centring of music in pulse and tonality, it invited an acquaintance with musical cultures in which those elements had not been subject to western development, as in Young's studies of Indian singing or Reich's of west African drumming.

But folk music also had much to offer composers who did not want to offload their western baggage, as Berio's music shows. Like many composers, he began by looking at folk music through Stravinsky's glasses: his *Folk Songs* (1964), written for the many voices of Berberian, are something like *Pribautki* plus show-biz. But as he involved himself more deeply with past musical languages, so he began to use folk melodies as memes, as bearers of meaning to be analysed, brought into contact with one another, mused upon, imitated. In *Coro* (1976–7) the mood changed from cabaret to dream, or nightmare, and in the viola concerto *Voci* (1984) Berio created a fantasy portrait of Sicilian folk music, which is 'certainly the richest, the hottest, and the most complex of our Mediterranean culture',[60] while in the *Duetti* for junior violinists and their teachers (1979–82) he created imaginary folk musics. His fascination with folk cultures that are not his own (he was born in Liguria, not in Sicily) is part of a wider fascination with musical traditions—wherever they spring from—as codes and manners of musical communication, both between people, and between people and the world. The resulting works are different, because their sources are different, but the procedures and the stance are the same, whether the composer is dealing with Sicilian folk music in *Voci*, with Schubert sketches in *Rendering*, or with a piece of his own in *Corale*.

As already mentioned, Ligeti has also learned much from many different kinds of folk music, as well as from that of his native Hungary, the far and the near often at the same time. This may have been in reaction to his youth, during which a sub-Kodály Romantic portraiture of folk music was the norm: when, after a gap of nearly thirty years, he returned to setting the Hungarian language, in the *Hungarian Studies* for chorus[61] (1983), it was with a delight in contrivance and African–Caribbean polymetres, as well as in the intervals and rhythms that the language, taught by folk music, wants to sing. This is the folk music of a Hungary on the moon, and it answers the same sort of ironic distance from folk culture in the Sándor Weöres poems.

Ligeti's interest in African music provides a striking parallel, or contrast, with Berio's. Both composers have warmly acknowledged a debt to Simha Arom's studies of Banda Linda polyphony in the Central African Republic,[62] but where Berio is concerned with how folk music is voiced, and with the evidence it carries of expression, communication, and culture, Ligeti is an abstracter. Berio, discovering a musical artefact, listens to what it says, or sings, about a human community and their relationship with the world; Ligeti looks at how it is made. It is significant that Berio should have given the title *Voci* to a work for instruments, whereas Ligeti's folk-music syntheses, even when vocal, have an instrumental exactitude.

For other composers, folk music has to do with home. It may provide a way of claiming identity, as it seems to be with Xenakis, in the accommodation to Balkan rhythms and modes he makes in much of his later music. It may be a way of saying something about your country, as in Finnissy's *English Country-Tunes*. It may offer models of economy, as in Kurtág. It may be an invitation beyond the norms of tuning and instrumentation, as also in Kurtág and in Ligeti. It may be a manifest difference, to be explored and honoured, as in the African music of Kevin Volans (b. 1949). It may be something to be brought into collision or co-operation with the

[60] Note with RCA RD 87898.

[61] For an analysis, see Luminita Aluas, 'Visible and Audible Structures: Spatio-Temporal Compromise in Ligeti's *Magyar etüdök, Tempo*, 183 (1992), 7–17.

[62] See Ligeti, 'Ma position comme compositeur aujourd'hui', 8–9; and Dalmonte and Varga, *Luciano Berio: Two Interviews*, 20 and 152.

standard apparatus of western music, as in Tan. It may, even if it is yours, seem puzzlingly and amusingly odd, as in Weir. Or it may just be deeply in the background of what you are, as in Birtwistle.

Brian Ferneyhough

To the tide of retrogression that arrived in the seventies, progress found an answer in Brian Ferneyhough (b. 1943). Born in England, but trained in the Netherlands and Switzerland, and subsequently active as a teacher in Switzerland, Germany, and the United States (at San Diego from 1987), Ferneyhough was an international figure before he was a national one: his big break came at the 1974 Royan Festival, and for some years he was more performed and more influential in continental Europe than in Britain. He seemed to fit into what was, by the mid-1970s, the almost empty category of the international avant garde. As with Hopkins, his critical attitude to the music of the 1950s was sharpened by the intensest appreciation of the lessons that could—and the challenge that must—be drawn from that music. There was no going back. He took over the role of intellectual and creative combatant that most of the leading composers of the 1950s had abandoned; he even taught at Darmstadt.

The importance to him of the Darmstadt adventure is evident in his scores of the 1960s—in, for example, the highly sophisticated rhythmic notation suggestive of the first book of Boulez's *Structures* or of Stockhausen's first Piano Pieces. But he may have identified more, at this time of his early twenties, with the music Boulez was writing at the same age. He similarly concentrated on small instrumental forms, always including the piano, and similarly achieved a wild, fresh energy that would, in his case, remain characteristic. The sources of that energy, though, were different. Where Boulez was in arms against the past, crashing through the models of Beethovenian sonata or French good taste, Ferneyhough's intensity is typically an intensity more of composition than of destruction. System is not in the way of expression: expression happens by, through and in system—or rather, by, through and in the entrammelling of a human being (first the composer, later the performer) with system. As Ferneyhough has said, for example, of his *Four Miniatures* for flute and piano (1965), 'the flute part contains several very specific rhythmic configurations whose purpose is to focus the performer's mind on that particular dimension at very precise junctures'.[63] Similarly, the purpose of complex musical architectures is to focus the composer's mind at the very precise juncture of inscription.

This understanding of system makes Ferneyhough's seeming adherence to musical progress questionable—both within the time frame of the individual work, and within the larger time frame of history. To take the latter first, he has never chosen,

---

[63] Interview with Philippe Albèra in *Contrechamps*, 8 (1988), 9.

as Boulez and Stockhausen chose and choose, to project his works as patterns or compendia for the future, and his few references to the past have concerned somewhat distant prototypes: Webern and the fantasias of Purcell in the case of his first major work, the Sonatas for string quartet (1967), or the polychoral music of sixteenth-century Venice and England. Such ancestors are, to be sure, significant. If, for all his internationalism, there is something English in Ferneyhough's music, this is less a rhythmic sharing with the language (which he has rarely set) than the continuing echo of an early approximation to the textures of Tudor and Stuart music—to polyphonies of strings (in the Sonatas, *Epicycle*, *Firecycle β*, and *Funérailles*) or voices (in the *Missa brevis*, *Time and Motion Study III*, and *Transit*)—but of an approximation conspicuously without the stylistic references that had become almost unavoidable in English music at the time. In rejecting, for example, Davies, he rejected one English tradition to come closer to another, for, like the composers of antiphons and masses in colleges and cathedrals under the first Tudors, he perpetuated—and, by hypertrophy, radicalized—devices that had been supplanted in the rest of Europe. He thus combined the belatedness of a Tavener or a Tallis with the newness and influence of a Dunstable. For himself, however, he has preferred to leave any historical message implicit. The past is not demanding consummation. The future is just what happens next.

So it may appear to be within the context of the individual work, among those completed before 1980. Ferneyhough's method appears to have been to assemble so many strategies—strategies of quantification and transformation having their roots in 1950s serialism—that his creative options were, to use his own word again, 'focused': hence the characteristic impression of musical figments of extreme articulacy and force, such as begin to arrive particularly in the solos of *Prometheus* for wind sextet (1967) and the duo for two violins in the Sonatas of the same year. The certainty of the gesture, at such moments, is absolute, but absolute by assertion rather than by demonstrable adherence to some convention or structure. The music is so because it wills itself so, and it convinces partly because it has nothing to prove beyond its own existence. It is not trying to tell us what the future of music must be. It is not even trying to tell us what the future of the piece must be. Ferneyhough's works of this early period are typically composed of discrete fragments (twenty-four in the Sonatas), and sometimes the ordering (*Cassandra's Dream Song*) or even the nature (*Sieben Sterne*) of the fragments may be alterable by performers. Being absolute by assertion, the music could, alternatively, have been absolute by assertion in a different way. Or it could have been different music that was absolutely asserted. (There are connections here with Stravinsky and with Birtwistle, in that the arbitrary becomes absolute in being composed. An example from Birtwistle is his 1984 *Still Movement* for strings, which takes a different route between points in his opera *Yan Tan Tethera*.) Facing the fact that his creative choices, however straitened, could have gone differently—that the lightning could have taken a different path—Ferneyhough contemplated the idea of making another, inevitably quite different realization of *Prometheus*, and he intended

Firecycle β, for an orchestra of strings and percussion (1969–71), to be accompanied by companion but dissimilar treatments of the same material: a *Firecycle α*, 'rather short and compact, with very dense and very complex activity, like, say, an astronomical object seen from afar' and a *Firecycle γ*, in which the listener would come inside the 'molecular structure' and observe the material becoming 'highly repetitive and almost characterless'.[64] A few years later he did achieve something similar, creating in *Funérailles II* a second context for items removed from *Funérailles I*.

During the interim he composed pieces that can be seen as models of his relationship with his material in the act of composition: solo pieces, in which the performer, like the composer, has to operate at a level of extreme awareness while negotiating a way through a multitude of rivalling and even conflicting demands; and *Transit* for vocal and instrumental ensembles (1972–5), in which imaginative perception is both the goal and the constant mode of being. If the earlier works had looked towards Boulez and, to a lesser extent, Stockhausen, those of the 1970s move on to the sites of the second-generation avant garde: the unaccompanied chorus, swarming with new vocal techniques, in *Time and Motion Study III* (first performed by Clytus Gottwald and his Schola Cantorum Stuttgart, who had gone this way, though never quite so arduously, with Kagel, Schnebel, and Holliger[65]), and the solo flute and cello, the bearers of so many new musical messages during the late 1950s and 1960s, in *Unity Capsule* (1975–6) and *Time and Motion Study II* (1973–6).

The opening of *Unity Capsule*, shown in Example 72, may suggest the problems, even in what is a relatively simply passage.[66] Ferneyhough's use of short note values, which gives his scores a characteristic scarified look, makes it possible for him to indicate continuity in the beaming, and may also sharpen the player's zest for speed—for speed quite deliberately dangerous when there is so much to be considered and done. Not only are the judgements of pitch, duration, and dynamic exceedingly fine, but Ferneyhough adds many further levels of demand and distinction. To paraphrase his own explanation of the notation,[67] the half-rhomb note-heads in the first bar indicate sounds with a great deal of breath noise; the block note-head on the voice line in the second bar indicates 'play with the mouth open and with full but diffuse respiration—as if your breath were cut off', while the circle in the next bar stands for a plosive produced by the tongue without breath. The inverted T shapes above the stave mean 'without tongue attack'; the rotating U shapes show the angle at which the instrument must be held to the lips; and the plus signs indicate percussive but silent depressions of the keys. There are also more conventional indications of fingering.

Not only all this (and later much more), but the piece also compresses into its capsuled unity a great many cross-references: for example, the 4–3–2 pattern of the

---

[64] Interview with Philippe Albèra in *Contrechamps*, 8 (1988), 19.

[65] See Clytus Gottwald, 'Brian F. oder Von Metaphysik der Positivismus', *Melos*, 44 (1977), 299–308.

[66] For a performer's view, see Kathryn Lukas, 'Cassandra's Dream Song & Unity Capsule', *Contact*, 20 (1979), 9–11. See also a fascinating account by Steven Schick in his 'Developing an Interpretive Context: Learning Brian Ferneyhough's *Bone Alphabet*', *Perspectives of New Music*, 32/1 (1994), 132–53.

[67] 'Unity Capsule: Un journal de bord', *Contrechamps*, 8 (1988), 140–8.

Ex. 72. Ferneyhough, *Unity Capsule* (1975–6)

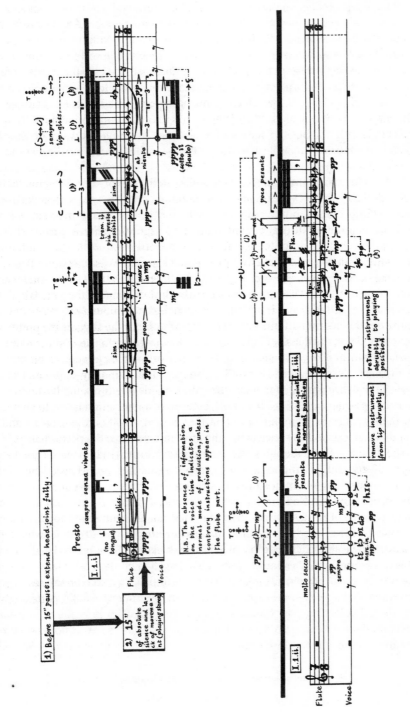

opening bars is echoed in the numbers of subsections within the first section (new subsections begin, as shown, with the fifth and seventh bars), and in the number of sections within the piece. Of course, the status of the information is in doubt, partly because there is so much of it, partly because some bits of it will cancel out others, and partly because it cannot be projected: for instance, the only bar in Example 72 likely to be definable as a length is bar 6. But the music is surely aware of its condition. Ferneyhough's hint that a bar can be measured only by means of an ungainly physical gesture is one of his black ironies, and his often quoted statement that his concern is with 'the positive nature of doubt' may be understood as a declaration that his music exists precisely in its imprecision—in the failures and the over-abundances of its performance.

Support for that would come from his preface to the earlier and far less intensively notated *Cassandra's Dream Song*: 'The notation does not represent the result required: it is the attempt to realize the written specifications in practice which is designed to produce the desired (but unnotatable) sound quality. A "beautiful", cultivated performance is not to be aimed at . . . Nevertheless, a valid realization will only result from a rigorous attempt to reproduce as many of the textural details as possible: such divergencies and "impurities" as then follow from the natural limitations of the instrument itself may be taken to be the intentions of the composer.' The difference in *Unity Capsule* is that the 'divergencies and "impurities" ' will come not only from the instrument but from the frantic nature of the task. As the composer has pointed out, the density of instructions 'often stops performers "remembering" too far ahead, and leaves them in a constant state of "surprise attack", as the horizon of memory closes around them'. For listeners, too, this may happen. Though Ferneyhough has protested that his 'structures, as linear entities, *can* be heard individually',[68] it may be that 'a "beautiful", cultivated' appreciation is less to be hoped for than a constant grappling, and that the only form will be the drive to understand—or at least to keep pace with—the drive immanent in the performance.

The flute was Ferneyhough's own instrument; it provided him with a great variety of effects; and, as a monodic source, it added a further level of useful constraint on a composer for whom 'texture and structure . . . are the two vehicles of expressive form'.[69] But he also found possibilities of highly charged virtuosity in the dramatic persona of a cellist wired-up so that vocal and instrumental sounds could be amplified and recorded: hence *Time and Motion Study II*, part of a series whose title is a pun on the efficiency tests to which British workers were subjected in the 1960s. This was Ferneyhough's nearest approach to Kagelian borderlands of instrumental theatre and social criticism. Similarly, *Transit* is unusually concrete: unusually generous with an almost Berio-esque or Birtwistlian sonorous appeal (in the chattering together of voices and instruments, or in the eruptions of brass), and unusually acknowledging of a world outside itself. Part of what makes Ferneyhough so problematic a pioneer is the close centring of each of his works on materials and issues

---

[68] Albèra interview, 38.   [69] 'Unity Capsule: Un journal de bord'.

which are proper to it alone. *Transit*, one of his very few vocal pieces, looks out. In its texts, in its layout (in concentric semicircles of instruments around the singers), in its form, and in its imagery, it concerns itself with the mind's penetration of the objective universe, even if this is perhaps only a metaphor for the mental and physical agilities working at pressure in the more abstract pieces.[70]

Funérailles for string septet and harp, completed in 1980, ends a period in Ferneyhough's output with a memorial which also has elements of the graphic (foretastes of the 'cathedral-under-the-sea' sonorities of *Mnemosyne*[71]), and which may evoke 'a rite taking place behind a curtain',[72] but which stands by and for itself—or rather, itselves, since its dual character absorbs any external reference into a force field between the two panels, which are to stand separately in a programme, like two matching doors. Matching but not equal. *Funérailles II* surely has to be played second, since not only does it heighten the experience by dearth, but it ends with a desperate, conclusive gesture as some of the string players take up percussion instruments.

Ferneyhough's next two works, the Second String Quartet (1980) and the quasi-sonata for piano *Lemma–Icon–Epigram* (1981), exude a supreme confidence, not least in removing themselves from the blasted, withered soundscapes of *Unity Capsule* and the *Time and Motion* series (busy deserts though those are) and from the associated notational complexity. This may have been a fruit of the composer's success. It may have come, as he has suggested, from the discovery that closings of the memory horizon could be engineered more subtly. It may have been stimulated by work on his only piece for full orchestra, *La terre est un homme* (1976–9), whose complement of a hundred and one players effectively precluded—for reasons of time in the composition if not practicality in the performance—the wealth of detail found in the immediately preceding compositions. The Second Quartet is a quartet on silence: not only the gaps that break up events and processes in the early part of the single movement, but perhaps also the silencing of differentiation that takes over as whistling high glissandos—magical sounds that had appeared in the Sonatas—come to dominate. The piece also enacts, as it grows from an opening violin cadenza, the move in Ferneyhough's output from the essentially solo music of the 1970s to the solo-plus-ensemble music of the 1980s and 1990s.

The Second Quartet marks a new clarity of utterance, with respect to how easily the memory horizon can be pushed back so that ten minutes can be perceived as a logical span. It may be significant that the composer, not prone to explications of technique, published an analysis of this piece,[73] for in a sense the music here is what can be analysed, whereas in *Unity Capsule* the music is what cannot be. Going into more detail than the composer, Richard Toop's analysis of *Lemma–Icon–Epigram*[74]—an analysis that belongs with Ligeti's of *Structures Ia* as a

[70] A valuable essay by James Erber accompanies the recording on Decca HEAD 18.
[71] Interview with Richard Toop included in the publisher's brochure for the *Carceri d'invenzione* cycle (London: Peters, 1993), 11.
[72] Note with Erato 88261.   [73] 'Deuxième quatuor à cordes', *Contrechamps*, 8 (1988), 149–62.
[74] 'Brian Ferneyhough's *Lemma–Icon–Epigram*', *Perspectives of New Music*, 28/2 (1990), 52–100.

modern classic of the genre (or classic of the modern genre)—indicates how the logic may be laid bare in terms of transformations (of note sets, durations, durational successions, time signatures, dynamics—all the usual quantities of 1950s serialism) that are individually quite simple but complex in their interworkings.

These two works, the quartet and the piano piece, fit appropriately into repertories not short on masterpieces, whereas their predecessors are more difficult to programme: it is hard to imagine, for example, a cello recital that could accommodate—withstand—*Time and Motion Study II*. Such considerations may have led Ferneyhough to the idea, adumbrated by *Funérailles*, of creating a whole concert of his own, the *Carceri d'invenzione* cycle (1981–6), named after Piranesi's engravings of 'imaginary dungeons'—or 'dungeons of imagination', to posit a pregnant secondary interpretation. What Ferneyhough admired in these architectural capriccios was a content 'hyper-loaded with expression, with explosive and implosive energy', generated by 'the tremendous multiplication of sometimes quite contrary perspectival lines'.[75] His assumption here that 'expression' has to do not with paralleling or eliciting emotions but with 'energy' is significant for his whole output: his writings and interviews are full of metaphors of force and tension, as in his suggestion that the first idea for a piece might come in the form of 'baroque constructions of levers and pivots which shift the coagulum of time to one side or the other'.[76] (On this idea of music as energy moving time, he has suggested that the finale of the *Carceri* series conveys 'situations in which alterations in the flow of time through and around objects or states become sensually (consciously) palpable'.[77]) Piranesi's designs may have looked to him like such musical embryos: 'baroque constructions' of stairways, vaults, towers, bridges.

The Piranesian heptalogy consists of the following works: *Superscriptio* for piccolo,[78] *Carceri d'invenzione I* for sixteen players, *Intermedio alla ciaccona* for violin, *Carceri d'invenzione II* for flute and twenty players, *Etudes transcendentales/Intermedio II* for soprano, flute, oboe, cello, and harpsichord, *Carceri d'invenzione III* for fifteen wind and three percussion, and *Mnemosyne* for bass flute and tape. It is a sequence that can, characteristically, be understood in several ways. There is an alternation of orchestras, in the three *Carceri d'invenzione*, with smaller formations. There is a flautist's descent, from thrilled solo initiation on the piccolo, through quasi-concerto (in *Carceri II*) and semi-concealment in a chamber group (playing flute, piccolo and alto flute in the *Etudes transcendentales*), to solo memorializing, when this player is the last on the field of action—a field whose final emptiness is accentuated by the fact that it echoes with recordings only of the player's own voice. There is a symmetry around the flute concerto. But there is also

[75] Toop interview, 6; see also Richard Toop, ' "Prima le parole . . ." (on the sketches for Ferneyhough's *Carceri d'invenzione I–III)*', *Perspectives of New Music*, 32/1 (1994), 154–75. For a painting of his own, similarly replete with contrary geometries, see the cover of Etcetera KTC 1070.

[76] Albèra interview, 34.

[77] 'The Tactility of Time', *Perspectives of New Music*, 31/1 (1993), 20–30.

[78] For an analysis see Richard Toop, '*Superscriptio* por flûte piccolo solo', *Entretemps*, 3 (1987), 95–106.

a stronger symmetry around the *Etudes transcendentales*, which are much longer than any of the other works, occupying almost a third of the total ninety-minute length.

These *Etudes* claim a high position not just in contemporary music but among the classics of the twentieth century, coming subsequent to *Pierrot lunaire* and *Le marteau sans maître*. Like the Schoenberg work, they set poems in German, by Ernst Meister and Alrun Moll; Ferneyhough has also drawn attention to the connection in saying that he was tired of 'the rather white sound' of the *Pierrot* ensemble (though later, in *On Stellar Magnitudes*, he was to write precisely for that ensemble) and wanted 'a hard-edged metallic quality'.[79] The relationship with Boulez's piece is more implicit, though marked by there being similarly nine movements in three interlocking cycles. Also, just as Boulez paid homage to Schoenberg in including a piece for voice and flute, so Ferneyhough does the same to place his work further along the line.

Another connection with Schoenberg and Boulez is in the reformulation of the ensemble from movement to movement—a reformulation to which Ferneyhough adds a redefinition of character. For example, the pianissimo adagissimo of the fifth number, shot through with regular rhythms, moves dramatically, through a sustained note on the cello, into the most song-like movement. Around this lyrical centre are pieces in which the vocal line is splintered or drawn into elaborate melismas, and the symmetry is enhanced by the location of movements in which the silence of the woodwind brings the harpsichord into relief: the third, in which the addition of pizzicato cello heightens the guitar-like nature of the harpsichord's broken chords and tremolos, and the eighth, for voice and harpsichord alone.

But the work's stature depends not on its catalogue of generalities but rather on its high density of significant incident. Beginnings and ends of movements are often brilliant: the cello cadenza at the end of the second song, the alarm call for piccolo, oboe, and cello in unison at the start of the last, the already mentioned link between the fifth and the sixth, and, most startling of all, the guttering close of the final song, as tiny instrumental fragments trail off into—or protest against—silence. What Ferneyhough might want to call 'energy' so often communicates itself as drama, or, one might simply say, as beauty: the supple vocalise on vowel sounds in the last movement, following a passage in which the singer has only been able to enunciate consonants. Also, though so much that happens must remain as wonderful bewilderment, threads of explicability are constantly pushing through to the surface, as in the passage from the second song shown in Example 73, where the oboe takes over the soprano's G, pushes it up a quarter-tone, and then, after another thought, pushes it on up another quarter-tone. Part of the point, not just in this piece, seems to be to have us oscillating between interpreting quarter-tones in this way as inflections (hence the importance of the glissando in Ferneyhough) and understanding them as distinct entities. On the larger scale, we may wonder how

---

[79] Toop interview, 7.

Ex. 73. Ferneyhough, *Etudes transcendentales* (1982–5): II

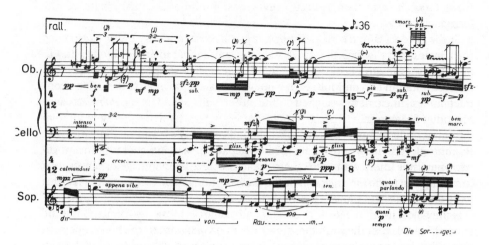

much the separate songs—and the separate pieces of the whole *Carceri* cycle—are inflections of one another, how much they are discrete.

Example 73 provides a simple instance of a gesture—the transferred and interrupted upward slide—existing not alone, as in the solo pieces of the 1970s, but within a context, whether in opposition to it, nascent from it, or declining into it. This shift may have to do with an alteration in how the composer has been able to view himself: not as a voice crying in the wilderness, but as an active, engaged participant in the musical world. On a less metaphorical plane, it is through embedded gesture that, for Ferneyhough, the work speaks, and declares its difference from the un-gesturing crystallinity that is the potential peril of an organization as ramified as his: 'Music is not dead material, nor yet abstract form. Still less is it meaningless maneuvering in an uncaring, arbitrary void. The idea of the figure seen as a constructive and purposive reformulation of the gesture should clear the path for aura, the visionary ideal of a work entering into conversation with the listener *as if it were another aware subject*'[80] (italicized in the original). Especially in a period of so much musical dumbness, Ferneyhough's works may indeed appear, in their rich networking, to have taken on life and consciousness. They have the recognizable familiarity and the unfathomable strangeness of other people. And his search for gestures and contexts for gestures may have something to do with the preponderance of the solo–ensemble contrast, within the *Carceri* cycle and in the works that followed: the Third Quartet (1987), which, like the Second, has solo incursions; the Fourth Quartet (1989–90), in which a soprano joins the ensemble;[81] and a sequence of chamber concertos that began with *La chûte d'Icare* (1988) and *Terrain* (1992).

[80] 'Il tempo della figura', *Perspectives of New Music*, 31/1 (1993), 10–19.

[81] When he was asked in an interview 'What music would you go out of your way to hear?', Schoenberg's Second Quartet was the only single work he mentioned; see Paul Griffiths, *New Sounds, New Personalities* (London, 1985), 81.

The notation in Example 73, typical of later Ferneyhough, is less fraught than in *Unity Capsule*, even though the composer compounds temporal complexity by introducing novel time signatures (2/10 earlier in this movement), which—along with the speeds, the irrational rhythms, and the quarter-tones—ensure that the work lives up to the difficulty of its Lisztian eponym. Difficulty is intrinsic to the music: Ferneyhough is writing under extreme conditions (the advanced development of notation and performance in western culture, the neglect of that development in so much new western music), and his music necessarily reflects and embodies the extremity. Also, as with Liszt, the strenuous may be seen as a route to the transcendent. For that is the music's ambition. Its concern with edges—not only the edges between movements but perhaps also the edge of the high treble, the edge between sound and word, the edge of achieveable speed—has to do with achieving that '*salto mortale*... over the end... of a composition, in such a way as to be able actually to modify, to change, to show in a different light the world outside the object itself'.[82] The work's fragmenting end may be in image of this leap by which it would enter the world, would attain 'a certain permanence'[83]—the permanence that led to the choice of poems having to do with death and survival.

Immortality is an option only for those who believe that something new and permanently valid can, still, be added to the world, beyond the round of commentaries destined to be covered by accretions of other commentaries. However that may be, Ferneyhough's confidence in at least the possibility of immortality is what makes him such a rare and vital figure in his time.

Morton Feldman

Like Scelsi and Nono, Feldman began to loom much larger in the musical world a few years before his death—and for similar reasons. His lack of an ideology had relegated him to the second rank in the ideological 1950s, when even Cage had had an ideology: the ideology of having no ideology. Also, as a big man, and a man of humour, he perhaps fitted too well the role of comfortable clown. But in the 1970s, when trust in ideologies faltered, here was a waiting hero: a composer who had been quietly making music by—as it seemed and seems—unaided intuition. According to a story of his own: 'My past experience was not to "meddle" with the material, but use my concentration as a guide to what might transpire. I mentioned this to Stockhausen once when he had asked me what my *secret* was. "I don't push the sounds around." Stockhausen mulled this over, and asked: "Not even a little bit?" '[84]

Using 'my concentration as a guide', Feldman had quickly gone on from the graph scoring of his *Projection* series, for the reason that he was interested in

[82] Toop interview, 6. [83] Ibid. 8.

[84] 'Crippled Symmetry', *RES: Anthropology and Aesthetics*, 2 (Cambridge, MA, 1981); reprinted with Hat Art 60801/2.

freeing sounds, not performers. (He did, however, return to graph scoring for works on a larger scale: *Out of "Last Pieces"*, *Atlantis*, and *In Search of an Orchestration*.) Before they could be freed, sounds first had to be identified—and he excelled in identifying harmonies that would, under the pianissimo lentissimo conditions of his music, sound delicate and detached. So he had begun to notate pitches, but to leave them just as note-heads, with no rhythmic indication, as Cage did in the *Music for Piano* series. Different players, or groups of players, would then proceed through their parts independently: this was the case in, for example, the *Durations* series for various ensembles (1960–1) or *Between Categories* for two quartets, each of tubular bells, piano, violin, and cello (1969). Such a rhythmic loosening would not have been possible in music for several performers without the assumption, always present in Feldman, that the music must be slow, so that there is never any question of linking a sound to what had gone before. Each must exist for itself, and in order to accommodate so many diverse existences, none must dominate: hence the second requirement almost constant in Feldman's music, that it be quiet. In the composer's words: 'the music seems to float, doesn't seem to go in any direction, one doesn't know how it's made, there doesn't seem to be any type of dialectic, going alongside it, explaining it. They [the audience] are not told how to listen, that is the problem. Most music listens for the public.'[85]

By the end of the 1960s Feldman had restored conventional rhythmic notation, and in the series *The Viola in my Life* (1970–1)—especially in the viola concerto that is its fourth and last member—had come near restoring a conventional progressiveness, at least on the scale of melodic gesture: *Rothko Chapel* for chorus with solo singers and instruments (1971) includes a melody he had written more than twenty years earlier. But this was a passing phase, and most of his subsequent works, though fully notated, maintain the instant-by-instant unfolding—as well as the quietness and the slowness—that had defined his world since the early 1950s. Asked by Heinz-Klaus Metzger if his gentle music was in mourning for the victims of the Holocaust, he came close to agreeing, but wanted to widen the question to include 'say, for example, the death of art'. 'I do in a sense mourn something that has to do with, say Schubert leaving me. Also I really don't feel that it's all necessary any more. And so what I tried to bring into my music are just very few essential things that I need. So I at least keep it going for a little while more.'[86]

If this suggests threads of music squeezed out against finality, the image is borne out by his output up to this point, since, though numerous, his works had tended to be brief and for small ensembles: many are for piano (or multiple pianos), whose sound—chordal, resonant, reducible to an extreme pianissimo without danger of breaking or fraying—particularly suited his purposes; others are for choice instrumental groupings; very few involve voices, and those few are mostly wordless. But in the early 1970s the pattern began to change, in dimensions of both size and

[85] Conversation with Heinz-Klaus Metzger and Earle Brown. A recording and a transcription are supplied with EMI C165 28954/7.

[86] EMI C165 28954/7.

scoring. There were suddenly more orchestral works, characteristically titled either with their scoring (*Cello and Orchestra, Piano and Orchestra, Oboe and Orchestra,* even just *Orchestra*) or with some pregnant semi-abstract phrase (*Elemental Procedures*). Partly this was a matter of opportunity. In 1971–2 Feldman had been resident in Berlin, and from that time onwards he was frequently commissioned by European orchestras and radio authorities.

But the other growth in his music—the growth in length—cannot be explained by market forces. At the end of the 1970s his works became immense: *Violin and Orchestra* (1979) plays for over an hour, *String Quartet* (also 1979) for over an hour and a half, *String Quartet II* (1983) for up to five and a half hours. The possibility of great length may have been opened by his soprano monodrama *Neither* (1977), to a text written for him by Samuel Beckett;[87] but a seventy-minute stage piece is not unusual, whereas a string quartet that goes on for hours without pause quite definitely is. So is the other monster in his output, the four-hour *For Philip Guston* (1984), which was one of several pieces he wrote at that time for a touring group that included the flautist Eberhard Blum, the percussionist Jan Williams, and the pianists Yvar Mikhashoff and Nils Vigeland. (Works of this period, demanding dedication, were often written for particular musicians, who included also the pianists Bunita Marcus, Aki Takahashi, and Roger Woodward, the singer Joan LaBarbara, and the violinist Paul Zukofsky.) 'My whole generation', he said, 'was hung up on the 20 to 25 minute piece. It was our clock. We all got to know it, and how to handle it. As soon as you leave the 20–25 minute piece behind, in a one-movement work, different problems arise. Up to one hour you think about form, but after an hour and a half it's scale. Form is easy—just the division of things into parts. But scale is another matter.'[88]

Feldman spoke of 'the contradiction in not having the sum of the parts equal the whole': 'The scale of what is actually being represented . . . is a phenomenon unto itself.'[89] At the beginning of his career he had, even more than Cage, been influenced by the New York painters of his generation and the one before,[90] and in his late works he may have wanted to achieve—as he did achieve—the kind of presence a large Rothko has by virtue of its scale: the grandeur and the strangeness that come simply from there being so much of it. (Yet, whether in Rothko or in Feldman, these gifts are not unearned: what they demand from their recipient is acceptance, not striving.) Another influence on Feldman's late music—or 'permission' for it, to use his own word—came from Islamic rugs, which he collected. On his floor there was, for instance, an Anatolian chequerboard piece 'with no systematic color design except for a free use of the rug's colors reiterating its simple pattern'.[91] Symmetry on one level, of geometry, is combined with asymmetry on another, of coloration—

[87] Beckett's sixteen-line 'libretto'—the only text he wrote for music—appears not to have been included in any collection of his writings. It is reproduced, in the original, with an extract from the score in Gottfried Meyer-Thoss, 'Facetten des Transluziden', *Musik-Konzepte*, 48–9 (1986), 122–34.

[88] Universal Edition brochure (1994).   [89] 'Crippled Symmetry'.

[90] In 'Crippled Symmetry', for example, he refers to Rauschenberg, Pollock, and Rothko.

[91] Ibid.

an asymmetry subtly complicated by the fact that the colours of rural rugs are uneven, because yarn was dyed in small quantities. According to his own account, it was out of such observations, rather than by glancing aside at the minimalism of younger New York contemporaries, that he began to work with repetitive pattern at the time his music grew.

And certainly the works of his last eight or nine years (works which must, in terms of duration, account for fully half his output) have little beyond repetition in common with those of Reich and Glass. Pulse, where it exists, is slow, and the music remains quiet. Most decisively, there is no process, but still a drifting. Tonal features return: they can hardly be avoided when there is so much repetition, and in some pieces—such as *Triadic Memories* for solo piano (1981), which can play for up to an hour and a half—Feldman made a feature of them. But the motive implications of common chords are resisted. 'Chords are heard repeated without any discernible pattern. In this regularity (though there are slight gradations of tempo) there is a *suggestion* that what we hear is functional and directional, but we soon realize that this is an illusion.'[92]

Feldman's repetitions also differ from most in his creation of a symmetry 'crippled' by asymmetry, whether from 'slight gradations of tempo', from changes of orchestral colour (in *The Turfan Fragments*) or from rhythmic notations which look exact but will inevitably be performed a touch inexactly. For instance, at the start of *Three Voices* (1982), shown in Example 74, the co-ordination of the top part with the other two is unlikely to be precise, and the imprecision—suggesting life, suggesting failing—seems to be wanted. Composing the piece shortly after the death of his closest painter friend, Philip Guston, Feldman had in mind a singer with two loudspeakers behind her. 'There is something kind of tombstoney about the look of loudspeakers. I thought of the piece as an exchange of the live voice with the dead ones—a mixture of the living and the dead.'[93] The dead would have to include the metrical regularity and the harmonic directedness that the music can no longer operate—'something . . . to do with . . . Schubert leaving me.'

Ex. 74. Feldman, *Three Voices* (1982)

---

[92] In 'Crippled Symmetry', for example, he refers to Rauschenberg, Pollock, and Rothko.
[93] Quoted in note with New Albion 018.

Franco Donatoni

Franco Donatoni (b. 1927), of the generation of Stockhausen, Boulez, Nono, and Berio, seemed destined to be one who came afterwards. He met Maderna in 1953, went to Darmstadt the next year, and abruptly turned from Italian neoclassicism to international modernism: 'Till I was thirty, I copied Bartók. After I met Maderna, I copied Boulez.'[94] 'Then', to continue this compact autobiography, 'I got interested in John Cage, had my negative period and so on.' This 'negative period', roughly coextensive with the 1960s, led him not only into indeterminacy but also into automatic procedures and the use of found material, as in *Etwas ruhiger im Ausdruck* (1967), which is scored for the quintet of *Pierrot lunaire*—a repeated fascination in Donatoni's instrumentation—but takes its material from another Schoenberg source: the eighth bar of the second of the Op. 23 Piano Pieces. 'There is something elusive in those few notes, something which evades what *must* happen and invites one to think about what *can* happen.'[95] Out of the invitation comes a chain of soft possibilities, leading up to Schoenberg's at the end.

It seems that then, gradually during the 1970s, Donatoni changed not his methods but their implication. Quotation and mechanism, instead of being grim compulsions, became occasions for playfulness and brilliance; the ending of music—which was noticed most particularly by Italian critics and composers during this period—became cause for carnival. Since 1977 Donatoni has regularly produced several new pieces each year, most of them for small ensembles or solo instruments—media which answer his demands for clarity and for the projection of notes and motifs through canons and other strictly organized trajectories.

Ex. 75. Donatoni, *Still* (1985)

Example 75 shows a passage from *Still* for 'soprano leggero' with pairs of flutes, violins and keyboards (1985), which looks to the little trio for the Three Boys in *The Magic Flute* for its text ('schweige still') and perhaps also for its musical elements:

[94] Interview with Denise Faquelle, published with Adda 581 143.
[95] Quoted in note with Etcetera KTC 1053.

turn figures and single notes, chromatic neighbours and bright, high orchestration. Donatoni works these into a characteristic skein of miniature musical machines, where individual moments are highly determined but in their succession seem improvised. This is true even of the detail. For example, in the five-part canon— whose entries, as indicated, come at intervals of three demisemiquavers—the line flips unpreparedly from one diminished seventh (G♯–B–D) to another (C–E♭–F♯–A), and the soprano jostles her three-note path to the inevitable B♭. Typical also is the slightly wonky effect of patterns that do not quite fit together: the canon establishes a dotted-semiquaver pulse by its entries and its marcatos, and the soprano falls in with this, if irregularly (at least her motifs always begin and end on a pulse); but the piano tries to set up a quaver unit. In combining rigidity with whimsy, and in prac- tising superb technical sophistication on cheerfully rudimentary ideas, Donatoni's post-1977 music suggests Nancarrow come alive on instruments.

Dissemination

As in the supply, so in the public spread of contemporary music, the present age is one of marked expansion. There are many more performers actively engaged in new music than was the case in the 1950s and 1960s, and the volume of commercial recordings has vastly increased, especially in the period since the arrival of the com- pact disc. Along with the change of quantity has come, inevitably, a change of nature. The old means of communication—public radio stations, festivals (such as the long-established Donaueschingen, and newer annual occasions in Huddersfield, in Strasbourg, and, during the 1980s, at the Almeida Theatre in London), mixed ensembles (the London Sinfonietta, the Ensemble Inter- Contemporain, the Ensemble Modern, etc.)—have continued, but now that so much new music is available on record, broadcasting and live performance have lessened in importance. Of course, new music goes on being commissioned by reg- ular orchestras, but, under the universal licence of postmodernism, such music has often tended to be restorative, so that the gap between the adventurous composer and the 'traditional public' (if such exists) has been left wide. Boulez's attempts to bridge that gap, during the late 1960s and early 1970s, when he was most active as a conductor, have had little follow-up—not, perhaps, because the task is impossi- ble, but rather because it implies a unitary musical culture in which nobody any longer believes.

The disintegration of music is manifest, of course, not only in the split between old and new, but in the diversity within the new. One effect of this is that perform- ers have had to become specialists, and thereby to define their own repertories. For example, of the two string quartets which became suddenly prominent in the early 1980s, the Arditti built their reputation in complex music, albeit of diverse kinds (Carter, Xenakis, Henze, Ferneyhough), while the Kronos preferred composers closer to repetition and folk music (Reich, Volans, Riley, Sculthorpe). Each could find an ancestor in Bartók, but among living composers, Nancarrow and Gubaydulina are among the few to have figured on the programmes of both. The new-music quartet is in itself a striking phenomenon of the post-1980 period, and perhaps marks not only a recovery of traditional genres and an enhancement of the interpreter's prestige, but also an emulation, willed or unwilled, of how popular music is presented and performed. Like a rock group, the Kronos Quartet tend to play what they have recently recorded; and like a rock group's, their records are often coherent anthologies, titled as such, and featuring their name more conspicuously than those of the composers concerned.

The belated appearance of a record-led market in new music seems to have had two major consequences. In the first place, it has facilitated and served the fracture of contemporary music: such an increase in the output of compositions and recordings is inevitably accompanied too by a division of the audience, and there are now numerous labels catering for particular constituencies. On the other hand, the market economy has intensified commercial exploitation of performers and composers whose spectacular success has its measure in record sales rather than in any of the less definable criteria of musical prowess. Certain composers—Adams, Glass, Pärt, Tavener—not only outsell their colleagues of longer reputations but can also outsell any single new Mozart release, and the occasional piece—Górecki's Third Symphony[96] in Great Britain in 1993—may even enter the popular hit parade. Previously, classical music was music which did not sell, and contemporary classical music was music which emphatically did not sell. Change here is one symptom of the loosening of boundaries between categories and audiences, the new dispensation under which there is no stable body of classics but rather, for each of us, a continuously evolved body of music that is important.

The new role (not rule) of the market need not be alarming. Record companies prove wonderfully unable to guess where the next runaway success will come from: often it has originated with a small outfit, and then the multinationals have fallen in behind to imitate or buy up. Also, the example of popular music, where the history of commercial exploitation is longer and the potential gains are much greater, suggests that homogenization, however good for business, cannot be sustained and will never overwhelm the repertory. There may always be those whose records sell in huge numbers: Madonna and Pärt, to take an unlikely couple from the 1980s. But—ignorant, as we all are, of the mechanisms of musical appeal, and run, after all, by people who are human beings and not only agents of the profit motive—the record industry will have to continue to support an unprecedented abundance and variety.

[96] See Wilfrid Mellers, 'Round and about Górecki's Symphony No. 3', *Tempo*, 168 (1989), 22–4, and in the same issue, 25–9, Tadeusz Marek and David Drew, 'Górecki in Interview (1968)—and 20 years after'.

Computers

The establishment of IRCAM in the late 1970s coincided with the peak of a period of creativity in computer sound synthesis and transformation, and on the crest of that wave, many of the leading practitioners, whether technician–composers or composer–technicians, went to Paris. Chowning was there. So was his fellow American David Wessel (b. 1942), whose *Antony* (1977) was one of the first and finest pieces to use the machinery developed at IRCAM by Giuseppe di Giugno (the 4A, predecessor of the 4X that was crucial to much of the institute's production in the 1980s, including Boulez's *Répons*). *Antony* neatly avoids the problem of the artificial quality of synthesized sound by avoiding entries and exits (very slow fades are the rule) and by concerning itself with great clusters, out of which distinct pitches gradually coalesce and disappear.

Among the European composers at IRCAM in the early days were Berio and Globokar, and with such a range of talent it well might have seemed that anything could happen: Boulez's call to arms has already been noted. But in the event, as was perhaps inevitable, many of the more celebrated personnel departed, and IRCAM became another electronic music studio, if one that was unusually well financed, and unusually able, therefore, both to embark on grand projects and to present itself to the public: a concert hall was built into the place; not only did it have its own orchestra, in the Ensemble InterContemporain, but it had too an impresario (Nicholas Snowman, who had managed the London Sinfonietta); and new works were taken on tour in France, across western Europe and to the United States. At least during the 1980s, IRCAM dominated computer music in Europe—but not entirely: at City University in London, for example, Alejandro Viñao (b. 1951) and others did important work; Viñao's *Son entero* for four voices and computer (1988) powerfully creates an electronic folk orchestra evocative of his native Cuba.

Partly because of IRCAM's public—even state—role, partly because it was set up as a rendezvous for experts in both conventional instruments and electronics, and partly because this was the way electronic music was going anyway, Boulez's institute quite quickly came to specialize not in small studies, such as had been characteristic of computer music, but in big concert pieces, usually with an instrumental soloist or ensemble and the 4X: examples include Boulez's *Répons* (first performed in 1980) and Berio's *Chemins V* for clarinet and electronics (also performed in 1980, but soon withdrawn; the version without electronics remained as *Sequenza IX*). Concern with instrumental sound, and with how it could be changed, naturally involved a study of timbre, which remained central to the IRCAM philosophy and practice. Younger composers who came to the studio in some numbers—among them Kajia Saariaho (b. 1952), Gérard Grisey (b. 1946), George Benjamin, and Jonathan Harvey (b. 1939)—were all influenced by this, and the influence stayed with them, to go into works made solely for instruments.[97] IRCAM thereby stimu-

[97] Three articles concerning Harvey's music are included in *Contemporary Music Review*, 1/1 (1984), an issue devoted to 'Musical Thought at IRCAM'. Saariaho's early pieces are considered, and copiously

lated some of the most intensive efforts at reimagining orchestral sound in the 1980s and 1990s; it also contributed to one of the great works of the period, since the electronic inserts for Birtwistle's *The Mask of Orpheus* were made there by the composer in collaboration with Barry Anderson.

Since the mid-1980s the growing availability of powerful computers and creative software has diminished the importance of IRCAM, or indeed of any institution; this is just one effect of the general centrifugal force in new music. As electronic equipment becomes normal and sophisticated, so the existence of electronic music as a category seems to be disappearing: the Kronos Quartet, for example, regularly play with amplification, and electronics have long been permanently on Stockhausen's agenda, even in works where electronic processing is not featured. In *Répons*—and in its successor piece . . . *explosante-fixe* . . . , for transformed flute with the same orchestra—the difference between the electronic and the natural is part of the point. This may soon seem a period feature.

Benjamin's IRCAM piece *Antara* for two electronic keyboards and ensemble (1987) suggests how, on the contrary, there need be no difference of creative approach or compositional effect between the synthesizer and the flute, which are, after all, simply machines of different ages. The work uses its electronic machines in order to—among other things—project into the concert hall a set of panpipes, while also stabilizing their sound and increasing their range. Panpipe sounds, digitally recorded and stored with their microtonal inflections, are sampled by a keyboard, which seems in the early part of the piece to be teaching new tunes, and new intonations, to the flutes and strings (see Example 76): as in contemporary Ligeti, the music uses the interplay between different tuning systems, while the engagement of human sound and human touch avoids the endemic problems in recorded computer music of a mechanization of timbre and rhythm. (Of course, finger rhythm is different from breath rhythm, and the music takes note of that. If breath

Ex. 76. Benjamin, *Antara* (1987)

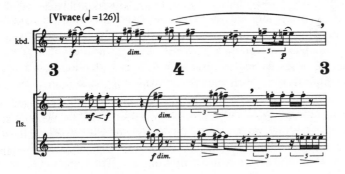

illustrated, in her 'Timbre and Harmony: Interpolations of Timbral Structures', *Contemporary Music Review*, 2/1 (1987), 93–133.

rhythm were wanted, it would be perfectly possibly to use a synthesizer controlled by a blown device.)

In a better world, *Antara* might be the overture to a new future for the orchestra, as an assembly of normal instruments, of normal instruments transformed—a technique adumbrated by Stockhausen in *Mixtur* and notably refined by Boulez, as well as by Saariaho in her *Lichtbogen* for nonet (1985–6) and *Io* for chamber orchestra (1986–7)—and of electronic instruments, producing together all kinds of new possibilities of harmony, timbre, and rhythm. But there are perhaps other constraints that will force orchestras into more conservative patterns. Meanwhile the evolution of computer music in and for itself, as a purely electronic art, is likely to be happening less in great institutions than in living rooms, and to be contributing to a rebirth of domestic music as a creative art, with many millions of composers pursuing their own fantasies, and communicating with others through computer networks.

Complexities

There are many complexities: complexities of density, whether the sounds be simultaneous or successive; complexities of event, concerning single sounds whose components are numerous and changing; complexities of relationship, which the composition may set up among its sounds; complexities of reference, to other compositions, other traditions, other histories; complexities of interpretation, which relatively elementary music may elicit, whether at the time of hearing or after; complexities of expression, in areas that are untoward or ambiguous; complexities of complexities. All have given rise to controversy, but at this point in musical history, the arguments seem like swordfights in the dark. No Birtwistle is likely to be persuaded to become a Pärt, no Pärt a Birtwistle, and their respective admirers are unlikely to change sides—certainly not at a time when the grounds of musical discrimination appear to have reduced themselves to matters of taste. The quietening of the intellectual disputes that raged between Cage and Boulez, or around the permissibility of Ligeti, is one of the dubious privileges of the postmodern age.

Besides, complexity on one level may well be simplicity on another. The intention of complex music seems clear: to absorb the listener's attention wholly for the duration. But simple music, which leaves space within that attention, thereby complicates communication: what are we meant to be doing while an A minor chord is being slowly arpeggiated? Birtwistle's music, like Beethoven's, has those elements of clarity, surprise, awkwardness, and incomprehensibility by which we recognize the mouthing of another human being. With it we may feel ourselves to be in a familiar situation, and therefore in a simple one. But Pärt's does not sound like anyone we are likely to meet. There is a great deal that something—what?—has forbidden it to say. Much that we know to be possible has been revoked, which places it in a very different category from music which may sound in some ways similar, but which was created with all the knowledge and experience available to its com-posers: plainsong, for example, or Notre Dame organum, or Vivaldi. Pärt's music, however simple in substance, is complex in that it stands before us inexplicably tongue-tied. We may feel that we have nothing to say in return.

Apologies for a complexity which resides in the substance of the music, rather than beyond and around it, have tended to rest on two grounds. According to the argument from history, the development of music is a development towards increasing refinement, density, and multiplicity—and there is some quasi-experi-mental support for that in the development of minimalism since 1964. According to the argument from life, we exist in complex worlds—we move at speeds, cope with abstractions, and deal with information flows to which the human animal has had only half a heartbeat of evolutionary time to adjust—and our music will reflect that if it is to seem real. But the historical justification can be turned around, since there have also been periods of sudden simplification: the arrival of diatonic perspective in the fifteenth century, or that of monody at the beginning of the seventeenth. In any event, the history of music, at least, never repeats itself, and it is hard to find useful precedents for a period in which the works of several hundred living com-posers (as well as many more hundreds of dead ones) are available at modest cost and inconvenience to most people in the western world. As for the argument from life, part of the complexity of our existences is that they contain periods of calm as well as rush, and perhaps this is the complexity we most need to understand and value: the complexity of Pärt together with Birtwistle.

But it is significant that the arguments for complexity, from history and from life, belong to composers of an older generation: Boulez, Babbitt, Carter. Those born during or since the Second World War have come to maturity in a musical world demonstrating the need for complexity (and for its less outspoken companion: newness) by the widespread absence of it, and the use of the word as a flag dates from the 1980s, from the time when it had become clear that minimalism, on the one hand, and postmodern repro, on the other, were not going to go away, and that—as Adams's *Harmonielehre* (1985) proved—they could easily be allies. This may help explain the embattlement which composers of complexity (understood now as a brutal but useful term for a school of musical thought and practice, not as a simple noun) may regrettably evince in their statements and public personae.

Complexity seems to have its home most fully and freely in particular countries: in the United States (thanks partly to the continuing example of Babbitt, partly to the fact that many composers are academics and that complexity is intellectually respectable, and partly just to the size of the recording business, which is able to sustain music of the most diverse kinds), in Britain (thanks to the impression made not only by Ferneyhough but also by Michael Finnissy), and in Germany (thanks perhaps to the failure of the Darmstadt flame quite to extinguish itself, and to the goad of Germanic musical history). However, it is the British group, if group it be, that has been most conspicuous since the early 1980s, in terms of teaching, of influ-ence and of the dissemination of their music. Michael Finnissy (b. 1946), who, unlike Ferneyhough, has made his career in England, has taught at various institutions, and been a model for his self-certainty and lack of compromise. Chris Dench (b. 1953) has become part of the musical life of Australia, as has Richard Barrett (b. 1959) in works written for the Elision Ensemble, whose splendiferous range of colours (with a prominent tuned percussion centre, including anklung, mandolin, and guitar, as well as full stretches of winds and strings) has produced a kind of sensuous complexity that may be uniquely Australian.[98]

Finnissy's output—in what is another contrast with Ferneyhough—is enormous; it is also exceedingly diverse, and would alone demonstrate what a poor label 'complexity' is. In his numerous piano works—most of them written for himself to play, and including several concertos as well as whole books of 'transcriptions' and other solo pieces—complexity is often a fair enough statement of the pressure of events within the music, and of the pressure of histories behind it. These histories would include the history of keyboard virtuosity, and its associate histories of determined eccentricity (Grainger and Ives are among the heroes Finnissy has celebrated in piano portraits) and festooning elaboration, as shown particularly, but not only, in his 'transcriptions', of music from Verdi to Gershwin—transcriptions which go, as the inverted commas are meant to indicate, so far as often to bury the original within the turmoil of following through what had been implicit or undecided or under-achieved. But not all Finnissy's music is like this. His String Trio (1986) is remarkable for its sustained stillness, its seeming hold of a waiting frenzy in tense check. And he has been able to travel in his music to even more offbeat destinations: to the setting of Japanese, to symphonic poetry in *Red Earth* (1988), to reconnoitres with Obrecht motets, and to Zola melodrama in his opera *Thérèse Raquin* (1992–3), where the enclosure of the family tragedy is equalled in the parlour setting for voices and piano, and where violent events are related, perhaps as in the String Trio, with a fastidious dispassion that is violent in itself. The opera is also an example of Finnissy's concern with folk music, which can—as most things can in his output—take different forms. The cycle of *English Country-Tunes* for piano (1977) wields immense power against a Merrie England interpretation of past reality, while in *Thérèse Raquin* the politer reference to French folksong is important in the portrayal of the weak husband's submissiveness.

The music of James Dillon (b. 1950) is also a lesson in the varieties of complexity, and in the fact that what may be most complex of all is the composer's inability or unwillingness to submit to—or his success in escaping from—the measures by which we would recognize style. We may be moving, with Dillon as with Ferneyhough, from a kind of first-order complexity, where the music just is complex (as it is, for example, in Dillon's First Quartet, of 1983), to a second-order complexity, where astonishment is as much at the composer's variety as at any

---

[98] The three composers mentioned in the latter part of this paragraph are, together with James Dillon, the subject of Richard Toop's 'Four Facets of "The New Complexity" ', *Contact*, 32 (1988), 4–50. For a response to this important article see Arnold Whittall, 'Complexity, Capitulationism and the Language of Criticism', *Contact*, 33 (1988), 20–3.

particular instance of that variety. Dillon's orchestra piece *helle Nacht* (1986–7) had suggested a mitigation of complexity by a kind of rude energy having parallels in Xenakis and as far back as *The Rite of Spring*. Yet his *Nine Rivers* cycle of pieces for various ensembles, begun in 1988, indicates that he is far from pursuing a single line of development.

There is, however, one great constant among composers of complexity, which is their focus not so much on large orchestral and electronic projects that might seem well designed to accommodate multitudinous events (though there are instances of those in Ferneyhough, Finnissy, and Dillon) but rather on solo instruments, and even on the instrument whose capacities for colour and range are most restricted: the flute, as in Dillon's *Sgothan* (1984) and the important sequence of pieces by Dench. This choice may have something to do with the beckoning example of Ferneyhough's several flute solos, and beyond them of Varèse's and Debussy's, but probably just as important is the challenge of creating complexity within limitation, and of thereby awakening prodigious energy in the acts both of composition and of performance. For complexity is by nature a virtuoso art, and finds its proper ensigns in virtuoso performers. Babbitt may, in the 1960s, have gone to the electronic studio in despair of hearing his music correctly played in the concert hall, but he soon came out again, and began writing pieces for virtuosos: for string quartets, for other chamber groups, and for the pianists Robert Taub and Alan Feinberg. In the same way, part of the thrill of the new complexity of the 1980s and 1990s is the thrill it has engendered in performers.

John Cage

There is no more powerful demonstration of the inexorability of progress in the 1950s and 1960s than its effect on an artist devoted to non-intention. Cage had accepted that new music demanded new ideas, and in the *Concert for Piano and Orchestra* he had spent them prodigally. His relatively few pieces after that had, almost every time, introduced new procedures, new means, new notations. Then in 1969 came a return: *Cheap Imitation*—originally a piano work, later orchestrated and adapted for solo violin—was his first fully prescribed composition since the time series of the mid-1950s. (The coincidence with Stockhausen's *Mantra* is striking.) This might have been a special case: Cunningham had choreographed Satie's *Socrate*, but could not get the rights to use Cage's transcription of the score; hence this 'cheap imitation', repeating Satie's rhythmic structure but transposing each phrase by chance. However, far from being an isolated exercise in musical economy, *Cheap Imitation* turned out to be the key to the manifold production of Cage's last two decades, for it embodied a truth that became inescapable as the 1960s receded: the truth that new ideas were no longer going to be so easy to find. Cage mentioned with approval Gunther Stent's conclusion that 'everything has been thought; all the fundamental discoveries have been made', and added: 'That doesn't mean that we don't need to compose new music, but new ideas on music are no longer necessary.'[99]

His choice of the word 'necessary', rather than 'possible', suggests how for him the postmodern condition was not a cause for anxiety but another liberation. 'I have been talking about abundance. I believe that what we can reasonably expect, within this state of stasis, is the interpenetration of . . . arts and . . . sciences . . . in a climate very rich with joy and—I am purposely using an expression frequent in Japanese texts—bewilderment.'[100] In his own work, the interpenetration resulted in a flowering of writings, prints, drawings, and watercolours, all based at root on principles of chance composition he had developed in music, while the release from the necessity of new ideas enabled him to return to the musical productivity he had known in the decade before *4' 33"*. In *Song Books* (1970) he created a vocal complement to the *Concert*: a collection of ninety *Solos for Voice* that covered a great variety of notational forms, and that could be performed individually or assembled in any way for a choral performance. In keeping with his professed belief, the ideas were not new, for the *Solos* repeated compositional methods he had introduced during the previous thirty years; but undoubtedly the music was.

Now that he was composing again, new ideas inevitably came despite their unnecessariness, and by the mid-1970s he was at work in several different areas. There were pieces for natural instruments—amplified plant materials in *Child of Tree* (1975), water-filled conch shells in *Inlets* (1977)—chosen partly because their acoustic properties would be unpredictable: 'In the case of *Inlets*, you have no control whatsoever over the conch shell when it's filled with water. You tip it and you get a gurgle, sometimes; not always. So the rhythm belongs to the instruments, and not to you.'[101] There were pieces for conventional instruments requiring extraordinary virtuosity: the *Etudes australes* for piano (1974–5), the *Etudes boréales* for cello and piano played as percussion kit (1978), and the *Freeman Etudes* for violin (1977–90). For all these pieces, pitches were chance-selected with the help of star charts (hence the titles of the first two sets), and Cage used chance operations also to determine—sometimes deliberately over-determine—other aspects: 'I had become interested in writing difficult music, etudes, because of the world system which often seems to many of us hopeless. I thought that were a musician to give the example in public of doing the impossible that it would inspire someone who was struck by that performance to change the world.'[102] There were composed musicircuses (see p. 161), most notably *Roaratorio* (1979), which combined Cage's own reading of mesostics extracted from *Finnegans Wake* with tapes and performances by Irish folk musicians. There were disintegrations of existing music, created by omitting notes and extending those that remained: generally he used old American music—hymntunes in the case of *Hymns and Variations* for twelve

---

[99] *For the Birds*, 219.   [100] Ibid. 220.
[101] Cole Gagne and Tracy Caras, *Soundpieces: Interviews with American Composers* (Metuchen, Scarecrow, 1982), 77.
[102] Note with Etcetera KTC 2016.

amplified singers (1979)[103] a source to which he seems to have been drawn in making *Apartment House 1776* for the bicentennial of the United States. There were works that were musicircuses and disintegrations at the same time: the *Europeras* composed out of the traditional operatic repertory. There were one-off events, such as *Il treno* (1978), three happenings on 'prepared trains'. There were efforts at making the orchestra a model of calm anarchy: the orchestral versions of *Cheap Imitation* (1972) were to be played without a conductor; *Etcetera* (1973) offers twenty players the choice of playing as soloists, on cardboard boxes, or joining any one of three conducted ensembles; *Quartets I–VIII* (1976), another hymntune piece, puts forward a different ensemble of four musicians for each phrase; *Thirty Pieces for Five Orchestras* (1981) again features small groups, but this time overlapping, as the five orchestras proceed independently.

Thirty Pieces for Five Orchestras is, as James Pritchett has pointed out,[104] one of the first compositions to profit, by reverse interpenetration, from the work Cage had begun to produce as a printmaker in 1978. Not only did he repeat, in making scores, a method he had used in making prints—that of placing marks through chance-placed holes in cardboard templates—but there is a similar effect of fragile drifting designs, achieved partly in the music by a new technique of placing each piece only loosely within a bracket of time, giving the period during which it must begin and the period during which it must end. He repeated this idea in *Music for* (1984–8), a set of parts to be put together as required (so that, for example, a string quartet might make *Music for Four*) and in the profusion of 'number' pieces that followed, each with a title that just states the number of parts, with a superscript if that number has already been used: hence *Four* for string quartet (1988), *Four²* for SATB chorus (1990), *Four³* for one or two pianos, twelve rainsticks, violin or oscillator, and silence (1991), and so on.

Example 77, from the flute part from *Two* for flute and piano (1988), shows how the time-bracket notation works. Each note could, at the maximum, endure for a minute and a quarter, or, at the minimum, be a staccatissimo some way between thirty seconds and forty-five seconds into the bracket; each could also be silent, if the player decided to end it before it had begun. Cage's comments suggest, whatever else, an objective delicacy: he spoke of sounds being 'brushed into existence'[105] and of music now conveying 'a feeling of not knowing where you are in sound, but rather floating'.[106] Also indicative, and typical of this series, is the reduction of events to single tones. Cage had been working with reduced compasses since *Hymnkus* (1986), for instruments playing notes within the ambit of a fifth; during the whole of *Two*, which lasts for up to ten minutes, the flautist plays only ten notes at three different pitches (the third is the Ab a minor third above the F). The piano part, of course unco-ordinated, is not much more active.

[103] See William Brooks, 'John Cage and History: *Hymns and Variations*', *Perspectives of New Music*, 31/2 (1993), 74–103.

[104] *The Music of John Cage* (Cambridge, 1993), 185.   [105] Quoted ibid. 200.

[106] Quoted in Revill, *The Roaring Silence*, 278.

Ex. 77. Cage, *Two* (1988): flute part

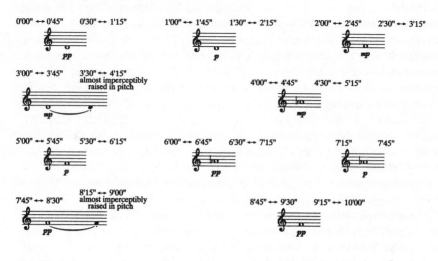

After the rush of the *Etudes* and the exuberance of *Roaratorio*, there is this predominant stillness in Cage's late music: a stillness of single sounds simply existing. So detached from flow, any sound—even a traditional chord—seems to be waiting and new.

Pierre Boulez

In the late 1970s Boulez drastically curtailed his conducting activities in order to devote himself to IRCAM and to composition, but his works have remained few, and those few all concerned with perfecting or proliferating earlier ideas. Revised versions of *Le visage nuptial, Improvisation sur Mallarmé III,* and *cummings ist der Dichter* appeared in the 1980s; most extraordinarily, a grand amplification of *Notations,* developing each of the piano miniatures into a movement for immense orchestra, was begun in 1977. Of the nominally new pieces, *Dialogue de l'ombre double* was a return to the materials and the situation of *Domaines,* but with the clarinettist now reflected in the mirror of the machinery designed at IRCAM for live manipulation of sound by computer; other works were based on the . . . *explosante-fixe* . . . skeleton, as *Rituel* had been, or on the six-note set obtained from the surname of Paul Sacher. Having used this to make a minor piece, *Messagesquisse* for cello with six cellos accompanying (1977),[107] Boulez then took it as the seed for his biggest project since *Pli selon pli—Répons* for six keyed-instrument soloists with

---

[107] For an analysis see Antoine Bonnet, '*Ecriture* and Perception: on *Messagesquisse* by Pierre Boulez', *Contemporary Music Review,* 2/1 (1987), 173–209.

electronics and chamber orchestra—and for the offshoots emerging as *Dérive* and *Dérive 2*.[108]

Répons was begun in 1980, and is itself partly a reworking of the *Eclat/multiples* idea of contrasting percussive with sustaining instruments, though with electronics coming in to collect and change sounds that otherwise could only linger and die as resonances. The complement is thus complex: a twenty-four-piece ensemble with roughly equal numbers of woodwinds, brass, and strings, six soloists placed around the audience (two pianos, harp, cimbalom, xylophone plus glockenspiel, vibraphone), and all the electronic equipment. Like most of Boulez's works apart from the piano sonatas, *Répons* is emphatically not a repertory piece. In terms of its gear, at least, it goes out on its own adventure, and its appearance, at the high noon of postmodernism, could be interpreted as a 'response' on behalf of the modernist challenge—a response that has been enthusiastically endorsed by Jean-Jacques Nattiez.[109]

Certainly Boulez has wanted to set himself at a distance from the kind of stylistic reference which, in its earlier guise as neoclassicism, he had been decrying since his student days. For example, in talking once about the rhythm of *Répons* he indicated that the two types long characteristic of his music—'chaotic and irregular' ('smooth time', as he often used to call it) and 'very regular rapid repeated notes' ('striated time')—are now joined by a third sort: 'Finally at the end there is a regularity, a kind of metre—but with much ornamentation. The ornamentation is in fact very irregular, but the metre itself is very regular.'[110] This he defended, in modernist form, as something netted into the basic substance of the piece: 'The harmony always gives this impression of something followed by its inverse; there is always a centre—an axis of symmetry. This symmetry of harmony corresponds in harmonic terms to a regular metre.' There is no question, he insisted, of stylistic pluralism. 'I accept and use the values I refused before . . . I feel now that there is no reason to exclude such things. But it is always necessary to use them according to the stylistic purpose of the piece.'

Yet such an interpretation raises problems. Modernism—and especially Boulez's modernism—had been defined not only by its explorations but by its refusals. If those refusals are reconsidered, even rescinded, the thrust away from western tradition begins to falter. Also, *Répons* is clearly the work of a composer with a history of his own. However special the work's apparatus, and however spectacularly that apparatus imposes itself (especially when, nearly seven minutes into the piece, the soloists at last enter with a grand arpeggio that is re-echoed both acoustically and electronically), there are obligations to particular ideas Boulez had already set in play (the harmonies of *Messagesquisse*, the timbral conflicts of *Eclat/multiples*). And

---

[108] See Susan Bradshaw's contribution to William Glock (ed.), *Pierre Boulez: a Symposium* (London, 1986).

[109] See the several essays on the piece collected in his *Le combat de Chronos et d'Orphée* (Paris, Bourgois, 1993), 159–217.

[110] Peter McCallum, 'An Interview with Pierre Boulez', *Musical Times*, 130 (1989), 8–10.

in relation to wider history—quite apart from the resurgence of metre—the music's mechanisms of transformation contrive an almost thematic continuity. Where in *Le marteau sans maître* the harmonies had been too fleeting and often too noise-trapped to decipher, those of *Répons* are spaciously prolonged, and melodies, as in *Messagesquisse*, are reduced to rudimentary linear statements of those harmonies. Also, the electronic manipulations (repositioning sounds in space, changing timbres, transposing figures) seem largely decorative when the live possibilities are already so various. If, as Boulez's technical assistant Andrew Gerzso has aptly put it, 'the score is full of answers to answers to answers to create a never ending mirror-like effect',[111] so too are the scores of *Eclat/multiples* and *Figures–Doubles–Prismes*. Computer machinery is not needed to produce that effect; computer machinery is needed, rather, to stake a claim for the unprecedented in a world which—inside his music as outside—was filling up with things revived.

Nothing, however, need be read into the fact that *Répons* has remained incomplete, since that is the common condition of Boulez's works. There was a first performance at the 1981 Donaueschingen Festival, when the piece played for under twenty minutes; it then grew by stages to reach three quarters of an hour by 1984.[112] Boulez suggested it ought to be twice that size, and so big enough to occupy an entire concert, but there it stopped, and his interest at IRCAM turned soon to a new version of . . . *explosante-fixe* . . . , which was unveiled in 1993 as a set of three movements: 'Transitoire VII', 'Transitoire V' and 'Originel', of which the last is an expansion of the little chamber flute concerto *Mémoriale* (1985). Except that there are three electrified flutes instead of a percussion sextet, the means are those of *Répons*, to which the work is, perhaps, a response. Computer treatment is now more integral, generating an amplified, anonymous thickness of flute sound, through and against which the other instruments play, and the ramifications of musical figures are pursued with a fantastic virtuosity that bewilders with density rather than speed and change. Whether the work will achieve its intended scale of eight movements must, in the light of Boulez's record through the four decades since *Le marteau sans maître*, be doubtful: it joined a catalogue of 'works in progress' already fat with the Third Piano Sonata, *Figures–Doubles–Prismes*, *Eclat/Multiples*, the orchestral *Notations*, and *Répons*, not to mention works unbegun, including a long-promised opera. With those works and projects, . . . *explosante-fixe* . . . may be another exemplification of the ultimate statement that there can be no ultimate statement.

Harrison Birtwistle

The process illustrated in Birtwistle's *Melencolia I*, by which a single note gradually gives rise to a whole musical world, was the process of other works of the late 1970s,

---

[111] 'Reflections on *Répons*', *Contemporary Music Review*, 1/1 (1984), 23–34.
[112] See Jameux, *Pierre Boulez*, 358.

including *Silbury Air* and . . . *agm* . . . for chorus and three instrumental groups (1978–9). . . . *agm* . . . , though based on fragmentary verbal phrases (the broken relics of Sappho's poetry) and written for fragmented ensembles, is music of unusual spaciousness and continuity in Birtwistle, and it may have been both a consummation and a dead-end. During the next year or so he produced only the Clarinet Quintet, perhaps his most inscrutable piece, and a choral item related to the Orpheus project, which had been interrupted in 1975, when it seemed the work might never be staged. But in the summer of 1981 a relatively small piece, *Pulse Sampler* for oboe and claves, opened new possibilities for him in the combination of melody and rhythm as independent but knocking entities, and soon afterwards he took up *The Mask of Orpheus* again: an examination of the work might well reveal how, as with *Siegfried*, the third act implies much more than a theatre interval separating it from the other two.

After finishing *The Mask of Orpheus*, in 1984, Birtwistle took the basic principle of *Pulse Sampler* on to a wider plane in *Secret Theatre*, which is scored for roughly the same ensemble as *Silbury Air* (the basic London Sinfonietta line-up of solo woodwind, brass, and strings, with piano and percussion), but which exists in quite its own world, partly because it starts boldly rather than with a slow birth, partly because of the intricate, constant play between an essentially melodic 'cantus' and an essentially rhythmic 'continuum' which is a clockwork of ostinatos (though in Birtwistle mechanical repetition is nearly always subject to a bit of shove, so that regularity is offset by distortions that make each new element different and interesting). Birtwistle has described the orchestral scores of his operas as being musical dramas without voices, saying of *The Mask of Orpheus* that 'the orchestra, even though it responds to the events on stage, has a life of its own',[113] and *Secret Theatre* is maybe the accompaniment to a concealed opera we do not need to see. But it also, like *Verses for Ensembles*, makes the concert platform into a stage. The 'cantus' is played by one or more soloists standing aside, the 'continuum' by the rest of the ensemble—though of course the two categories are not held separate: the 'cantus' is always in danger of devolving into faltering repetition, while the threat to the 'continuum' is that it become impressed too much by the free flow and largeness of the melody. The grand *Earth Dances* for large orchestra (1985–6) then moves the idea on to a further level of possibility, with multiple strata of both 'cantus' and 'continuum'. Both works introduce new textures (the rich low register of *Earth Dances*) and new gestures (such as the rippling downward staccato scale with which, in both works, a long expansion seems to deflate) that look towards *Gawain*, which was to work with continuous growth and continual repetition over a larger span.[114] Further steps were taken in a surprising turn to lyric music (always featuring the high soprano voice, and usually with a mixed ensemble) in settings of Rilke, haiku, Celan, and his own poems—verse whose pregnant images and fracturings

---

[113] Note in the programme for the 1986 English National Opera production.

[114] See Rhian Samuel's note on the music in the programme for the 1991 Covent Garden production and its 1994 revival.

could be exacerbated by music; 'delicate', for the first time, enters the vocabulary of words for describing Birtwistle. After *Gawain* there were more Celan songs and a Jaan Kaplinski set.

Meanwhile, the first performances in 1986 of *The Mask of Orpheus*, *Earth Dances*, and the 'mechanical pastoral' *Yan Tan Tethera* brought the composer belated recognition, and perhaps satisfaction. His next major work, *Endless Parade* for trumpet with shadowing vibraphone and accompanying string orchestra (1986–7), is effulgent, exultant, and therefore simpler, with the trumpet's melody repeatedly returning to an initiatory signal before going off on new trajectories, and with the different roles more firmly and permanently established than had been the case in *Secret Theatre*. The next piece he wrote for the soloists of the London Sinfonietta, *Ritual Fragment* (1990), strikes a different tone—it was written as a memorial to Michael Vyner, the ensemble's long-faithful artistic director—but its public address is no less direct, perhaps because again it presents melody not as communal chant, as in *Secret Theatre*, but as solo declamation.

This time there are ten soloists, who take their turns to stand and enunciate at the focus of the semicircle in which the others are placed, then return. According to the composer, what they play as soloists is 'a continuous line',[115] though where the 'cantus' of *Secret Theatre* had welded disparate instrumental voices into a unity, *Ritual Fragment* makes it possible for each instrument to make its statement in its own way, with its own rhetoric of gesture and motif. In Example 78, which shows most of the horn's eulogy, the solo instrument begins by echoing the stentorian rising tenth that has just been announced by the bass trumpet (which, in its own solo, will majestically reclaim the gesture) before going on to the emphatic D that is properly its own. The bassoon has one of Birtwistle's de-characterized melodies in even values and narrow intervals—the kind of line that could go on for ever, always the same and always different (cf. Example 52)—while the trumpet and the viola, at the final climax, jump out with memories of highly characterized ideas from their solos. The piano and the double bass are, as is clear from this example, signalling instruments; the cello and the double bass, also unable to move, occasionally seem to converse with the soloist (the cello here could be recalling the horn to its correct path), but more generally underpin the harmony. And it is now sustained harmony, rather than rhythmic ostinato, that provides the 'continuum'—harmony that tends to underrate rhythmic precision, just as the percussed and pizzicato rhythms of earlier Birtwistle scores had underplayed harmony. In placing melody against melody in a harmonic echo chamber, *Ritual Fragment* has a new ease, and yet its gestures—in Example 78, the signals, the solo pronouncement, and the memories—are keenly asserted. The move from a rhythmic to a harmonic background provided the last fundamental necessity for the composition of *Gawain*.

Birtwistle's understanding of music as theatre is very apparent in *Ritual Fragment*, as it was in *Verses for Ensembles* and *Secret Theatre*, and was to be again

---

[115] Preface to the score.

Ex. 78. Birtwistle, *Ritual Fragment* (1990)

in *Five Distances for Five Instruments* (1992), for a spaced wind quintet. But instruments are actors too, or masks, in works which do not project the players as stage presences. *Antiphonies* for piano and orchestra (1992), for example, includes roles for a tuba humming to itself in long, slow melody, for trombones whose brutish interjections are their only contributions to the opening minutes, for piccolos wheeling in the upper air, for a trumpet whose bright line comes out of *Endless Parade* by way of *Ritual Fragment*, and of course for the piano, which can lead a chorus within the orchestra—aligned with the bright metal of vibraphones, bells, glockenspiels, and harps, or with the clattering wood of marimbas and temple blocks—or else stand outside as an alternative space for musical ideas: acting that part, it suggests the piano of *Petrushka*. As so often, the piece finds new contexts for old ideas, such as the staccato scalar deflations, the deep-bass quakes of *Earth Dances*, or a breezing line from high woodwinds recalling *Secret Theatre*. As so often, too, there are refrain elements and ideas that come only once, such as a sequence of quiet, lifting gestures for the strings, divided into thirty parts to create widely spaced harmonies at once monumental and mysterious. Birtwistle's ability to go on exploring a wholly individual sound world, and to face history with robust confidence (here Stravinsky, in *Gawain* Wagner), leaves room for doubt about the demise of the great composer.

Luciano Berio

Berio is the great rememberer. So perhaps are all composers—especially at a time when sudden acts of forgetting (such as occasioned total serialism or minimalism) are very much less likely than exhaustive recollections, and when music absorbed in its own behaviour (as Ferneyhough's might seem to be) has to adopt extreme measures in order so to particularize itself as not to remind us of anything outside. This is the age of memory. But what Berio remembers is not the substance of the past; it is language, culture, history. And his remembering goes on not before the music is composed but as it proceeds, as if the music itself were remembering— remembering what the flute meant to Debussy, remembering what a major third has been in a universe of melodic and harmonic languages, remembering forms and textures, remembering possibilities of narration, from those of elementary signalling to those of unfolding complex stories in the theatre. The chamber-orchestra piece *Requies* (1984–5), a beautiful (but then that is a word claimed by almost everything Berio has produced) memorial to Berberian, seems to mimic the process of remembering a melody, recalling snatches, trying them out in different ways, finding its conclusion in a question. Music which does not imitate but remembers, and which even seems conscious of itself remembering, posits not only a past but a present, and a relation between the two. To quote a phrase from Dante that Berio and Sanguineti used in *Laborintus II*, and that the composer has further recalled in interview:[116] 'Music is all relative'. It asks 'the ever-open question of how man relates to the world',[117] and as it does so, its answers become themselves part of the world, so that every new work enters a widened field of relations, and widens it still more. The all-embracing inclusivity—of music's past and far-flung traditions, and of its possibilities as an instrument of cognition (including cognition by emotional sympathy, by rational inquiry and by speculative fantasy)—is what makes Berio so humane a figure in contemporary music.

Because his concern is with relations—with processes rather than objects—his music is unusually difficult to excerpt. The objects, as already mentioned, may come from different sources, and Berio welcomes them arriving with the aromas of their origins; specific in his music are the processes—both the processes we infer from how the objects appear (processes of transcription) and the processes executed within the music (processes of transformation). But some of this may be evident in Example 79, a short passage from the middle of his orchestral piece *Formazioni* (1985–7), where the horns introduce a nineteenth-century Romantic curve, echoed by the strings, and then the oboe enters with something like a folksong. The connection between these two comes most of all, perhaps, in the ocean swell of the harmony, which very often in Berio remembers the melody—keeps notes in store, and as it re-selects them, forever makes possible new melodies. One may note that the most recent *Sequenze* for exclusively monodic instruments—*VII* for oboe (1969), *IX* for clarinet (1980), and *X* for trumpet (1984)—all found ways to retain a harmonic reckoning: in *VII* a drone, in *IX* a computer (though this was abandoned, and surely the work's quasi-Bachian implicit harmony is enough— together with the harmony of clarinettish histories, from Mozart to Stockhausen by way of Brahms and Woody Herman, it brings about), in *X* an undamped piano which the trumpet tones cause to vibrate. In *Formazioni* there is again a drone, a middle-register E, that only very slowly dissolves during the course of the piece (it is still intermittently there in the example). Music remembers its most primitive past—drone, pulsation, repetition—as integral to its present sophistication.

Within the narrower history that is Berio's output, *Formazioni* has a notable place among his essays in remembering the traditional orchestra—and, of course, transforming it. As in many works from *Allelujah I* onwards, a transformation of sound is secured by a transformation of seating: there are 'formations' of brass on either side of the platform (powerfully interlocutory at the great climax soon after Example 79), and woodwind ensembles at front and rear (engaging in subtler dialogues across the main body of strings). A signature feature, found too in *Voci* (1984) and *Concerto II (Echoing Curves)* (1988–90), is the placing of a group of violins at the back, from where they can make striking penetrations, as when they answer the piano soloist in *Concerto II*. Whereas in the 1950s and 1960s Berio, like most composers, transformed the orchestra by radically changing its make-up, in the 1980s and 1990s a reconfiguring of standard resources—achieved by virtuosity of

---

[116] *Luciano Berio: Two Interviews*, 23.   [117] Ibid. 21.

orchestration as well as by changing the platform layout—is enough. *Formazioni* is scored for a quite normal large orchestra; Berio subsequently made a demonstration of the lesson by revising *Epifanie* for more practical resources as *Epiphanies*.

However, the most startling display of his ability to find new sound worlds latent in the conventional, even classical, orchestra is *Rendering* (1988–90), in which late Schubert sketches for a D major symphony are realized in Schubertian style and joined—with only a celesta added to the orchestra—by music which bends away from Schubert, or rather which ripples out over the larger memory field available to Berio. Transcription and composition are not different activities: even the most mechanical arrangement will take on a trace of the arranger; even the most radical new departure will be in some measure a revision. For the transcriber–composer, self-transcription is a waiting fascination, pursued in the *Chemins* series, which has continued through *Corale* (1980–1), on *Sequenza VIII* for violin, and *Chemins V* (1992), on *Sequenza XI* for guitar. If in some of Berio's arrangements of other music his own voice is, nevertheless, rather quiet (as in the Mahler songs, or the clarinet concerto he made from a Brahms sonata), these works are perhaps to be seen as balancing, and perhaps facilitating, the adventure going on at the same time in *Formazioni*.

The charge against Berio's music of memory might be that it cannot forget, that it is committed to evolution, not revolution; and what may be his most powerful works have come about when he has engaged with that charge: in the middle movement of *Sinfonia*, in the finale of *Un re in ascolto*, and in the magnificent *Ofanim* (1988–92). This is the most important piece he has produced so far with his Tempo Reale Audio Interactive Location System (TRAILS), developed at the Tempo Reale institute he founded in Florence in 1987 to carry on the work he had begun at IRCAM. Just as *Formazioni* works with orchestral space, so *Ofanim* works with electronic space: with illusions of space contrived by electronic sound, and with moving sound through space. The work's title, meaning 'wheels' in Hebrew, alludes to the dramatic rotations engineered by TRAILS, over the heads of the audience and of the performers: antiphonal groups of singing children and instrumentalists, the former alternating between Ezekiel's fiery vision (of lightning, whirlwind, strange creatures, the voice of God, and, again, great wheels flying through the air) and the Song of Songs. All the while a solitary woman is crouched on the stage. When everyone else has stopped, she rises to sing, and what she sings is an unyielding lament, also taken from Ezekiel: 'Thy mother is like a vine in thy blood . . . and she appeared in her height in the multitude of her branches. But she was plucked up in fury, . . . and the east wind dried up her fruit.' We may want to think here of Berio remembering folksong, remembering Weill, remembering Monteverdi, remembering Verdi. Or it may seem that the music shames such a response—almost shames itself—by the directness of its force.

POSTLUDE

The half-century journey from Boulez's Flute Sonatina to Berio's *Ofanim* is a journey not just from one time to another but from one kind of time to another. To Boulez in the 1940s, time was a railway track, and the composer's duty was to be on the train, preferably driving the engine. The view to the sides was irrelevant. Shostakovich, Britten, Poulenc, Copland, Dallapiccola: such other voices of the 1940s could not be heard by those on the history express. Even Stravinsky and Schoenberg could not be heard.

But though it may be hard still to sympathize with the young enthusiast's intolerance and ungenerousness, there was something brave and inspiriting about the late modernist adventure. Otherwise it could hardly have commanded such widespread attention and support, nor could it have resulted in works which took music to the edges of the possible so quickly and in so many different directions: *Le marteau sans maître*, *Gruppen*, the Barraqué Sonata, *Tempi concertati*, *Movements*, *4' 33"*, *Partitions*, *Oiseaux exotiques*, and *Il canto sospeso* make an extraordinary bunch of works to have come out of one decade, the 1950s. The changes they brought cannot be unsaid. Even the splitting of time—for now we look back not along one pair of ever parallel rails but into a tangle of ribbons blowing behind us and constantly changing in what they reveal of themselves (what they reveal, therefore, of us)—even this splitting into so many simultaneous histories was implicit in the 1950s, in the divergences among the works just mentioned.

It was in the early 1960s, though, that the idea of a single way forward became untenable, even as music acquired again qualities of richness and diversity: this was the time of *Chronochromie*, of *La mort de Virgile*, of *Kontakte*, of *Epifanie*, of *Pli selon pli*. And towards the end of the 1960s composers began to look seriously at what 'progress' had left out of account: harmonic continuity, pulse, expressive gesture, theatre, the past. Hence *Requiem Canticles*. Hence *Sinfonia*. Hence *Punch and Judy*. Hence *Hymnen*. Hence *Die Soldaten*. And hence the vitality of early minimalism.

Yet after those few years of hope and chaos, at the end of the 1960s and into the early 1970s, music entered a relatively barren period—a period, perhaps, of exhaustion, and of confusion caused by the absence of any generally agreed aim or aesthetic. The doubtfulness of that time was, I think, reflected in the first version of this book, which is one reason why a thorough-going revision was necessary, because now the atmosphere is very different. What happened in the mid-1980s was quite extraordinary: *The Mask of Orpheus* and *Earth Dances*, *Un re in ascolto* and *Formazioni*, *Saint François d'Assise*, the *Kafka-Fragmente*, the *Carceri d'invenzione*, *Prometeo*, *Nixon in China*, the late works of Feldman and Cage. As to the reason—

well, music is not isolated from the rest of life, and may turn as life turns from dogma to openness, from the institutional to the personal, from the mechanical to the natural, from invented histories to discovered ones. It need no longer worry us that the way ahead is unclear (though it may worry us if some prefer the ways behind). Our business is with now.

REPERTORY

'LP' indicates a black-disc recording; numbers otherwise refer to CDs.

Hans Abrahamsen (1952–)
Publisher: Hansen

String Quartets Nos. 1 and 2 have been recorded by the Kontra Quartet (Da Capo 9006), *Winternacht* and *Walden* by the London Sinfonietta (Paula 37), and *Universe Birds* on Kontrapunkt 32016.

John Adams (1947–)
Publishers: Associated to 1985, Boosey & Hawkes thereafter

Among early works, *Phrygian Gates* is recorded by Ursula Oppens on Music & Arts 604 (with Carter). Most later works are available on Elektra Nonesuch (*Grand Pianola Music*, 79219; *Nixon in China*, 79177). Simon Rattle conducts *Harmonielehre* on EMI 555 051.

AMM
The only recording of an improvisation involving Cardew is on LP Mainstream 5002.

Milton Babbitt (1916–)
Publishers: Associated, Boelke-Bomart, Peters

An approach might be made by way of the piano works from 1947 to 1985, recorded by Robert Taub on Harmonia Mundi 905 160, the quartets (No. 2, LP Nonesuch H 71280; No. 3, Music & Arts 707; No. 4, CRI 587, No. 5 Music & Arts 606), or the electronic pieces (*Ensembles for Synthesizer*, LP Columbia MS 7051; *Philomel* with Bethany Beardslee, New World 307, or with Judith Bettina, Neuma 450 74, whose other tracks include Varèse's *Poème électronique*). A variegated anthology, including Beardslee in *Vision and Prayer*, is provided on CRI 521. Also important are the recordings of *All Set* for jazz ensemble (Elektra Nonesuch 79222), the Piano Concerto with Alan Feinberg (New World 346), and *Sextets* with *The Joy of More Sextets*, played by Feinberg and Rolf Schulte (New World 364).

Jean Barraqué (1928–73)
Publisher: Bärenreiter

The Piano Sonata has been recorded by Claude Helffer (LP Valois MB 952) and Roger Woodward (LP EMI EMSP 551 or LP Unicorn UNS 263). *Séquence* and *Chant après chant*, with Josephine Nendick, appear on LP Valois MB 951. Paul Méfano has conducted recordings of . . . *au delà du hasard* (LP Astrée 50 1979) and *Le temps restitué* with the Concerto (Harmonia Mundi 905 199).

Richard Barrett (1959–)
Publisher: United Music Publishers

Anthology recording by the Elision Ensemble on Etcetera 1167.

Gerald Barry (1952–)
Publisher: Oxford University Press
Anthology recording on NMC 021.

George Benjamin (1960–)
Publisher: Faber
Several works have been recorded on Nimbus, including *Ringed by the Flat Horizon, A Mind of Winter*, and *At First Light* (5075), *Antara* (5167, with works by Boulez and Harvey), and *Sudden Time* (1432), most with the composer conducting.

Luciano Berio (1925–)
Publishers: Suvini Zerboni to 1958, Universal thereafter
Among rather few recordings made before the mid-1960s, the first performance of the *Serenata*, with Severino Gazzelloni as solo flautist and Boulez conducting, is preserved on LP Véga C30 A139. Recordings made by the original *Sequenza* performers including Cathy Berberian's of *III* (Philips 426 662, Wergo 6021), Vinko Globokar's of *V* (Wergo 6021), Walter Trampler's of *VI* (LP RCA RK 11530, with *Chemins II* and *III*), Heinz Holliger's of *VII* (Philips 426 662), Carlo Chiarappa's of *VIII* (Denon CO 75448, with *Corale* and the violin *Duetti*, and Eliot Fisk's of *XI* (MusicMasters 67150). Berberian also recorded *Chamber Music* (Philips 426 662), *Circles* (Wergo 6021), *Visage* (Musica d'Oggi 105 1017, with Elise Ross in *Passaggio*), *Epifanie* and *Folk Songs* (Stradivarius 10017), and *Recital I* (RCA 62540).

Berio features as conductor on several of these discs, and also on LP CBS 61079 (*Sinfonia*), LP RCA RL 11674 (*Nones, Allelujah II*, and the Concerto for two pianos), LP RCA RL 12291 (*Points* and other works), DG 423 902 (*Coro*), RCA RD 87898 (*Corale* with Chiarappa, *Voci* with Aldo Bennici, and *Requies*), Philips 432 889 (Verdi songs with José Carreras), and Teldec 74002 (Mahler songs with Thomas Hampson). Other notable recordings include those of *Tempi concertati* on Attacca/Babel 9057 4 (ASKO Ensemble) and of the *Sinfonia, Formazioni*, and *Folk Songs* on Decca 425 832 (Riccardo Chailly conducting). In the 1980s Boulez recorded the *Sinfonia* with *Eindrücke* on Erato 2292 45228, and a group of concertante pieces from *Chemins II* to *Corale* on Sony SK 45862 (Ensemble InterContemporain).

Philips 426 662 and Wergo 6021 offer the most useful anthologies of earlier Berio; the Chailly record, *Coro*, and the disc with *Voci* and *Requies* carry the story on into the 1970s and 1980s.

Harrison Birtwistle (1934–)
Publisher: Universal to 1994, Boosey & Hawkes thereafter
The few recordings made before the late 1970s include versions of *Tragœdia* (LP Argo ZRG 759), of *The Triumph of Time* under Boulez with *Chronometer* (LP Argo ZRG 790), and of *Verses for Ensembles, Nenia*, and *The Fields of Sorrow* with the London Sinfonietta under David Atherton (LP Decca HEAD 7). The London Sinfonietta later recorded *Punch and Judy*, again with Atherton (Etcetera 2014), *Silbury Air, Carmen Arcadiae Mechanicae Perpetuum*, and *Secret Theatre* under Elgar Howarth (Etcetera 1052), and *Meridian, Melencolia I* with Antony Pay, and *Ritual Fragment* under Oliver Knussen (NMC D009). Larger works recorded include . . . *agm* . . . under Boulez (Erato 2292 45410, with Kurtág), *The Triumph of Time* and *Gawain's Journey* under Howarth (Collins 13872), *Earth Dances* under Peter Eötvös (Collins 20012), and *Nomos, An Imaginary Landscape*, and *Antiphonies* (Collins 14142). *Verses for Ensembles* reappeared with *Refrains and Choruses* and *For O, for O, the Hobby-Horse is Forgot*

under James Wood (Etcetera 1130); *Endless Parade* has been recorded by Håkan Hardenberger with Howarth conducting (Philips 432 075).

The NMC disc is outstanding, but nothing here is without interest, and the old recordings of *Verses for Ensembles* and *The Triumph of Time* remain valuable.

Benjamin Boretz (1934–)

Publishers: Lingua, Open Space

Recordings include solo improvisations (Open Space 2), a coupling of *Group Variations I* with duo improvisations (Open Space 5), and a volume of ensemble improvisations (Open Space 6).

Pierre Boulez (1925–)

Publishers: Amphion, Heugel, Universal (most works)

The earliest recording available is that of the first and only performance of *Polyphonie X* (Col Legno AU 031 800); the same set includes *Poésie pour pouvoir* and *Structures II*, also recorded at their premières, the latter work involving the composer as pianist with Yvonne Loriod. Early recordings of the Sonatina were made by Severino Gazzelloni with David Tudor (LP Véga C30 A139) and with Frederic Rzewski (LP RCA 1312); there is also an early account of *Structures I* by the Kontarskys on LP Véga C30 A278, preceding their recording of both books on Wergo 6011. The recording of the Second Piano Sonata by Maurizio Pollini is on LP DG 2740 229; Charles Rosen recorded the other two sonatas on LP CBS 72871, and Claude Helffer all three on Astrée E 7716. Later performances appear in Boulez anthologies: CBS MK 42619 (*Notations*: Pi-Hsien Chen, *Structures II*: Chen and Bernhard Wambach), Erato 2292 45648 (Sonatina and First Sonata: Sophie Cherrier and Pierre-Laurent Aimard) and DG 445 833 (*Notations and Structures II*). Another of these post-1985 miscellanies, Erato 2292 45494, includes the final versions of *Le visage nuptial* and *Le soleil des eaux* with *Figures–Doubles–Prismes*, all conducted by the composer. Still with Boulez conducting, there is an earlier recording of the definitive *Le soleil* (Stradivarius 10029) and one of the 1958 version (EMI CDM 7 63948). Parts of the *Livre pour quatuor* are available on LP Erato STU 70580 and LP Mainstream 5009.

Boulez's four recordings of *Le marteau sans maître* provide a fascinating history of growing ease and breadth: they were made, all with French ensembles, in 1957 (LP Véga C35 A67), 1964 (Adès 14 073), 1973 (LP CBS 73191, with a 1969 *Livre pour cordes*) and 1985 (CBS MK 42619), the 1964 version being the most electric. There are also recordings of performances under Robert Craft (LP Philips A 01488 L) and Bruno Maderna (Stradivarius 10028). The latter disc includes too a recording of *Figures–Doubles–Prismes* under Maderna and a 1959 performance of the first two *Improvisations sur Mallarmé* under the composer, who made two recordings of the complete *Pli selon pli*, in 1969 (LP CBS 72770) and 1981 (Erato ECD 88074).

Domaines, with Michel Portal on clarinet and Diego Masson conducting, is on Harmonia Mundi 190 930, *Eclat/Multiples* and *Rituel*, both under Boulez, on Sony SK 45839. Of the later anthologies, Erato 2292 45648 includes *cummings ist der Dichter*, *Dérive* and *Mémoriale* (Boulez and the Ensemble InterContemporain) with *Dialogue de l'ombre double* (Alain Damiens), and Erato 2292 45493 has *Rituel*, *Messagesquisse*, and *Notations I–IV* (all Barenboim). Another version of this last score has Abbado conducting (DG 429 260). DG 445 833 offers the definitive ... *explosante-fixe* ....

A basic Boulez selection might start with the 1964 *Marteau* and the Pollini recording of the

Second Sonata, the 1981 *Pli selon pli*, the pairing of *Eclat/Multiples* and *Rituel*, and the Erato disc spanning from the Sonatina to *Dialogue*.

Benjamin Britten (1913–76)
Publishers: Boosey & Hawkes to 1966, Faber thereafter

Much of Britten's music was recorded under his own baton by Decca. The Third Quartet is played by its original performers, the Amadeus, on Decca 425 715.

Earle Brown (1926–)
Folio, a group of seven works including *December 1952*, is published by Associated and recorded on LP EMI 1 C 165–28 954/57 Y (Ensemble Musica Negativa).

Gavin Bryars (1943–)
Publisher: Schott

The Sinking of the Titanic has been recorded three times, in 1975 (LP Obscure 1), in 1990 (Crépuscule TWI 922), and in 1994 (Point 446 061), each time with the composer's participation. The 1975 version is coupled with *Jesus' Blood Never Failed Me Yet*, which was re-recorded in an enlarged version in 1993 (Point 438 823). Many later works are available on ECM.

Sylvano Bussotti (1931–)
Per tre sul piano is published by Universal and recorded on LP EMI EMSP 551 (Roger Woodward).

John Cage (1912–92)
Publisher: Peters

Cage participated directly in just a few of the many recordings of his music: as lecturer in *Indeterminacy* (Smithsonian Folkways 40804/5), as a participant in the 1958 retrospective at which the *Concert* had its first performance, with David Tudor as soloist (Wergo 6247), as co-performer with Tudor in *Cartridge Music* (LP Mainstream 5015) and *Variations IV* (LP Everest 6132), as pianist in *Cheap Imitation* (LP Cramps CRSLP 6117), and as reciter in two versions of *Roaratorio* (Mode 28/9, Wergo 6303). Another primary document is Tudor's recording of the third and fourth books of the *Music of Changes* (LP New World 214).

Much of the other music for piano and prepared piano has been recorded on Wergo by Joshua Pierce, including the *Sonatas and Interludes* (60156), whose other interpreters include John Tilbury (LP Decca HEAD 9) and Aki Takahashi (Denon C37 7673). The *Sixteen Dances* have been recorded by the Ensemble Modern (RCA 09026 61574), the *String Quartet in Four Parts* by the LaSalle (DG 423 245, with quartets by Lutosławski, Mayuzumi and Penderecki), and Arditti (Mode 27, with *Four*), and the Concerto for prepared piano by Yuji Takahashi (LP Nonesuch H 71202).

Recordings of later works, so dependent on the instantaneities of performance, have to be justified by particular care. A multi-piano version of the *Music for Piano* series by several Hungarian musicians is coupled with *Thirty Pieces for Five Orchestras* on LP Hungaroton SLPD 12893. Frances-Marie Uitti's cello recital (Etcetera 2016) includes *26' 1.499"* for string player, the cello solo from the *Concert for Piano and Orchestra*, *Variations II*, and the *Etudes boréales*. There are full-scale recordings of the *Concert* by the Ensemble Musica Negativa (LP EMI 1 C 165–28 954/57 Y) and the SEM Ensemble (Wergo 6216), and of *Atlas eclipticalis* by these same ensembles (LP DG 137 009 and again Wergo 6216). *Aria* is sung by its destined performer, Cathy Berberian, on LP Mainstream 5005, and *Music for Amplified Toy Pianos* is played by the Gentle Fire on LP EMI 065 02 469. The recording of *HPSCHD* (LP Nonesuch H 71224) has a claim as sanctioned by the composer and issued with his directions for chance-composed playback.

Among works after *Cheap Imitation*, the *Song Books* were recorded by the Schola Cantorum Stuttgart (Wergo 6074); extracts appear with earlier and later vocal solos on Joan LaBarbara's *Cage* album (New Albion 035). Paul Zukofsky's selection (CP² 103) includes *Cheap Imitation*, *Chorals*, and some of the *Freeman Etudes*, which Irvine Arditti offers complete (Mode 32 and 37). Grete Sultan recorded the *Etudes australes* written for her (Wergo 6152), and Uitti the *Etudes boréales* (Mode 1–2 as well as Etcetera 2016). The *Thirty Pieces for String Quartet* and *Music for* are played on Mode 17 by the Arditti Quartet. Apart from that ensemble's *Four* (Mode 27), recordings of the late number-title pieces include versions of *Five* and *Seven²* on a Barton Workshop double album including earlier works (Etcetera 3002), two different accounts of *Thirteen* played by Ensemble 13 (CPO 999 227), and one of *Fifty-Eight* (Hat Art 6135).

Cornelius Cardew (1936–81)
Publishers: Experimental Music Catalogue, Peters

Two paragraphs of *The Great Learning* were recorded by the Scratch Orchestra (LP DG 2561 107), and selections from the 1973–4 piano albums by the composer (LP Cramps CRSLP 6106).

Elliott Carter (1908–)
Publishers: Associated to 1985, Boosey & Hawkes thereafter

The four quartets have been recorded by the Arditti (Etcetera 1065 and 1066) and the Juilliard (Sony S2K 47229, with the Duo for violin and piano). The Duo also appears in a compilation with instrumental pieces both earlier (Cello Sonata) and later (*Riconoscenza, Scrivo in vento, Enchanted Preludes, Con leggerezza pensosa, Gra*) on Bridge 9044. Other anthologies of chamber works include Elektra Nonesuch 79183 (the Cello Sonata and the Sonata for flute, oboe, cello, and harpsichord, together with the Double Concerto featuring Paul Jacobs and Gilbert Kalish) and ECM 1391 (Triple Duo, *Esprit rude/Esprit doux, Riconoscenza, Enchanted Preludes*). Charles Rosen pairs the two big piano works, the Sonata and *Night Fantasies*, on Etcetera 1008; also noteworthy are performances of the former piece by Jacobs (Elektra Nonesuch 79248, with *The Minotaur*) and of the latter by Ursula Oppens (Music & Arts 604, with Adams).

Oppens has also recorded the Piano Concerto, coupled with the Variations, Michael Gielen conducting (New World 347). The later concertos have both been recorded by their original soloists: the Oboe Concerto by Heinz Holliger under Michael Gielen (Col Legno AU 031 800) and Boulez (Erato ECD 75553, with *A Mirror on Which to Dwell* sung by Phyllis Bryn-Julson, *Penthode*, and *Esprit rude/Esprit doux*), and the Violin Concerto by Ole Böhn under Oliver Knussen (Virgin 91503, with the Concerto for Orchestra and *Three Occasions*). *A Mirror* is sung by its original singer, Susan Davenny Wyner, with Boulez's performance of *A Symphony of Three Orchestras* on LP Columbia M 35171. The other two late vocal works were also recorded by their first interpreters: Jan De Gaetani and Thomas Paul for *Syringa* (CRI 610) and Martyn Hill for *In Sleep, in Thunder* (Wergo 6278, with the Triple Duo played by its original team, the Fires of London). Bridge 9014 brings together the vocal triptych with earlier Frost songs. Among historical recordings featuring original performers, the Double Concerto is done by

Ralph Kirkpatrick and Charles Rosen on LP EMI ASD 601, and Leonard Bernstein conducts the Concerto for Orchestra on LP CRI 469.

A useful start could be made with Etcetera 1065 (Quartets Nos. 1 and 4), Elektra Nonesuch 79183 and Virgin 91503.

John Chowning (1934–)

Stria and other works are available on Wergo 2012.

George Crumb (1929–)
Publisher: Peters

Ancient Voices of Children is recorded on Elektra Nonesuch 79149 (Jan De Gaetani), and *Black Angels* on Elektra Nonesuch 79242 (Kronos).

Peter Maxwell Davies (1934–)
Publishers: Boosey & Hawkes, Chester, Schott

The Pierrot Players made two recordings: LP Mainstream 5001, including *Antechrist*, and LP HMV ASD 2427 (or LP Angel S 36558), including *Revelation and Fall*. Among recordings by the group's successor, the Fires of London, are LP L'Oiseau-Lyre DSLO 2 (*Antechrist, Missa super L'homme armé, Hymnos, From Stone to Thorn*), Unicorn-Kanchana 9052 (*Eight Songs for a Mad King*), Unicorn-Kanchana 2068 (*Vesalii Icones*), Unicorn-Kanchana 2044 (*Fantasia on a Ground and Two Pavans* and other realizations), and Unicorn-Kanchana 2038 (*Ave maris stella, Image Reflection Shadow*). *O magnum mysterium* was recorded in 1963 with Cirencester forces (LP Argo ZRG 5327), and there was an early recording of the Second Taverner Fantasia under Sir Charles Groves (LP Argo ZRG 712, with *Points and Dances* from *Taverner* played by the Fires). Also valuable are Jan De Gaetani's recording of *Dark Angels* (LP Nonesuch H 71342) and Simon Rattle's of the First Symphony (LP Decca HEAD 21). Davies himself has, since the late 1980s, conducted much of his music for Collins, including *Worldes Blis* (13902), *St Thomas Wake* (13082), the Second Symphony (14032), the Third Symphony (14162), and the Fourth Symphony with the Trumpet Concerto featuring John Wallace (11812). An alternative version of this last work is provided by Håkan Hardenberger and Elgar Howarth on Philips 432 075. The *Seven In Nomine* and suite from the film scores, under Nicholas Cleobury, are on Collins 10952.

Of the Pierrot Players and early Fires recordings, those of *Eight Songs* and *Vesalii Icones* have the virtue of availability. *Worldes Blis* is a crucial work; the Trumpet Concerto well represents the later Davies.

Chris Dench (1953–)

A remarkable anthology of flute music, played by Laura Chislett, is on Etcetera 1146. The Elision Ensemble include *Driftglass* on RCA CCD 3011.

James Dillon (1950–)
Publisher: Peters

Richard Bernas conducts orchestral and percussion works on NMC 004. *Sgothan* has been recorded by Pierre-Yves Artaud (Fontec 3253) and Laura Chislett (Vox Australis 007), *Spleen* by James Clapperton (Musical Nova 7), and *Del cuarto elemento* by Irvine Arditti (Montaigne 789 003).

Franco Donatoni (1927–)
Publishers: Suvini Zerboni to 1977, Ricordi thereafter

There are several anthology recordings, including Stradivarius 33315 (Gruppo Musica Insieme di Cremona), Etcetera 1053 (Nieuw Ensemble), Adda 581 133 and 581 143 (both 2E2M), and Harmonic 8616 (Luca Pfaff). The Cremonese disc has the widest chronological spread, from *For Grilly* to *Arpège*, but the French and Dutch performances are livelier; *Etwas ruhiger im Ausdruck* is on the Nieuw Ensemble's disc, *Still* on the second by 2E2M. Solo pieces often appear in mixed recitals, such as Irvine Arditti's on Montaigne 789 003 (*Argot*). *Tema* and *Cadeau* are played by the Ensemble InterContemporain under Boulez on Erato 45366 (with Ligeti), *Cloches* by the ASKO Ensemble on Attacca/Babel 9057 (with Berio, Francesconi, and Maderna).

Pascal Dusapin (1955–)
Publisher: Salabert

Short pieces from the 1980s are presented by the group 'Accroche-Note on Harmonic 8721. There are also recordings of *Roméo et Juliette* (Accord 201 162) and *Medeamaterial* (Harmonia Mundi 905 215), both based on the first productions, and of Quartets Nos. 2 and 3 by the Arditti (Montaigne 782 016).

Morton Feldman (1926–87)
Publishers: Peters to 1969, Universal thereafter

Early recordings are included on LP CBS Odyssey 3216 0302 (by performers including the composer, David Tudor, Russell Sherman, and the Composers Quartet) and Edition RZ 1010 (Tudor playing 1950s pieces—*Intermission V, Intersection III, Piano Pieces 1956 A* and *B*—in the 1950s), of which the latter also features the composer in recordings made in the 1970s (*Intermission V* again, *Extensions III, Piano Three Hands* with John Tilbury). Feldman also appears, as conductor and pianist, on CRI 620 (*False Relationships and the Extended Ending, The Viola in my Life I–III, Why Patterns?*), and there are later recordings of music from his last decade featuring members of his Buffalo group on Hat Art 2 6080 (*Crippled Symmetry* and *Why Patterns?*), 4 61041/4 (*For Philip Guston*), and 3 6120 (*For Christian Wolff*). Other recordings made by musicians close to the composer, or under his supervision, appear on LP Mainstream 5007 (*Durations I–IV* with Tudor and others), LP CBS Odyssey Y 34138 (*For Frank O'Hara* with Jan Williams and others), LP EMI 1 C 165–28 954/57 Y (*The Straits of Magellan, For Franz Kline*, and *Between Categories*, played by the Ensemble Musica Negative), CP² 101 (Paul Zukofsky and Marianne Schroeder in *For John Cage*), CP² 102 (Zukofsky and Ursula Oppens in *Spring of Chosroes*), and New Albion 018 (Joan LaBarbara in *Three Voices*). Another recording of documentary importance is Leonard Bernstein's of . . . *Out of 'Last Pieces'* (LP Columbia MS 6733).

Many more recordings have appeared since the composer's death, and include Hat Art 6101 (with early pieces played by Frances-Marie Uitti and Nils Vigeland), Etcetera 2015 (piano works, including *Triadic Memories*, performed by Roger Woodward and collaborators), Col Legno WWE 2 CD 31873 (a much slower *Triadic Memories* from Markus Hinterhauser), Col Legno WWE 2CD 31874 (*Crippled Symmetry*, also with Hinterhauser), Hat Art 6035 (piano works, including *Palais de Mari*, performed by Schroeder), Montaigne 782 018 (Ensemble Recherche in 1970s pieces), New Albion 039 (*The Rothko Chapel* and again *Why Patterns?*), Clarinet Classics 0009 (Roger Heaton and Simon Limbrick in *Bass Clarinet and Percussion*), and Elektra Nonesuch 79320 (Aki Takahashi and the Kronos in *Piano and String Quartet*).

This last disc and the LaBarbara *Three Voices* would usefully supplement the selections from earlier periods on RZ 1010 and CRI 620.

Brian Ferneyhough (1943–)
Publisher: Peters

The principal recordings are Etcetera 1070 (*Superscriptio, Intermedio alla ciaccona*, the *Etudes transcendentales*, and *Mnemosyne* from the *Carceri*, together with *La chûte d'Icare*), LP Stil 31085 83 (three performances of *Cassandra's Dream Song* and two of *Unity Capsule* by Pierre-Yves Artaud), and Montaigne 789 002 (the Arditti in the first three quartets and *Adagissimo*). The *Time and Motion Studies* are available on, respectively, Attacca/Babel 8945 1 (Sparnaay), LP Musicaphon BM 30 SL 1715 (Taube), and Cadenza 800 895 (Schola Cantorum Stuttgart), and *Transit* is performed under Elgar Howarth on LP Decca HEAD 18. Other works to have been recorded include *Prometheus* (Sonor on CRI 652), *Funérailles* (under Boulez on Erato 88261), *Lemma–Icon–Epigram* (Massimiliano Damerini on Frequenz 011 058), *Carceri d'invenzione IIb* (Roberto Fabbriciani on Europa 350 229), and *Bone Alphabet* (Steven Schick on Newport Classic 85566).

Michael Finnissy (1946–)
Publishers: United Music Publishers to 1987, Oxford University Press thereafter

The composer's recording of *English Country-Tunes* is on Etcetera 1091; Etcetera 1096 offers *Cátana, Contretänze* and the String Trio. NMC 002 is a recital disc by Finnissy.

Stefano Gervasoni (1962–)
Publisher: Ricordi

Works recorded include *Su un arco di bianco* (UMMUS 106) and *Tre intermezzi* (RCA 74321 16229).

Philip Glass (1937–)
Publisher: Dunvagen

Earlier works are recorded on Elektra Nonesuch 79326 (*Two Pages, Music in Fifths, Music in Similar Motion*), Elektra Nonesuch 79325 (*Music with Changing Parts*), and Virgin 91311 (*Music in Twelve Parts*). There are two recordings of *Einstein on the Beach*, associated with the original production of 1976 (CBS M4K 38875) and with the revival of 1992 (Elektra Nonesuch 79323). Of the later operas, there are recordings of *Satyagraha* (CBS M3K 39672), *The Photographer* (CBS MK 37849), and *Akhnaten* (CBS M2K 42457).

Vinko Globokar (1934–)
Publisher: Peters

Globokar's recital record LP DG 137 005 includes his *Discours*. Among other recordings of works from the late 1960s and early 1970s are Harmonia Mundi 90933 (*Fluide, Ausstrahlungen, Atemstudie* played by Holliger) and Harmonia Mundi 905 214 (*Discours II* and *Echanges*, both with the composer).

Sofya Gubaydulina (1931–)
Publishers: Soviet publishers to 1979, Sikorski thereafter

Larger works recorded include *Stufen* and '*Stimmen ... Verstummen*', both conducted by Rozhdestvensky (Chandos 9183), *The Hour of the Soul* with Marek Pekarski (Col Legno 0647

290), *Offertorium* with Gidon Kremer (DG 427 336, with *Hommage à T. S. Eliot*), and *Pro et contra* conducted by Tadaaki Otaka (BIS 668). There are recordings of *Seven Words* with various other works on MCA 68005, Wergo 6263, and Berlin Classics 1113. String Quartets Nos. 1–3 and the String Trio are played by the Danish Quartet on CPO 999 064; there is also a recording of the Second Quartet by the Arditti on Montaigne 789 007 (with Kurtág and Lutos awski).

Jonathan Harvey (1939–)
Publisher: Faber

Of the composer's IRCAM projects, *Mortuos plango, vivos voco* is on Erato ECD 88261 and *Bhakti* on NMC 1. Frances-Marie Uitti plays the Cello Concerto and other pieces on Etcetera KTC 1148.

Hans Werner Henze (1926–)
Publisher: Schott

Operas recorded include *Boulevard Solitude* (Cascavelle 1006), *Der junge Lord* (DG 445 248), *Elegy for Young Lovers* (LP DG 138 876, excerpts), *The Bassarids* (Koch Schwann 314 006), and *The English Cat* (Wergo 6204). Symphonies Nos. 1–6 exist in recordings by the composer (DG 429 854); No. 7 has been recorded with the *Barcarola* by Simon Rattle (EMI CDC 7 54762). The five quartets are played by the Arditti on Wego 60114. Other works recorded include *Chamber Music 1958* (Koch Schwann 310 004), *Das Floss der 'Medusa'* (LP DG 139 428–9), *El Cimarrón* (Koch Schwann 314 030), *Der langwierige Weg in die Wohnung der Natascha Ungeheuer* (LP DG 2530 212), Violin Concerto No. 2 (LP Decca HEAD 5), and *La Cubana* (Wergo 60129).

Lejaren Hiller (1924–)
The *Illiac Suite* is recorded on Wergo 60128.

Heinz Holliger (1939–)
Publisher: Schott

A span of chamber works from *Glühende Rätsel* to the Quintet for piano and wind is on Accord 201 922; other chamber works appear on ECM 833 307 (*Studie über Mehrklänge* played by the composer, *Trema*, Duo for violin and cello) and Wergo 6084 (String Quartet and Chaconne for cello). *Siebengesang*, with Holliger, and *Der magische Tänzer* are on DG 445 251; the first performance of *Pneuma* is on Col Legno AU 031 800. Extracts from the *Scardanelli-Zyklus* are sung by the Schola Cantorum Stuttgart on Wergo 6084; a complete performance under the composer's direction is on ECM 1472/3.

Bill Hopkins (1943–81)
Publishers: Schott, Universal

Two Pomes, Sensation, Pendant, and *En attendant* are performed on NMC 014 by musicians including Alison Wells, Alexander Balanescu, and Richard Bernas.

Mauricio Kagel (1931–)
Publishers: Peters, Universal

Works recorded include the String Sextet (LP Véga C30 A278), *Transición II* (LP Mainstream 5003), *Match* (LP DG 104 933), *Musik für Renaissance-Instrumente* (LP DG 104 933), the String

Quartet (Montaigne 789 004), *Der Schall* (LP DG 2561 029), *Ludwig van* (LP DG 2530 014), *Unter Strom* (LP DG 2530 460), *Staatstheater* (LP DG 2707 060), and *Exotica* in two performances (DG 445 252 and Koch Schwann 3 1391).

Oliver Knussen (1952–)
Publisher: Faber

Where the Wild Things are and *Higglety Pigglety Pop!* are available on video disc (Pioneer PA 88 212); the former is also on CD (Arabesque Z 6535 L). Other recordings include Unicorn-Kanchana 2010 (Symphonies Nos. 2 and 3, *Ophelia Dances* book 1, *Coursing*) and Virgin 59308 (*Hums and Songs of Winnie-the-Pooh*, *Océan de terre*, Variations for piano, *Songs without Voices*). Many of the performances are conducted by the composer, who has also recorded Birtwistle, Carter, Takemitsu, and Wolpe.

György Kurtág (1926–)
Publisher: Editio Musica Budapest

A half-dozen discs provide virtually all the Kurtág available. *The Sayings of Péter Bornemisza* is recorded by Erika Sziklay and Loránt Szücs on Hungaroton 31290 in a programme including the Eight Piano Pieces Op. 3 (two performances, by Zoltán Kocsis and István Antal), the Eight Duos for violin and cimbalom, and the Four Pilinszky Songs. Other works from before the mid-1970s appear on LP Hungaroton 11846 (String Quartet, Op. 1, Wind Quintet, *In Memory of a Winter Sunset*, selection from *Játékok* played by the composer and his wife). Op. 1 is recorded with the later quartets, *Twelve Microludes*, and *Officium breve*, by the Arditti on Montaigne 789 007 (with Gubaydulina and Lutosawski).

Messages of the Late Miss R. V. Trusova is sung by Adrienne Csengery, with Boulez conducting, on Erato 2292 45410 (with Birtwistle), and by Rosemary Hardy, with Peter Eötvös conducting, on Sony SK 53290 (with Christine Whittlesey in *Scenes from a Novel* and Hermann Kretzschmar in . . . *quasi una fantasia* . . .). The Csengery–Boulez recording is combined with performances by her of *S.V. Remembrance Noise*, the *Attila József Fragments, Scenes from a Novel* and the last song of *Requiem for the Beloved* on Hungaroton 31576. She also recorded the *Kafka-Fragmente* with András Keller (Hungaroton 31135).

The most various compilation is the recording of the 1993 Salzburg Festival 'portrait concert', which includes miniatures of the 1970s as well as the larger works of 1987–91: . . . *quasi una fantasia* . . . , *Op. 27 No. 2, Grabstein für Stephan,* and *What is the word* (Col Legno WWE 31870).

Helmut Lachenmann (1935–)
Publisher: Breitkopf & Härtel

Gran torso is available in recordings by the Berne Quartet (Col Legno 0647 277) and the Società Cameristica Italiana (Edition RZ 1003), the latter with the composer's recording of *Guero*. This and other piano works are played by Roland Keller on Col Legno AU 31813. There are three similar programmes of chamber music including *Pression* and *Allegro sostenuto*, on CPO 999 102, Accord 202 082 and Col Legno WWE 31863. Another selection of chamber pieces, including *temA*, is on Montaigne 782 023. The first performance of *Schwankungen am Rand* appears on Col Legno AU 031 800; of later orchestral works, *Ausklang* and *Tableau* appear on Col Legno WWE 31862, and *Tanzsuite mit Deutschlandlied* with *Reigen seliger Geister*, both featuring the Arditti Quartet, on Montaigne 782 019.

György Ligeti (1923–)
Publishers: Peters, Schott (most works), Universal

A long run of Wergo recordings includes many made when the works concerned were new— though not in the case of the pre-1956 compositions included on 60131 (*Musica ricercata* and other piano pieces, with *Monument–Selbstportrait–Bewegung*) and 60079 (the two quartets, played by the Arditti). The First Quartet has also been recorded by the Hagen (DG 431 686) and by the Voces Intimae on a record with *Musica ricercata* and later works (BIS 53). Other early works available include the Cello Sonata, played by Matt Haimovitz (DG 431 813), and the choruses *Éjszaka* and *Reggel*, included in a collection of the composer's unaccompanied pieces sung by the Groupe Vocal de France (EMI CDC 7 54096).

The Wergo series continues with 60161 (*Glissandi, Artikulation, Volumina, Continuum*, Ten Pieces for wind quintet, Two Studies for organ), 60162 (*Atmosphères, Lux aeterna, Ramifications*, Chamber Concerto), 60045 (*Aventures* and *Nouvelles aventures*, Requiem), 60163 (Cello Concerto, *Lontano*, Double Concerto, *San Francisco Polyphony*: these last two works are in performances under Elgar Howarth and also available on BIS 53), 60100 (harpsichord pieces, *Monument–Selbstportrait–Bewegung* played by Antonio Ballista and Bruno Canino, the Horn Trio performed by its original practitioners: Saschko Gawriloff, Hermann Baumann and Eckart Besch), 6170 (*Le Grand Macabre*), and 60134 (Etudes Nos. 1–6 played by Volker Banfield). Other useful compilations include DG 423 244 (*Aventures, Ramifications*, and the Chamber Concerto all under Boulez, the Second Quartet played by another première team, the LaSalle, and *Lux aeterna*), Decca 425 623 (Ten Pieces, Chamber Concerto, *Melodien*, Double Concerto, with David Atherton and the London Sinfonietta), Col Legno 031 815 (piano and harpsichord music), Sony SK 58945 (Cello Concerto, Chamber Concerto, Violin Concerto, with Peter Eötvös and the Ensemble Modern), and DG 439 808 (Cello Concerto, Piano Concerto, Violin Concerto, with Pierre Boulez and the Ensemble InterContemporain).

Since its première under Hans Rosbaud, recorded on Col Legno AU 031 800, *Atmosphères* has won the attention of other distinguished conductors, including Leonard Bernstein (LP Columbia MS 6733), Seiji Ozawa (LP RCA SJV 1513), and Claudio Abbado (DG 429 260). There are also alternative recordings of the Chamber Concerto from Hungarian (LP Hungaroton 11807) and Canadian (UMMUS 102) ensembles, of *Monument–Selbstportrait–Bewegung* by the Kontarskys, who had recently given the first performance (LP DG 2531 102), of the Horn Trio by two French (Erato ECD 75555 and Montaigne 782 006) and one US group (Bridge 9012), and of the Etudes Nos. 1–6 by Pierre-Laurent Aimard, the composer's preferred executant (Erato ECD 75555). Garth Knox plays a movement of the Sonata for viola on Montaigne 782 027.

A fair survey would be provided by a selection such as Wergo 60131, Wergo 60163, DG 423 244, and Erato ECD 75555—though that would be to ignore the claims of *Le Grand Macabre* and the later concertos.

Otto Luening (1900–)
Publisher: Peters

Fantasy in Space and *Invention on a 12-Tone Theme* are on CRI 611 (with Ussachevsky's *Sonic Contours*), *Gargoyles* on LP Columbia MS 6566, and *Concerted Piece* on LP CRI 227.

Witold Lutosławski (1913–93)
Publisher: Chester

The composer's recordings include versions of Symphonies Nos. 1 and 2 (EMI 65076) and No. 3 (Philips 416 387); Nos. 3 and 4 have also been recorded by Esa-Pekka Salonen (Sony SK 66280). There are versions of the String Quartet by the LaSalle (DG 423 245), the Arditti (Montaigne 789 007), the Hagen (DG 431 686), and the Kronos (Elektra Nonesuch 79255).

Nicholas Maw (1935–)
Publisher: Faber

Odyssey is conducted by Simon Rattle on EMI CDS 7 54277.

Olivier Messiaen (1908–92)
Publishers: Durand, Leduc (most works), Universal

The composer recorded most of his organ music including the *Messe de la Pentecôte* and the *Livre d'orgue* (EMI CDZD 7 67400, with earlier cycles), and the *Méditations sur le mystère de la Sainte Trinité* (Erato ECD 71594). His few recordings as pianist include the *Quatre études de rythme* (LP78 Columbia LFX 998–9), a crucial document apparently not reissued. Largely he left piano recordings to his wife, Yvonne Loriod, who made versions of *Cantéyodjayâ* (LP Véga C30 A139), the *Quatre études* and the *Petites esquisses d'oiseaux* (Erato ECD 71589), the *Catalogue d'oiseaux* (LP Véga VAL 11 and later Erato ECD 71590), and *La fauvette des jardins* (Erato ECD 71590). Among the concertante pieces, she is heard in recordings of the first performances of *Réveil des oiseaux* (Col Legno, AU 031 800), *Oiseaux exotiques* (LP Véga C30 A65), and *Un vitrail* (Montaigne WM 332, recorded at the composer's eightieth birthday concert conducted by Boulez, and including also *Oiseaux exotiques, Sept haïkaï* and *Couleurs*), as well as on LP Supraphon SUA ST 50749 (*Réveil, Oiseaux exotiques*), and Koch Schwann 311 232 (*Oiseaux exotiques, Un vitrail, La Ville d'En-haut*), Adès 14073 (*Sept haïkaï* with works by Boulez and conducted by him), Erato ECD 71584 (*Sept haïkaï* and *Des canyons*), Erato ECD 71587 (*Couleurs* with *Et exspecto* conducted by Boulez), DG 445 827 (*La Ville d'En-haut*, conducted by Boulez, with *Chronochrome* and *Et exspecto*), and DG 445 947 (*Concert à quatre*). She recorded *Harawi* with Rachel Yakar (Erato ECD 75501). She also took part in several recordings of *Turangalîla*, including those under Ozawa (LP RCA SB 6761–2) and Myung-Whun Chung (DG 431 781), and one of *La Transfiguration*, under Antal Dorati (Decca 425 616).

Other pianists who have recorded Messiaen include Paul Jacobs (the *Quatre études* on LP Elektra Nonesuch 71334), Peter Donohoe (in *Turangalîla* under Simon Rattle on EMI CDS 7 47463 8, in *Oiseaux exotiques, Sept haïkaï, Couleurs, Un vitrail,* and *La Ville* under Reinbert de Leeuw on Chandos 9301), Paul Crossley (in *Oiseaux exotiques, Couleurs,* and *Des canyons* under Esa-Pekka Salonen on CBS M2K 44762), Peter Hill (complete solo music on Unicorn-Kanchana, including *Cantéjodjayâ* and the *Quatre études* on 9051 and the *Catalogue d'oiseaux* on 9062, 9075, and 9090), and Robert Sherlaw Johnson (*Harawi* with Noelle Barker on Argo ZRG 606). Other organists include Jennifer Bate (complete recording on Unicorn-Kanchana, with *Le livre du Saint Sacrement* on 9067/8) and Gillian Weir (complete recording on Collins 70312). Other singers include Jane Manning (*Harawi* on Unicorn-Kanchana 9034).

Saint François was recorded at the·original performances under Ozawa (Cybélia 833/6). There are recordings under Chung of *Eclairs* (DG 439 929), and of the *Concert à quatre, Un sourire,* and earlier works (DG 445 947). The Piece for piano and string quartet appears on Montaigne 782 027.

All the Erato recordings mentioned above were issued in a seventeen-disc set that also includes the *Cinq rechants* (ECD 71597) and a conversation between the composer and

Claude Samuel (ECD 75505). This set could be supplemented by the discs listed in the last paragraph, by *La Transfiguration*, by a *Turangalîla* and by the composer's organ recordings, to provide an almost complete Messiaen. Less formidable selections of post-1945 works might start with the Rattle *Turangalîla*, the Loriod *Quatre études* and *Petites esquisses* (the early Preludes are also included), and the eightieth-birthday concert.

Meredith Monk (1943–)

Recordings on ECM include *Dolmen Music* (1197), *Turtle Dreams* (1240), and *Atlas* (1491/2).

Conlon Nancarrow (1912–)
Publisher: Schott

The Studies for Player Piano, up to 1988, are recorded on Wergo 60165 (42, 45, 48, 49), 60166/7 (1, 2, 7–13, 15–19, 21, 23–5, 27–9, 33–4, 36, 43, 46–7, 50) and 6168 (3–6, 14, 20, 22, 26, 31–2, 35, 37, 40–1, 44). Of the late instrumental pieces, the Arditti have recorded String Quartet No. 3 (Gramavision R21S 79440), the Ensemble Modern Piece No. 2 (RCA 09026 61180), and Ursula Oppens her Two Canons for Ursula (Music & Arts 699).

Luigi Nono (1924–90)
Publishers: Schott to 1963, Ricordi thereafter

Several works of the 1950s are available in closely contemporary performances under Bruno Maderna: these include *Composizione No. 1*, *España en el corazon*, *Memento*, and *Composizione No. 2* (Arkadia 027 1), *Y su sangre* (LP RCA VICS 1313), and *Il canto sospeso* (Stradivarius 10008). There are also early performances of *Polinfonica–monodia–ritmica* (LP Time 58002), *Due espressioni* under Hans Rosbaud (Col Legno AU 031 800), *Incontri* under Boulez (LP Véga C30 A66), and *Varianti* with Rudolph Kolisch as soloist and Rosbaud conducting (LP DG 0629 030). Later recordings of works from this period include those of the *Variazioni canoniche* under Gielen (Astrée E 8741), *Polifonica–monodia–ritmica* (Artis 032), *España en el corazon* and *Memento* under Horst Neumann (Berlin Classics 002 141), *Liebeslied* (DG 429 260) and *Il canto sospeso* (Sony SK 53 360) under Abbado, and *La victoire de Guernica* under Adolf Burkhardt (Vox Pop 4016/7).

Works of the next decade were presented around its end by Wergo, in recordings available on 6038 (*Ha venido*, *La fabbrica illuminata*, *Auschwitz*), 6229 (*Omaggio a Emilio Vedova*, *Sul ponte di Hiroshima*, *Per Bastiana*), LP 60026 (*Sarà*), and LP 60051 (*Djamila Boupachà*, *Canciones a Guiomar*), with Gielen, Maderna, and Clytus Gottwald the conductors. A Maderna performance of *Per Bastiana* is also included on the Arkadia disc. There are later performances of *Canciones* under Richard Dufallo (LP Columbia MS 7281) and of *La fabbrica illuminata* by Silvia Montanari (Artis 032).

Most of the electronic–political frescos of the late 1960s and early 1970s were recorded pretty immediately; they include *A floresta è jovem* (LP Harmonia Mundi MV 30 767 and LP DG 253 1004), *Contrappunto dialettico* (DG 423 248), *Un volto e del mare* (LP Philips 6521 027), and *Y entonces comprendió* (LP DG 2530 436). The re-release of *Contrappunto* is in company with *Como una ola* and . . . *sofferte onde serene . . .* , both with Maurizio Pollini; Abbado conducts. An alternative performance of *Como una ola*, with Giuseppe La Licata playing and Herbert Kegel conducting, is on Berlin Classics 002 141, and Artis 032 includes an alternative . . . *sofferte . . .* played by Aldo Orvieto, as well as *Con Luigi Dallapiccola*. These last two works—the former excellently played by Markus Hinterhauser—are also recorded on Col

Legno WWE 31871 with *Das atmende Klarsein*. *Fragmente–Stille* is available in a recording by the LaSalle, who had recently given the first performance (DG 415 513), and in one by the Arditti in a coupling with '*Hay que caminar*' (Montaigne 789 005). The latter work is included with Gidon Kremer's recording of the piece written for him, *La lontananza nostalgica* (DG 435 870), of which Irvine Arditti gives a fuller account on Montaigne 782 004 (Arditti and his quartet also worked with Nono).

Other works of the 1980s were also recorded by musicians with whom Nono had collaborated, including Roberto Fabbriciani and Ciro Scarponi (recordings of *A Pierre* on LP Edition RZ 1004 and Ricordi 1003), and Giancarlo Schiaffini (recordings of *Post-prae-ludium No. 1* on Ricordi 1003 and Artis 032); Fabbriciani also recorded a fragment from *Das atmende Klarsein* (Europa 350 229); all three play in *Quando stanno morendo* (Ricordi 1003). *Donde estás, hermano?* was recorded by the female vocal quartet for whom it was written, Bel Canto (Aulos 66034), and Gielen recorded the two last orchestral works, *A Carlo Scarpa* and *No hay caminos* (Astrée E 8741).

The Maderna recordings should be sought out for the earlier works; to them could be added in the first place Col Legno WWE 31871, DG 423 248, Montaigne 789 005, and Ricordi 1003.

Nuovo Consonanza (1965–80)

Improvisations of 1967–75 are recorded on Edition RZ 1009.

Pauline Oliveros (1932–)

She publishes her own scores, and in some cases recordings. Other recordings include Mode 40 (*St. George and the Dragon, In memoriam Mr. Whitney*).

Arvo Pärt (1935–)

Publisher: Universal

Much of Pärt's later music has appeared on a series of ECM records beginning with *Tabula Rasa* (1275), *Arbos* (1325), and *Passio* (1370).

Harry Partch (1901–76)

Most works remain unpublished. Two CRI releases—7000 (*Castor* and *Windsong*) and 7001 (*The Bewitched*, recorded at the 1957 première)—are transfers from the almost complete recorded edition made between 1953 and 1962 by the composer and his ensemble, and previously released independently by him on his Gate 5 label. Later recordings in which Partch was involved include LP Columbia MS 7207 (*Castor* and *Daphne*) and LP Columbia M2 30576 (*Delusion of the Fury*). There are posthumous recordings of *Revolution in the Courthouse Park* (Tomato R2 70390) and *Daphne* (Mode 33), the latter by Newband, who have care of the instruments.

Krzysztof Penderecki (1933–)

Publisher: Schott

Muza 017 includes Polish recordings of String Quartet No. 1, the *Threnody* and the St Luke Passion; this last work has also been recorded by the composer (Argo 430 328). An alternative version of the quartet is on the LaSalle's disc with Cage, Lutos awski, and Mayuzumi (DG 423 245), an alternative *Threnody* on Conifer 168. Col Legno AU 031 800 incudes the first performance of *Anaklasis*.

Horatiu Radulescu (1942–)

The few recordings include Edition RZ 1007 (*Clepsydra* and *Astray*, both using 'sound icons') and Montaigne 782 030 (*Inner Time II*).

Steve Reich (1936–)

Publishers: Universal to 1970, Boosey & Hawkes thereafter

Most of Reich's music is available in recordings by or with his own ensemble, or made with his blessing. Releases on Elektra Nonesuch include 79101 (*The Desert Music*), 79138 (*Sextet* and *Six Marimbas*), 79169 (*It's gonna rain, Come out, Piano Phase, Clapping Music*), 79170 (*Drumming*), 79176 (*Different Trains* and *Electric Counterpoint*), 79220 (*The Four Sections* and *Music for Mallet Instruments*), and 79295 (*Tehillim* and *Three Movements*), on ECM 168 (*Violin Phase, Music for a Large Ensemble*, and *Octet*), 1129 (*Music for Eighteen Musicians*), and 1215 (*Tehillim*), and on DG 427 428 (*Drumming, Music for Mallet Instruments, Six Pianos*) and 439 431 (*Music for Mallet Instruments* and *Variations*). Where the earlier music is concerned, DG 427 428, with recordings made in 1974, has the value of contemporaneity, as does Robi Droli 5108 (*Four Organs* and *Phase patterns*, both recorded in 1970).

Recordings more distant from the composer include Argo 440 294 (Piano Circus in *Four Organs*), Argo 430 380 (Piano Circus in *Six Pianos*), Hungaroton 31358 (Amadinda in *Music for Mallet Instruments, Music for Pieces of Wood*, and *Sextet*), EMI 47331 (Ransom Wilson in *Vermont Counterpoint* and *Eight Lines*), and Clarinet Classics 0009 (Roger Heaton in *New York Counterpoint*).

Wolfgang Rihm (1952–)

Publisher: Universal

A valuable sequence of CPO recordings offers lieder featuring Richard Salter and Bernhard Wambach (999 049), the *Musik für drei Streicher* (999 050), *Fremde Szenen I–III* played by the Beethoven Trio (999 119), *Kein Firmament* played by the Ensemble 13 (999 134), and *Die Eroberung von Mexiko* (999 185). Also important are the recordings of *Die Hamletmaschine* (Wergo 6195), of String Quartets Nos. 3, 5, and 8 by the Arditti (Montaigne 782001), of the Viola Concerto, *Dunkles Spiel*, and other orchestral works (Cadenza 800 886), of *Frau/Stimme* (Col Legno AU 031 800) and of *Gesungene Zeit* (DG 437 093). The discs devoted to lieder and to quartets are outstanding.

Terry Riley (1935–)

In C is revived by Piano Circus on Argo 430 380.

Frederic Rzewski (1938–)

Publisher: Zen-On

In the 1960s he made recordings of Boulez and Stockhausen, and his participation later in that decade in Musica Elettronica Viva and Nuova Consonanza is documented on LP Mainstream 5002 and Edition RZ 1009 respectively. Of his compositions, *Coming Together* and *Attica* are recorded by Group 180 on Hungaroton 12545. Later works recorded by the composer include *The People United Will Never Be Defeated!* and Four North American Ballads (Hat Art 6089), Four Pieces and the third ballad (Vanguard 08 9199 71), and the Piano Sonata and *De profundis* (Hat Art 6134). There are alternative versions of *The People United* by Ursula Oppens (Vanguard OVC 8056), and of the ballads by Kathleen Supové (CRI 653).

Kaija Saariaho (1952–)

Publisher: Hansen

Records include Finlandia 374 (*Verblendungen, Litchbogen, Io, Stilleben*) and Ondine ODE 804 (*Nymphaea, Du cristal, . . . à la fumée*).

Giacinto Scelsi (1905–88)

Publisher: Salabert

A few of the numerous Scelsi recordings do nothing for the composer; others valuably fill gaps; some are magnificent. Among those in the second category are the performances of orchestral pieces on three Accord discs: 200612 (*Quattro pezzi, Uaxuctum, Anahit*), 201112 (*Hurqualia, Chukrum, Hymnos*), and 200402 (*Aion, Konx-Om-Pax, Pfhat*). The exceptional releases include the Arditti double album of the five quartets with the String Trio and *Khoom* (Salabert 8904/5), Frances-Marie Uitti's recordings of *Trilogia* and *Ko-tha* (Etcetera 1136), Michiko Hirayama's recording of the *Canti del Capricorno*, which were written for her (Wergo 60127), a collection of mostly solo pieces under the title *Okanagon* (Hat Art 6124), and another anthology by members of 2E2M (Adda 581 189).

Alfred Schnittke (1934–)

Publishers: Peters, Sikorski (most works), Sovetsky Kompozitor, Universal

Soviet recordings include Rozhdestvensky's of the first three symphonies (Melodiya 10 00062, 00063, 00064). Symphony No. 4 has been recorded by Okko Kamu (BIS 497) and No. 5 by Neeme Järvi (BIS 427); there are many other Schnittke recordings on the same label. Gidon Kremer takes part in recordings of the Concerto Grosso No. 1 (DG 429 413), the Violin Concertos Nos. 1–2 (Teldec 94540), the Concerto Grosso No. 5 (DG 437 091), and the Beethoven Violin Concerto with cadenzas by Schnittke (LP Philips 6514 075). Other important recordings include those of *Life with an Idiot* (Sony S2K 52 495), *Minnesang* and the Concerto for chorus (Chandos 9126), String Quartet No. 3 by the Kronos (Elektra Nonesuch 79181) and the Britten (Collins 12982), and String Quartet No. 4 by the Alban Berg (EMI CDC 7 54660, with Rihm).

Arnold Schoenberg (1874–1951)

Publishers: Boelke-Bomart, Israeli Music Publishers, Marks, C. F. Peters, Schott, Shilkret

There are several recordings of Schoenberg's two post-1945 chamber works, the String Trio and the Phantasy for violin and piano. Of his other compositions, Boulez's complete recording of the choral music (Sony S2K 44571) includes *A Survivor from Warsaw*, the Three Folksongs, *Dreimal tausend Jahre*, *Psalm 130*, and the *Modern Psalm*. A volume of Robert Craft's complete Schoenberg includes these last two works and the canon 'Gravitationszentrum eigenen Sonnensystems' (LP CBS 77223). There is also a recording of the *Modern Psalm* under Michael Gielen (Wergo 60185).

Dmitry Shostakovich (1906–75)

Publishers: Soviet imprints

There are so many recordings as to defy cataloguing, let alone the heavier task of selection. A quick guide is all that will be attempted here. All the post-1945 symphonies have been recorded by Haitink (Decca) and Rozhdestvensky (Melodiya); there are also notable performances under Barshai (No. 14 on Russian Disc), Bernstein (No. 9 on CBS and DG, No. 14 on Sony), Flor (No. 10 on RCA), Kondrashin (No. 13 on Russian Disc), Masur (No. 13 on Teldec), Mitropoulos

(Nos. 9 and 10 on CBS), Mravinsky (No. 10 on Praga, Nos. 10 and 12 on Erato, Nos. 11 and 15 on Russian Disc), Oistrakh (No. 9 on Russian Disc), Rattle (No. 10 on EMI), Rostropovich (Nos. 9, 10, 11, and 15 on Teldec), Solti (No. 9 on Decca), and Stokowski (No. 11 on EMI). All the quartets have been recorded by the Borodin (EMI), Brodsky (Teldec), and Fitzwilliam (Decca) quartets. The two violin concertos are coupled by Dmitri Sitkovetsky (Virgin), and No. 1 has been recorded by Viktoria Mullova (Philips); the two cello concertos are offered together by Natalia Gutman (RCA) and Heinrich Schiff (Philips), and separately by Rostropovich (No. 1 on CBS, No. 2 on DG); Piano Concerto No. 2 is played by the composer on EMI 54606, and has also been recorded by his grandson (Chandos) and Bernstein (CBS). There is a pairing of the Violin Sonata and the Viola Sonata on Melodiya, played by Oleg Kagan and Yuri Bashmet, both with Sviatoslav Richter; the Viola Sonata has also been recorded by Kim Kashkashian and Robert Levin (ECM). Of the last song cycles, the orchestral version of the Tsvetayeva Poems exists in a recording by Julia Varady and Haitink (Decca), and the Michelangelo Suite and Lebyadin Verses were recorded by Fischer-Dieskau and Ashkenazy (also Decca).

Karlheinz Stockhausen (1928–)
Publishers: Universal to 1969, Stockhausen Verlag thereafter

Recordings on the composer's own CD label are of performances conducted or supervised by him, many of them originally released by DG. They include 1   (*Chöre für Doris, Choral, Drei Lieder*, Violin Sonatina, *Kreuzspiel*), 2   (*Formel, Spiel, Schlagtrio, Punkte*), 3   (*Etüde, Studie I* and *II, Gesang der Jünglinge, Kontakte*), 4   (*Kontra-Punkte, Zeitmasze, Stop, Adieu*), 5   (*Gruppen, Carré*), 6   (*Zyklus, Refrain, Kontakte* with instruments), 7   (*Momente*), 8   (*Mixtur*), 11   (*Prozession, Ceylon*), 12   (*Stimmung*), 13   (*Kurzwellen*), 14   (*Aus den sieben Tagen*), 15   (*Spiral, Pole*), 16   (*Mantra*), 18   (*Sternklang*), 19   (*Trans*), 20   (*Am Himmel wandere ich . . .*), 21   (*Ylem*), 22   (*Inori*), 23   (*Atmen gibt das Leben . . .*), 24   (*Musik im Bauch, Tierkreis* on musical boxes), 25   (*Harlekin*), 26   (*Sirius*), 27   (*Amour, In Freundschaft, Traum-Formel*, played by Suzanne Stephens), 28   (*Amour, In Freundschaft*, pieces derived from *Samstag, Montag*, and *Dienstag*, played by Kathinka Pasveer), 29   (*Der Jahreslauf*), 30   (*Donnerstag aus Licht*), 31   (*Unsichtbare Chöre* from *Donnerstag*), 32   (*Laub und Regen, Tierkreis, In Freundschaft*, pieces derived from *Donnerstag, Samstag, Montag, Dienstag*, and *Freitag*, played by Suzanne Stephens), 33   (*Aries*, Piano Piece XIII), 34   (*Samstag aus Licht*), 35   (*Tierkreis* for instruments, pieces derived from *Samstag* and *Montag*), 36   (*Montag aus Licht*), 37 and 38 (excerpts from *Montag*), 39 (classical concertos with cadenzas by Stockhausen), 41   (*Oktophonie* from *Dienstag*), 42   (*Synthi-Fou* from *Dienstag*), and 43   (pieces derived from *Donnerstag, Samstag* and *Dienstag*, played by Markus Stockhausen).

The Piano Pieces have been recorded by Aloys Kontarsky (I–XI: Sony S2K 53346, with *Mikrophonie I–II*) and Bernhard Wambach (I–XIV: Koch Schwann 310 009, 015 and 016). There are also important recordings of VI by David Tudor (LP Véga C30 A278), of I–VIII and XI also by Tudor (Hat Art 6142), and of X by Frederic Rzewski (LP Wergo 60010, with performances of *Zyklus* by Christoph Caskel and Max Neuhaus). Among other valuable early recordings not included in the composer's complete edition are those of *Punkte* by Boulez (AU 031 800), *Kontra-Punkte* by Boulez (LP Véga C30 A66) and Maderna (LP RCA VICS 1239), *Zeitmasze* by Boulez (LP Véga C30 A139) and Craft (LP Philips A 01488 L), *Zyklus* and *Refrain* featuring Caskel and the Kontarskys (LP Time 58001), *Kontakte* featuring Caskel and Tudor (Wergo 6009), *Momente* in its 1965 state conducted by the composer (LP Wergo 60024), *Mikrophonie I* and *II* in their original recordings (Sony S2K 53346, with Kontarsky in the Piano Pieces), *Mixtur* (LP DG 137 012), and *Spiral* by Holliger (LP DG 2561 109). *Mixtur* is coupled with

Telemusik, while the other tape piece of the 1960s, *Hymnen*, is on LP DG 2707 039. Recordings by the composer's live electronic ensemble include—besides the versions of *Kurzwellen*, *Aus den sieben Tagen*, and *Mikrophonie I* already mentioned—LP Vox STGBY 615 and LP DG 2530 582 (*Prozession*), LP DG 139 461 (*Opus 1970*), LP EMI Electrola C 165 02 313/4 (*Spiral, Pole, Japan*, and *Wach* from *Für kommende Zeiten*), and LP Chrysalis CHR 1110 (*Ceylon* and *Zugvogel* from *Für kommende Zeiten*). Among other recordings of intuitive pieces by musicians close to the composer are Harmonia Mundi 190 795 (Musique Vivante in *Setz die Segel* and *Verbindung* from *Aus den sieben Tagen*) and LP Wergo 325 (Michael Vetter in *Spiral*). Most of the recordings with which the composer has been involved since the early 1970s are now on his own label; an exception is that of the reduced version of *Michaels Reise um die Erde* with Markus Stockhausen as soloist (ECM 1406).

The small—and, not only for that reason, intriguing—category of recordings from outside the Stockhausen circle includes Wambach's of the Piano Pieces, another disc featuring Wambach with Mircea Ardeleanu and Fred Rensch in *Zyklus*, *Refrain*, and *Kontakte* (Koch Schwann 310 020), *Kontakte* again with Avery and Stephen Schick (Music & Arts 648), *Stimmung* sung by Singcircle (Hyperion 66115), *Kurzwellen* and *Setz die Segel* played by Negative Band (LP Finnadar CS 9009), and *Spiral* played by Eberhard Lum (Hat Art 6132). *Dr. K*, originally available on a celebration disc from Universal Edition (LP UE 15043), has been re-recorded by the California Ear Unit (New Albion 019).

Hat Art 6142, Wergo 6009, and Stockhausen 5 have special claims as presenting the only pre-1969 performances generally available; Stockhausen 3 and 4, together with Koch Schwann 310 016 and 009 (Wambach's recordings of Piano Pieces I–XI), would add other essential works of this period. A choice from what is available of the later Stockhausen might include discs 16 and 19 in his own series, together with the full *Donnerstag*, its middle act (ECM 1406) or an operatic pot-pourri (Stockhausen 28, 32 or 43, or Koch Schwann 310 015, which offers the Piano Pieces from *Donnerstag*, *Samstag*, and *Montag*). The main absences would then be those of the 1965 *Momente*, *Telemusik*, and *Hymnen*.

Igor Stravinsky (1882–1971)
Publisher: Boosey & Hawkes

The composer's recordings, made during the period 1957–66 and re-released on Sony SM2K 46291/46302, include performances of the *Ebony Concerto*, the Concerto in D, *Orpheus*, the Mass, *The Rake's Progress*, the Cantata, the Septet, the Shakespeare Songs, *In memoriam Dylan Thomas*, the *Canticum sacrum*, the *Greeting Prelude*, the *Choral-Variationen*, *Agon*, *Threni*, *Movements*, *Monumentum*, *A Sermon*, *The Dove Descending*, the Eight Instrumental Miniatures, the *Elegy for J.F.K.*, and *Introitus*. There are also early recordings by him of the *Ebony Concerto* (LP Columbia ML 4398), the Concerto in D (LP RCA LM 1096), *Orpheus* (LP RCA LM 1033), the Mass (LP RCA LM 17), *The Rake's Progress* (LP Fonit-Cetra DOC 29, recorded at the initial performances; LP Columbia ML 4723/5), the Cantata (LP Columbia ML 4899), and the Septet, Shakespeare Songs, Four Songs, and *In memoriam Dylan Thomas* (LP Columbia ML 5107).

The Sony collection includes most of the other post-1945 compositions: the *Epitaphium*, the Double Canon, *The Flood*, *Abraham and Isaac*, the Variations, the *Requiem Canticles*, and *The Owl and the Pussy-Cat*; where necessary, Robert Craft conducts. There are also historical recordings by Peter Pears of *In memoriam Dylan Thomas* (Col Legno AU 031 800), by Craft of the *Canticum sacrum* and *Choral-Variationen* (Adès 13 293), by Mravinsky of *Agon* (Melodiya 224), and by Boulez of *A Sermon* (Montaigne TCE 8800). Boulez's later recordings include a volume of songs, among them the Shakespeare set, *In memoriam Dylan Thomas*, the *Elegy for J.F.K.*, and the Wolf instrumentations (DG 431 751), and a volume of instrumental pieces with the *Ebony Concerto*, *Epitaphium*, Double Canon, and Eight Instrumental Miniatures (LP DG 2531 378). The following are also noteworthy: a further recording under Riccardo Chailly of *The Rake's Progress* (Decca 411 644), performances of the Mass and *Canticum sacrum* sung by Westminster Cathedral Choir (Hyperion 66437), a programme conducted by James Wood of other choral pieces, including the *Tres sacrae cantiones*, *The Dove Descending*, and *Introitus* (Hyperion 66410), a Soviet recording of *Movements* (LP Melodiya C10 18073–4), and Fischer-Dieskau's recordings of *Abraham and Isaac* and *Elegy for J.F.K.* (Orfeo S 015 821).

Tōru Takemitsu (1930–)
Publisher: Salabert to 1978, Schott thereafter

Several works of the 1950s and 1960s are contained on three JVC discs: 1007 (*Arc*, *Dorian Horizon*), 1008 (Yuji Takahashi and Toshi Ichiyanagi playing piano works), and 1009 (*Vocalism A.I.*, *Kanshō*). The piano music is also covered by Roger Woodward (Etcetera 1103) and Kami Ogano (Philips 432 730); other recordings of the earlier works include Denon 79441 (*Requiem* and *November Steps* conducted by Wakasugi), BMG BVCC 5048 (*Requiem* and *Dorian Horizon* conducted by Ozawa), DG 423 253 (*Ring, Sacrifice, Valeria, Stanza I*), Philips 420 257 (*November Steps* conducted by Haitink), and Philips 432 176 (*November Steps* conducted by Ozawa). Pianists who have recorded *For Away* include, besides Woodward and Ogano, Yuji Takahashi (Wave C25G 00032) and Aki Takahashi (Toshiba EWCC 33 3322). There are selections of later orchestral pieces on Virgin 91180 (Knussen) and RCA 09026 61574 (Richard Stoltzman and Tadaaki Otaka).

Tan Dun (1957–)
Publisher: G. Schirmer

There are two discs of orchestral music: Koch 3 1298 (*On Taoism, Orchestral Theatre I, Death and Fire*) and Fontec 3276 (*On Taoism, Orchestral Theatre I, Orchestral Theatre II*), both with the composer as vocalist and conductor. CRI 655 offers smaller pieces: *Eight Colors, Snow in June, Circle with Four Trios*. Less conventional resources appear in *Nine Songs* (CRI 603) and *Paper Music* (Parnassus 81801).

Edgard Varèse (1883–1965)

Déserts has been recorded by Craft (LP CBS S 75106), Boulez (LP CBS IM 39053), and the ASKO Ensemble (Attacca/Babel 9263, with the *Poème électronique*), *Nocturnal* by Maurice Abravanel (Vanguard OVC 4031). The *Poème* is also available on LP CBS S 75695 and Neuma 450 74 (with Babbitt).

Alejandro Viñao (1951–)

Wergo 2019 offers the Triple Concerto and *Son entero*, Musidisc 244 942 three works for soprano and computer.

Kevin Volans (1949–)
Publisher: Chester

Discs include United 88034 (*White Man Sleeps* and other works with harpsichords and percussion), Collins 141 720 (Quartets Nos. 4–5 played by the Duke), and Argo 440 687 (Quartets

Nos. 2–3 played by the Balanescu). The Kronos have recorded movements from *White Man Sleeps* (Elektra Nonesuch 79163) and Quartet No. 2 (Elektra Nonesuch 79253).

Judith Weir (1952–)
Publishers: Novello to 1987, Chester thereafter

King Harald's Saga, The Consolations of Scholarship, and *Missa del Cid* are on United 88040; *Blond Eckbert* is on Collins 14612; other works recorded include *An mein Klavier* (NMC 002, played by Michael Finnissy), *Scotch Minstrelsy* (Abacus 109), *The Art of Touching the Keyboard* (Merlin 891 706), and *Airs from Another Planet* (Lorelt 103).

David Wessel (1942–)
Anthony is on Wergo 282 030.

Stefan Wolpe (1902–72)
Publishers: McGinnis & Marx, Peer-Southern

Battle Piece has been recorded by Geoffrey Douglas Madge (CPO 999 055, with *Form IV*) and Marc-André Hamelin (New World 354). Other pianists to have made recordings include Peter Serkin (*Form IV* on New World 354) and Katharina Wolpe (*Form* and *Form IV* on Largo 512). There are chamber works on Koch 3 7112 (Violin Sonata, Oboe Quartet, Trio in Two Parts), Col Legno AU 31809 (Saxophone Quartet, *From Here on Farther*), Bridge 9043 (Quintet with Voice, Piece in Three Parts under Knussen), Elektra Nonesuch 79222 (Saxophone Quartet), CRI 587 (String Quartet), and LP Elektra Nonesuch 78024 (*Enactments*, Second Piece for Violin Alone). The Symphony is on CRI 676.

Iannis Xenakis (1922–)
Publishers: Boosey & Hawkes to 1966, Salabert thereafter

Early recordings are preserved on Col Legno AU 031 800 (*Metastaseis* at its first performance, under Hans Rosbaud), Chant du Monde LDC 278 386 (*Metastaseis* and *Pithoprakta* under Maurice Le Roux, *Eonta* under Konstantin Simonovic, with Yuji Takahashi), Denon CO 1052 (*Herma* and *Evryali* played by Yuji Takahashi), Salabert 8906 (*Oresteia*), LP Erato ERA 9119 (*Terretektorh* under Charles Bruck), and Adès 14 122 (*Nuits* under Marcel Couraud). Electronic pieces of this period appear on LP Nonesuch H 71246 (*Diamorphoses, Concret PH, Orient–Occident, Bohor*) and LP Ereato STU 70530 (*Diamorphoses, Orient–Occident*). There are later performances of *Eonta* on Teldec 2292 46442 (with Rolf Hind) and Attacca LIVE 1 (with Aki Takahashi in a programme also including later works), and of *Nuits* on Arion 68084. *Kraanerg* has been recorded by Roger Woodward (Etcetera 1075).

    Among records covering works from different parts of the composer's career are Montaigne 782 005 (Arditti Quartet and Claude Helffer in *Herma, ST/4–1,080262, Nomos alpha, Evryali, Ikhoor, Mists, Tetras, Tetora*, and other pieces), Erato 2292 45770 (members of the Ensemble InterContemporain in *Nomos alpha, Phlegra, Thallëin, Jalons, Keren*), and Attacca LIVE 1 (ASKO Ensemble in *Palimpsest, Waarg*, and *Echange*, as well as *Eonta*). Of the later orchestral works, only *Jonchaies* has been recorded (LP Erato STU 71513 and Col Legno AU 31830), while *Pleiades* has been recorded by Les Percussions de Strasbourg (Harmonia Mundi 905 185 and Denon CO 73678), Kroumata (BIS 482), Makoto Aruga (Sony 32DC 691), and the ensemble Pléiades (Erato 2292 45019).

    The Chant du Monde disc, an essential, would need to be supplemented by the Nonesuch collection of electronic pieces, by *Nuits* and the *Oresteia* music, and by the ASKO anthology for the later music.

LaMonte Young (1935–)

An early recording from *The Tortoise, his Dreams and Journeys* is on LP Shandar 83 510. *The Well-Tuned Piano* is played by the composer on Gramavision R255 79452, *The Second Dream of the High-Tension Line Stepdown Transformer* appears on Gramavision R21S 79467, and *Stompin' Live*, a performance by the composer with his Forever Bad Blues Band, is on Gramavision R2 79487.

Bernd Alois Zimmermann (1918–70)
Publisher: Schott

A good survey is provided by the concertos on Philips 434 114 (Heinz Holliger in the Oboe Concerto, Heinrich Schiff in the *Canto di speranza* and the Cello Concerto, Håkan Hardenberger in *Nobody Knows*) and by the chamber music on DG 437 725 (*Perspektiven, Présence, Monologe, Intercommunicazione*, featuring the Kontarskys with Saschko Gawriloff and Siegfried Palm, all musicians close to the composer). *Die Soldaten* (Teldec 9031 72775) is a survey all by itself. Other recordings include those of the Viola Sonata (AU 031 800), *Photoptosis* (LP Wergo 60062), and the *Requiem für einen jungen Dichter* (Wergo 60180).

BIBLIOGRAPHY

This list is centred on, but not limited to, works in English; the original-language editions of translated books are not generally noted, except where composers' writings of interviews are concerned. The latter will be found in the second part of the list, the first being concerned with more general works; the order, within the subdivisions in both parts, is chronological, in order to show the history of the literature, and in particular which are the earliest and which the latest contributions, for there may be reasons to cherish both. To offer a further, more empirical guide, the most important books are marked with an asterisk. As the footnotes will have indicated, a great deal of the period's musical literature rests in uncollected articles; the list that follows would therefore have to be supplemented by, most particularly, the specialist journals and reviews, some of which—such as *Die Reihe* or *Perspectives of New Music*—were or are crucial media of information and debate.

1. GENERAL BOOKS

Surveys and Dictionaries

HODEIR, ANDRÉ, *La Musique depuis Debussy* (Paris: Presses Universitaires de France, 1961), English trans. *Since Debussy* (New York: Grove, 1961).*

LANG, PAUL HENRY (ed.), *Problems of Modern Music* (New York: 1962).

SAMUEL, CLAUDE, *Panorama de l'art musical contemporain* (Paris: Presses Universitaires de France, 1962).

LANG, PAUL HENRY, and BRODER, NATHAN (eds.), *Contemporary Music in Europe* (New York, 1965).

DIBELIUS, ULRICH, *Moderne Musik 1945–1965* (Munich, 1966).

MELLERS, WILFRID, *Caliban Reborn* (New York: Harper & Row, 1967).

BARTOLOTTO, MARIO, *Fase seconda* (Turin: Einaudi, 1969).

ROSSI, NICK, and CHOATE, ROBERT A., *Music of Our Time* (Boston: Crescendo, 1969).

VOGT, HANS, *Neue Musik seit 1945* (Stuttgart: Reclam, 1972; 2nd edn. 1982).

COOPER, MARTIN (ed.), *The New Oxford History of Music*, x: *The Modern Age 1890–1960* (London: Oxford University Press, 1974).

NYMAN, MICHAEL, *Experimental Music: Cage and Beyond* (London: Studio Vista, 1974).

VINTON, JON (ed.), *Dictionary of Twentieth-Century Music* (London: Thames & Hudson, 1974).

SMITH BRINDLE, REGINALD, *The New Music* (London: Oxford University Press, 1975; 2nd edn. 1987).

SCHMIDT, CHRISTIAN MARTIN, *Brennpunkte der Neuen Musik* (Cologne: Gerig, 1977).

WHITTALL, ARNOLD, *Music since the First World War* (London: Dent, 1977).

MERTENS, WIM, *American Minimal Music* (London: Kahn & Averill, 1983).

GRIFFITHS, PAUL, *The Thames and Hudson Encyclopaedia of 20th-Century Music* (London: Thames & Hudson, 1986).

JOHNSON, TOM, *The Voice of New Music: New York City 1972–1982* (Eindhoven: Het Apollohuis, 1989).

KOSTELANETZ, RICHARD, *On Innovative Music(ian)s* (New York: Limelight, 1989).

MORTON, BRIAN, and COLLINS, PAMELA, *Contemporary Composers* (Chicago: St James, 1992).

BORIO, GIANMARIO, *Musikalische Avantgarde um 1960* (Laaber: Laaber, 1993).

BOSSEUR, DOMINIQUE and JEAN-YVES, *Révolutions musicales: La Musique contemporaine depuis 1945* (Paris: Minerve, 1993).

SCHWARTZ, ELLIOTT, and GODFREY, DANIEL, *Music since 1945* (New York: Schirmer, 1993).

Catalogues and Handbooks

HILLER, LEJAREN A. JR, and ISAACSON, LEONARD M., *Experimental Music: Composition with an Electronic Computer* (New York, 1959).

BASART, ANN P, *Serial Music: A Classified Bibliography of Writings on Twelve-Tone and Electronic Music* (Berkeley and Los Angeles: University of California Press, 1961).

KARKOSCHKA, ERHARD, *Das Schriftbild der neuen Musik* (Celle: Moeck, 1966).

CROSS, LOWELL M., *A Bibliography of Electronic Music* (Toronto: University of Toronto Press, 1967).

DAVIES, HUGH (ed.), *Répertoire international des musiques électroacoustiques/International Electronic Music Catalog* (Cambridge, Mass.: MIT Press, 1968).

CAGE, JOHN, and KNOWLES, ALISON, *Notations* (New York: Something Else, 1969).

MATHEWS, MAX V., and others, *The Technology of Computer Music* (Cambridge, Mass., 1969).

ROADS, CURTIS (ed.), *The Music Machine: Selected Readings from* Computer Music Journal (Cambridge, Mass.: MIT Press, 1989).

Essays and Interviews

BECKWITH, JOHN, and KASEMETS, UDO (eds.), *The Modern Composer and his World* (Toronto: University of Toronto Press, 1963).

SCHWARTZ, ELLIOTT, and CHILDS, BARNEY (eds.), *Contemporary Composers on Contemporary Music* (New York: Holt, Rinehart & Winston, 1967).

STÜRZBECHER, URSULA, *Werkstattgespräche mit Komponisten* (Cologne: Gerig, 1971).

MARGER, BRIGITTE, and BENMUSSA, SIMONE (eds.), *La Musique en projet* (Paris: Gallimard, 1975).

ZIMMERMANN, WALTER, *Desert Plants: Conversations with 25 American Composers* (Vancouver, 1977).

BATTCOCK, GREGORY (ed.), *Breaking the Sound Barrier: A Critical Anthology of the New Music* (New York: Dutton, 1981).

KOLLERITSCH, OTTO (ed.), *Zur 'Neuen Einfachkeit' in der Musik* (Vienna: Universal, 1981).

GAGNE, COLE, and CARAS, TRACY, *Soundpieces: Interviews with American Composers* (Metuchen, NY: Scarecrow, 1982).

DELIO, THOMAS, *Circumscribing the Open Universe* (Lanham, Md.: University Press of America, 1984).

—— (ed.), *Contiguous Lines* (Lanham, Md.: University Press of America, 1985).

GRIFFITHS, PAUL, *New Sounds, New Personalities* (London: Faber & Faber, 1985).

DUFALLO, RICHARD, *Trackings: Composers Speak* (New York: Oxford University Press, 1989).

FORD, ANDREW, *Composer to Composer: Conversations about Contemporary Music* (London: Quartet, 1994).

RAHN, JOHN (ed.), *Perspectives on Musical Aesthetics* (New York: Norton, 1994).*

2. BOOKS ON AND BY INDIVIDUAL COMPOSERS

Milton Babbitt

Perspectives of New Music, 14/2 + 15/1 (1976).
BABBITT, MILTON, *Words about Music*, ed. Stephen Dembski and Joseph N. Straus (Madison: University of Wisconsin Press, 1987).*
MEAD, ANDREW, *An Introduction to the Music of Milton Babbitt* (Princeton: Princeton University Press, 1994).*

Jean Barraqué

Entretemps, 5 (Paris, 1987).
Musik-Konzepte, 82 (Munich: text + kritik, 1993).

Luciano Berio

Contrechamps, 1 (Paris: L'Age d'Homme, 1983).
DALMONTE, ROSANNA, and VARGA, BALINT ANDRAS, *Luciano Berio: Two Interviews* (London: Boyars, 1985).*
OSMOND-SMITH, DAVID, *Playing on Words: a Guide to Luciano Berio's* Sinfonia (London: Royal Musical Association, 1985).
STOÏANOVA, IVANKA, *et al.*, *Luciano Berio: Chemins en musique* [= *Revue musicale* 375–7] (Paris: Richard-Masse, 1985).
HALL, GEORGE (ed.), *BBC Berio Festival at the Barbican* (London: BBC Concerts, 1990).
OSMOND-SMITH, DAVID, *Berio* (Oxford: Oxford University Press, 1991).
BERIO, LUCIANO, *Remembering the Future* (Cambridge, Mass.: Harvard University Press, forthcoming).

Harrison Birtwistle

HALL, MICHAEL, *Harrison Birtwistle* (London: Robson, 1984).
BBC Birtwistle Festival (London: BBC Concerts, 1988).

Pierre Boulez

GOLÉA, ANTOINE, *Rencontres avec Pierre Boulez* (Paris: Julliard, 1958).
BOULEZ, PIERRE, *Penser la musique aujourd'hui* (Paris: Gonthier, 1964), English trans. *Boulez on Music Today* (London: Faber & Faber, 1971).
—— *Relevés d'apprenti* (Paris: Seuil, 1966), English trans. *Stocktakings from an Apprenticeship* (Oxford: Oxford University Press, 1991).*
—— *Par volonté et par hasard: Entretiens avec Célestin Deliège* (Paris: Seuil, 1975), English trans. *Conversations with Célestin Deliège* (London: Eulenburg, 1977).*
PEYSER, JOAN, *Boulez: Composer, Conductor, Enigma* (London: Cassell, 1977).
GRIFFITHS, PAUL, *Boulez* (London: Oxford University Press, 1978).
STAHNKE, MANFRED, *Struktur und Ästhetik bei Boulez* (Hamburg: Wagner, 1979).

BOULEZ, PIERRE, *Points de repère* (Paris: Bourgois, 1981), English trans. *Orientations* (London: Faber & Faber, 1986).

JAMEUX, DOMINIQUE, *Pierre Boulez* (Paris: Fayard, 1984), English trans. (London: Faber & Faber, 1991).

HÄUSLER, JOSEF (ed.), *Pierre Boulez: Eine Festschrift zum 60. Geburtstag am 26. März 1985* (Vienna: Universal, 1985).

HIRSBRUNNER, THEO, *Pierre Boulez und sein Werk* (Laaber: Laaber, 1985).

GLOCK, WILLIAM (ed.), *Pierre Boulez: A Symposium* (London: Eulenburg, 1986).*

STACEY, PETER F., *Boulez and the Modern Concept* (Aldershot: Scolar, 1987).

JAMEUX, DOMINIQUE, *et al.*, *Répons/Boulez* (Paris: Actes Sud, 1988).

BOULEZ, PIERRE, *Jalons (pour un décennie)* (Paris: Bourgois, 1989).

—— *Le Pays fertile: Paul Klee* (Paris: Gallimard, 1989).

Boulez at the Barbican (London: BBC Concerts, 1989).

BOULEZ, PIERRE, and CAGE, JOHN, *Correspondance et documents*, ed. Jean-Jacques Nattiez (Winterthur: Amadeus, 1990), English trans. *The Boulez–Cage Correspondence* (Cambridge: Cambridge University Press, 1993).*

KOBLYAKOV, LEV, *Pierre Boulez: A World of Harmony* (Chur: Harwood, 1990).*

AGUILA, JÉSUS, *La Domaine Musical: Pierre Boulez et ringst ans de création contemporaine* (Paris: Fayard, 1992).

HÄUSLER, JOSEF, *Pierre Boulez in Salzburg* (Salzburg: Eidolon, 1992).

MULLER, THEO (ed.), *Jeux de Boulez* (Rotterdam: Kunststichting, 1994).

Benjamin Britten

EVANS, PETER, *The Music of Benjamin Britten* (London: Dent, 1979).

KENNEDY, MICHAEL, *Britten* (London: Dent, 1981).

WHITTALL, ARNOLD, *The Music of Britten and Tippett* (Cambridge: Cambridge University Press, 1982; 2nd edn. 1990).

CARPENTER, HUMPHREY, *Benjamin Britten: A Biography* (London: Faber & Faber, 1992).

John Cage

HOOVER, KATHLEEN, and CAGE, JOHN, *Virgil Thomson* (New York: Yoseloff, 1959).

John Cage (New York: Peters, 1962).

CAGE, JOHN, *Silence: Lectures and Writings* (London: Calder & Boyars, 1968, repr. Boyars).*

—— *A Year from Monday: New Lectures and Writings* (London: Calder & Boyars, 1968, repr. Boyars).*

TOMKINS, CALVIN, *Ahead of the Game* (Harmondsworth: Penguin, 1968).

KOSTELANETZ, RICHARD (ed.), *John Cage* (London: Allen Lane, 1971; rev. New York: Da Capo, 1991).*

CAGE, JOHN, *M: Writings '67–'72* (London: Calder & Boyars, 1973, repr. Boyars).

CHARLES, DANIEL, *Gloses sur John Cage* (Paris: Union Générale d'Editions, 1978).

Musik-Konzepte: Sonderband John Cage (Munich: text + kritik, 1978).

CAGE, JOHN, and CHARLES, DANIEL, *For the Birds* (London: Boyars, 1981).*

GRIFFITHS, PAUL, *Cage* (London: Oxford University Press, 1981).

CAGE, JOHN, *Empty Words: Writings '73–'78* (London: Boyars, 1980).

—— *Themes & Variations* (Barrytown: Station Hill, 1982).

John Cage: Etchings 1978–1982 (Oakland: Crown Point, 1982).

GENA, PETER, and BRENT, JONATHAN (eds.), *A John Cage Reader* (New York: Peters, 1982).

CAGE, JOHN, *X: Writings '79–'82* (London: Boyars, 1987).

Revue d'esthétique, NS 13–15 (1987–8).

John Cage: The New River Watercolors (Richmond: Virginia Museum of Fine Arts, 1988).

FLEMING, RICHARD, and DUCKWORTH, WILLIAM (eds.), *John Cage at Seventy-Five* (Lewisburg: Bucknell University Press, 1989).

KOSTELANETZ, RICHARD (ed.), *Conversing with Cage* (London: Omnibus, 1989).

BOULEZ, PIERRE, and CAGE, JOHN, *Correspondance et documents*, ed. Jean-Jacques Nattiez (Winterthur: Amadeus, 1990), English trans. *The Boulez–Cage Correspondence* (Cambridge: Cambridge University Press, 1993).*

CAGE, JOHN, *I–VI* (Cambridge, Mass.: Harvard University Press, 1990).

Musik-Konzepte: Sonderband John Cage II (Munich: text + kritik, 1990).

REVILL, DAVID, *The Roaring Silence: John Cage: A Life* (London: Bloomsbury, 1992).

CAGE, JOHN, *Composition in Retrospect* (Cambridge, Mass.: Exact Change, 1993).

KOSTELANETZ, RICHARD (ed.), *John Cage: Writer* (New York: Limelight, 1993).

KOSTELANETZ, RICHARD (ed.), *Writings on John Cage* (Ann Arbor: University of Michigan Press, 1993).

PRITCHETT, JAMES, *The Music of John Cage* (Cambridge: Cambridge University Press, 1993).*

Rolywholyover: A Circus (Los Angeles: Museum of Contemporary Art, 1993).

Cornelius Cardew

CARDEW, CORNELIUS, *Scratch Music* (London: Latimer, 1972).

—— *Stockhausen Serves Imperialism* (London: Latimer, 1974).

Elliott Carter

EDWARDS, ALLEN, *Flawed Words and Stubborn Sounds: A Conversation with Elliott Carter* (New York: Norton, 1971).

The Writings of Elliott Carter, ed. Else and Kurt Stone (Bloomington: Indiana University Press, 1977).

SCHIFF, DAVID, *The Music of Elliott Carter* (London: Eulenburg, 1983).*

RESTAGNO, ENZO (ED.), *Carter* (Turin: Edizioni di Torino, 1989).

Peter Maxwell Davies

PRUSLIN, STEPHEN (ed.), *Peter Maxwell Davies: Studies from Two Decades* (London: Boosey & Hawkes, 1979). [Collection of articles originally published in *Tempo*]

GRIFFITHS, PAUL, *Peter Maxwell Davies* (London: Robson, 1981).*

BAYLISS, COLIN, *The Music of Sir Peter Maxwell Davies: An Annotated Catalogue* (Beverley: Highgate, 1991).

SEABROOK, MIKE, *Max: The Life and Music of Peter Maxwell Davies* (London: Gollancz, 1994).

Franco Donatoni

DONATONI, FRANCO, *Questo* (Milan: Adelphi, 1970).
—— *Antecedente X* (Milan: Adelphi, 1980).
CRESTI, RENZO, *Franco Donatoni* (Milan: Suvini Zerboni, 1982).
DONATONI, FRANCO, *Il sigaro di Armando* (Milan: Spirali, 1982).
Entretemps, 2 (Paris, 1986).
CASTAGNOLI, GIULIO, *Portrait: Note su Franco Donatoni* (Turin: Compositori Associati, 1988).
DONATONI, FRANCO, *In-oltre* (Brescia: L'Obliquo, 1988).
MAZZOLA NANGERONI, GABRIELLA, *Franco Donatoni* (Milan: Targa Italiana, 1989).
RESTAGNO, ENZO (ed.), *Donatoni* (Turin: Edizioni di Torino, 1990).

Franco Evangelisti

Musik-Konzepte, 43–4 (Munich: text + kritik, 1985).

Morton Feldman

FELDMAN, MORTON, *Essays* (Kerpen: Beginner Press, 1985).
Musik-Konzepte, 48–9 (Munich: text + kritik, 1986).

Brian Ferneyhough

MELCHIORRE, ALESSANDRO (ed.), *I quaderni della Civica Scuola di Milano*, viii (Milan, 1983).
Contrechamps, 8 (Paris: L'Age d'Homme, 1988).
FERNEYHOUGH, BRIAN, *Collected Writings*, ed. James Boros and Richard Toop (London: Gordon & Breach, forthcoming).*

Vinko Globokar

GLOBOKAR, VINKO, *Einatmen Ausatmen* (Hofheim: Wolke, 1994).

Hans Werner Henze

HENZE, HANS WERNER, *Essays* (Mainz: Schott, 1964); expanded as *Musik und Politik: Schriften und Gespräche 1966–1975*, ed. J. Brockmeier (Munich, 1976), English trans. *Music and Politics* (London: Faber & Faber, 1982); further expanded as *Musik und Politik: Schriften und Gespräche 1955–1984* (Munich, 1984).
GEITEL, KLAUS, *Hans Werner Henze* (Berlin, 1968).
SCHULTZ, K. (ed.), *Hans Werner Henze: eine Auswahl* (Bonn, 1976).
RESTAGNO, ENZO (ed.), *Henze* (Turin: Edizioni di Torino, 1986).
REXROTH, DIETER (ed.), *Der Komponist Hans Werner Henze* (Mainz: Schott, 1986).
HENZE, HANS WERNER, *Die englische Katze: Arbeitstagebuch* (Frankfurt, 1988).
PETERSEN, PETER, *Hans Werner Henze: Ein politischer Musiker* (Hamburg: Argument, 1988).
SCHOTTLER, WOLFRAM, *Die Bassariden von Hans Werner Henze* (Trier: Wissenschaftlicher Verlag, 1994).

Mauricio Kagel

SCHNEBEL, DIETER, *Mauricio Kagel: Musik, Theater, Film* (Cologne: DuMont, 1970).
Musique en jeu, 27 (Paris, 1977).
KLÜPPELHOLZ, WERNER, *Schubert im Schosse Goethes in den Armen Freuds* (Berlin: Deutsche Oper, 1980).
KLÜPPELHOLZ, WERNER, *Mauricio Kagel 1970–1980* (Cologne: DuMont, 1981).
KAGEL, MAURICIO, *Worte über Musik* (Munich: Piper, 1991).
KLÜPPELHOLZ, WERNER (ed.), *Kagel . . . /1991* (Cologne: DuMont, 1991).

György Kurtág

SPANGEMACHER, FRIEDRICH (ed.), *György Kurtág* (Bonn: Boosey & Hawkes, 1989).
Contrechamps, 12–13 (Paris: L'Age d'Homme, 1990).

Helmut Lachenmann

Musik-Konzepte, 61–2 (Munich: text + kritik, 1988).

György Ligeti

NORDWALL, OVE, *György Ligeti: Eine Monographie* (Mainz: Schott, 1971).
GRIFFITHS, PAUL, *György Ligeti* (London: Robson, 1983).*
Ligeti in Conversation (London: Eulenburg, 1983).*
MICHEL, PIERRE, *György Ligeti: Compositeur d'aujourd'hui* (Paris: Minerve, 1985).
RESTAGNO, ENZO (ed.), *Ligeti* (Turin: Edizioni di Torino, 1985).
SABBE, HERMANN, *György Ligeti* [= *Musik-Konzepte,* 53] (Munich: text + kritik, 1987).
György Ligeti (Vienna and Graz: Universal, 1987).
Contrechamps, 12–13 (Paris: L'Age d'Homme, 1990).
BURDE, WOLFGANG, *György Ligeti: Eine Monographie* (Zurich: Atlantis, 1993).

Witold Lutos awski

VARGA, BALING ANDRAS, *Lutos awski Profile* (London: Chester, 1976).
STUCKY, STEPHEN, *Lutos awski and his Music* (Cambridge: Cambridge University Press, 1971).
Musik-Konzepte, 71–3 (Munich: text + kritik, 1991).
NIKOLSKA, IRINA, *Witold Lutos awski* (Stockholm: Melos, 1993).
RAE, CHARLES BODMAN, *The Music of Lutos awski* (London: Faber & Faber, 1994).

Olivier Messiaen

MESSIAEN, OLIVIER, *Technique de mon langage musical* (Paris: Leduc, 1944), English trans. *Technique of my Musical Language* (Paris: Leduc, 1957).
ROSTAND, CLAUDE, *Olivier Messiaen* (Paris: Ventadour, 1957).
MESSIAEN, OLIVIER, *Conférence de Bruxelles* (Paris: Leduc, 1958).
GOLÉA, ANTOINE, *Rencontres avec Olivier Messiaen* (Paris: Julliard, 1960).

MARI, PIERRETTE, *Olivier Messiaen* (Paris: Seghers, 1965).

SAMUEL, CLAUDE, *Entretiens avec Olivier Messiaen* (Paris: Belfond, 1967), English trans. (London: 1976); expanded as *Olivier Messiaen: Musique et couleur: Nouveaux entretiens* (Paris, Belfond, 1986), English trans. *Olivier Messiaen: Music and Color* (Portland: Amadeus, 1994).*

WAUMISLEY, STUART, *The Organ Music of Olivier Messiaen* (Paris: Leduc, 1968).

JOHNSON, ROBERT SHERLAW, *Olivier Messiaen* (London: Dent, 1975; 2nd edn. 1989).

NICHOLS, ROGER, *Messiaen* (London: Oxford University Press, 1975; 2nd edn. 1986).

MESSIAEN, OLIVIER, *Conférence de Notre-Dame* (Paris: Leduc, 1978).

REVERDY, MICHELE, *L'Œuvre pour piano d'Olivier Messiaen* (Paris: Leduc, 1978).

PÉRIER, ALAIN, *Messiaen* (Paris: Seuil, 1979).

HALBREICH, HARRY, *Olivier Messiaen* (Paris: Fayard/SACEM, 1980).

Musik-Konzepte, 28 (Munich: text + kritik, 1982).

GRIFFITHS, PAUL, *Olivier Messiaen and the Music of Time* (London: Faber & Faber, 1985).*

MESSIAEN, OLIVIER, *Conférence de Kyoto* (Paris: Leduc, 1986).

RÖSSLER, ALMUT, *Beiträge zur geistigen Welt Olivier Messiaens* (Duisburg: Gilles und Francke, 1986).

MESSIAEN, OLIVIER, *Les Vingt-deux concertos pour piano de Mozart* (Paris: Séguier-Archimbaud, 1987).

MICHAELY, ALOYSE, *Die Musik Olivier Messiaens* (Hamburg: Wagner, 1987).

REVERDY, MICHELE, *L'Œuvre pour orchestre d'Olivier Messiaen* (Paris: Leduc, 1988).

MASSIN, BRIGITTE, *Olivier Messiaen: Une poétique du merveilleux* (Aix-en-Provence: Alinéa, 1989).

Saint François d'Assise [special issue of *L'Avant-Scène Opéra*] (Paris: Premières Loges, 1992).

HILL, PETER (ed.), *The Messiaen Companion* (London: Faber & Faber, 1995).*

Conlon Nancarrow

GANN, KYLE, *The Music of Conlon Nancarrow* (Cambridge: Cambridge University Press, 1995).

Luigi Nono

DEGRADA, FRANCESCO (ed.), *Al gran sole carico d'amore* (Milan: Ricordi, 1974).

STENZL, JÜRG (ed.), *Luigi Nono: Texte, Studien zu seiner Musik* (Zurich: Atlantis, 1975).

Musik-Konzepte, 20 (Munich: text + kritik, 1981).

SPANGEMACHER, FRIEDRICH, *Luigi Nono: Die elektronische Musik* (Regensburg: Bosse, 1983).

CACCIARI, MASSIMO (ed.), *Luigi Nono: Verso Prometeo* (Venice: Biennale, 1984).

RIEDE, BERND, *Luigi Nonos Kompositionen mit Tonband* (Munich: Katzbichler, 1986).

Contrechamps, special number (Paris: L'Age d'Homme, 1987).

CACCIARI, MASSIMO, and REXROTH, DIETER (eds.), *Luigi Nono: Prometeo* (Frankfurt: Alte Oper, 1987).

RESTAGNO, ENZO (ed.), *Nono* (Turin: Edizioni di Torino, 1987).

KROPFINGER, KLAUS (ed.), *Komponistenportrait Luigi Nono* (Berlin: Festwochen, 1988).

LINDEN, WERNER, *Luigi Nonos Weg zum Streichquartett* (Kassel: Bärenreiter, 1989).

KOLLERITSCH, OTTO (ed.), *Die Musik Luigi Nonos* (Vienna and Graz: Universal, 1991).

SPREE, HERMANN, *'Fragmente–Stille an Diotima': Ein analytischer Versuch zu Luigi Nonos Streichquartett* (Saarbrücken: Pfau, 1992).

Bibliography 359

ZEHELEIN, KLAUS (ed.), *Luigi Nono* (Stuttgart: Tage für Neue Musik, 1992).
FENEYROU, LAURENT (ed.), *Luigi Nono: Ecrits* (Paris: Christian Bourgois, 1993).
HÄUSLER, JOSEF (ed.), *Brennpunkt Nono* (Salzburg: Residenz, 1993).
TAIBON, MATEO, *Luigi Nono und sein Musiktheater* (Vienna: Böhlau, 1993).

Pauline Oliveros

GUNDEN, HEIDI VON, *The Music of Pauline Oliveros* (Metuchen, NJ: Scarecrow, 1983).

Harry Partch

PARTCH, HARRY, *Genesis of a Music* (New York: Da Capo, 1974).*
—— *Bitter Music*, ed. Thomas McGeary (Urbana, Ill.: University of Illinois Press, 1991).

Krzysztof Penderecki

SCHWINGER, WOLFRAM, *Krzysztof Penderecki: His Life and Works* (London: Schott, 1989).

Henri Pousseur

POUSSEUR, HENRI, *Fragments théoriques sur la musique experimentale* (Brussels): i (1970), ii (1972).
—— *Musique/Sémantique/Société* (Tournai: Casterman, 1972).
Musik-Konzepte, 69 (Munich: text + kritik, 1990).

Steve Reich

REICH, STEVE, *Writings about Music* (Halifax: Press of the Nova Scotia College of Art and Design, 1974).*

Wolfgang Rihm

REXROTH, DIETER (ed.), *Der Komponist Wolfgang Rihm* (Mainz: Schott, 1985).
WILKENING, M. (ed.), *Komponistenportrait Wolfgang Rihm* (Berlin: 1988).
RIHM, WOLFGANG, *Ausgesprochen: Gesammelte Schriften, Reden und Gespräche* (Winterthur: Amadeus, 1992).

Giacinto Scelsi

Musik-Konzepte, 31 (Munich: text + kritik, 1983).
ANGERMANN, KLAUS (ed.), *Giacinto Scelsi: In Innern des Tons* (Hofheim: Wolke, 1993).

Alfred Schnittke

BURDE, TAMARA, *Zum Leben und Schaffen des Komponisten Alfred Schnittke* (Kludenbach: Gehann, 1993).

Arnold Schoenberg

LEIBOWITZ, RENÉ, *Schoenberg and his School* (New York: Philosophical Library, 1949, repr. Da Capo, 1975).

RUFER, JOSEF, *The Works of Arnold Schoenberg* (London: Faber & Faber, 1962).

Arnold Schoenberg Letters, ed. Erwin Stein (London: Faber & Faber, 1964).

MACDONALD, MALCOLM, *Schoenberg* (London: Dent, 1976).

ROSEN, CHARLES, *Schoenberg* (London: Boyars, 1976).

STUCKENSCHMIDT, H. H., *Schoenberg: His Life, World and Work* (London: Calder, 1977).

NEWLIN, DIKA, *Schoenberg Remembered: Diaries and Recollections (1938–76)* (New York, 1984).

RINGER, ALEXANDER L., *Arnold Schoenberg: The Composer as Jew* (Oxford: Oxford University Press, 1976).

Dmitry Shostakovich

KAY, NORMAN, *Shostakovich* (London: Oxford University Press, 1971).

BLOKKER, ROY, and DEARLING, ROBERT, *The Music of Shostakovich: The Symphonies* (London: Tantivy, 1979).

VOLKOV, SOLOMON, *Testimony: The Memoirs of Dmitry Shostakovich* (London: Hamish Hamilton, 1979).

NORRIS, CHRISTOPHER (ed.), *Shostakovich: The Man and His Music* (London, 1982).

ROSEBERRY, ERIC, *Shostakovich* (London: Midas, 1982).

Dmitri Schostakowitsch: wissenschaftliche Beiträge, Dokumente, Interpretatione, Programme (Duisburg, 1984).

HULME, DEREK C., *Dmitri Shostakovich: A Catalogue, Bibliography and Discography* (Oxford: Oxford University Press; 2nd edn. 1991).

WILSON, ELIZABETH, *Shostakovich: A Life Remembered* (London: Faber & Faber, 1994).*

Karlheinz Stockhausen

STOCKHAUSEN, KARLHEINZ, *Texte* (Cologne: DuMont): i (1963), ii (1964), iii (1971), iv (1978), v (1989), vi (1989).

HEIKINHEIMO, SEPPO, *The Electronic Music of Karlheinz Stockhausen* [= *Acta musicologica fennica*, 6] (Helsinki, 1972).

WÖRNER, K. H., *Stockhausen: Life and Work* (London: Faber & Faber, 1973).*

COTT, JONATHAN, *Stockhausen: Conversations with the Composer* (London: Robson, 1974).*

HARVEY, JONATHAN, *The Music of Stockhausen* (London: Faber & Faber, 1974).

MACONIE, ROBIN, *The Works of Karlheinz Stockhausen* (London: Oxford University Press, 1976; 2nd edn. 1990).*

Feedback Papers, 16 (1978).

HENCK, HERBERT, *Karlheinz Stockhausen's* Klavierstück X: *A Contribution toward Understanding Serial Technique* (Cologne: Neuland, 1980).

Musik-Konzepte, 19 (Munich: text + kritik, 1981).

FERRARI, LUIGI (ed.), *Samstag aus Licht* (Milan: Teatro alla Scala, 1984).

Karlheinz Stockhausen: Music and Machines (1954–1970) (London: BBC, 1985). [programme book with notes by Richard Toop]

TANNENBAUM, MYA, *Conversations with Stockhausen* (Oxford: Oxford University Press, 1987).*

FIORAVANTI, ROSSANNA (ed.), *Montag aus Licht* (Milan: Teatro alla Scala, 1988).

Contrechamps, 9 (Paris: L'Age d'Homme, 1988).

MACONIE, ROBIN (ed.), *Stockhausen on Music: Lectures and Interviews* (London: Boyars, 1989).

NEVILL, TIM (ed.), *Towards a Cosmic Music: Texts by Karlheinz Stockhausen* (London: Element, 1989).

CONEN, HERMANN, *Formel-Komposition: Zu Karlheinz Stockhausens Musik der siebziger Jahre* (Mainz: Schott, 1991).

BLUMRÖDER, CHRISTOPH VON, *Die Grundlegung der Musik Karlheinz Stockhausens* (Stuttgart: Steiner, 1992).

KURTZ, MICHAEL, *Stockhausen: a Biography* (London: Faber & Faber, 1992).*

Igor Stravinsky

CRAFT, ROBERT, *Conversations with Igor Stravinsky* (London: Faber & Faber, 1959).*

STRAVINSKY, IGOR, and CRAFT, ROBERT, *Memories and Commentaries* (London: Faber & Faber, 1960).*

VLAD, ROMAN, *Stravinsky* (London: Oxford University Press, 1960; 3rd edn. 1979).

COSMAN, MILEIN, and KELLER, HANS, *Stravinsky at Rehearsal* (London, 1962).

STRAVINSKY, IGOR, and CRAFT, ROBERT, *Expositions and Developments* (London: Faber & Faber, 1962).*

LANG, PAUL HENRY (ed.), *Stravinsky: A New Appraisal of his Work* (New York, 1963).

WHITE, ERIC WALTER, *Stravinsky: The Composer and his Works* (London: Faber & Faber, 1966; 2nd edn. 1979).*

BORETZ, BENJAMIN, and CONE, EDWARD T. (eds.), *Perspectives on Schoenberg and Stravinsky* (Princeton: Princeton University Press, 1968).

STRAVINSKY, IGOR, and CRAFT, ROBERT, *Themes and Conclusions* (London: Faber & Faber, 1972).*

CRAFT, ROBERT, *Stravinsky: The Chronicle of a Friendship* (London: Gollancz, 1972; 2nd edn. Nashville: Vanderbilt University Press, 1994).

HORGAN, PAUL, *Encounters with Stravinsky: A Personal Record* (London, 1972).

STRAVINSKY, VERA, and CRAFT, ROBERT, *Stravinsky in Pictures and Documents* (London: Hutchinson, 1979).*

GRIFFITHS, PAUL, *Igor Stravinsky: The Rake's Progress* (Cambridge: Cambridge University Press, 1982).

STRAVINSKY, IGOR, and CRAFT, ROBERT, *Dialogues* (London: Faber & Faber, 1982).*

SCHOUVALOFF, ALEXANDER, and BOROVSKY, VICTOR, *Stravinsky on the Stage* (London: Stainer & Bell, 1982).

CRAFT, ROBERT (ed.), *Stravinsky: Selected Correspondence*, 3 vols. (London: Faber & Faber, 1982, 1984, 1985).

DRUSKIN, MIKHAIL, *Igor Stravinsky: His Life, Works and Views* (Cambridge: Cambridge University Press, 1983).

TOORN, PIETER C. VAN DEN, *The Music of Igor Stravinsky* (New Haven: Yale University Press, 1983).

Strawinsky: Sein Nachlass, sein Bild (Basel: Kunstmuseum, 1984).

CRAFT, ROBERT (ed.), *Dearest Bubushkin: Selected Letters and Diaries of Vera and Igor Stravinsky* (London: Thames & Hudson, 1985).

PASLER, JANN (ed.), *Confronting Stravinsky* (Berkeley: University of California Press, 1986).

HAIMO, ETHAN, and JOHNSON, PAUL (eds.), *Stravinsky Retrospectives* (Lincoln, Nebr.: University of Nebraska Press, 1987).

WALSH, STEPHEN, *The Music of Stravinsky* (London: Routledge, 1988).*

ANDRIESSEN, LOUIS, and SCHÖNBERGER, ELMER, *The Apollonian Clockwork: On Stravinsky* (Oxford: Oxford University Press, 1989).*

STUART, PHILIP, *Igor Stravinsky: The Composer in the Recording Studio: A Comprehensive Discography* (London: Greenwood, 1991).

CRAFT, ROBERT, *Stravinsky: Glimpses of a Life* (London: Lime Tree, 1992).

GRIFFITHS, PAUL, *Stravinsky* (London: Dent, 1992).*

Tōru Takemitsu

OHTAKE, NORIKO, *Creative Sources for the Music of Toru Takemitsu* (Aldershot: Scolar, 1993).

Edgard Varèse

CHARBONNIER, GEORGES, *Entretiens avec Edgard Varèse* (Paris: Belfond, 1970).

OUELLETTE, FERNAND, *Edgard Varèse* (London: Calder & Boyars, 1973).

Musik-Konzepte, 6 (Munich: text + kritik, 1977).

Iannis Xenakis

XENAKIS, IANNIS, *Musiques formelles* (Paris: Masse, 1963; 2nd edn., Paris: Stock, 1981), English trans. *Formalized Music* (Bloomington, Ind.: Indiana University Press, 1971; 2nd edn., Stuyvesant, NY: Pendragon, 1991).

——*Musique–architecture* (Tournai: Casterman, 1971; 2nd edn. 1976).

L'arc, 51 (Aix-en-Provence: 1972).

XENAKIS, IANNIS, and REVAULT D'ALLONNES, OLIVIER, *Les Polytopes* (Paris: Balland, 1975).

XENAKIS, IANNIS, *Arts/sciences: Alliages* (Tournai: Casterman, 1976), English trans. *Arts/Sciences: Alloys* (Stuyvesant, NY: Pendragon, 1985).

VARGA, BALINT ANDRAS, *Beszélgetések Iannis Xenakisszal* (Budapest: Zenemükiadó, 1980), German trans. *Gespräche mit Iannis Xenakis* (Zurich and Mainz: Atlantis, 1995).

FLEURET, MAURICE (ed.), *Regards sur Iannis Xenakis* (Paris: Stock, 1981).

MATOSSIAN, NOURITZA, *Xenakis* (London: Kahn & Averill, 1986).

Musik-Konzepte, 54–5 (Munich: text + kritik, 1987).

RESTAGNO, ENZO (ed.), *Xenakis* (Turin: Edizioni di Torino, 1988).

HOFFMANN, PETER, *Amalgam aus Kunst und Wissenschaft: Naturwissenschaftliches Denken im Werk von Iannis Xenakis* (Frankfurt: Lang, 1994).

XENAKIS, IANNIS, *Kéleütha: Ecrits*, ed. Alain Galliari (Paris: L'Arche, 1994).

La Monte Young

YOUNG, LA MONTE, and ZAZEELA, MARIAN, *Selected Writings* (Munich: Heiner Friedrich, 1969).

YOUNG, LA MONTE, and MACLOW, JACKSON, *An Anthology* (Munich: Heiner Friedrich; 2nd edn. 1970).

Bernd Alois Zimmermann

ZIMMERMANN, BERND ALOIS, *Intervall und Zeit: Aufsätze und Schriften zum Werk* (Mainz: Schott, 1974).

Contrechamps, 5 (Paris: L'Age d'Homme, 1985).

KONOLD, WULF, *Bernd Alois Zimmermann* (Cologne: DuMont, 1986).

INDEX

WITHDRAW